This book is given
in honor of
Scott & Brad Hines
by
Mom & Dad
May 1999

EXCERPTS FROM A CUT ABOVE . . .

I still say, when people ask me how one gets to be a director, that you don't wait to be asked—go direct something! Even if it's in Super 8...the most important step in becoming a director is to find out if you are a director, and the way to find that out is to go and make a film and see if you can tell a story in a cinematic way.

—*James Cameron*

I like to set an atmosphere on my pictures. We're lucky SOB's to be doing what we're doing. Somehow it was ordained, and not to enjoy it is insane. I've been on pictures, some recently, that were really very painful, grueling and problematic with personalities and other matters. It made me not want to come to work, and I hate that. It means I've lost a certain amount of control. I think it enhances the actor's ability to perform if the atmosphere is tight for him. The director is there to father the bad moment if it comes up. But if the set is not happy, if there isn't a joyous feeling of being at work, then somewhere I've made a major mistake.

—*Richard Donner*

Film is your liberation, it's your demon, it's your nemesis, it's everything. It's your life.

—*Oliver Stone*

. . . packaging is obviously important in this world. I basically have just sort of gone wherever the hell something has gotten my attention, and then everything will fall wherever it falls. And when the dust clears, you take a look at your career, and you see what it is in retrospect. But it's the process, the examination of ideas and characters that you're pursuing, and stories that you want to tell. It's just purely the passion of it. When it's all said and done, who the hell knows? Reflection is less interesting to me than the pursuit.

—*Barry Levinson*

Anybody who tells you they're not influenced by past or current directors is probably fibbing. It's almost impossible not to be influenced. Me, I take the attitude that if it's a good shot and I can use it, I'll steal it. I have no shame. My goal is to make the best movie possible.

—*John Badham*

It did seem to me, in many ways, very fragmented, very internal, and reflected things that only I thought about at any great length. I may have just overestimated how unique I am. It turned out that everybody has these thoughts.

—*Steven Soderbergh*

You know, Hollywood is a strange place. One day you're on a billboard, the next day you're on a milk carton.

—*Mario Van Peebles*

If young film students come in to see me for advice, I ask if they've ever made a film. If they say no, I forget about them. Because if they really want to be a director, then somehow they've gotten ahold of an 8mm camera and shot 10 minutes somewhere. That's a good way to learn. I remember judging a student film festival one year. I saw a film by a nine-year-old that showed inventiveness and thought about what he was doing.

—*Arthur Hiller*

. . . any kind of movie that makes me feel something is a good movie . . . because that's what it's all about!

—*Harry Hurwitz*

I said to David Lean, who was then an editor, "How about you direct a picture and I'll produce it?" And he said, "That would be wonderful. What shall we make?" So together we found GREAT EXPECTATIONS. I went to Arthur Rank and said, "Arthur, David and I want to make GREAT EXPECTATIONS" and he said, "Okay, how much?" We said, "Three hundred and fifty thousand pounds," and he said, "Okay, go away and make it." And that was it. That applied to all those pictures—nobody saw any rushes or had anything to say. We had our freedom

—*Ronald Neame*

I'm from the streets of Long Island City. I am a pop culture sponge.

—*Joel Schumacher*

Ultimately, every decision and choice you make is filtered through your own personal set of tastes and preferences and idiosyncrasies. But I think what you might be getting at is that the personality of a particular film can't be solely attributed to one person. It was interesting there for a while having the director be considered God, but now that it's out that he isn't, we've all survived.

Is it a relief to you guys that the director isn't God after all?

I don't know, I haven't been at it long enough. To me, I look at the job as trying to get the most out of all the people you work with, trying to get them to do things beyond what they might normally do. And the better you are at doing that, then the better all the people you're working with, actors, technicians and craftsmen, will be at their jobs. And by definition, that seems to contradict any theory of the director as sole author of a film.

—*Martin Brest*

A CUT ABOVE
50 Film Directors Talk About Their Craft

Michael Singer

foreword by Leonard Maltin

PUBLISHING COMPANY
Los Angeles, CA

A CUT ABOVE, 50 Film Directors Talk About Their Craft
Copyright © 1998 by Michael Singer

LONE EAGLE PUBLISHING COMPANY, LLC™
2337 Roscomare Road, Suite Nine
Los Angeles, CA 90077-1851
Tel: 800-FILMBKS • Toll Free Fax: 888-FILMBKS
www.loneeagle.com & www.eaglei.com

Printed in the United States of America
Cover design by Lindsay Albert
Book design by Carla Green

Library of Congress Cataloging-in-Publication Data

Singer, Michael
A cut above : 50 film directors talk about their craft / by Michael Singer ; foreword by Leonard Maltin.

p.   cm.
ISBN 1-58065-000-7
1. Motion Pictures—Production and direction. 2. Motion picture producers and directors—interviews. I. Title.
PN1995.9.P7S56   1998
791.43'0223'0922—dc21   98-34631
                                                                          CIP

Distributed to the trade by National Book Network, 800-462-6420

Lone Eagle Publishing Company is a registered trademark.

For Yuko, Miyako and Kimiko

CONTENTS

FOREWORD
by Leonard Maltin

Directors are rarely unwilling to talk about their work. Most of them enjoy being interviewed, and this being the era of media hype, they're called upon to talk to reporters more often than ever at press junkets around the world.

It's much harder to find a really good interviewer—someone who knows both the contemporary film scene as well as movie history, someone who's worked in the business and understands the daily doings on a set or a distant location, someone who knows not just what to ask, but how to pose a follow-up question that gets to the heart of the matter.

Michael Singer is just such a person. A career professional in the field of film publicity, his resume speaks for itself: in his capacity as home-office publicist, he's worked on scores of movies from the early 1970's to the present. As a unit publicist, he's written countless presskits—useful, gracefully composed, well-informed—which have serviced hundreds of journalists and TV producers (not to mention anyone doing research on those movies for years to come). Directors like Oliver Stone and Joel Schumacher ask for him time and time again.

In short, Michael knows movies, and he loves them. That said, it should come as no surprise that the interviews in this book are not dry or predictable. They're lively, intelligent conversations, peppered with opinions and fueled by curiosity.

It's hard for me to pick a favorite. I learned things from every one I read—even the directors I thought I knew inside and out.

One of Michael's favorites is the interview with second unit director Noël Howard, and I must concur. It's not only sharp and funny; it's an opportunity to meet, vicariously, an unsung hero of movie history.

That's typical of Singer. He doesn't want to simply restate the obvious. He seems to go into each interview eager to find something new—and when he does, he wants to share it with all of us.

What better recommendation could there be for reading this book?

Leonard Maltin is best known for his appearances on television's *Entertainment Tonight*, where he has worked since 1982. He is also the editor of the annual paperback reference *Leonard Maltin's Movie & Video Guide*, and a number of other books on film. He is currently film critic for *Playboy* Magazine, and contributes regularly to a number of other publications. He also teaches at the University of Southern California.

KEY TO FILMOGRAPHIES

The following abbreviations and symbols are used in the directors' filmographies which appear at the end of each interview:

(AF)	=	Animated Feature
(AHVF)	=	Animated Home Video Feature
(ATF)	=	Animated Telefeature
(CCD)	=	Cable Concert Documentary
(CMS)	=	Cable Miniseries
(CPF)	=	Cable Television Performance Film
(CTD)	=	Cable Television Documentary
(CTF)	=	Cable Telefeature
(FCD)	=	Feature Concert Documentary
(FD)	=	Feature Documentary
(HVCD)	=	Home Video Concert Documentary
(HVD)	=	Home Video Documentary
(HVF)	=	Home Video Feature
(HVPF)	=	Home Video Performance Film
(MS)	=	Miniseries
(PF)	=	Performance Film
(S)	=	Serial
(TCD)	=	Television Concert Documentary
(TD)	=	Television Documentary
(TF)	=	Telefeature
(TPF)	=	Television Performance Film

★	=	after a film title denotes a directorial Academy Award nomination
★★	=	after a film title denotes a directorial Academy Award win
☆	=	after a film title denotes a directorial Emmy Award nomination
☆☆	=	after a film title denotes a directorial Emmy Award win

INTRODUCTION

For the past fifteen years I've had the pleasure and rare opportunity to interview more than fifty directors who have been responsible for some of the most memorable movies of this century. Many of these interviews appeared in the annual editions of my reference book, *Film Directors: A Complete Guide*, whose audience has mainly been the professionals in the entertainment industry.

Now, with great encouragement from my publisher, we have decided to publish these interviews as a compilation, so that filmmakers, movie buffs, fans, students and movie lovers in general will have a chance to read about these diverse filmmakers. Each interview has a new introduction, placing the filmmaker and the chronology of the interviews in proper perspective. The interviews herein were conducted from 1982 until just before my June 1998 deadline. Part of the fun in re-reading the earlier ones is to consider where the filmmakers went from that point in time, some following an absolutely predictable path, others veering as far off the road as possible.

However, as can be deigned from the subtitle of this book, "interview" isn't nearly as accurate a word as "discussion." For in each meeting with all of the filmmakers who were kind enough to lend me their time, I merely wanted to sit and talk about their lives in the movies, their approach to work, their hopes, their regrets. If my approach seems somewhat non-judgmental, well, that's absolutely correct. As a career unit publicist, I've spent enough time on sets to know just how terrifyingly, agonizingly difficult is the director's task. I certainly have my opinions as to what constitutes good and bad film, but I came to praise these directors, not to bury them.

The directors featured herein represent a cross-section of both U.S. and international filmmakers, running the gamut from the most commercial to the stubbornly independent. It was never my intention to only interview those at the top of their field. Rather, I wanted the filmmakers to characterize the reality of the motion picture industry, meaning that some of them are brilliant and others are, perhaps, just proficient . . . but all of them have struggled to keep working in one of the most competitive crafts on earth.

After finishing this book, the reader will obviously pick up on some of my favorite obsessions . . . most notably, the twin demons of pigeonholing, and perhaps even worse, the wicked spectre of ageism. Despite the fact that most directors are perfectly capable and desirous of working in many genres, the reality is that the a filmmaker who successfully makes an action picture is usually besieged by action movie scripts, the helmer who took the industry by storm with a comedy is offered every new comedy to come down the freeway. Pure and simple, it's utter nonsense, indicative of a painful lack of imagination on the part of many in the awesome positions of responsibility in the motion picture industry.

And then there's the accepted notion that as soon as a director reaches the age of 70 or so, they're to be applauded, honored, awarded, and led out to pasture for the duration of their lives. It's enough to make you wince, or maybe even cry, that it's been nearly 20 years since Billy Wilder has made a movie, and almost a decade has elapsed since Robert Wise has been behind a camera. It's easy for me to sit at my computer and discount such salient details as insurance and changing trends, but on the other hand, Akira Kurosawa (88) is reportedly planning a new production in Japan—where Kon Ichikawa (83) and Shohei Imamura (72) are also still active—and Manoel de Oliveira (90!) works non-stop in Portugal. I'm not suggesting that foreign film industries are any more supportive of their senior directors than in the United States, but it seems a particular shame, even a national tragedy, that our industry's elders aren't awarded for their greatness by supporting their active artistry. End of lecture.

Writing new introductions for this book sparked my memory of each and every one of these meetings and conversations, all of which were inspiring and educational in their own way. If they reveal a sense of the proverbial blood, sweat and tears that goes into the making of each and every motion picture—whether brilliant or banal—then I've performed my task.

—*Michael Singer*
San Francisco/Los Angeles
August 1998

50 FILM DIRECTORS TALK ABOUT THEIR CRAFT

$\mathcal{M}$ICHAEL $\mathcal{A}$PTED

In some respects, Michael Apted is one of the world's most unconventional directors. No one else glides so blithely back and forth between commercial American films, and decidedly uncommercial documentaries, which he makes with enormous skill. Intelligence and commitment have been the hallmarks of Apted's career. One of England's most prolific television directors in the 1960s and '70s, Apted moved into features there with THE TRIPLE ECHO, STARDUST and AGATHA. Moving Stateside, COAL MINER'S DAUGHTER, one of 1980's biggest hits, won recognition not only for its Academy Award-winning star, Sissy Spacek, but also for the man who directed her in that most American of films.

Since then, Apted has divided his energies between numerous major studio efforts—among them CONTINENTAL DIVIDE, GORKY PARK, FIRSTBORN, CRITICAL CONDITION, GORILLAS IN THE MIST, CLASS ACTION, THUNDERHEART, BLINK, NELL and EXTREME MEASURES—and several extraordinary documentaries in both England and the U.S. These have included the remarkable 28 UP and its successor 35 UP, BRING ON THE NIGHT (a provocative portrait of Sting's musical and personal transitions), the highly political INCIDENT AT OGLALA and MOVING THE MOUNTAIN (the former about the plight of Native Americans, the latter about the Tien An Men Square massacre in China) and most recently, INSPIRATIONS.

MICHAEL SINGER: *One searches in vain for consistent patterns in your career. Rather than make one big-budget film after another, you've chosen to direct such off-the-beaten-track projects as KIPPERBANG, 28 UP and BRING ON THE NIGHT. You seem to have made some radical decisions.*

MICHAEL APTED: Well, I wonder if these decisions aren't made for you. I did CONTINENTAL DIVIDE after COAL MINER'S DAUGHTER, which I liked and was pleased with, but it wasn't a big hit. Then GORKY PARK, which I was also pleased with, was disappointing at the box office. I always look for interesting material, wherever it may be. If it means going to England, if it means doing documentaries, then I'll do it. I'm of the school that likes to work and doesn't like

3

this endless hanging around with the notion that every movie you make is the be all and end all. I come from television, learned the business in television, and what was exciting about that was the sheer volume of work. It meant you could be more experimental. You could take more risks, because your whole career didn't hang on the last job. That's why I want to keep working—I don't want to do trash—but I want to keep working. I went to England to do 28 UP, for example. Who would have thought that would have done anything? I did it as a labor of love. . . financially, it was a ridiculous thing to have done. But it was something that I had spent a lot of time developing over the years, and of course it turned out to be something which brought me an enormous amount of prestige, really, much more than any movie since COAL MINER'S DAUGHTER. So what I'm saying is that you can never second guess what's going to happen. If you sit around thinking that your next film is going to be KING LEAR, your masterpiece, then you're going to be very disappointed. I think a successful film is a question of luck. We were lucky with COAL MINER'S DAUGHTER because it was the right time. It was a good film, but it also hit the marketplace just at the time when country music was entering the culture, with Willie Nelson, Crystal Gayle and Dolly Parton coming into the mainstream. It also hit perfectly for Sissy Spacek's career. Now, if it had come out two years earlier or two years later it might not have had the same heat. I think we were unlucky with GORKY PARK. . . it came out at the wrong time. As many things contributed to making COAL MINER'S DAUGHTER a hit as worked against GORKY PARK. You have to take the rough with the smooth. But you have to get out there. You have to look for material. I consider myself a working director on all different fronts.

Q: *As a result, it seems that the work you've done on a small scale has enhanced your reputation among critics and the industry itself.*

A: It's possibly true. I could have sat around and done what I thought was going to be a big commercial success. But the choice I made was not to do that, but to try and go off to do low-budget and more obscure projects. And it's funny how things work out. The things that are the most inauspicious in terms of commercial viability are the things that turned out for me to be the most successful. I mean, nobody wanted COAL MINER'S DAUGHTER. I imagine every American director in the industry had turned it down. Everybody thought I was crazy to do 28 UP. The same with BRING ON THE NIGHT. It didn't make any sense in terms of keeping my status as a Hollywood director.

Q: *I know that you've always had a healthy respect for popular music, what with STARDUST and COAL MINER'S DAUGHTER. How did your involvement with Sting and BRING ON THE NIGHT come about?*

A: It was really down to him. I knew David Manson socially, who had worked at A&M and produced BIRDY for them, and he was given kind of a watching brief over the idea of putting together a Sting film. And Sting knew of me too. . . he had seen 28 UP and knew that I did COAL MINER'S DAUGHTER and STARDUST I think what interested him about me was that I hadn't done just feature films, but documentaries as well. I went to see Sting and I was knocked out by him. I was extremely intrigued with his personality. He seemed so organized, so smart, so business-like. I was very impressed with his attitude and also extremely impressed at how talented he was. . . how well he understood music, how well he handled his band. I think we shared a background and a shared interest. Although I'm ten years older than he is, there is an enormous similarity in our backgrounds and what happened to us in a socio-economic sense.

Q: *Every article written about Sting presents a different portrait of the man. How open was he in allowing you to capture him?*

A: Well, I don't know. You'll have to be the judge of that. He gave us access to some extremely private, intimate moments. He's only been a big star for a few years. I'm not sure if he's entirely figured out who and what he is and what kind of access he wants to give you. There's certainly in many ways a kind of aloofness, a coldness, which was very much part of his persona with The Police. Now, the idea of doing BRING ON THE NIGHT with his new band was to break that down to an extent and make himself more emotionally acceptable. I think it goes very deep into himself. . . it's not just a musical change. How much I was able to get under his skin as I could with the people in 28 UP, I'm not so sure.

Q: *28 UP is a very different kind of documentary, one which has ten you almost a lifetime to make.*

A: I made it when the subjects of the film were ages 7, 14, 21 and 28. What you have is the interweaving of four generations of these people.

Q: *Why did you feel compelled to return once again to these people?*

A: Because I thought it was unique in the history of film. . . this kind of detailed coverage of what is, without being banal, the greatest drama in the world—which is growing up and getting through the day. It happened by chance. The original film, 7 UP, didn't set out as a massive project of following these people's lives. The original film was part of a series of documentaries for British television called World In Action. It was made in 1964 and dealt with the possibility of the English class system changing. Because there was a feeling in the early Swinging Sixties that eight hundred years of the English class system was, perhaps, beginning to be moved. We had The Beatles, we had the beginnings of real popular culture. And there was a suggestion that maybe that ghastly class system—the born-to-rule thing which had built up and practically destroyed my country—was falling apart. So what we did was take fourteen kids from different social backgrounds and just have them talk about what they wanted to do, their thoughts about money, sex, race. You could see very clearly that kids from privileged backgrounds knew exactly what they were going to do, while kids from the other end of the social scale hadn't a clue about what was going on, irrespective of their talents or abilities. Out of the mouths of babes came some awful truths—that the English class system was alive and well. So it created a bit of a stir, because of the simple ingenuousness of it all. To cut a long story short, we went back at age 14 to see how they were doing, and filming was a nightmare. It was a teenage mind you were trying to deal with, and they were monosyllabic. But we had created something, so I went back when they were 21 and now again when they're 28. It's a kind of family thing by now.

Q: *Is this something which could continue?*

A: I think so. I'll go on with it as long as the people are prepared to talk.

Q: *There's been some cross-pollination of documentary and drama in your films, particularly* COAL MINER'S DAUGHTER *and* GORKY PARK. *Were you conscious of that?*

A: I think so. I don't really believe in the auteur theory, I don't see anything thematic, but on the other hand obviously there are a lot of conscious choices that I make. All I'm interested in when I make films is verisimilitude, finding something interesting and creating an atmosphere or putting a slice of color onto film. I don't know what else there is to do. I'm not interested in special effects or hardware films, but I came to America because I wanted to make mainstream movies. You see, I grew up in the Sixties and fell in love with European cinema. I knew nothing about American film at all, but was brought up on Bergman, Reshals, Godard, Truffaut—that was my whole life. Then, in the Seventies, American film became something wonderful. Great movies. . . THE GODFATHER, TAXI DRIVER, MEAN STREETS, NETWORK, DOG DAY AFTERNOON, NASHVILLE. . . just wonderful movies, which people went to see by the millions-whereas the great European movies were made for a small minority of people in art houses. American cinema in the Seventies seemed to be what I dreamed about, which was to touch millions of people. The real thing, it seemed, was to make films that in some small way would change people, or entertain and educate them in the best possible way. And I think American cinema has lost that.

Q: *Why?*

A: I don't know. . . there are certain obvious reasons. . . films are so expensive, people are much more nervous about what they put in the marketplace, more interested in popcorn than intelligence. There's been an enormous failure of nerve. Well, it's alright for me to sit here and say that, but it's not my money. Nevertheless, the studios have lost faith in intelligent movies. And yet, when you can pull it off, like TERMS OF ENDEARMENT, the rewards are colossal. And you sense a hunger for it in audiences.

Q: *So you're not without hope?*

A: No. For every intelligent film that's released, it's another hurrah.

F I L M O G R A P H Y

M I C H A E L   A P T E D

b. February 10, 1941 - Aylesbury, Buckinghamshire, England

NUMBER 10 (TF) Granada TV, 1968, British

BIG BREADWINNER HOG (TF) Granada TV, 1968, British

YOUR NAME'S NOT GOD, IT'S EDGAR (TF) Granada TV, 1968, British

IN A COTTAGE HOSPITAL (TF) Granada TV, 1969, British

DON'T TOUCH HIM, HE MIGHT RESENT IT (TF) Granada TV, 1970, British

SLATTERY'S MOUNTED FOOT (TF) London Weekend TV/Kestrel Films, 1970, British

THE DAY THEY BURIED CLEAVER (TF) Granada TV, 1970, British

BIG SOFT NELLIE (TF) Granada TV, 1971, British

THE MOSEDALE HORSESHOE (TF) Granada TV, 1971, British

ONE THOUSAND POUNDS FOR ROSEBUD (TF) Granada TV, 1971, British

ANOTHER SUNDAY AND SWEET F.A. (TF) Granada TV, 1972, British

JOY (TF) BBC, 1972, British

SAID THE PREACHER (TF) BBC, 1972, British

THE STYLE OF THE COUNTESS (TF) Granada TV, 1972

THE REPORTERS (TF) BBC, 1972, British

BUGGINS' ERMINE (TF) Granada TV, 1972, British

KISSES AT FIFTY (TF) BBC, 1973, British

HIGH KAMPF (TF) BBC, 1973, British

JACK POINT (TF) BBC, 1973, British

THE TRIPLE ECHO Altura, 1973, British

POOR GIRL (TF) Granada TV, 1974, British

A GREAT DAY FOR BONZO (TF) Granada TV, 1974, British

STARDUST Columbia, 1975, British

WEDNESDAY LOVE (TF) BBC, 1975, British

THE COLLECTION (TF) II Granada TV, 1976, British

STRONGER THAN THE SUN (TF) BBC, 1977, British

THE SQUEEZE Warner Bros., 1977, British

AGATHA Warner Bros., 1979, British

COAL MINER'S DAUGHTER Universal, 1980

CONTINENTAL DIVIDE Universal, 1981

KIPPERBANG P'TANG YANG, KIPPERBANG MGM/UA Classics, 1983, British

GORKY PARK Orion, 1983

FIRSTBORN Paramount, 1984

28 UP (FD) First Run Features, 1984, British, originally filmed for television

BRING ON THE NIGHT (FCD) The Samuel Goldwyn Company, 1985

CRITICAL CONDITION Paramount, 1987

GORILLAS IN THE MIST Universal, 1988

THE LONG WAY HOME (TCD) Yerosha Productions/Granada TV/CBS Music Video Enterprises, 1989, British

CLASS ACTION 20th Century Fox, 1991

35 UP (FD) The Samuel Goldwyn Company, 1991, British, originally filmed for television

INCIDENT AT OGLALA (FD) Miramax Films, 1992

THUNDERHEART TriStar, 1992

BLINK New Line Cinema, 1994

MOVING THE MOUNTAIN (FD) October Films, 1994, British

NELL 20th Century Fox, 1994

EXTREME MEASURES Columbia, 1996

INSPIRATIONS (FD) Clear Blue Sky Productions, 1997

ALWAYS OUTNUMBERED (CTF) HBO NYC/Palomar Pictures, 1998

$\mathcal{J}$OHN $\mathcal{B}$ADHAM

There was much ado in 1997 about the 20th anniversary of a film called SATURDAY NIGHT FEVER, a massive success in its own time, which had developed a whole new following with a newer generation. Sure, there was the camp value of those terrifically tacky mid-'70s disco styles paraded in the film by star John Travolta and the rest of the cast. But there was something more afoot... in fact, it was rediscovered that SATURDAY NIGHT FEVER was a fine, observant movie about youthful angst and dead end futures, well-acted by Travolta and company, and seamlessly directed by John Badham.

In recent years, Badham has become known as a hardcore action specialist, his visceral impulses put into service of such films as BLUE THUNDER, WARGAMES, STAKEOUT, BIRD ON A WIRE, THE HARD WAY, POINT OF NO RETURN, ANOTHER STAKEOUT, DROP ZONE, NICK OF TIME and INCOGNITO. Several of the above—most notably WARGAMES, the two STAKEOUT films, BIRD ON A WIRE and THE HARD WAY—mixed comedy and thrills to good advantage. But in fact, some of Badham's best films have been in different venues. including heartfelt comedy and/or drama (THE BINGO LONG TRAVELING ALL STARS AND MOTOR KINGS, WHOSE LIFE IS IT ANYWAY?, AMERICAN FLYERS), classic horror (DRACULA), or family fantasy/adventure (SHORT CIRCUIT).

The following discussion with Badham reveals an unpretentious filmmaker who just loves to make movies, unapologetically in the mainstream and without intentions of swimming anywhere else.

MICHAEL SINGER: AMERICAN FLYER *had been circulating the studios for quite some time. How did it come to you or how did you come to it?*

JOHN BADHAM: It came to me from Warner Bros. I had expressed a lot of interest in the subject matter, and I'm a big fan of Steven Tesich. I like the way he draws human beings and thought that it would be exciting to tell this story, which is a very personal relationship between two brothers set against the background of the largest bicycle race in the United States.

Q: *I assume that the elements are different enough so that people won't have a sense of deja-vu watching another Steve Tesich bicycle race movie á la BREAKING AWAY.*

A: You won't think you're seeing the same movie, or even a similar movie. The differences are really quite enormous. The Coors Classic that we filmed is a major world class race that traverses almost 1500 miles up and down the Rocky Mountains, and this bears only vague relationship to the rather small local race that was depicted in BREAKING AWAY.

Q: *Who plays the brothers?*

A: The actors are relatively new—to films, anyway. Kevin Costner plays the older brother and David Grant, the younger brother. They're both tremendously talented actors. There is also a wonderful appeal in having actors who are unknown to the audience. You discover them as you're watching the movie. It's like meeting a new friend.

Q: *What lured you into filmmaking in the first place? How about a brief chronology of John Badham's life and times?*

A: I was born in England, and my mother remarried an American who brought us to the United States when I was about five. I was raised in Alabama, where he lived. I went to Yale as an undergraduate—I had been involved with theatre in high school, and got involved again at Yale. My mother had been an actress. She had studied at the Royal Academy in London and had a radio and television talk show in Birmingham, Alabama, when I was growing up. So my interest in theatre continued while I was an undergraduate, and then I went to the Yale Drama School as a director. I think I started out wanting to be an actor, but sometime during my Yale career found out that I was not very good, and that maybe I could get involved in something where at least I could meet some girls. . . I noticed that there were always girls surrounding those guys who were directing, so it looked like a good opportunity. I took a Master's Degree from the school as a theatre director, but by that point I had developed an interest in film. After graduating, instead of going to New York or applying to a college somewhere to teach, I came to California. . . largely on the strength of the fact that my sister Mary, who was nine years old and playing in the backyard in Alabama, had been discovered to star in TO KILL A MOCKINGBIRD, for which she got an Academy Award nomination. I thought, what the hell. She knows some people out there. Maybe I should go there and see what's going on. So I came out. After about four months of looking around Los Angeles for a job, I would have taken any kind of a job, even pumping gas.

Finally, feeling like somebody crawling across the desert trying to find an oasis, I took a job in the Universal mailroom. I found myself there with a lot of people who also had Master's Degrees and said they wanted to be directors and producers. There was some guy in there named Walter Hill who wanted to be a director, and some red-headed guy named Mike Medavoy who wanted to run a studio, and several others who have become producers over the years. We sort of fanned out of the mailroom as we found other jobs in other parts of the studio. Medavoy and I went into the casting department and trained as casting directors. I was a casting director on shows like The Chrysler Theatre, Run For Your Life and various half-hour shows. I eventually made friends with a terrific producer named William Sackheim, and became his assistant and then associate producer. Eventually, I started directing little things for him. And when I say little, I mean little—like inserts of ashtrays. The first shot I ever did with a professional crew was an insert of a transistor radio hanging from a rifle in a police car. I was petrified. I had more anxiety over that little insert than you can imagine. And the biggest compliment was that they let me do another insert!

Over a period of a year, I did more and more complicated things and finally another producer, David Levinson, agreed to let me direct an episode of a series called The Senator, which was part of The Bold Ones series. It was a very good beginning to my directing career because the show was so prestigious. Afterwards, I did a lot of television-hour shows, half-hour shows, and finally movies of the week.

Q: *At a time when TV movies were as similar as apples on a fruitstand, you made two—The Law and The Gun—which really stood out. Did you specifically look for material on television which would rise above the norm?*

A: I think I learned from various people the clear lesson that, if you're interested in doing bigger and better things, you'd better have very good material. No matter how good a director you think you are, if you don't have wonderful scripts to start with you're never going to be able to distinguish yourself. That kept me away from lots and lots of movies or television shows that would have just kind of added to a mediocre credit list. I tried early on not to work just to be working, and to save my money so if I didn't work for a month or two, my family wouldn't scream and the creditors wouldn't bang down my front door. That was a very good decision, because I avoided doing a lot of turkey movies of the week.

Q: *You also seemed, aesthetically, to be not so much directing for television as for film. Were you conscious of that at the time?*

A: I think I was just conscious of trying to make the most exciting piece of work that I could, whether I was doing a halfhour or an hour or a two-hour show.

Q: *Do you think that television is just about the best training ground for a newcomer?*

A: I don't know if it's the best training ground, but it's a damn sight better than anything else that I know of. I see a terrible mistake being made constantly by beginning directors who have some writing talent. They get to the position in the movie business where they're able to get a chance to direct. And they get into deep trouble right away because they don't have any real training or background. You know, you can read all the books you want and see all the movies you want and talk to all the directors you want, but until you get out on the floor it's a mind boggler unlike anything you've ever seen. The responsibilities are enormous. If you start out doing an hour or a half-hour television show, the risks are much less. First of all, you can get through it a lot easier. Doing a lot of those shows is like operating a well-oiled machine. A director can barely know what he's doing and get through it. It may not be great, but he can get through it. Directing a full-length feature, however, is much, much harder. The fact is, the beaches are littered with the bodies of first-time feature directors, some of whom are friends of mine who have a hard time getting another directing job. These directors should have learned their craft in television before jumping in with the big boys.

Q: *It seems that, more and more, young writers and directors are turning up their noses at television.*

A: Well, I can tell you that at Universal on any given day at the time I was there, Steven Spielberg, Richard Donner, Michael Ritchie, Jeannot Szwarc and myself would be directing shows. We were all learning our craft and getting to a place where we were really in a position to do features.

Q: *Do you have any mentors who have in some way influenced your work?*

A: Anybody who tells you they're not influenced by past or current directors is probably fibbing. It's almost impossible not to be influenced. Me, I take the attitude that if it's a good shot and I can use it, I'll steal it. I have no shame. My goal is to make the best movie possible. Whatever it takes, I'll do. I'm not ashamed to admit that I looked at BULLITT any number of times to study the car chase, and see what I could learn about shooting action. Even when I was doing BLUE THUNDER I would go back to BULLITT and look at it. I'm not ashamed to admit that Michael Ritchie's techniques of documentary filmmaking that you see in DOWNHILL RACER and THE CANDIDATE are techniques that I admire tremendously and learned from him.

Q: *I'd like to talk about some of your features. When you were shooting SATURDAY NIGHT FEVER, did you have any idea that you were creating a cultural icon of the Seventies?*

A: Nobody had any intention of making cultural icons. No one knew that we were going to unleash upon the world a major new star. Everyone was hoping that we'd make a good little picture. The initial budget was $2.5 million, and even in 1977 that was a real tough New York picture to make for so little money. We were going with a relatively unknown director, a relatively unknown star and material culled from the pages of New York Magazine. We were blessed with five new songs from The Bee Gees, who at the time had gone into a kind of decline and hadn't really done anything for a while. They were viewed by the brass at Paramount as not being very good songs and having nothing to do with disco. I had never been in a disco up to two weeks before we started shooting the film. My experience with dance was my mother sending me to dance class when I was in grammar school. It was all very new to me. Before the movie was released, Paramount was scared to death of the profanity and begged the producer, Robert Stigwood, to delete most of it. Stigwood, bless him, wouldn't alter a single frame of the film. By the end of the first weekend of release, we knew we had a pretty nice hit going, and it never stopped. It was like The Little Engine That Could, just chugging and chugging, on and on. And before you knew it, we had a $300 million worldwide gross.

Q: *Would you make WHOSE LIFE IS IT ANYWAY? again exactly as you made it?*

A: What I would do differently are some things that I wanted to do originally. First of all, I wanted to get the actors and myself to work for scale. I wanted to make it at an economic level where it really didn't matter how well or badly it did, because the economic risk would have been small enough so that if it had a small audience, it really wouldn't have mattered. On the other hand, MGM was trying its best to re-establish itself as a major studio and not appear as if they had to do only low-budget shows. I would hate like hell to have to give up the most magnificent set I ever had built for me (until the time of the WARGAMES set), but I guess I could have made it work in a real hospital in a practical situation.

Q: *Watching* WARGAMES *again on cable, it was apparent that couched within a very entertaining framework was one of the most potent anti-nuke messages seen in a feature film. Yet, people tend to think of it as more of straight entertainment than as a "message" film.*

A: Well, it's interesting how when something serious intrudes into what up until that point had been an entertaining film, the serious aspects are overlooked. People tend to dismiss it, thinking, "It's just an action film." We thought that if we made the film entertaining we could slip in a little seriousness at the end. But when people talk about the film they don't view it with the same gravity as some of the other nuclear-themed films that appeared at the time. But, of course, nobody saw those films, so how could they have gotten the message that was put forth so seriously?

F I L M O G R A P H Y

J O H N   B A D H A M
b. August 25, 1939 - Luton, England
THE IMPATIENT HEART (TF) Universal TV, 1971
ISN'T IT SHOCKING? (TF) ABC Circle Films, 1973
THE LAW (TF) Universal TV, 1974
THE GUN (TF) Universal TV, 1974
REFLECTIONS OF MURDER (TF) ABC Circle Films, 1974
THE GODCHILD (TF) MGM TV, 1974
THE KEEGANS (TF) Universal TV, 1976
THE BINGO LONG TRAVELING ALL STARS AND MOTOR KINGS Universal, 1976
SATURDAY NIGHT FEVER Paramount, 1977
DRACULA Universal, 1979
WHOSE LIFE IS IT ANYWAY? MGM/United Artists, 1981
BLUE THUNDER Columbia, 1983
WARGAMES MGM/UA, 1983
AMERICAN FLYERS Warner Bros., 1985
SHORT CIRCUIT TriStar, 1986
STAKEOUT Buena Vista, 1987
BIRD ON A WIRE Universal, 1990
THE HARD WAY Universal, 1991
POINT OF NO RETURN Warner Bros., 1993
ANOTHER STAKEOUT Buena Vista, 1993
DROP ZONE Paramount, 1994
NICK OF TIME Paramount, 1995
INCOGNITO Warner Bros., 1997
SORROW FLOATS (CTF) Showtime, 1998

$\mathcal{P}$AUL $\mathcal{B}$ARTEL

One of Hollywood's authentic oddball mavericks, Paul Bartel carved a niche in the hearts of audiences with his unique blend of the macabre and the comic. His sometimes marvelously weird sensibilities were seen to best advantage in such films as PRIVATE PARTS, DEATH RACE 2000, EATING RAOUL and the delightfully titled LUST IN THE DUST and SCENES FROM THE CLASS STRUGGLE IN BEVERLY HILLS. Even Bartel's more mainstream projects—THE LONGSHOT and NOT FOR PUBLICATION would be in this category—were definitely off kilter, which automatically limited their chances for wide reception by audiences.

When not directing and acting in his own projects, Bartel can often be seen performing in several of his colleague's films, including HOLLYWOOD BOULEVARD, PIRANHA, ROCK 'N' ROLL HIGH SCHOOL, GET CRAZY and HEART LIKE A WHEEL.

I chatted with Bartel in his West Hollywood apartment shortly after the successful release of EATING RAOUL. . . unfortunately, the hoped-for sequel to that film that Bartel mentions at the end of the interview has yet to come to pass. . .

MICHAEL SINGER: *Let's talk about death.*

PAUL BARTEL: Always a pleasure.

Q: *It seems to me that death is at the heart of most of your films. But it's treated in such a gleeful way that it takes the edge off. Are you particularly interested in death as a subject in film?*

A: No, I don't think I am consciously interested in death. I am interested in comedy. And I think, probably, at the heart of a lot of comedy is fear of one kind or another. Surely fear of death is one of those main fears. Yes, in terms of DEATH RACE 2000, the whole idea of inflicting death more or less capriciously seemed to me a good basis for comedy. The premise of the movie was so grim that the only way I could deal with it was to exaggerate it outrageously, artificialize it and not take it seriously. That was also true of the premise of PRIVATE PARTS, much less so in CANNONBALL, where I really wasn't very interested in the premise of the movie at all. I'm interested in the horror genre, the suspense genre, and death is certainly an important aspect of those.

Q: EATING RAOUL *is a film that revels delightedly in a kind of hip bad taste.*

A: That comes from a blending of Dick's [Blackburn, Bartel's collaborator] and my sensibilities plus the sensibilities of the actors. The impetus for making EATING RAOUL, from my standpoint, was to do a film in which Mary Woronov and I could co-star. And because we aren't big names, we wanted to do something that would attract attention by its outrageousness and would entertain an audience on its own merits. I think that it catered to the aesthetics of the film, the desire to be outrageous and appeal to a young, hip audience. I would certainly be interested in making a more genteel comedy, but those are much harder to sell. Outrageousness is an exploitive quality in film.

Q: *Nevertheless,* EATING RAOUL *was in many ways a comedy of manners.*

A: There's a synthesis of a genteel approach and raunchy and outrageous material, which was the basic production concept of the movie.

Q: EATING RAOUL *had one of the best senses of Los Angeles, from a comic point of view, that I've seen in a long while. Did you grow up here?*

A: No, I'm an East Coaster, from New Jersey. But I lived in New York for awhile and I think of myself as essentially a New Yorker with a New York sensibility.

Q: *But your approach to L.A. in* EATING RAOUL *is sort of a love/hate thing, a city both repugnant and vastly entertaining.*

A: Well, I'm very fond of L.A. I do find plenty of food for satire here. But I'm not one of those New York L.A. haters. I really love it most of the time.

Q: *When did you know you were going to be a filmmaker?*

A: I got interested in animation at a very early age. I used to go to the movies a lot and my favorite films were animated films. I loved Saturday cartoon matinees, the UPA films. When I came out to California for the first time, going to UCLA, I thought I wanted to be an animation director. But the bottom was falling out of the market for good, ambitious, sophisticated animation. And also, I became a little more interested in theatre and acting, as well as writing and live-action films. But animation was my first love and I still appreciate it.

Q: *Is it correct to assume that there's a certain influence of animated films on your live-action features?*

A: It is certainly an element in the mix, specifically in EATING RAOUL and DEATH RACE 2000. Much less so in CANNONBALL and PRIVATE PARTS.

Q: *How did you get your first feature,* PRIVATE PARTS, *financed and made?*

A: The administration at MGM at that time wanted to produce a series of very low-budget non-union pictures, and PRIVATE PARTS was one of them.

Q: Were you pleased with the distribution? How much of the country saw PRIVATE PARTS?

A: Most of the major cities. But the title, which was chosen by the president, was a major miscalculation and the absence of any star names in it pretty much killed the film's chance for reaching a wide audience.

Q: What was your original title?

A: BLOOD RELATIONS.

Q: Was DEATH RACE 2000 your concept or Roger Corman's?

A: Roger Corman's. When I came into it there was an unworkable script. We spent a year rewriting, abandoning and then putting it back into production again.

Q: Can I assume that the original idea was not intended to be as funny as it turned out to be?

A: It was always intended to have a comic element. The first script was very bizarre and not particularly funny. Then Chuck Griffith brought a great deal of comedy into it, and my input was also basically comic. Roger was of two minds about it. He wanted it to be funny, but he didn't want it to be essentially a comedy and was trying to make a hard action film with comic overtones.

Q: Did you have to fight for your vision?

A: Yes. I got in a certain number of things that I wanted. He ultimately had control of the editing, so he took out a lot of stuff that I would have liked to have had in. The finished film is very much a synthesis of his vision and mine. And people seem to enjoy the film, so I'm not unhappy with it.

Q: It really has become one of the most popular cult films of the seventies. MAD MAX and THE ROAD WARRIOR would be unthinkable without it.

A: George Miller told me that DEATH RACE 2000 was a big influence on MAD MAX. I like MAD MAX, but I think THE ROAD WARRIOR is the absolute apotheosis of that genre. I can't imagine any more perfect realization of that kind of movie. It's not my favorite kind of film, but THE ROAD WARRIOR is one of my favorite movies and George is high on my list of favorite directors.

Q: You are often talked about in the same category as John Waters. You both celebrate bad taste and revel in a kind of junk nostalgia. Does that comparison bother you at all?

A: No, but I don't think it's particularly accurate. I met John recently and I think he's quite wonderful. In fact, we wrote a fairly large part for John in this new Paul and Mary Bland picture. He's very funny, and I think his movies are wonderfully funny and satirical, but I don't particularly identify. I see why people think that we are in some ways similar, but I think that my attitude toward the audience is different than his.

Q: In what way?

A: I think he is more concerned with shocking and scandalizing than I am.

Q: I went to see EATING RAOUL on opening night at a theatre in Westwood, and you were outside before the start of the film handing out promotional cookies which had a bite taken out of them. That seemed to be taking directorial involvement with a film's distribution several steps beyond what I've seen. Is working on the fringes of the industry something that you'd like to continue to do?

A: Well, I'd like to continue to be involved in the production of the kind of low-budget film which permits risk taking and innovation. I would also like to participate in some of the mainstream productions with their economic benefits. My ideal would be to alternate between the two—do a low-budget, non-union picture independently and then work on a big-budget studio film.

Q: Can you talk about your new project?

A: It's a light comedy about yellow journalism and political corruption in New York entitled NOT FOR PUBLICATION. It has none of the dark underpinnings of EATING RAOUL. It's a big change of pace. And indeed, the sequel to EATING RAOUL, which Dick is going to direct with me producing, is itself a much lighter film than EATING RAOUL. There's only one murder in it—and it's very early in the picture.

F I L M O G R A P H Y

PAUL   BARTEL
b. August 6, 1938 - Brooklyn, New York
PRIVATE PARTS MGM, 1972
DEATH RACE 2000 New World, 1975
CANNONBALL New World, 1976
EATING RAOUL 20th Century Fox International Classics, 1982
NOT FOR PUBLICATION The Samuel Goldwyn Company, 1984
LUST IN THE DUST New World, 1985
THE LONGSHOT Orion, 1986
SCENES FROM THE CLASS STRUGGLE IN BEVERLY HILLS Cinecom, 1989
SHELF LIFE Northern Arts Entertainment, 1994

$\mathcal{M}$ARTIN $\mathcal{B}$REST

There must be a method behind Martin Brest's madness. . . although he's directed only four films in the last 14 years, three of them hit the critical and box office bullseye (with the fourth not yet released at the time of this writing).

Brest first came to national attention in 1984 with the release of BEVERLY HILLS COP, which was not only an overwhelming box office success, but won over critics as well with its offbeat characterizations, fast action and skewed sense of humor. (It may be difficult to recall all this now in light of the more conventional approaches of the film's two sequels, neither of which were directed by Brest).

Brest had already charmed audiences with his first big-studio feature, the relatively low-budget and low-keyed GOING IN STYLE—starring George Burns, Art Carney and Lee Strasberg—as well as his first film, HOT TOMORROWS, a highly-praised satire made under the auspices of the American Film Institute. The years that followed GOING IN STYLE were fraught with some anxieties, as Brest worked on and was forced to leave the production of WARGAMES, hard times which were certainly forgotten by the end of BEVERLY HILLS COP's first week of release.

Brest's next two features also hit the jackpot: the delightful action-comedy MIDNIGHT RUN (1988), which featured terrific chemistry between the antagonistic protagonists portrayed by Robert De Niro and Charles Grodin; and SCENT OF A WOMAN (1992), a serio-comedy featuring one of Al Pacino's most enjoyable performances, for which Brest received an Academy Award nomination as Best Director.

Most recently, Brest finally returned to the screen at the helm of MEET JOE BLACK, an re-consideration of DEATH TAKES A HOLIDAY, starring Brad Pitt and Anthony Hopkins.

MICHAEL SINGER: *When you were announced as director of* BEVERLY HILLS COP *a lot of people scratched their heads and wondered how you would reconcile your somewhat offbeat sensibilities with such a sweepingly commercial project.*

MARTIN BREST: Well, before production started I don't think anybody thought it was going to be a particularly big, sweepingly commercial movie. It was just an action comedy that everybody hoped would achieve some success.

Q: *Even though Eddie Murphy had at that point been established as a major star?*

A: As absurd as it sounds now, there were concerns coming from some quarters about whether or not Eddie could carry a movie on his own, because he hadn't done it before. Of course, all of us involved in the production knew that he could not only carry it, but toss it across the Pacific Ocean if he wanted to.

Q: *How did you get involved with* BEVERLY HILLS COP?

A: I had heard about the project years before from Don Simpson. Apparently there had been four writers before Don Petrie, Jr., whose draft the studio decided to go with. At that point, Sylvester Stallone was to star, and I was hired as director.

Q: *How long did that proceed before Eddie Murphy came into the picture?*

A: A couple of months.

Q: *Obviously the script had to be reworked drastically then.*

A: Well, Eddie came on only a couple of weeks before shooting. But since we were still trying to solve story and pacing problems, we never really had time to tailor to Eddie until the first day of shooting. Essentially, we were re-writing every day.

Q: *The creative process must have been intensified day by day.*

A: The writing process didn't stop until the last take of the last shot, literally. It was like putting together a puzzle where the picture on the puzzle was constantly changing. The plotline of the story was always in flux.

Q: *How collaborative was it between you and the cast on a daily basis?*

A: I would encourage the actors to come up with things for their characters that could add to the story and humor. The worst thing for me would be somebody who just wanted to show up and say their lines. That's not what we needed on this particular movie.

Q: *That sounds like the key to some of those weirdly original characters, like Bronson Pinchot's art dealer.*

A: It's no news that casting is one of the most, if not the single most, important contribution a director can make to the determination of a project's personality. The casting director and myself looked for actors that audiences were not very familiar with, who could substantially contribute to what was on the page. . . and maybe even take what was on the page, throw it out, and come up with something even better.

Q: Do you think there was any kind of particular change in how people viewed you after BEVERLY HILLS COP? Do you think some liked you more because you had directed such a wonderfully successful film, or that some felt that a little of you got lost in such a project?

A: That would be hard for me to say. Why do you think they might feel that?

Q: Because HOT TOMORROWS to GOING IN STYLE to BEVERLY HILLS COP seems, perhaps, a slightly illogical progression in your career.

A: Actually, the first movie I made while a student at NYU shared a similar sense of mischievous fun with BEVERLY HILLS COP. But every movie is different. It's not my ambition to adhere to a specific style. The interesting thing about different projects is how you really have to solve a multitude of problems and research all the emotions that a particular project examines. It's exciting to do different things each time.

Q: Several directors I've spoken with have gone out of their way to reject the auteur theory. They made a point of indicating that they have to re-adjust and re-make themselves for each project. Do you have any thoughts on this?

A: Ultimately, every decision and choice you make is filtered through your own personal set of tastes and preferences and idiosyncrasies. But I think what you might be getting at is that the personality of a particular film can't be solely attributed to one person. It was interesting there for a while having the director be considered God, but now that it's out that he isn't, we've all survived.

Q: Is it a relief to you guys that the director isn't God after all?

A: I don't know, I haven't been at it long enough. To me, I look at the job as trying to get the most out of all the people you work with, trying to get them to do things beyond what they might normally do. And the better you are at doing that, then the better all the people you're working with, actors, technicians and craftsmen, will be at their jobs. And by definition, that seems to contradict any theory of the director as sole author of a film.

Q: HOT TOMORROWS brought you a lot of attention, playing in festivals and the like. . .

A: It ran on what you might call the eccentric circuit.

Q: Did it become a calling card of sorts in Hollywood?

A: I don't know if you could call it a calling card, but if one wants to direct movies, it helps to have a movie that you've directed to get you to the next step.

Q: Was GOING IN STYLE a script that you wrote on spec and then shopped around?

A: No. Actually, it was a reversal of the classic case. After I finished at AFI, I found an unpublished short story written by a carpenter from New York. He just read it into a little cassette tape recorder. I heard the tape and loved the story, and I brought it to Warner Bros., wanting to direct it. The project was put into development, and my first job as a director was to go out and find a writer for it. At the time, I couldn't find a writer whom I felt would capture the qualities I was hoping to bring out of the material, so I went back to Warner Bros. and had to sell myself as the writer—which they were more reluctant about than hiring me as the director! I sort of did it backwards. Instead of having a script and then trying to get to direct it, I was the director who then had to convince the studio to let me write it.

Q: *How did you feel walking onto the set of* GOING IN STYLE *as a 27-year-old director working with George Burns, Art Carney and Lee Strasberg?*

A: I was nervous going to the set the first day, not necessarily because of the stature of the actors, but because I'd hardly ever seen a real Hollywood movie being filmed, let alone being put in the position of having to direct one. But once I got there and started working it just felt very natural and it went very, very smoothly.

Q: WARGAMES *was a film that you started directing, but left after a few weeks' shooting. Was it a project that you conceived yourself?.*

A: No, a completed script was brought to me. I liked it, and worked on the project for a year and a half. I worked on the script, did the casting, all the technical research, had the sets built, even filmed for three weeks.

Q: *What happened?*

A: Well, I don't know. It's funny. At the time I thought we were making what could have been a great piece of American entertainment. I was very confident of the job we were doing. However, there were some people who had problems with my work. The major reason for my dismissal that they circulated at the time was that I was incapable of making the movie fun. However, after BEVERLY HILLS COP came out, the parties in question scrambled for an alternate excuse because that one didn't seem to be appropriate anymore.

Q: *How different a film of* WARGAMES *do you think you would have made?*

A: Without diminishing the contribution of an esteemed colleague, the feeling I have is that the finished movie as it stands now is sort of the television version of the film we were making.

Q: *When you left the project it must have been quite a blow to your ego.*

A: It was very painful. Had I a string of five movies behind me that were moderately successful, it might not have been such a problem. But only having one small movie to my name, and then being fired from my second film, made things very difficult.

Q: *Did friends and colleagues rush to your support, or was there a discernible shying away?*

A: My friends were very supportive. The community as a whole, I guess, didn't know what to think.

Q: *How long was it between leaving* WARGAMES *and getting onto* BEVERLY HILLS COP?

A: About a year and half.

Q: *You must have had a nice feeling of, if not revenge, than at least vindication when* BEVERLY HILLS COP *was released.*

A: Well, it was nice to know I wasn't nuts. Throughout the whole WARGAMES experience I would say to myself, "Am I crazy or are they crazy? We're making a really good movie here, what's the problem?" I never could figure out what all the negativity was about. And then, after I was fired, naturally—being a semi-reasonable person—I said to myself, "Gee, maybe I stink, maybe the work was lousy, maybe what I thought was going to be good and entertaining wasn't." You really do start to doubt yourself, unless you're totally deluded. I was lucky to get an opportunity to see that my instincts about making a movie that's fun and entertaining were not totally unreliable.

Q: *Is it fair to say that comedy is the genre in which you feel most comfortable?*

A: I would like to make all kinds of movies, although I don't think that I'd like to make a movie that was totally devoid of humor. I think even a serious movie, with a serious message, is best served, and is kept in a better balance, with a little bit of humor. There's really no genre that I wouldn't consider.

F I L M O G R A P H Y

M A R T I N   B R E S T
b. 1951 - Bronx, New York
HOT TOMORROWS American Film Institute, 1977
GOING IN STYLE Warner Bros., 1979
BEVERLY HILLS COP Paramount, 1984
MIDNIGHT RUN Universal, 1988
SCENT OF A WOMAN ★ Universal, 1992
MEET JOE BLACK Universal, 1998

$\mathcal{J}$AMES $\mathcal{C}$AMERON

Considering James Cameron's reputation as one of the most fearsome and unforgiving taskmasters in motion pictures, the circumstances that befell this humble interviewer during a meeting with Cameron at his Los Angeles home should have resulted in the apocalyptic fireworks oft-described by journalists and co-workers. But truth, thank God, is stranger than fiction.

Having completed a wonderfully productive, nearly one-hour-long interview with Cameron, I swept up my tape recorder perched in between myself and the subject, and noted with disbelieving horror that the "pause" button had remained on for the duration, the only time up to then and since, over the course of more than 200 interviews, that I ever made such a stupid and careless mistake. This would have caused embarrassment under any circumstance with any director, but despite Cameron's complete affability during the interview, I had already heard stories of what lurked just underneath, waiting to be unleashed by a moment of incompetence. For a moment, flop sweat mounting, I considered saying nothing at all, reconstructing the interview to the best of my ability as soon as I lurched through the door of my apartment. . . alas, realizing that it would be an impossible task and unfair to Cameron.

And so, loins girded, I admitted my egregious error.

A long, terrible moment passed, Cameron saying nothing. I expected the worst, and had little doubt that it would surpass my greatest fears.

Finally, he nodded slightly, and uttered words more shocking than my imagination could have invented.

"Okay. . . let's have some coffee and do it again," he said quietly, with not a hint of justified sarcasm lurking underneath those words, and headed upstairs to pour a couple of cups of java.

I blinked, regained consciousness, and when Cameron returned, switched off that goddamned pause button, and watched the tape roll, with the filmmaker exceeding himself in both honesty and eloquence the second time around.

In the 11 years that have passed since, the mythology of James Cameron has increased dramatically, particularly with the legend-in-its-own-time TITANIC, his magnum opus, and by the way, the highest grossing motion picture made, the recipient of 14 Academy Award nominations and the winner of 11 of those little statuettes (with Cameron taking home three of them personally, for directing, co-editing and co-producing the film), an all-time record shared with 1959's BEN-HUR.

Described as "uncontrollable" by studio executives and alternately excoriated and praised by those who work with him, the method and the madness seem to be one and the same. Cameron is indeed driven, but the results speak for themselves. Yes, his films are brilliantly engineered pieces of popular entertainment, but Cameron nonetheless carries forth central and highly personal themes into nearly all of his films. . . the ultimate failure of technology, and the human resourcefulness that must overcome when the machine breaks down. . . particularly the transformational power of love. For when one wipes away the future-tech veneer of Cameron's films, revealed beneath is a very old-fashioned romantic. And TITANIC was the ultimate (and most obvious) expression of this quixotic aspect of Cameron, staged in a magnificently detailed past rather than the fanciful and terrifying future depicted in THE TERMINATOR, ALIENS, THE ABYSS and TERMINATOR 2: JUDGMENT DAY.

For TITANIC, Cameron marshaled all of his monumental skills in the pursuit of haunting cinematic poetry, creating as satisfying a moviegoing experience as audiences had experienced for longer than many could remember. As for the budget. . . who, in the end (especially in light of the film's subsequent fortunes), could care less? It wasn't our money. . . and as Anthony Lane noted in his rave review of TITANIC in The New Yorker, "If you have to spend $200 million on a movie, this is the way to do it."

In the following conversation, Cameron discussed his beginnings and hopes for the future, sometimes accurately, and occasionally not. . . such as when he claimed that after ALIENS, "I've pretty much gone as far as I can go in the science fiction genre. I can't imagine doing a film that's bigger or more complicated or has more imagery." But then again, at that point, T2 was still five years away!

MICHAEL SINGER: *When did you first know that you wanted to make movies?*

JAMES CAMERON: When I first saw 2001: A SPACE ODYSSEY. That film awakened in me a sense of wonder about film as art. I had always seen film as entertainment, because I spent my formative years going to the local movie grind house as much as possible, spending all of the lunch money that I had saved during the week to go to at least two movies on weekends. But when I saw 2001, it was the first time—at the age of 14 or 15—that I actually thought film could be something elevated beyond that. I became aware of the role of music in a film, and the impact that it could have in creating some sort of emotional effect. And, also, of course, I wanted to know how the special effects were done. There are things in 2001 that will stand 500 years from now as being important contributions to art. The idea of the ape throwing the bone and jump-cutting to a spaceship in orbit, summing up four million years of human development in a single cut, is something that's absolutely brilliant. . . brilliant outside of any consideration of film as art. . . it's just art. It says something that's very powerful. When I first saw it, I stumbled out of the theatre, realized that I was back on earth after Kubrick's "trip" sequence, and threw up on the sidewalk. It really affected me that much. Now, to my knowledge, 2001 was one of the first films that had a really definitive book about the making of the film, so one thing led to another and I was finding out how the sets were built, how the director works with actors, how special effects are done and so forth. It may seem like a strange door to enter by to some people, because it's certainly not the normal procedure. Usually, you learn about this kind of stuff from art appreciation classes. But this was one-stop-shopping for me—I got a Super 8 camera and started doing my own very simple, special effects shots, double exposures and that sort of thing. I got together with other amateur filmmakers—none of us were any good whatsoever—and that just kindled a technical awareness of film. I still say, when people ask me how one gets to be a director, that you don't wait to be asked—go direct something! Even if it's in Super 8. . . the most important step in becoming a director is to find out if you are a director, and the way to find that out is to go and make a film and see if you can tell a story in a cinematic way. Some people have wonderful ideas, but the gap between those ideas and the execution of those ideas on film is the gap they'll never be able to close. But some people do it instinctively, and those are the people who should continue. Of course, I shouldn't pontificate, because my course into it was so bizarre and convoluted.

Q: *You taught yourself by doing and reading and watching other movies? You had no formal training at all?*

A: No. I think the true and proper schooling for a filmmaker is sitting in a movie theatre watching film, even if that means you go to see it two or three times. Basically, the only real training that's of any value is watching other movies and seeing how they're done, and reaching a point where you can extrapolate backwards from watching a shot as to how it was achieved—and then go and do it yourself and see how your results compare. I don't think it's something that can be taught in classrooms, really. Don't get me wrong—I would have loved to have gone to film school, because I think I would have had access in a very easy and direct way to the kind of information that I needed. But the important thing, I think, is training you eye and your mind to analyze film.

Q: *At the time you were teaching yourself filmmaking, you were already starting to write as well?*

A: The writing probably came first, because in high school I wanted to be a novelist. I had story ideas, and would always be working on them, writing notes and scenes. It taught me a lot about basic narrative structure and characterization. And once again, it was self-taught to an extent. I took English and creative writing in college, and that of course was helpful to formalize ideas and give names to things that I was already thinking about. Concurrent with that, I was doing a lot of illustrating for myself. I taught myself to draw human figures from Marvel comic books—not exactly the formal school, but there was a period of time when I wanted to become a comic book illustrator. It's interesting, because I think there's a very strong connection between comic books and films—a lot of critics would jump on that and say, "There's a very strong connection between comic books and your films!" But I mean that in a broader sense, which is that if you look at the way comic book illustrators work, their visual language is the same as the cinematic grammar that is generally used by directors. They can jump from a close-up of an eye to a wide shot of a landscape, and they tell stories in individual cuts. If you look at a comic book, you can almost visualize it as separate set-ups within a scene. For my mind, there is almost no difference between a comic book and a storyboard for a scene. So that kind of training of breaking up a story into separate individual images was really helpful for telling a story on film.

Q: *So your visual and dramatic sensibilities were developing simultaneously, which resulted in the fact that the visual and dramatic elements in your films always seem to be on an equal footing.*

A: I think the balance sways back and forth from one scene to the other. There are some scenes that devote themselves almost entirely to some sort of visual exercise, and there are other scenes that are so straightforward and dramatic that the visuals become almost secondary. But the overall balance is that the two should be mixed in equal parts. And I think that's really the best kind of film—it's certainly the best kind of science fiction fill in the sense that too many of them have subordinated character and story to creating another world. That's fine for a small segment of the audience who are primarily visual people, but on the whole, as a very simple generalization, I think people like people. Audiences have to relate to people that they're seeing within a fill, or they have no emotional attachment. It's possible to see and enjoy a fill that has no direct emotional involvement, but I think you get more out of a movie when the characters are accessible and you can feel for their problems.

Q: *Some have suggested that you've restored the good name of science fiction and fantasy rims because you've injected character back into them after years of special effects with stick figures for people. And yet, the best science fiction writers were always concentrating on characters in their stories and novels.*

A: Sure. I think what's happening now in the last few years is what happened to science fiction literature in the late 1930s and early 1940s, when you had John W. Campbell, who was the editor of several science fiction magazines, forcing his writers to write as if it were proper literature first and scientific analysis second. There was an evolution that brought science fiction literature forward into the idea of literature first and speculative fiction second. I think that film might be doing the same thing, and I think that's the only way it will ever find its true and proper audience—which is everybody. As far as I'm concerned, science fiction shouldn't be relegated off to the corner of the spectrum. Science fiction is for everybody. We live in a technological world. Before it used to be you only had to know how to turn on your TV and how to drive your car. Now, if you can't speak computer, you're not going to be a citizen of the next decade. So to say that science fiction is just for the pencil-neck nerds with the calculators on their hips is to really miss the point, because what it's addressing is our relationship to technical advancement. It's about where we are in our world and where we're going. To me, science fiction is a pet genre, and I think that part of what Gale [producer/writer Gale Anne Hurd] and I have tried to do in THE TERMINATOR and ALIENS is to broaden its base in a sense, make it more respectable to people who otherwise wouldn't like that sort of film.

Q: *Tell me how you passed through young adulthood and into the professional movie world.*

A: It was a pretty circuitous route. Having moved to the Los Angeles area from Canada at 17, I enrolled in junior college. I thought I wanted to be the next Jacques Coasteau, so I took marine biology for a semester. Somewhere along the way I found out that I'd probably be counting fish eggs at some hatchery in Oregon for the rest of my life. I discovered physics and astronomy—I took four semesters of physics and really enjoyed it. But them I got bored with the whole process entirely, dropped out, and decided to see the world in all its glory—which involved working as a truck driver for about two or three years. This wasn't wasted time, though. I was spending a lot of time writing and drawing on my own, and was driving to pay the rent. I was married at the time and my first wife had absolutely no inkling of the fact that this would ever lead anywhere other than working an 8-5 job indefinitely. She thought that art and writing were just quirky hobbies. I was living in Orange County at the time, and it could have been Nebraska from the standpoint of the film business—there's no direct connection, even though it's just 15 miles away. Then one day, out of the blue, a friend of mine called up and said that he had this consortium of dentists who wanted to do a tax write-off investment for a film and did I have any ideas? One of the ideas we presented to these guys was science fiction. It was the one we felt was the least probable they would want to go ahead with, but STAR WARS had just been released and was doing phenomenal business, and they thought they were going to cash in. They, like us, didn't understand that you can't get there from here. We had to shoot a 10- or 12-minute pilot for the feature, and we wanted to shoot it exactly as if it were a piece of the finished movie, partly to demonstrate to the investors that we were responsible filmmakers—which, of course, we weren't—and partly because we wanted to have fun. In fact, one of the funniest things I can recall was that the entire first day of shooting was spent trying to load the camera. We decided that we had to shoot in 35mm, so we went down to Mark Armistead (camera rental), and they were very nice. We were obviously total bumbling rubes that just fell off the turnip truck, but they rented us $30,000 worth of equipment. No problem. We didn't want to admit that we didn't know how to load the camera, so we just took it all and figured that being technically oriented, we would work it out. Basically, we wound up sort of disassembling the camera and putting it back together to figure out how it worked so we could put film in it and get it to crank through. And then the very first shot we did was this really complicated matte shot that I wouldn't even try to do now—and it worked perfectly! We didn't know were weren't supposed to be able to do it, so we did it. In a way, I think you learn better that way. We were sharing half a building which we were using as a studio, and one of the secretaries from the other half of the building came in and saw me sitting in the hallway reading a book on filmmaking. She thought it was a joke. While the crew and actors were sitting on the set, I was looking for how-to pointers! The project never did develop, and about a year later, when I was using the film as a sample real, I got hired to work on the Roger Corman film, BATTLE BEYOND THE STARS. I wound up working in special effects, process projection, motion control. Somehow, I made the transition to art director. They fired the original art director and looked around for some suicidal volunteer to take over and try to finish the remaining 32 out of 35 sets that needed to be designed and built in a period of about a week. I got a lot of practical experience out of that, so I went on to be production designer on another film, then did the special effects for John Carpenter's ESCAPE FROM NEW YORK. After that, I asked Roger if I could direct for him, which seemed to be the natural place for me—because about that point I had a dawning awareness that directing was the only place where you got perfect confluence of the storytelling, visual and technical sides. Roger told me to start doing second units, so he put me on a picture called GALAXY OF TERROR for a couple of weeks, where I did mostly slimy monster shots. And the day I finished second unit on GALAXY OF TERROR, I got offered PIRANHA II: THE SPAWNING.

Q: You shot your version of PIRANHA II and then the producer sort of shot his, correct?

A: It was kind of the ultimate director's nightmare. In fact, somebody on the crew said to me while we were shooting, "The best consolation of making this is that we'll never be this bad again!" The Italian producer was pretty unscrupulous. First he tried to fire me, but we were on a distant location and it didn't work. So I finished shooting, but the producer called himself a second unit director and shot new scenes that weren't in the script—mostly involving topless women. He basically cut the film himself back in Rome. I was supposed to go there and supervise post-production, but because he tried to fire me earlier, I guess he felt he didn't owe me anything. I wound up scrounging some money and going to Rome on my own to find out what he was doing with the picture. He wouldn't show it to me once I got there. There's a semi-amusing anecdote here. When I was in Rome on preproduction working on the script, I wanted the female protagonist in PIRANHA II to break into the morgue using a credit card. The producer didn't understand how it could be done, so I went to the front doors of his office, had him lock the doors and then broke in using a credit card. Well, three or four months later, I wound up back in Rome trying to see my movie. He won't show me the film, but since I know the security people and they still think I am working for the producer, I just said, "Hi, how ya' doing?" and got in. I rode the elevator to the top floor, took out my credit card just the way I showed him, broke into the office, taught myself how to run their strange flatbed editing console, and showed myself the movie, reel by reel. Then I'd go and have meetings with the producer and try to talk him into changing and fixing the film. He couldn't figure how I knew what was going on! Then I'd go back in and make the changes myself—driving the editor buggo. There were actually some things in the film that I managed to change that they didn't have time to change back.

Q: Did they ever find out what was going on?

A: They never did. But the end result was the film was pretty much his and it was pretty bad. It wasn't the way I intended it to be, even when we were shooting. Let alone the limitations of filming a movie in Jamaica with an Italian crew when you've got three hurricanes wiping out your schedule, and that sort of thing.

Q: At that point, I'm sure you were already looking towards better times. Had you already written THE TERMINATOR?

A: When I was in Rome the second time, I had gotten sick with some kind of fever and was languishing in my hotel room for a couple of days with nothing to do but stare at the ceiling. I came up with my basic story idea of THE TERMINA-TOR at that time, and when I got back to L.A. and PIRANHA II was all over, I called Gale and told her about it, wrote the treatment, and she agreed to take it around to the studios. We actually got the basis of the deal from Hemdale from the treatment. Then I wrote the script in fairly short order—about four weeks, I think—and it was pretty much the script that we shot.

Q: THE TERMINATOR *surprised a lot of people. Were you conscious of trying to make a breakthrough science fiction film while it was in production?*

A: We thought we were making the movie that you eventually saw. In other words, I think some films go through a metamorphosis while they're being made, and they get skewed in a different direction. But THE TERMINATOR wound up as pretty much the film we started out with, and I don't think we were trying to set the world on fire, either. I just came up with a way of juxtaposing futuristic elements with a kind of everyday reality.

Q: *Was the distributor aware that they had something more than a run-of-the-mill action grinder?*

A: I think they saw it as a very straightforward exploitation action movie, like a Charles Bronson or Chuck Norris movie that plays for two or three weeks, pays for itself and keeps the machinery rolling. I don't think they ever thought it was really something special. The head of publicity for Orion at that time—not currently—literally described the picture as a "down-and-dirty exploitation picture. "We said, "No, it's a science fiction film and you should sell it that way." He said, "Don't be ridiculous, it's not a science fiction film. If you sell it as a science fiction film you'll be betraying that audience." I said, "Why, because it doesn't have a space-ship in it? It's about time travel and robots, and you can't get two more science fictional concepts than that in one movie." Anyway, there was a sort of fundamental difference of opinion about what the film was, and we were finally vindicated by the critics. It wasn't until the critics supported the film that Orion really decided that maybe it was something worthy of promotion. Unfortunate, but true.

Q: *When did you write your draft of* RAMBO?

A: The chronology went something like this—I had written the script for THE TERMINATOR, we went through a number of casting scenarios, and finally cast Arnold Schwarzenegger. He wanted to do the picture, but we had to wait for him to go off and do CONAN THE DESTROYER first. So I had four or five months of free time before THE TERMINATOR started production, and I'd already done a lot of my preparation and storyboard work. I literally had nothing to do. I asked my agent to get me some writing assignments and the only two meetings that I had were with the people who wanted to do RAMBO and the people who wanted to do ALIENS. And I got both assignments, which was bizarre, because I had never gone out on the writer's trail of pitch sessions. I'm still, to this day, a terrible pitcher. I can't get up on the desk and tap dance the way some writers can. I think what happened was that I agreed to do both assignments on the same day, and I was offered them within a few days of each other. The producers of both projects knew each other, so I got them all on a conference call to make sure they all knew that I was writing for someone else at the same time—which I guess they thought was pretty strange behavior because what writers are supposed to do is not tell and take them both! So I wound up writing what was then FIRST BLOOD II: THE MISSION, which became RAMBO: FIRST BLOOD PART II later. I wrote two drafts and a polish of that, plus a treatment and two-thirds of the script for ALIENS in that particular period of time.

Q: *Your FIRST BLOOD II was, I'm sure, conceptually quite different from what emerged in the final version of RAMBO.*

A: Yes. I was responding to the first film which I thought was pretty good-both in taking the assignment and in trying to find a way into the story and the character. I wanted to try and preserve some aspects of Rambo's original character, and so in my approach to it, we first see him in the psychiatry wing of a VA hospital. He's just been kicked and kicked by the system to the point where he's just completely outside normal society. It was supposed to be a serious approach to character from a psychological standpoint, and when Rambo goes back to Vietnam, it's a very surreal moment—almost like a flashback. In my version, the character was a very haunted and tormented guy, not a superhero at all. Also the story I wrote was a buddy movie—Rambo and one other guy, a kind of high-tech all-American new soldier of the Eighties, like one of those conscienceless Special Forces guys who just goes in and does his duty with all the trick weapons. Rambo, on the other hand, was a kind of atavistic character who could eat leeches and run around barefoot in a jungle and have a mental communion with the way the Vietnamese live. What I tried to do with the story was show how he becomes like the Viet Cong, where he winds up being a very primitive tribal-like fighter, against a massive technological war machine—in this case the Russians. None of this stuff wound up in the final film. It became a very straightforward action thriller, with a lot of ultra-patriotic political overtones thrown in by Sylvester Stallone. The other major difference was that when you met the POWs Rambo was there to rescue, they were real people. You learned about them—you cared. And when Rambo went back to save them, it was an emotional moment. In the final film, I felt like he was going back to pick up a six-pack of beer. It's frustrating.

Q: *It seems though, that you were ultimately able to get a couple of elements from your FIRST BLOOD II script into ALIENS.*

A: Right.

Q: *The notion of somebody returning to. . .*

A: . . . face their deepest fear, or that moment of trauma on which their character has fixated. I've known people who have gotten into serious traffic accidents that completely changed their lives, and they fixate on that moment. They can't get past it, they can't grow until they've addressed it in some way. The idea of psychological catharsis, I thought, was really interesting. I thought it was something that people would respond to at a subconscious level. So there's a lot of that in the approach to the Ripley character in ALIENS. In a way, I finally got to do my RAMBO in ALIENS, but I don't like to say that, because people think, "Yeah, Sigourney Weaver with a machine gun got to do RAMBO in ALIENS." But that's not what I'm talking about I'm talking about the first third of ALIENS, where she's wrestling with having just escaped from something, being permanently bonded to it in a sense of destiny—like Rambo and his terrible experiences in Vietnam.

Q: *You also managed to get in the notion of the high-tech soldier who ultimately has to revert to the most basic survival techniques in order to live.*

A: Exactly. I think a lot of what ALIENS is about is addressing the fact that we rely very heavily on technology, and we come to rely less and less on our own basic skills and effort of will. In ALIENS, we see that get stripped away. . . the weapons and technology and communication all break down. It's not an anti-technology message, because Ripley uses a machine at the end to prevail. But it's really more about how we're deceived by technology instead of relying on ourselves.

Q: *You were an admirer of Ridley Scott's ALIEN. Didn't that intimidate you when you embarked on creating your own, and ultimately very different, sequel?*

A: I was in equal parts intimidated and seduced by it. On the one hand, yes, it's intimidating to follow in the footsteps of a classic. But on the other hand, there was enough support and energy coming out of that film that I felt I could go beyond. I think I was probably just having too much fun to really think in negative terms. For me, the opportunity to do ALIENS was to take a lot of what I liked from the first film and weld it together with my own imagery. I wanted to do a film that was consistent with my own style, as opposed to try and do a retread of Ridley Scott's style. To that end, although I'd seen his film a couple of tunes in the past, I ran it for myself and a couple of the special effects people only continued on once, very early in pre-production. And I never went back to it again. I didn't have a print laying around that I'd study once in a while, or go through frame by frame. I think that in every sequel, what you wrestle with is the division between homage and being enslaved to the vision of the first film. And of course, Ridley Scott's vision was so overpowering. That was seductive, as well. I like the way he did things. It was hard sometimes to do shots differently. And of course, there are a couple of place in ALIENS where I intentionally mimicked his style, just to sort of create a subconscious memory of the first film in the audience's mind. The end result, I think, is that the two films aren't directly comparable as one being better than the other. They're different stylistic experiences. And from what I heard, Ridley really liked ALIENS.

Q: *You've been praised for your handling of actors, both by the critics and the actors you've worked with.*

A: For me, working with actors is the most fun and the most challenging aspect of the work right now, because I feel like I've gotten to the point where I'm pretty comfortable with the technical aspects. The special thrill is creating characters, putting words into their mouths. . . because that's when it changes. And of course, what you look for when you cast is a change for the better. I've always looked for actors who are very creative and are willing to bring in a lot of ideas, and who are also willing to have those ideas thrown out if they're inappropriate. I've had the opportunity to work with some very enthusiastic actors, who have a genuine excitement for what they do and the person that they're playing. I think it's only when actors start feeling insecure about the project, about the director, about what they're being asked to do, that they start going into behavior patterns that are apparently egotistical—but are really, I think, more defensive. I've been fortunate in never having worked with a really difficult star. I can always deal with an actor on the basis of having written a character and knowing what's going on in that character's head, which makes me helpful to the actor. It makes them look better, and it makes their work more satisfying.

Q: *The police station scenes in* THE TERMINATOR *and the Colonial Marine group sequences in* ALIENS *have an improvisational quality. How do you work with actors to get that naturalistic tone?*

A: Well, in the case of the police station scenes in THE TERMINATOR, they were pretty much word-for-word from the script. In ALIENS, there was a little more flexibility, but the basis for all the lines was pretty much there. In ALIENS, it was a real exercise in ensemble work—for me and for the actors. I got all the actors who played Marines together two weeks before shooting started and we did half a day, each day, of rehearsal from the script, and half a day of military maneuvers in the Pinewood Studios garden—which involved Marine Corps calisthenics, rifle drill, march runs with packs, things like that. We basically created the psychological illusion that they were an actual platoon. And another thing that helped and this was by design—was that the actor I cast to play the sergeant, Al Matthews, was a real Marine Corps sergeant in three consecutive combat tours of Vietnam. So he's a pretty hardened vet, and brought a lot of reality to both his own character and to everybody else's as well. If one of the actors dropped their rifle, he would run over and scream in their face, "Your rifle is your life, soldier! Give me fifty!" And the actor would get down and do fifty push-ups in front of the other actors. I think that helped. It created an environment where the people were very close to their characters, and if they said something in an improvisational way, it was accurate. I think it was a perfect blend of what was written and what was created from scratch. The whole scene where they're putting on their armor, and the sergeant is walking through the group talking, was made up by Al and myself on the set just at that moment. And every take was completely different. He had more rap at his fingertips than I could have used in four movies.

Q: *You were trying, in a way, to hook into the audience's collective unconscious memory of all those movies that they've watched through the years on television and in movie theatres?*

A: Yes, and I think it worked. I think people feel very comfortable with those characters and with those situations. The idea of the green new lieutenant, hardened old sergeant, wisecracking private, quiet Steve McQueen character—who in this happens to be a woman, Vasquez—it's all there. And it's all there in a very barefaced way. But the fact that it's in a completely new context makes it, I think, interesting. And it's kind of a fun rediscovery. Also, I like the basic clarity of the 1940's filmmaking narrative structure. It wasn't plagued by a lot of ambiguities. It was before the discovery of the antihero. When they told a story, you knew what they meant to say. When I walk out of a theatre these days, fifty percent of the time I don't know what the movie was about. And I don't like that feeling. For my own personal taste, I like to have a certain clarity of intention. I think you have to have something to hope for. When you watch a football game, you're cheering for your team to make a touchdown. And for an audience to invest themselves in a film, I think they have to understand what the ground rules are. I also see a lot of films these days that don't have an ending. They have great characters, set pieces that are fun, but the endings seem to be modular—they could have done it differently. The best films, to me, are the ones that can have only one ending. When I hear people shooting different endings for a movie I say, "God, how can you do that?" For me, the ending comes first and then you write backwards, and all the threads converge on that. And when it happens, there's a rightness about it that resonates through the rest of the film.

Q: *You took a giant leap between* PIRANHA II *and* THE TERMINATOR, *and then between* THE TERMINATOR *and* ALIENS. *How did you handle such large increases in budget and responsibility?*

A: The interesting thing about my subjective experience of each one of these three films was that from the standpoint of my process, of what I do in real time on the set, there was almost no difference between them. I still wound up completely destroying my wardrobe, like I do on every film crawling around on the floor setting up low angles, in TERMINATOR, I was crawling around in the gutters of downtown Los Angeles. In ALIENS, I was crawling around the slime-covered floors of Pinewood sound stages.

Q: *Do you think you'll soon be moving outside of the science fiction/fantasy field?*

A: I think with ALIENS I've pretty much gone as far as I can go in the science fiction genre. I can't imagine doing a film that's bigger or more complicated or has more imagery. The challenge doesn't exist anymore. Now I think the challenge would be to do a small ensemble picture and have it be as compelling as one that has the sort of sturm und drang aspects of THE TERMINATOR and ALIENS.

Q: *Are you kind of director who never reads his reviews?*

A: The thing I like about film reviewing and film critics is that it creates dialogue, and you get to hear very specific and articulately voiced feedback. In that sense, critical analysis of a film is very important. It's pointless to say I'm just making movies for myself and I'm not going to pay any attention to what critics say, because you try to do certain things that make a film function on various levels and you never really get any articulate feedback on it—except through written criticism of the film. That's the only time anybody sits down and expends enough energy to actually formalize their response to the movie. Your friends won't do it. They'll say, "Yeah, great movie, let's go play racquetball." I've been fortunate in that even PIRANHA II was well reviewed by one of the two reviewers who wrote about it. I think on THE TERMINATOR and ALIENS we were running about 80% favorable. But even the negative reviews I read very carefully because I think there are lessons there. The thing that is constantly fascinating to me about movies is the disparity between the intention of a scene and the way it's interpreted subjectively by different people.

Q: *So you continue to educate yourself?*

A: Yes, I'm all over the place. You have to. I mean, if I was to sit here and say, "I've made three movies, I know everything there is to know about filmmaking," it would be ridiculous. I'd like to hope that I can be like John Huston, just keep making movies as long as I live. You're always learning. You're always discovering something new.

F I L M O G R A P H Y

J A M E S   C A M E R O N

b. August 16, 1954 - Kapuskasing, Ontario, Canada
PIRANHA II - THE SPAWNING   Saturn International, 1983, Italian-U.S.
THE TERMINATOR   Orion, 1984
ALIENS   20th Century Fox, 1986
THE ABYSS   20th Century Fox, 1989
TERMINATOR 2: JUDGMENT DAY   TriStar, 1991
TRUE LIES   20th Century Fox, 1994
TITANIC ★★   Paramount/20th Century Fox, 1997

$\mathcal{H}$ENNING $\mathcal{C}$ARLSEN

In the 1960s, when Scandinavian cinema began to explode onto sophisticated American screens, much of what was seen emanated from Sweden and
such notable filmmakers as Ingmar Bergman, Bo Widerbergh, Jan Troell and
Mai Zetterling. But something was also stirring in the state of Denmark at that
time, and its name was Henning Carlsen.

The fact is that Carlsen was the first Danish filmmaker to win real international fame and acclaim since the great Carl Dreyer. Curiously enough, Carlsen's
first and next-to-most-recent film—respectively, DILEMMA and THE WOLF AT
THE DOOR—were shot in English. The rest, with one French exception, were
Danish or other Scandinavian-language films, virtually all of them award-win-
ners at various international film festivals (approximately 25 such prizes in all).

It's ironic, and sadly indicative of the poor distribution of foreign-language
films in the United States throughout the '70s, '80s and '90s, that of Carlsen's 14
distinguished works, only DILEMMA, THE CATS, HUNGER, PEOPLE MEET AND
SWEET MUSIC FILLS THE HEART and THE WOLF AT THE DOOR have been
seen in this country's theatres. That error was corrected with retrospectives of
Carlsen's entire body of work at both the Museum of Modern Art in New York
and the American Cinemateque in Los Angeles in 1991, the year of our conversation. Unfortunately, his most recent film, TWO GREEN FEATHERS (1995)—
which like HUNGER is based on a work by Knut Hamsun—also failed to find a
U.S. distributor, just as Carlsen has remained unsuccessful in his campaign to
mount a production of Kurt Vonnegut's novel Jailbird, based on a fine script by
Buck Henry.

Nonetheless, Carlsen remains unafraid to shy away from what he calls "crazy"
projects, tilting at windmills and determined to take the rest of us on his quest.

MICHAEL SINGER: *You spent years making documentary films. . . How did you come
to make your first feature?*

HENNING CARLSEN: It was linked to my activities as a documentary and
industrial filmmaker. A very big Danish industrial company asked me to make a

documentary about their first 25 years. I wrote a very ambitious screenplay called DANFORS AROUND THE CLOCK AROUND THE WORLD, the fact that they were always active 24 hours a day somewhere on the map. So the owner of the company said, "Okay, first you make a sequence on the factory and then you go to South Africa and make a sequence there, and then show me how the mix between factory and foreign sequences works when it's cut together." So we went to South Africa, and cut this sort of pilot for him, and he said okay, go ahead. So myself and the cinematographer,

Henning Kristiansen, made an enormous trip which took us to Egypt, India, Thailand, Singapore, Australia and then back to Johannesburg in South Africa. And when we came back there I suddenly realized that something had happened. This was in 1958, and apartheid was only 10 years old. The local branch manager of Danfors took us to the company on a Saturday afternoon, and there was an old black man who was helping us there. The week was finished, and this old man was packed to go home. The branch manager—who must have been 30 or 32 years old—said to this old man, who must have been 70 or so, "Okay, you can go home now. . . be a good boy." And this young chap telling this distinguished old black man to "be a good boy" was just a shock to me. Then I started to take a harder look around and discovered what was really going on. When I returned to Denmark to finish the film, I started to read about South Africa, and that was when I read Nadine Gordimer for the first time. I decided that if ever I should get the possibility of making a feature film, South Africa would be my subject.

Q: How did that actually come about?

A: My mother died, and my sister and I inherited a house, which we sold. I got half the money, and decided to use it to make this picture. I returned to South Africa to do research in January 1962, and met Nadine for the first time. I suddenly had the idea to make a film of Nadine's book A World of Strangers, which was eventually titled DILEMMA for the film. I called her and she said "Fine, let's do it." And while we were working on the screenplay, the book was banned in South Africa. But we made the film, still the only Nadine Gordimer novel to be adapted for the big screen.

Q: And it was made illegally?

A: Illegally, yes. I think I lost 18 kilos in six weeks, and smoked 60 cigarettes a day.

Q: And you're alive to tell about it. When you were out in the streets of Johannesburg— because there are several exterior sequences in the movie—what did you tell the authorities you were doing?

A: Well, most of it was shot from a van, with a camera on a tripod and curtains on the windows. But one window was open, and it sort of functioned as a one-way mirror. For instance, you remember a shot of two policemen looking at the passport of a black man? They were less than one meter from us, and Henning Kristiansen, my cameraman, was having trouble getting them in focus because they were so close. We were scared that they would hear the sound from the Arriflex inside the van.

Q: Was it shot in 16mm or 35mm?

A: 35mm black and white.

Q: DILEMMA very strongly revealed your background as a documentary filmmaker. Much of it was shot in a strongly impressionistic style. Your most recent film, however, reveals a very different aesthetic.

A: Yes, with THE WOLF AT THE DOOR I tried to link the style of the film with the style of its subject, which was the work of Paul Gauguin.

Q: HUNGER is probably your most famous film, and it's still amazingly unsettling to watch. The only other films I can think of that get so close to such unsympathetic protagonists are those by Scorsese. What was your own attitude toward the "hero" of HUNGER?

A: You know, when you sit down to read a book, the world around you disappears. Particularly when you read a book which is written in a kind of "first person" style. So I felt like I was Knut Hamsun's protagonist when I made the picture, with Per Oscarsson, who played the role, more or less replacing me. The film was also made in a "first person" style. Actually, HUNGER was one of the first adult books I ever read, and when I re-read it I was convinced that it could make a powerful picture. That was at a time of my career where I knew that if I decided what picture I wanted to make, I could actually decide when it would start shooting.

Q: And it was HUNGER that first brought you squarely into international recognition?

A: Well, DILEMMA made me famous in a certain way because when it was discovered that I had shot the film illegally, it was a big scandal, at least in Europe and England. And DILEMMA won first prize at the Mannheim Film Festival.

Q: Were you able to find distribution for DILEMMA in England and the U.S.? After all, it was shot in English.

A: I was rushing around London trying to find a distributor for the picture, and I couldn't understand why I was having problems because it was a good movie that was highly acclaimed by international critics, and so on. Until one day, a British distributor said to me, "But Mr. Carlsen, have you not understood that your picture is a hot potato in London?" It was even a hot potato in the United States. It finally got distributed in England by a company called Contemporary Film. The owner was a very liberal person named Mr. Cooper. I think they had a branch connected with a company in America, which distributed the film in 16mm.

Q: It must be frustrating to you that you had three consecutive films distributed to great acclaim in the U.S.—HUNGER, PEOPLE MEET AND SWEET MUSIC FILLS THE HEART and THE CATS—and then none of your movies were seen in America until THE WOLF AT THE DOOR. With only three exceptions your films have won awards at several international festivals, and your work has been continually recognized in Europe. And yet, you suffered through 20 years of non-distribution in the United States.

A: That's true. And it's a fate many foreign directors have suffered with the decreasing interest in foreign cinema that we saw in the U.S. in those years. But if you say that I've made 13 films, and four of them have been distributed in America, that's actually a very high percentage for European filmmakers.

Q: *You're now working with Buck Henry on a film adaptation of Kurt Vonnegut's JAILBIRD, which is considered an important work. And of course, you mean for this to be an American production shot in English.*

A: Well, if you look up the word "important" in my computer's dictionary, it has different meanings. Important can mean a big book, without meaning a well known book. I think JAILBIRD is an important book, but it's very rare that I meet people who have read it.

Q: *At the moment of this interview, you' re seeking financing, is it more difficult because of the fact that only four of your 13 films have been seen in the U.S.?*

A: Absolutely. And it makes it even tougher that the Hollywood establishment doesn't like writers and directors who have grown pubic hair.

Q: *This subject of age discrimination in the film industry has become quite controversial as of late. There's an obsession in this country with youth. If you're a film school graduate, and they showed your student film at a little festival, every studio is dying to give you a development deal. If you've been around for 20 or 30 years, made 15 or 20 films and won awards all over the world, it is true that sometimes the color of your hair will be used against you.*

A: But it's not all American. It's also the case in my own country. I think there's so limited money for filmmaking that they want to put the money up for young people, and I can't honestly blame them.

Q: *Do you see yourself as a Danish filmmaker, or a filmmaker who happens to be from Denmark?*

A: The latter.

Q: *Does this get you into trouble in your own country?*

A: It does in a way. Because you know, all small societies proclaim that if you stick up your nose over the surface, they'll cut it off. But I feel that my true roots are in the fact that images started to move, and that transcended all national borders.

Q: *You have one of the world's greatest collections of magic lanterns, and I understand that you are both writing a book and preparing a documentary film on the roots of the moving image.*

A: Yes. . . perhaps even more than a documentary. . . a fantasy.

Q: *When did this obsession with the foundation of film begin?*

A: I think it started before I even was conscious of the fact that I wanted to become a filmmaker. I was fascinated from the beginning by the fact that you could throw a picture up on a wall, that you could transform a picture from being a slide or a roll of perforated film to something on a wall or a screen. There was a magic lantern in the basement of my parents' house in Aalborg, and it was never used by us because it was completely outdated. I mean, nobody used a magic lantern after the turn of the century. But there it was, and actually, I stole it. And that was the first sample in my collection. Then when I moved to Copenhagen, I often saw magic lanterns in antique shops, and I started to buy them whenever I could. A part of my collection was stolen in 1980, but when I moved to Paris for three years to prepare a picture I rebuilt it. I was fascinated by the fact that throughout time, artists have been trying to fight against the fact that their art, sculptures and pictures were inanimate. But even on the prehistoric wall paintings, the artists were expressing the movements of the animals. And they were not made as decorations, but a kind of communication. Mankind has been overrun by a search no, an urge—to beat nature, to create and present movement.

Q: *To me, that's the most mysterious thing of all about film. . . . this preservation of what no longer exists. It's very frightening in a way.*

A: Yes, it is. But one of the new problems we are now facing is that it turns out that this preservation is not eternal. You've got to do something about it all the time if you want to keep it. Otherwise, they just disappear.

Q: *Getting back to JAILBIRD, how did you come to the idea of making the film, and how did you become associated with Buck Henry on this venture?*

A: To the first question, I can say that I have been a great admirer of Vonnegut as a writer for years, and have read everything he has written that's been available in Europe. Only four of his books have been translated into Danish, including JAILBIRD, but the translations are so bad that I went back to the English originals. What happened was, I had a project which I was supposed to begin shooting after THE WOLF AT THE DOOR, which was one of those projects I had been dreaming of for years and years. I suddenly got a message two weeks before we were supposed to begin pre-production that the picture was not going to happen. Obviously, I became rather depressed, and for some time I didn't know what to do next. Then suddenly one day, my eyes fell on my copy of JAILBIRD. It just sort of jumped out at me. And I thought, yes, why not JAILBIRD as a movie? You know, I have a tendency to choose impossible projects. I mean, making an illegal picture in South Africa about apartheid in 1962 was a crazy idea, making a film of HUNGER was a completely crazy idea, and even THE WOLF AT THE DOOR, a movie about Gauguin, was another crazy idea. So I felt that since so many of my projects had been crazy, why not try another one?

Q: *And your involvement with Buck Henry?*

A: I had originally thought of Buck Henry acting as the film's main character, because I had met him in Copenhagen years ago. Then I remembered that he was also a very highly accomplished screenwriter, so I called and asked him if he would be interested in writing the screenplay. He said that he would have to re-read the book. After a couple of weeks Buck called me back, and after the lawyers and agents had made their homework, he was ready to start.

Q: *With the radical time shifts and spanning of the years, JAILBIRD is not an easy book to adapt.*

A: No, it isn't, but I think that Buck has done marvelous, wonderful work.

Q: You've worked before with English-speaking writers, like Nadine Gordimer and Christopher Hampton, who adapted the screenplay you had written with Jean-Claude Carriere for THE WOLF AT THE DOOR, but Buck Henry is the first American you've worked with. Is there any difference?

A: Yes, there's a big difference. The Anglo-Saxon approach is different from the European, because European writers and authors have the feeling that what they're about to create is divine, and should not be touched. The American way, which allows for much more change, is more fresh. Now, you've asked me about why JAILBIRD, and why Buck Henry, but there's one question you haven't asked.

Q: Okay, ask it for me.

A: Here it is: "Why do you think, Henning Carlsen, that a Dane should come and make this picture, which is entirely American?"

Q: I was too polite to ask that. But it's a good question.

A: It's a very good question. And the answer is that for one thing, it's my initiative. I brought it to where it is. Another justification is that it may be interesting to have a foreigner look at the history of this country with fresh eyes. Perhaps I'm looking at this country in a way that no American would. When I did a film in France, it turned out to be more French than most French pictures.

Q: As a matter of fact, some of the best films ever made about America have been made by foreigners. Has Kurt Vonnegut been involved at all with the project?

A: No, except for one meeting that I had with him at the Algonquin Hotel before we started writing, and another more recently after we finished writing. I said to him at the first meeting, "There are two reasons why I wanted to meet you. The first is that we will be shooting some of the film in New York, and I had a nightmare that you would be in the crowd, watching us shoot, before I had even shaken your hand. The second reason is that I want to be the one to tell you that I'm going to violate your book." He asked what I meant by that, and I said "I'm going to cut things out, add new things, change other things, and that's a violation. Any film adaptation of a book is a violation. Normally, I work only with dead poets and authors, but since you are alive, I should tell you this." Vonnegut then said something wonderful. . . "You cannot violate my book," he told me, "because it will always be there. . . on the bookshelves in the library, in people's homes, in the bookstores. So my position is go ahead start on it from scratch and do whatever you want."

Q: Has Vonnegut now read the screenplay? And if so, what's his response?

A: He wrote a beautiful letter to Buck in which he expressed his appreciation of Buck's work with the book, ending with "God bless you and Henning Carlsen." And that despite the fact that we have violated his book completely, exactly as we said we would. You see. . . I learned when I made HUNGER from Knut Hamsun's novel that you can only be faithful to a book by betraying it.

F I L M O G R A P H Y

H E N N I N G   C A R L S E N

b. June 4, 1927 - Aalborg, Jutland, Denmark

DILEMMA *A WORLD OF STRANGERS* Minerva Film/Bent Christensen Filmproduktion, 1962, Danish

EPILOGUE Bent Christensen Filmproduktion/Constantin Films, 1963, Danish

THE CATS National Showmanship, 1964, Swedish

HUNGER Sigma III, 1966, Danish-Norwegian-Swedish

PEOPLE MEET AND SWEET MUSIC FILLS THE HEART Trans-Lux, 1967, Danish-Swedish

WE ARE ALL DEMONS Nordisk Film/Sandrews/Teamfilm/Henning Carlsen Film, 1969, Danish-Swedish-Norwegian

ARE YOU AFRAID? Henning Carlsen Film, 1971, Danish

OH, TO BE ON THE BANDWAGON! Henning Carlsen Film/Nordisk, 1972, Danish

A HAPPY DIVORCE CFDC, 1975, French-Danish

WHEN SVANTE DISAPPEARED Dagmar Filmproduktion, 1976, Danish

DID SOMEBODY LAUGH? Dagmar Filmproduktion/Sam-Film, 1978, Danish

YOUR MONEY OR YOUR LIFE Dagmar Filmproduktion, 1982, Danish

THE WOLF AT THE DOOR *OVIRI* International Film Marketing, 1986, Danish-French

TWO GREEN FEATHERS *PAN* Northern Light Productions/Zentropa Entertainment/Dagmar Film/Multimedia, 1995, Norwegian-Danish-German

$\mathcal{G}$ILBERT $\mathcal{C}$ATES

A noted producer and director of motion pictures, television and theatre—Gilbert Cates has also distinguished himself with two terms as one of the Directors Guild of America's most effective and outspoken presidents, the current Dean of the UCLA School of Theater, Film and Television, and as the man who restored dignity to the annual presentations of the Academy Awards as its best producer in memory.

As the president of the DGA, Cates faced familiar issues of strikes and contracts, and the more insidious new ones of colorization and other technological horrors, head-on, usually producing positive results for filmmakers' rights.

God knows where Cates has also found the time to direct, but that he has, perhaps most notably in the arena of telefeatures, where he has specialized in sensitive dramas that emphasize character and story over pyrotechnics. Cates has received Emmy nominations for CONSENTING ADULT, DO YOU KNOW THE MUFFIN MAN? and ABSOLUTE STRANGERS, his other fine work for the small screen also including TO ALL MY FRIENDS ON SHORE, JOHNNY, WE HARDLY KNEW YE, HOBSON'S CHOICE, CHILD'S CRY and INNOCENT VICTIMS. His best features are still his first two: the lovely I NEVER SANG FOR MY FATHER and SUMMER WISHES, WINTER DREAMS.

MICHAEL SINGER: *You have quite a background in theatre, television and film. Can you give me a bit of history?*

GILBERT CATES: I went to Syracuse University, majored in theatre and received a Master's Degree. The first job that I got when I left the university was as a page at NBC, and from there I became the assistant stage manager of a Broadway show called Shinbone Alley. New York then was much different than it is today, because television was just burgeoning and theatre was still very active. There were many more jobs available per person than there are now, so it was much easier to break in. Oddly enough, after Shinbone Alley I got involved with game shows. I did about thirty pilots, shows like Quick on the Draw, Camouflage and Across the Board. One little footnote is that the first television game show done in color was Haggis Baggis which I directed. It was amazing—the cameras were humongous. Then from game shows, I directed a pilot for the series called "Hootenanny," and from that I did a series with my brother Joe called "International Showtime," which featured Don Ameche as host. I directed and executive produced it for four years all over the world, covering circuses and other extravaganzas. That was actually the first project which gave me the opportunity to direct a movie, because having had this experience with the circus, I did a feature documentary called RINGS AROUND THE WORLD for Columbia Pictures, which also starred Don Ameche.

Q: *You were still involved with theatre, though.*

A: Around that time I produced about eight plays on Broadway, directed two or three of them, and had only two hits. One was "You Know I Can't Hear You When the Water's Running" —Marty Balsam won the Tony Award for that, and it was also with Eileen Heckart, George Grizzard and Melinda Dillon. The other was "I Never Sang For My Father" with Lillian Gish, Hal Holbrook and Teresa Wright. Later, because I had made RINGS AROUND THE WORLD for Columbia Pictures, they agreed to let me make I NEVER SANG FOR MY FATHER as a movie. Their only requirement was for me to get Gene Hackman to play the son, which I did. . . and he was nominated for an Academy Award for that role. I continued to do a lot of films and plays for television. My favorite was AFTER THE FALL with Christopher Plummer and Faye Dunaway. . . and then I moved to LA ten years ago.

Q: *Can versatility actually be a problem in your profession?*

A: The most difficult part of my involvement in show business has been that every time I work in one area, people only think that I can work in that one area. For a period of time I was just a Broadway producer and director. For another period of time I was just working in television, and for another period just in features. I'd rather be able to. . . like a little bee. . . go around and get a little nectar here, a little nectar there.

Q: *Would you say that directors are stereotyped the way actors are?*

A: I tell you, it's worse. I've said this many tunes. I've lectured about it many times. When an actor is stereotyped as a comedian and someone says he can't do a straight pan, at least the actor can read for the role. But as a director, you're dead. People can't think beyond what it is that you've done last. There was a period when I only got scripts that had to do with sickness. When I did I NEVER SANG FOR MY FATHER it dealt with geriatrics. Then I did TO ALL MY FRIENDS ON SHORE with Bill Cosby, which dealt with sickle cell anemia. Then I did a movie with Natalie Wood playing a disabled person called THE AFFAIR. Then I did THE KID FROM NOWHERE, which dealt with Down's Syndrome. Stereotyping is rampant. Now, if you become a big star there's no problem. If Barbara Streisand wanted to read portions of the Bible and the telephone book she could get financing for ten million bucks to do it. The problem today is that in California, most people's sense of history is what happened last year. There are no, or very few, historical perspectives used to help the decision-making process. As a result, whatever your last two films were is your history, so if your last two films were comedies, you are a comedy director. I did THE LAST MARRIED COUPLE IN AMERICA followed by OH GOD! BOOK II, and then for a year all I got were comedy scripts.

Q: Do you have a preference for working in television or theatrical films?

A: Not really. The material is most important to me. However, there are no real blockbusters in television. If a movie does a hundred million dollars it is such a part of our consciousness that everything that follows is affected by it. If a director does a theatrical movie that really goes through the roof and gets great critical response, it stays with people. In television, if you do two-hour movies, it's hard to have a big blowout. It's over in a night. A movie, however, seeps into the collective unconscious. It plays in theatres, then after a period of time it goes into commercial television networks, then it may go to pay television and syndicated television. Then it will be released as a videocassette. All this takes a period of two or three years. And there's the merchandising that accompanies it. It's not unlike having a major ailment that affects your whole body. But somehow, a television show, no matter how many people see it. . . so what? Everyone watches and then the next night they watch something else. Now there are seminal exceptions to that rule. ROOTS is a magnificent example, and so, perhaps, is BRIAN'S SONG. I'm proud, though, that the television movie which I directed called CONSENTING ADULT had a dramatic effect on the gay community. So it did have a major impact on a segment of the American public.

Q: You seem to have no problem switching back and forth between television movies and feature films, although often that field seems more segmented.

A: At one time television companies loved getting feature directors, because it gave the films a sense of importance and style. However, that was more than compensated by the fact that they were afraid that feature directors needed more time, that they were going to go over budget, that they weren't as reliable, and so now it's kind of mixed.

Q: So do you, in fact, prefer working in features?

A: I'll give you one short answer if you'll let me give you the long one as well. The answer simply is that I prefer directing material that I really love. I loved doing CONSENTING ADULT and I loved doing AFTER THE FALL. Those were both for television. I've never done a project that I haven't liked—or that I havn't started out liking. I ended up not liking them as much, but I've been fortunate that I've never done a project for the money alone. Now, if all things are equal, and I have material I like and I have a chance to do it as a television movie or as a feature, I would rather do a feature, because you have more time.

Q: Is there more artistic freedom in features?

A: I don't think so. You read stories all the time about directors having their films recut or destroyed. You've got these major traumas involving some big directors. It doesn't often happen in television, though. I think the reason is that there is no money to let it happen. There's no opportunity for indulgence. You finish a television movie, typically, and you have twelve weeks tops to deliver the finished print. Usually it's ten weeks to deliver the print. That gives you four weeks to do a rough. After six weeks you show it to an executive. You've got a week or ten days to lock it, and a month to finish it. So oddly enough, on the whole there may be less interference in television. Now, of course there are things you can't do in television, but that's not so much interference by the network as much as the reality of the medium.

Q: As a veteran director and outgoing president of the Directors Guild of America, I'm sure you've had your share of battles with executives.

A: You know, making a movie is an adventure. I love Truffaut's quote—"Making a movie is like going on a voyage. You can't wait to begin the voyage, and halfway through it you can't wait until it's over." There is a continuous battle between people who know how to make movies and people who think they do and know little or nothing about the process, and therefore can only damage a director's working process. I know this is true, because I've seen it myself first hand over and over again. What I'm saying is that the executive who is smart and wants to get the best product that he can is aware of what I'm saying. They are concerned about the script, which they should be. They're concerned about the director, the three or four key actors involved in the show, and the budget. Once they make that agreement you're on your own. Now, they watch dailies to be sure you're shooting the script, and that's fine. But there are people who have flop after flop, and it's just not a surprise to anybody but them. There are people I wouldn't do a picture for. Life is just too short.

Q: What are some of the important issues facing the DGA at this time?

A: I think one of the major issues has to do with the distortion of completed films—and I can't think of adjectives harsh enough to describe people who alter films after their release. You know, this business of colorization is just one small illustration. Fortunately, it's caught the public imagination, and as a result we've used it as a vehicle to get other things done. We were also against panning and scanning, but no one would listen. I've done one picture in scope, and it's terrible what happens when it goes on television. They say that the FCC doesn't allow letterboxing, which allows the entire image to be seen without the panning and scanning, but that's baloney—because the FCC has no effect on cable and they have no effect on videocassettes. Then there was the business of speeding up and slowing down films, and no one was interested in that either. So we've been trying for a long time to have an effect on these things which have limited interest on the part of the public, which ultimately dictates politicians' and business peoples' interest. Colorizing presented us with that opportunity. It became a lightening rod incident, and we're playing it for all it's worth. But it lakes a great deal out of our treasury, both financially and emotionally, to get laws changed.

Q: It amazes me that there's so little respect for the artist's intent in this country.

A: In Europe, there's something called the droit morale, which is the law where the individual governments, e.g., France, Germany and England, recognize the artist's primacy over financial interests—so that in those countries, when the movie's finished, no one can change it. In our country, we historically recognize the importance of private property, and we recognize that importance not only as it relates to real estate, but films as well. Consequently, it's possible for a Ted Turner to buy HOW GREEN WAS MY VALLEY and colorize it. Worse than that, it's possible for him to buy it, colorize it, and take a new copyright on it! Then he has a new piece of material. It is unconscionable in a civilized society that this should be allowed to happen. The concept is. . . I paid for it, it's mine. I can do what I want with it. We don't have a concept of trusteeship here. There's nothing wrong with someone owning a Modigliani—you can own it, you can sell it, you can realize a profit on it. There's nothing wrong with you photographing it and selling prints. But there is something wrong with taking a Modigliani and changing its color, or cutting it and making four little Modiglianis out of it. Well, legally we don't recognize that here, and that's a tragedy. That is probably the Guild's biggest artistic and intellectual pursuit.

Q: *And I understand that there's worse yet that technology has to offer in terms of changing or distorting existing films.*

A: Do you know about the Craig 5000, which now can actually regenerate an actor's face and arrange for that face to say lines? Technically, they'll be able to redo a scene with a dead actor. They can even reproduce an actor's voice and have him say something they invent. They can have Clark Gable say "Frankly my dear, I don't give a crap." They can make whole new movies with Clark Gable! Now, when Elliot Silverstein, who is chairman of the DGA's President's Committee to investigate these matters went out to look at the computer, he found out that the only it can't do yet is duplicate folds in clothing. But they can reproduce Spencer Tracy's face, or anyone else's. It is cannibalism of the worst kind. Colorizing is not the worst that can happen. The worst is yet to be dealt with. It's terrible.

Q: *It seems a tragedy that high technology has turned out to be the enemy of art rather than its partner.*

A: Well, Socrates made the point that if man can conceive it, it will happen. To the degree that we develop abilities, we have to utilize those abilities. That's man's nature. Part of the terrible fear of atomic weapons is that conceptually, at some point they are going to be used. Logically, over a period of ten thousand years, over a period of fifty million years—or maybe a week—if we have it we are going to use it. The only way to prevent these horrible things from being used to legislate against them, and we're committing a lot of money in the Guild to this. I think it's justified.

F I L M O G R A P H Y

G I L B E R T   C A T E S

b. June 6, 1934 - New York, New York
RINGS AROUND THE WORLD (FD) Columbia, 1967
I NEVER SANG FOR MY FATHER Columbia, 1970
TO ALL MY FRIENDS ON SHORE (TF) Jemmin & Jamel Productions, 1972
SUMMER WISHES, WINTER DREAMS Columbia, 1973
THE AFFAIR (TF) Spelling-Goldberg Productions, 1973
ONE SUMMER LOVE DRAGONFLY American International, 1976
JOHNNY, WE HARDLY KNEW YE (TF) Talent Associates/Jamel Productions, 1977
THE PROMISE Universal, 1979
THE LAST MARRIED COUPLE IN AMERICA Universal, 1980
OH, GOD! BOOK II Warner Bros., 1980
COUNTRY GOLD (TF) CBS Entertainment, 1982
HOBSON'S CHOICE (TF) CBS Entertainment, 1983
BURNING RAGE (TF) Gilbert Cates Productions, 1984
CONSENTING ADULT (TF) ☆ Starger Company/David Lawrence and Ray Aghayan Productions,
    1985
CHILD'S CRY (TF) Shoot the Moon Enterprises/Phoenix Entertainment Group, 1986
BACKFIRE New Century/Vista, 1987
FATAL JUDGMENT (TF) Jack Farren Productions/Group W Productions, 1988
MY FIRST LOVE (TF) The Avnet-Kerner Company, 1988
DO YOU KNOW THE MUFFIN MAN? (TF) ☆ The Avnet-Kerner Company, 1989
CALL ME ANNA (TF) Gilbert Cates Productions/Mianna Pearce Productions/Finnegan-
    PinchukProductions, 1990
ABSOLUTE STRANGERS (TF) ☆ Absolute Strangers Co./Gilbert Cates Productions, 1991
CONFESSIONS: TWO FACES OF EVIL (TF) Cates-Doty Productions, 1994
INNOCENT VICTIMS (TF) Kushner-Locke Company/Cates-Doty Productions, 1996

$\mathcal{M}$ARTHA COOLIDGE

What's heartening about Martha Coolidge's career is that she's occasionally scored, sometimes failed, but continues in her quest to expand both her horizons and her talents in all directions. Her career was really kicked off by VALLEY GIRL, one of 1983's nicest surprises. . . a funny, incisive and touching film that utterly disarmed audiences with its dead-on depiction of L.A. life during a time now used as a backdrop for period pieces, and by being one of the first movies to demonstrate what Nicolas Cage was capable of doing on screen. However, Coolidge's first effort—NOT A PRETTY PICTURE—was a widely praised and very controversial film about rape that won awards at the American and Mannheim Film Festivals.

It's not been a smooth road since for Coolidge. Following VALLEY GIRL, both JOY OF SEX and THE CITY GIRL were little seen and distributed, and REAL GENIUS—a wonderful comedy that had both smarts and style—was remarkably underrated. Another tepid feature (PLAIN CLOTHES) and two TV movies followed, until Coolidge hit paydirt once again in 1991 with RAMBLING ROSE. This powerful tale of 1930s Georgia, written by Calder Willingham from his novel, won Oscar nominations for both Laura Dern and her mother Diane Ladd, the film a terrific showcase not only for them and the rest of the cast, but for Coolidge as well.

Since then, Coolidge's work has followed a typically unpredictable path, whether an offbeat inter-cultural love story for cable television (the charming CRAZY IN LOVE), ethnic comedy-drama (LOST IN YONKERS, ANGIE), childhood fantasy (THREE WISHES) or senior comedy (OUT TO SEA, one of the better Lemmon/Matthau post-GRUMPY OLD MEN pairings).

MICHAEL SINGER: *It seemed to me that you transcended the basic youth/sex genre with* VALLEY GIRL *and turned it into something different from what might originally have been intended.*

MARTHA COOLIDGE: Well, it was [producers and co-writers] Andy Lane and Wayne Crawford's project and they always intended it to be a love story. They were a little worried that the girls wouldn't come off as real, and that's why they wanted me to direct it. I think that as a woman I was able to bring some reality to the girls, which is very important. I mean, I learned something from Roger Ebert and Gene Siskel on T.V., when they said that in all the other teenage comedy sex pictures the girls don't even have names! That is really shocking. Andy and Wayne were genuinely concerned about that. . . they wanted it to be better than it could have been. And I think the people who were genuinely surprised were the distributors. I don't think they expected a real movie.

Q: *How involved were you with the development of* VALLEY GIRL?

A: Well, they did a rewrite with me and then added scenes. I wanted certain scenes in there, like Nicolas [Cage] and Deborah's [Foreman] breakup scene at the door. It wasn't in the script. I said, you can't have a love story where the couple breaks up without showing them breaking up. There was somewhat of a lack of focus, but they had written the script quickly. So we worked on it together before we shot it.

Q: *A lot of people who knew of you before* VALLEY GIRL—*basically from* NOT A PRETTY PICTURE, *which is a very different kind of movie—were surprised to see your name connected with a title as commercial as* VALLEY GIRL. *Of course, it turned out better than expected. Are you surprised by what's been happening to you since it was released?*

A: Oh no, I'm ready. I'm definitely ready. But on the other hand, it's always a surprise, I think, when things bring the unexpected. There are always surprises, and I'm not entirely used to it yet either. Somebody asks me how success feels, and I am shocked—is he talking to me? And then I thought, hell, I guess he's right. I'm working, which I'm glad to be doing, but I don't think it's been long enough for me to tell what it feels like. I'm ready, but when you're working on a movie and faced with a million problems, it doesn't make any difference whether you're successful or not. You're just working on a movie faced with a million problems.

Q: *Your newest film is* NATIONAL LAMPOONS JOY OF SEX. . .

A: You know I have another picture, don't you? It's called THE CITY GIRL.

Q: *That's something you've been working on for a long time, isn't it?*

A: Two and a half years, but it's finished. It's very different from VALLEY GIRL and JOY OF SEX—a serious, dark picture about singles life in an urban city. It's about a young woman photographer who has modern romantic ideas—mostly sexual ideas—about men. And she has a boyfriend who is not like her fantasies. He's not cool, not hip and not beautiful in a way that she fantasizes. She's a photographer for kind of a hip publication not unlike L.A. Weekly combined with Interview—she does fashion and rock and roll and kind of new wave lifestyle pictures. She finally breaks up with her boyfriend and tries to go and live out her fantasies in the club life of Toronto. And nothing works out. It's very funny, but also a dark, multi-layered, very interesting movie. I really like it. It's totally independent, shot partly in L.A. and mostly in Toronto. Peter Bogdanovich bought it—he's the executive producer. It shut down in Canada, we ran out of money, the producers didn't know what to do. I tried to raise the money many times over until Peter saw it. He loved the picture, fully appreciated the kind of ordeal that I'd been through and bought it himself.

Q: *Your newest film, a comedy based on Alex Comfort's book, The Joy of Sex, has been through about a dozen producers.*

A: And a lot of writers too.

Q: *Was the final script the product of a number of those writers?*

A: Only one—Kathleen Rowell, who also wrote THE OUTSIDERS, so this is a real change of pace for her. Now JOY OF SEX is about two high school kids who decide that they want to have their first sexual experience. But since they're both very romantic, they want a romantic sexual experience. But they both keep getting sidetracked, and nothing works out. It's not a farce, but a very funny, naive and sweet picture.

Q: *With that name—National Lampoon—in front of the title, one immediately wonders about excessive raunch.*

A: No. The most intensive raunch is a scene where these guys are lighting their farts, but that's not in detail.

Q: *What the hell, if it was good enough for Bergman in FANNY AND ALEXANDER, I guess it's good enough for JOY OF SEX. Did you have any trepidation when you were asked to direct the film?*

A: Well, I was being offered a lot of youth comedies, and they were generally not good. I realized that I wanted to go ahead and work right away, for several reasons. One is that I spent so many years not working, and two, I needed to make some money too. So I figured okay, I'll do it. . . and I'm thrilled I'm doing comedy. I think comedy is extremely difficult to do. Kathleen is a very good friend of mine and we were going to develop something together. And it was one of my agents at William Morris who said that JOY OF SEX was coming up and could be available, and that Kathleen wrote it. I mean, we were talking about doing something else, and she wasn't available to write it because she was working on JOY OF SEX. So it just seemed to make sense.

Q: *As a woman working on a big studio film, did you find yourself getting special treatment?*

A: I don't think that people treated me any differently than any other picture I've done . . . people have generally respected me. Except they called me "Ma'am," which is strange. I think it stems from the old Hollywood tradition of calling the director "Sir."

Q: *Where are you from, and when did you start making movies?*

A: I'm from New Haven, Connecticut, and I made my first film in my first year at college. And I really loved it. I had lots of friends, older than me by a year or two, who already were making films. I was directing theatre and acting, so I was already in the theatre world. I acted in a film that summer, then made four films in my sophomore year. Then in the third year I went into independent study, because they didn't really have a film department, and made a 16mm film as opposed to 8mm. Then I left school, went to New York, and worked in commercials and documentaries—mostly assistant editor, then editor, script girl, you know, everything. I also went to night school in film—NYU, the School of Visual Arts and Columbia Graduate School. At Columbia, in the spring of 1968, I was doing a 25-minute 16mm film with Michael Brandon about a guy who was drafted and was afraid to go to Vietnam. And then the whole school was shut down by the riots. I didn't get my film finished that year, and ended up emigrating to Montreal to write and produce for television. I finally came back to NYU Graduate School in the master's program, and directed three or four films there, produced several and edited quite a few in 35mm. In my last year I produced my first film that got distribution, PASSING QUIETLY THROUGH, and directed my documentary DAVID: OFF AND ON. A teacher at NYU saw that film and hired me to direct an hour-long documentary about a free school in Long Island which became a special on PBS. I got very active in the New York film community and ended up getting a grant to make my next picture, which I called OLD FASHIONED WOMAN—it was a portrait of my grandmother and has been on PBS a lot. Then I got more grants and inves- tors, and did NOT A PRETTY PICTURE. By then I was pretty well established in New York, I'd won a lot of prizes in the nontheatrical film world, lots of festivals, and started the Association of Independent Video and Film Makers with two other people. But I really, really wanted to make theatrical films. . . not to put down the films I made—I love them and I'd always like to be able to do it that way. But I wanted to work with actors. After NOT A PRETTY PICTURE, I decided to chuck it all and move to Los Angeles. Even though I was over-experienced in a way, I was an AFI intern with Robert Wise on AUDREY ROSE, which was a very interesting experience. I learned a lot. Finally, after going back and forth for a year, Francis Coppola and company come back from doing APOCALYPSE NOW in the Philippines and said they wanted to work with me. So I went into development on PHOTOPLAY, a rock and roll love story, which ended up being two and a half years of my life. After it got shelved, and several other development deals fell through, I got kind of disillu- sioned and moved back to Canada and immediately directed a mini-series for the CBC. Then I got THE CITY GIRL, which I told you about before. I've also written a screwball comedy with Colleen Camp called TWELVE'S A CROWD, which Peter Bogdanovich wants me to direct for his company.

Q: *You're one of the top women directors working in this town. How do you see yourself as far as that position is concerned?*

A: I must say that I do very clearly see myself as a pioneer, as I do the other women directors. There is absolute truth to the fact that one woman's success is another woman's success. The guy who hired me to do VALLEY GIRL went around and hired another woman director for his next picture. Also, I turned down a picture at a studio and they turned around and hired another woman who had never done a feature before.

Q: *Are you afraid that producers are going to typecast women directors?*

A: I'm not afraid of it. They do that. I think it's good that I'm doing comedy, because comedy can break through some sexual lines. I really want people to see THE CITY GIRL because I think that will break through some other pre-conceived ideas. It's so much a woman's picture I can't even tell you. And it's not what any- body expects from a woman. It's absolutely a woman's picture — not soft, not light, not silly, not easy, not without violence and not without an edge. You know, a movie takes a lot out of you, and you can only make so many in your life. I want to do some comedies, and I want to do some serious pictures and I want to do some big pictures. I don't necessarily mean $40 million . . . when I say big, I mean big in scope. And I think you can say that I want to prove that I can do those things, that a woman can do things on that scale. I'd like to do science fiction, deal with special effects. I'm not a director because I want to do movies that stay in the Valley—I mean, when I approached the Valley, I approached it the way I would an historical subject. You have to get to know your material.

Q: How have attitudes changed toward women directors?

A: In the past, a woman was not hired, in general, to do the kind of "B" pictures that young male directors were hired to do, and that generally had to do with the attitudes of the people financing those pictures. There are a couple of exceptions-Barbara Peeters and Stephanie Rothman. But in general, I found that in the past the attitude of the independent financiers was much worse than even the studios, who would at least talk to a woman director. They were open to political and societal pressure to take women seriously, whereas the cliched independent who chews on a cigar and worked his way up from nothing and thinks the woman should stay in the kitchen is not going to hire a woman—and he does what he wants with his money, you know? That's a very simplified explanation for why I think it's harder for women in the independents. Therefore, women directors in general have to make a leap that in many cases a male director doesn't, which is from educational films, documentaries, little things for television or children's films to—suddenly—features. The VALLEY GIRL's are very hard to come by, almost unheard of for a woman. That's why I was so thrilled. I was being offered a commercial, independent, low-budget picture.

Q: Do you think male directors are judged by different standards than women directors?

A: Yes. How many times has a woman done a picture that wasn't that good or wasn't a hit, and they said "Well, I'll never work with a woman again." Imagine if they said that about a man! "I'll never work with a man again"? Because he didn't have a hit? I really hope to God that if I ever make a really awful picture, they'll give me the space to do it in.

Q: Do you think things have finally and truly changed?

A: They're changing. It's in the process and it's going to take a long time. I feel that it's a movement, and women changing their role in our society is simply an aspect of the social movement. But the point is, that women have seriously been changing their role in society for the last eighty years, and there is tremendous historical resistance to it, in women as well as men. There may be brilliant, talented women out there, but they are not as prepared by their background and their childhood and their histories to be leaders. Or something even more complicated than a leader, like a director—which is an in-between position—a person who is both under and over a lot of creative people. It's a very lonely, isolated position. But it is changing.

F I L M O G R A P H Y

M A R T H A   C O O L I D G E

b. August 17, 1946 - New Haven, Connecticut
NOT A PRETTY PICTURE Films Inc., 1976
VALLEY GIRL Atlantic Releasing Corporation, 1983
JOY OF SEX Paramount, 1984
THE CITY GIRL Moon Pictures, 1984
REAL GENIUS TriStar, 1985
PLAIN CLOTHES Paramount, 1988
TRENCHCOAT IN PARADISE (TF) Ogiens-Kate Company Productions/The Finnegan-Pinchuk
    Company, 1989
BARE ESSENTIALS (TF) Republic Pictures, 1991
RAMBLING ROSE Seven Arts/New Line Cinema, 1991
CRAZY IN LOVE (CTF) Ohlmeyer Communications/Karen Danaher-Dorr Productions, 1992
LOST IN YONKERS Columbia, 1993
ANGIE Buena Vista, 1994
THREE WISHES Savoy Pictures, 1995
OUT TO SEA 20th Century Fox, 1997

$\mathcal{J}$OE $\mathcal{D}$ANTE

Joe Dante's unexpected and sometimes outrageous films usually portray the "real" world's collision with supernatural and otherworldly forces in ways that are alternately humorous and horrifying, perhaps best exemplified in his superhits GREMLINS and GREMLINS 2: THE NEW BATCH, as well as his marvelous werewolf tome, THE HOWLING.

A director who has stubbornly adhered to his own peculiar sensibilities throughout his career, Dante graduated from Roger Corman's stable of directors at New World Pictures, where he directed HOLLYWOOD BOULEVARD (with Allan Arkush) and THE HOWLING. He then worked on two Steven Spielberg productions, directing a much-praised episode of TWILIGHT ZONE-THE MOVIE and the hugely successful GREMLINS. Dante followed with EXPLORERS, a fantasy adventure in which Earth kids discovered extra-terrestrial teens different in body but not in spirit. Although the film didn't quite catch on, it has a considerable league of fans. Continuing to mine the comic/fantasy vein, Dante followed with INNERSPACE, THE 'BURBS, GREMLINS 2: THE NEW BATCH and the delightful MATINEE, featuring John Goodman as a horror movie schlockmeister patterned after the immortal William Castle. He then turned his attentions to two cable television movies—RUNAWAY DAUGHTERS, a contribution to Showtime's REBEL HIGHWAY series of AIP homages—and HBO's THE SECOND CIVIL WAR.

At the time of writing, Dante was returning to the big screen with a high-tech new fantasy, DreamWorks's SMALL SOLDIERS.

MICHAEL SINGER: *I admire the way your films hook into the icons and iconography of pop culture.*

JOE DANTE: It's the only culture we've got now.

Q: *Can you elaborate on that a little?*

A: I noticed while I was doing EXPLORERS that some of the kids I spoke with didn't like to watch black and white films. I asked why not, and they said, "I dunno, just something about it." Even pop culture is now decaying in a much faster way than literary culture. Culture such as it is has become so immediate that the idea of doing anything with real longevity that has anything to do with specific pop culture is pretty risky.

Q: *Where does that leave filmmakers who need to draw on their own pasts and love for the pop cultures that existed during their childhoods?*

A: Well, I've done that a lot but I've tried to do it in a non-specific way. If people are watching a picture and they know where something comes from, if they've seen the movie that it refers to, then that's one added level of interest or understanding. But the impact of the work can't be limited to knowing that. It has to be something that's broad enough, an archetype, to still make its point, even if people don't know what it's in reference to.

Q: *Does this mean that even The Three Stooges are going to go out of fashion?*

A: Well, The Three Stooges seem to be somewhat resistant to the ravages of time. And with colorizing, which makes everything look like hand-colored lobby cards come to life, I'm sorry to say that probably sometime in the future almost everything will be colorized. Therefore, the idea of people not watching a film because it looks old and in black and white will probably pass away. But unfortunately, that's closing the door on a particularly brilliant chapter in movie visuals.

Q: *It's a blood curdling thought.*

A: It certainly is. The new Alfred Hitchcock TV show, where they've colorized all the introductions, is about the worst process I've ever seen because the colors are not in the places they're supposed to be. They're all blurry and smeary. Then the Hal Roach Company has another process, and they colorized the old Topper. Roland Young's mustache keeps moving all over his face.

Q: *So we're not talking about perfect technology.*

A: No. We're talking about movies that were not designed to be in color. If movies were designed to be in color they were shot a certain way and lit a certain way. You just can't take a black and white image and put color into it and expect it to have the same impact. Especially since there's no one around to tell what colors they should be. I don't particularly need to see the yellow flowers on Billie Burke's table that draw my attention away from her face. It's no accident that all the great stars came from the black and white era, because those were the movies where you watched people's faces.

Q: *Do you have hopes of making a movie in black and white?*

A: I'd love to make a black and white movie, but the problem is that now it's so economically unviable that you have to be making a self-appointed art picture. Some people have gotten away with it—Woody Allen movies and RAGING BULL— I can't wait to see what these pictures will look like when they're colorized.

Q: *You've been both praised and criticized for the strain of humor which runs through your films, which to some seems at odds with the horror. Where does it come from, and are you aware of the prospect of the horror and the comedy clashing?*

A: I don't know where it comes from. . . it comes from me, I guess. . . it's the way I see the world. But the prospect of it being a problem actually didn't occur to me until I did THE HOWLING, and the executives started to complain that they didn't know if it was supposed to be a comedy or a horror picture. It's probably the most sustained dramatic movie that I've ever done, but it still has moments of humor in it. Things that are funny in one place are not funny in another. Like if objects appear in places they don't belong. Or, as Lon Chaney used to say, a clown is funny in the circus ring but he's not funny at your door at midnight. To me that dichotomy has always been interesting. I think it's just a particular way of looking at things.

Q: *Also, horror and humor seems to create a certain tension which audiences sometimes don't really know what to do with.*

A: I think you need to give people something to think about in a movie. One way of doing it is to keep them offbalance and make comparisons between types of emotions that are going on within a given scene. The only scene in GREMLINS where people didn't know how to react at all was when Phoebe Cates' character told the story of what happened to her father. There was quite a bit of unhappiness about it on the part of the studio, because they didn't know whether to laugh or be horrified by the story. Actually, it's my favorite scene in the picture.

Q: *Do you think American audiences, raised on the moral certainties of television, don't know how to react to any form of ambiguity in feature films?*

A: I think they may be a little threatened by ambiguity and not welcome it, because they're not accustomed to it. I remember Family, which was a very popular T.V. show in its time. It raised some very complex issues, usually three stories at a time, and then completely solved them by the end of the show. It gave you the impression that nothing in life was really unsolvable and nothing really has any consequence, because everything you do could be wrapped up in an hour. I think that's kind of a tenet of television— that you don't leave things hanging and you don't keep people wondering. But I always thought that movies have somewhat more lasting impact on people, and the need to sew everything up isn't quite as strong. It helps to be able to see things twice and find something you didn't see before. A really interesting movie is one that you can watch over and over, because there are pleasures in it that are so transcendent that you can reenjoy it, and those pleasures build upon themselves. Eventually, you can see it a third or fourth time and that's all there is to see in the movie. Then there are other films that people have been watching since they were made, like CITIZEN KANE or MAGNIFICENT AMBERSONS, and the reason is because each time you see the movie something has changed in you, and there's something else in the movie that you didn't see. Because everything isn't all clear-cut, and the motivations aren't all by rote. And I think that's the secret of really good writing, letting the audience do some of the work. People tell me they like EXPLORERS better the second time. I have a problem with EXPLORERS, because I didn't get to finish the picture, and every time I look at it I see things that I know I could have fixed if I had the time.

Q: *You were compelled to release* EXPLORERS *before you added finishing touches?*

A: It was released during a summer that a lot of movies came out before they were finished, and this film was no exception. None of the people who were distributing it thought that it was very important for the film to be finished.

Q: *Were these just technical imperfections?*

A: No, not really. One of the things that people least understand is postproduction, which is the part where you find your movie. There's the movie you set out to make, and then there's the movie that you made because of the various things that were heaped upon you, like weather and schedules. Then, post-production is where you actually pick one of the several movies that it can be, and hone it down to what you want it to be. That's what the idea of previews is supposed to be. Since our preview came only a week before the picture opened, we didn't have much time to do anything. It's my favorite picture that I've done for various reasons. I just don't know if any of them are apparent.

Q: *Why is it your favorite?*

A: EXPLORERS is a very personal movie. GREMLINS, on the other hand-into which I managed to insert a lot of personal ephemera—was somebody else's project. In the case of EXPLORERS, I didn't initiate it, but it was something that I believed in. Without my realizing it, it ended up becoming sort of an extension of myself. I guess the whole tone of the picture and maybe even some of the things that are wrong with it, are things that sprang out of me and into the movie.

Q: *Do you think the second half of* EXPLORERS *was almost too original?*

A: I think that in order for the second half to work, the first half has to be the way it is. It was always intended to be a very quiet, even gentle movie. The fact that the kids go into space, expecting to find the answer to everything and all the aliens have to offer is a hollow imitation of the world they just left is, I think, sort of an interesting antidote to the superpower alien movies that we see, where people look up and a bright light comes on and they're ennobled and it's like they've found God. If this kid in EXPLORERS goes looking for God in outer space he's not going to find Him there.

Q: *But at the end, he's still looking.*

A: Of course he's still looking. He has to keep looking. But he just wasn't looking in the right place, because he was looking where his culture told him to look. There's a lot of interesting themes in the picture, some of which are apparent and some of which are fudged. It's the only movie I've ever made that I'd like to re-cut.

Q: *Would that ever be possible?*

A: Actually the home video version is a little different. I got to tidy up a couple of things.

Q: *Some of the images were wonderful, like the Tilt-A-Whirl becoming a spaceship.*

A: The funny thing about EXPLORERS is that kids under the age of fifteen understood, somehow, the very points that the adults found most vague. They honed into it, sort of on a psychic level, and that was very rewarding. After all, a lot of kids who saw PETER PAN slept by the window waiting for him to come.

Q: *Your films seem to be informed by a visual sensibility based, at least in part, on cartoons. How conscious are you of that?*

A: It's not really something that I sit down and plan. A real influence is something that's part of you, and so much of directing is changing the plans that you originally have. You should have asked Frank Tashlin this question, someone who started out in cartoons and moved into live action. Because with me it would have to wind up being the other way around, if it ever happens. I think the most cartoon-like thing I ever did was the TWILIGHT ZONE episode. Even the actors acted like cartoons, and it was a lot of fun— probably the most fun I ever had.

Q: *Do you want to work outside the horror/sci-fi/fantasy genre?*

A: Sure. It's not something I feel exclusively tied to, although it could be that whatever it is that I need to work out on film just seems to work out better within that context.

F I L M O G R A P H Y

J O E   D A N T E

b. Morristown, New Jersey
HOLLYWOOD BOULEVARD co-director with Allan Arkush, New World, 1976
PIRANHA New World, 1978
THE HOWLING Avco Embassy, 1980
TWILIGHT ZONE - THE MOVIE co-director with John Landis, Steven Spielberg & George Miller, Warner Bros., 1983
GREMLINS Warner Bros., 1984
EXPLORERS Paramount, 1985
AMAZON WOMEN ON THE MOON co-director with John Landis, Carl Gottlieb, Robert K. Weiss & Peter Horton, Universal, 1987
INNERSPACE Warner Bros., 1987
THE 'BURBS Universal, 1989
GREMLINS 2 THE NEW BATCH Warner Bros., 1990
MATINEE Universal, 1993
REBEL HIGHWAY: RUNAWAY DAUGHTERS (CTF) Drive-In Classics Cinema/Showtime, 1994
THE SECOND CIVIL WAR (CTF) HBO Pictures/Baltimore Pictures, 1997
SMALL SOLDIERS (AF) DreamWorks Pictures, 1998

$\mathcal{R}$ICHARD $\mathcal{D}$ONNER

Dick Donner's irrepressible energy has infused his hugely entertaining films for nearly 40 years. Audiences love his movies. Sometimes, the critics do too, but they're beside the point. Donner's all-American gusto genuinely transcends critical response, and if there's been a misstep or two along the way, there's always another movie to make and a few more million to please around the world.

After laboring through (but loving) his experience in the salt mines of television and low-budget features, Donner's skills really started to emerge in the 1976 supernatural thriller hit, THE OMEN. Two years later, SUPERMAN brilliantly confirmed his talent for combining visual spectacle with valid emotion. More than just a comic book movie, SUPERMAN displayed considerable filmmaking poetry in its epic tale of the immortal hero from planet Krypton, moving audiences to both tears and cheers. It is now, justifiably, considered a classic of big-time American moviemaking.

Donner's numerous features since then have been a decidedly mixed bag, both in subject matter and results. They range from the intimate drama of INSIDE MOVES and RADIO FLYER, the large-scale fantasies of the medieval romance LADYHAWKE and the Steven Spielberg/Donner-produced ode to childhood, THE GOONIES, as well as comedies (THE TOY, SCROOGED), an enjoyable comedy-western (MAVERICK), straight-up thrillers (ASSASSINS, CONSPIRACY THEORY) and his gigantically popular policier LETHAL WEAPON and its three blockbuster sequels.

This brief conversation was held during a midnight "lunch" hour on a West Hollywood set, and despite the lateness and demands of his shooting schedule, Donner happily discussed his refreshingly unpretentious philosophy of filmmaking.

MICHAEL SINGER: It's rare for directors to make sequels to their own successful films. What compelled you to take on LETHAL WEAPON 2?

RICHARD DONNER: I was sequelized on SALT AND PEPPER, THE OMEN and SUPERMAN. I never wanted to do a sequel. Usually, you create something and when it's done, the challenge is over. But my relationship with Mel Gibson, Danny Glover, Joel Silver, Warner Bros., and the entire crew is so exciting that when the studio suggested the sequel, I became very interested. At first I was just going to produce LETHAL WEAPON 2, but the more we talked about it, the more possessive I became. For the first time, I really didn't want to give it up to anybody. Now I know why. With LETHAL 2, I literally did not like to have weekends off. It's an experience that you wish you had all the time in the motion picture industry.

Q: You're noted for creating happy sets and a good working environment.

A: I like to set an atmosphere on my pictures. We're lucky SOB's to be doing what we're doing. Somehow it was ordained, and not to enjoy it is insane. I've been on pictures, some recently, that were really very painful, grueling and problematic with personalities and other matters. It made me not want to come to work, and I hate that. It means I've lost a certain amount of control. I think it enhances the actor's ability to perform if the atmosphere is tight for him. The director is there to father the bad moment if it comes up. But if the set is not happy, if there isn't a joyous feeling of being at work, then somewhere I've made a major mistake.

Q: Some directors, like Michael Curtiz and Otto Preminger, liked to create environments of fear because they felt that actors and crew worked best under that kind of pressure.

A: I was an assistant director years ago in live TV, commercials and documentaries. I worked for some very talented tyrants and learned from their ability to create. But I also learned some of the problems that I felt emanated from their attitude and how they handled people. I like to have a light, open atmosphere around me on the set. If the person who makes coffee comes around and has a thought or suggestion, I'm the first one to listen. Because it may be wonderful or it may not. If it's wonderful, I'll be the first to tell him I love it and why, and if it's not, I'll tell him that as well.

Q: THE OMEN was a major turning point in your career. Were you aware of that at the time?

A: I've always taken a film because I wanted to make that specific film, but every project has the potential to be the turning point in your career. THE OMEN was a phenomenal break for me, but while I was making it, I hated it and swore I was going to go back to television. Nothing's ever tight when you start a film. You're starting too early even if you've prepared for two years. You get laryngitis, you can't say "action," your dailies aren't tight, the actors you cast are wrong, you · have the wrong cameraman. . . I mean, everything is wrong. But once you've done a few films and know when the momentum is really starting to pick up, you start to feel a little confident. On THE OMEN, I never felt it—every frame of that film was a challenge. I came out of the first assemblage with the same editor I'm working with now, Stuart Baird, and I said, "It's a dismal failure." Then we sat down in the cutting room day in and day out and the picture started to take shape. My confidence began to grow during that editorial process. As the process started to become a comfortable one, I still had my insecurities, but I knew there would come a time within the film where I hit my pace and everything would start to be tight. In retrospect, I went back and looked at THE OMEN, and realized where I had found my pace—Gregory Peck gave it to me at a certain point. We had a fairly rough scene to do and were at each other's throats. Mr. Peck didn't believe in what I wanted, did it reluctantly, and voiced that reluctance to everybody. But the next day in dailies, he came over, whispered in my ear and said, "It couldn't have been better."

Q: *As big as the challenge of* THE OMEN *was, what was facing you on* SUPERMAN *must have been monumental. How did you approach the task?*

A: Blind faith. Every picture is blind faith. When I read a screenplay, I've shot it. It was one of the great advantages that I had in TV that I could prepare an hour show in a day. I could cast it in the morning and if I had the time, I could have the location on the backlot and shoot the next day. What I read I see. Of course, when I get behind the camera, I may see it totally different, but I'm secure in my mind because I've already seen the picture. On SUPERMAN, I surrounded myself with a set full of technical geniuses—like Geoffrey Unsworth, the greatest cinematographer in the world, and John Barry, the greatest production designer in the world— both gone now. I provoked the crew and broke barriers. In England, there was a set way of making movies. Everybody stayed within the parameters of their own departments. Well, on SUPERMAN, every night everybody was invited into my office for input on everything. By the time the picture was over, all the barriers had been broken. There were cheers in dailies when we saw something come to life that we had all talked about.

Q: *What is the difference in how you approach spectacles and more intimate films?*

A: None. They're all exactly the same. It could be a story of two people sitting in a living room—that's as much a challenge as making SUPERMAN.

Q: *So* INSIDE MOVES *and* THE GOONIES *presented the same challenge to you?*

A: Totally. INSIDE MOVES was an emotional challenge for me, the catharsis of a lot of my thoughts and problems. THE GOONIES was a challenge to be able to take myself back in life and see things through the eyes of a child again. Steven Spielberg and I were like kids on that. It was a fight to see who was the youngest.

Q: *It's perfectly logical, then, that you could go from the large-scale films you've been doing to smaller pictures like* INSIDE MOVES *and your better known TV movies, like* SARAH T.?

A: Yes. . . if I could find something special in that area, I'd love to do it. In the interim, my desire in life is to entertain. I truly love to come out of a motion picture and feel entertained. You read Time Magazine and find out that the planet's only got 200 years left. I'll read it in Time but I don't want to go to a movie and see it. I love the escape of motion pictures. I'm happy to be alive and like to convey that in the things I do.

F I L M O G R A P H Y

RICHARD DONNER

b. 1939 - New York, New York
X-15 United Artists, 1961
SALT AND PEPPER United Artists, 1968, British
LOLA TWINKY American International, 1970, British-Italian
LUCAS TANNER (TF) Universal TV, 1974
SENIOR YEAR (TF) Universal TV, 1974
A SHADOW IN THE STREETS (TF) Playboy Productions, 1975
SARAH T. - PORTRAIT OF A TEENAGE ALCOHOLIC (TF) Universal TV, 1975
THE OMEN 20th Century-Fox, 1976
SUPERMAN Warner Bros., 1978, U.S.-British
INSIDE MOVES AFD, 1980
THE TOY Columbia, 1982
LADYHAWKE Warner Bros., 1985
THE GOONIES Warner Bros., 1985
LETHAL WEAPON Warner Bros., 1987
SCROOGED Paramount, 1988
LETHAL WEAPON 2 Warner Bros., 1989
RADIO FLYER Columbia, 1992
LETHAL WEAPON 3 Warner Bros., 1992
MAVERICK Warner Bros., 1994
ASSASSINS Warner Bros., 1995
CONSPIRACY THEORY Warner Bros., 1997
LETHAL WEAPON 4 Warner Bros., 1998

$\mathcal{T}$AYLOR $\mathcal{H}$ACKFORD

With a strong background in television journalism and documentaries—
and an Academy Award for a previous short film—Taylor Hackford brought sen-
suality and intense emotion to AN OFFICER AND A GENTLEMAN, one of 1982's
most successful films, and only his second feature following the music-scene-
based THE IDOLMAKER. The film brought an Academy Award to Louis Gossett,
Jr. as Best Supporting Actor and a Directors Guild of America nomination to the
director himself.

Since then, Hackford has directed seven feature in various genres, including romantic thriller (AGAINST ALL ODDS), action thriller (WHITE NIGHTS), romantic drama (EVERYBODY'S ALL-AMERICAN), sweeping multi-generational
melodrama (BOUND BY HONOR, aka BLOOD IN. . . BLOOD OUT), suspense
(DOLORES CLAIBORNE) and supernatural thriller (DEVIL'S ADVOCATE). The
last two releases were solid hits, which must have been a relief to Hackford
following the limited release and cool reception afforded his three-hour Chicano
epic BOUND BY HONOR, a tremendously ambitious effort which has found an
enthusiastic audience via its video release. This film, more than any other in
Hackford's body of work, can be directly related to his journalistic and documentary background. Also a result of Hackford's life as a documentarian is the
1996 Academy Award winner WHEN WE WERE KINGS, which magnificently
chronicled the 1974 Muhammad Ali/George Foreman "Rumble in the Jungle" in
Zaire. In essence, Hackford "godfathered" the project, overseeing its production, conducting interviews and then editing the material more than 20 years
after it was shot.

Hackford consistently demonstrates a strong hand with both performance
and visuals, and his career has managed to be just as unpredictable enough to
be truly interesting. Just when you think he's settled into a mainstream Hollywood pattern, Hackford cracks the mold and goes off into other directions.

MICHAEL SINGER: *You keep a pretty low profile in this day of celebrity directors. Is that intentional, or is publicity just not something you think much about?*

TAYLOR HACKFORD: It's intentional. So far, I haven't had a need, and certainly don't have a desire, to do a lot of self-promotion. I've been lucky in that I've been able to make films—that's what I need to do. And because of AN OFFICER AND A GENTLEMAN, I've been able to start developing projects, which is important to me. I haven't had to go out and beat my chest and get articles written about me. I didn't hire a publicist, although I was approached by many, because I just didn't feel a need. Luckily, the DGA nominated me for their directors' award, which was an incredible honor for me. Everyone at the time said, "You've got to hire a publicist to go after the Academy so you can also get nominated for an Oscar." Frankly, it was probably more important to me to have been nominated by the DGA because they are my peers. Also, it's only my second film. I'm interested in building a body of work and not burning out on one or two films. If I find I can't get work, maybe then I'll have to go out and beat the bushes; but for the time being I'd rather keep a low profile.

Q: *You said that you "need" to make films. Of course, most filmmakers make movies because that's the only thing they want to do, but you had been in news and broadcast journalism. What turned you around? Had you always been interested in film, or was there a calling at some particular point?* .

A: Well, I think it has to do with evolution. I'd gone to college and majored in International Relations—I've always been very political. I was in the Peace Corps. . . I thought I was going to be a lawyer. . . and the evolution in terms of changing that whole career outlook took a number of years. I started hanging out with some film students when I was a senior at USC, and got turned on to film and the power of the media. I loved feature films. For periods of my life I went to 15 films a week, which is a lot of film on a regular basis. But since my background was political and I was very knowledgeable about politics, I went into the only area that I was interested in, which was a combination. I started working at a public television station simultaneously doing investigative and political reporting. I also did rock and roll shows, because of my extensive background in music. It was kind of incongruous that the two things would fit together, but at KCET, where I worked, they were very understaffed and you had to do a lot of things. I've always been a real glutton for work. I love work, and given the opportunity, when some of the producers were doing one piece a week, I was doing five because I thought, "what an opportunity!" And it was, in fact, my film school. To me, I wasn't being exploited—I was exploiting an opportunity to go out and get a lot of experience, which I did. But you know, in the back of my mind always—although it was a bit of a dream at the time—was the thought that it would be wonderful to make dramatic films. A number of the long documentaries that I did were portrait documentaries that were actually composed. I mean, they were documentaries in the sense that they were based on real people, but I spent enough time with those people so that I kind of composed them in a structural way. And those were much more dramatic than the normal kind of informational documentary. In those films, there was really something of substance, in getting someone who is a real person to let down his guard and reveal himself. It's immensely more difficult if you make it through and they do reveal themselves on camera. Much more difficult than working with actors, believe me, because normal barriers are very, very strong.

An actor is trained to open up and let his insides come out. Real people don't want to do that. They have a barrier up and they want you to think of them as nice people. But "nice" people can be mean at times, or crazy, or depressed, and no one really wants to show that other side of themselves to the world in a film. If you're skilled enough to get them to do it, I think it's an immense accomplishment. I use that skill now when I work with actors. I consider myself a performance director. I work with actors, I want performances, I want to do story films that have real changes in character, you cannot, in films today—at least in films that I want to make—separate who the real person is from the actor. What I'm trying to do is reveal the actors in their roles, and that hearkens back to when I was making documentaries—trying to make those people I was dealing with reveal themselves. You've got to draw from your own experiences. And that's what I do.

Q: *After the documentaries, you left KCET and started making short films, didn't you?*

A: I made one short film. You know, at a certain point working at a job. . . and I'm not making excuses, KCET was not a way station for me. . . I had a terrific time, able to do literally hundreds of mini-docs and news stories and rock and roll and jazz shows. . . but at a certain point. . . well, it was funny. We'd been doing an investigative show, a real good one, I think. We won a Peabody Award, I won a couple of Emmys, other producers on the show had won Emmys. It was a hard-hitting show. But, any time you go after people, you're going to get sued a lot. It puts a lot of pressure on a little television station. There was a policy change at the station where they leaned toward doing the kind of soft human interest features that commercial television was doing. And I said, jeez, what are we doing? We've got a good investigative unit, we're being recognized for what we're doing, why change? But it was clear that the pressure was just too much, and that they wanted to follow along the lines of commercial television. So I said the hell with it, and quit. I had to make a decision: either I was going to get a job working in news on commercial television as a network reporter, or I was going to take this dream of working in dramatic film and see if I could do it. You know, at a certain point you have to pretty well put up or shut up. I went out and starved for awhile, about six or seven months, waiting for a dramatic film. I kept myself alive by doing the NASA coverage of the Jupiter shot. It was a bread and butter job, but it was fun. Finally, I got a job doing a short film for an organization that wanted to make sex education films for high schools. They wanted a documentary, but I convinced them that if I made it look like a documentary, only write it and cast it with actors, it would be more effective. They agreed, and I made a half-hour film called TEENAGE FATHER. It was made for classrooms, but it turned out really well. We showed it on television, in a movie house here, and it won an Academy Award for Best Dramatic Short. When people saw it, they said, well, this guy can probably work with actors, and that was my ticket. Then I was able to do THE IDOLMAKER.

Q: *Considering your background in music, was THE IDOLMAKER a project that you initiated or was it brought to you?*

A: It was a project that was brought to me. Because of TEENAGE FATHER I got an agent. . . two agents really: Fred Specktor and Stephanie Brody of CAA, and they worked their asses off. They heard about THE IDOLMAKER—Gene Kirkwood and Howard Koch, Jr. had it at United Artists and were looking for a director. I met them, they saw my short film, liked it, heard about my background in music and hired me. They already had a screenplay, but not one the studio wanted to go ahead with. When I came in they wanted me to do a rewrite. I went through two drafts, the studio gave us a go, and we made the picture.

Q: *That was a fairly expensive looking movie, although I suspect it was very moderately budgeted.*

A: It was between $4.5 and $5 million. I think we got a lot of production value on the screen. Getting your first feature is a feat, and I felt incredibly lucky in that I knew the period very, very well. I taught the history of rock and roll at the Alternative College at USC. I have a real background in music and also, I'd done the concert films. It was a very nice opening film for me. At the same time I'm from California—I'm not Italian, nor am I from New York, and it was a film based in that milieu. When you've done documentaries, you become very respectful of accuracy and reality. With films like MEAN STREETS around—and I mention that because I think it's a fabulous movie and one that really reflected that kind of New York milieu—you have a lot to live up to. So I went to New York and South Philadelphia, spent time in the Bronx, went to Brooklyn with Ray Sharkey, basically observing. Sometimes an outside point of view can really help. On the other hand, no one could have made MEAN STREETS the way Marty [Scorsese] did because he knew it so well. What I'm saying is that it was a terrific opportunity and I didn't take it likely.

Q: *My only quibble with THE IDOLMAKER—and I'm sure you've heard this before—is that I wish the music had been more faithful to the actual sound of what was coming out of Philadelphia in the early 1960's.*

A: I've got to take the heat on that one, because the music coming out of Philadelphia in the early 1960's to me, is one of the low points of rock and roll. I mean, Bobby Rydell was actually quite good, but this film was based in part on the careers of Frankie Avalon, Fabian and Bob Marcucci. And frankly, it would seem to me to be a one joke film if I'd put either the actual songs that Avalon and Fabian sang, or songs like it, into the film. You're right, there was a definite decision made not to go for total simplistic accuracy there, and we were trying to do something that would have some relevance today. Jeff Barry, who wrote the music, did a terrific job and of course, he did write some of the best songs ever in rock and roll after that period. We didn't use any synthesizers. We didn't use any kind of instrumentation that wasn't available then. Looking back on it, we suffered from doing a film that in essence, wasn't the Bob Marcucci story, or the Frankie Avalon and Fabian story. But it was close enough to it that it got tagged with that. Inevitably, people looked at it and said, well, this isn't exactly the Frankie Avalon and Fabian story. On the other hand, people who didn't like those guys put it down as a Frankie Avalon/Fabian story. We ended up falling between the cracks when in fact, we were trying to make a film about a manager and his artists, which I think is a very interesting subject. From my point of view, as a first time director, it was a great experience.

Q: *When you were making AN OFFICER AND A GENTLEMAN, did you have any inkling of its eventual success as a monster hit?*

A: Not at all. I don't think anybody who was working on the film did. Oftentimes studios will say, "Oh, this is a sure thing, this is going to be a monster." Unless they're doing SUPERMAN, or something like that, and even then it's never guaranteed, studios don't really know what's going to be a hit or not. I sincerely doubt whether Chartoff, Winkler and John Avildsen, when they were making ROCKY said, "This is going to be a hundred million dollar film." They might have believed in it—you have to believe in the film when you're going along. No one had any expectations for the ROCKY's, the OFFICER AND A GENTLEMAN's, even STAR WARS and certainly E.T., which was turned down by other studios. You make the movie as best you can and try to put as much on the screen of what's inside of you. Then you turn it out there and hope for an audience. With THE IDOLMAKER, we never got that audience. The audiences that did see the film loved it, but we were never able to sell it enough to get them in the theatres despite the good word-of-mouth. With AN OFFICER AND A GENTLEMAN, Paramount was very smart. I have to give Don Simpson a lot of credit when he was head of production at Paramount. He liked the script—no one else at Paramount liked it, they didn't want to make it—but Don Simpson liked it, brought me in to direct the film and was a guiding force. He believed in it, but I don't think he thought it was going to be a big, successful movie. When it was finished, Frank Mancuso looked at it. He really had the sense that it could probably do big business. He designed a marketing campaign that I think was brilliant, and responsible for the business that it did. He's a very smart man, a very good marketer—the best. The film was good. I think it would have been successful. How successful I don't know—I think they did a lot to maximize its success.

Q: And the word-of-mouth took care of the rest?

A: But they started the word-of-mouth! They screened the movie like crazy all over the country for everybody who would look, which was wise. You may be losing five bucks for one person, but if they go out and tell ten other people and five of them come, you made out pretty well. Mancuso understood that.

Q: Was it an easy shoot for you?

A: No, it was hell. I loved it in the sense that we had a wonderful location and a good script to work with and a fabulous cast. But it was very difficult, very hard physically since we were in the Pacific Northwest on the Olympic Peninsula, where it rained all the time. There were immense personality conflicts on the film. The studio did not give us a great deal of support and wanted to fire me about six weeks into the film. The producer was not supportive at all, did everything he could to work against me on this. On every level, it was a hard film to do. But at the same time, there was a lot of vitality happening. And it worked. I must say, that to Richard [Gere] and Debra's [Winger] credit, when the studio wanted to fire me they said that they wouldn't work with another director. Paramount's a real tough outfit, but they're also a good studio—they know how to make movies. But in reality, I must tell you that at least in the making of the movie, it was not a particularly thrilling experience in the sense of having a lot of backup and support. On the other hand, I was able to make a movie I wanted. When it came to editing, Paramount did back me up. The movie that's up there is my film on every level, and I have no complaints there. Threats to the contrary, they did ultimately support me. At the same time, I gave them a good movie.

Q: *I know very little about AGAINST ALL ODDS except that it's supposedly based upon Jacques Tourneur's OUT OF THE PAST. When you went into production your film was also titled OUT OF THE PAST. Does the change in title signify a deliberate attempt to break away from the earlier version?*

A: Yes. The idea of doing a remake is a tough one to begin with, but this is so different from the original. If a film has been done well, to do it again in the same period is a mistake. I felt the original film had wonderful characterizations—Robert Mirchum, Kirk Douglas and Jane Greer were great—but the story was convoluted and fell apart at the end. I updated it to the present. I took the core relationship from the original film—with a very strong man and a very dangerous woman—and plugged it into a brand new story. I wanted to do a film about power in Los Angeles. And I believe that somebody could go to these two movies on the same night and see two different films. For that reason, I didn't want it to be called OUT OF THE PAST. I didn't want people to come expecting to see the old movie redone. When the writer and I got finished, we looked at each other and said, "It's too bad we even called this a remake because it's so different." The bottom line is that those three characters are still there, and that was from the old film. Certain purist critics will say, "Oh God, the old films can never be improved upon," and we'll have to take the heat, something you don't have to do with an original screenplay. Hopefully, people will be open enough to see that there is some real value in this and difference from the original. It has some homage in it, but mostly it's taking the old film as a jumping-off point and really moving into new territory.

Q: *Are there any attempts to match or update the film noir style?*

A: Not at all. I used Don Thorin again, my cinematographer on AN OFFICER AND A GENTLEMAN, but this has a very different look from OFFICER. It's a hard-edged, sharp style. It's tough to make a film in Los Angeles—I mean, so many films have been made here to begin with and television treats it every day. So to look at L.A. from a different perspective is hard. Finding locations which haven't been seen before is difficult. I think we've done it with this film. You really see the city from a unique point of view. A whole third of the film takes place in Mexico, in the Yucatan Peninsula. That should be very interesting because we started in Cozumel, on a little island called Isla Mujeres, and then we shot in two Mayan ruins which have never been filmed before. There's an immense amount of production value, and a sense of adventure from the audience's point of view. But there's no sentimentality in the L.A. footage, no mythologizing. I think too many people who have made films here come in and see this never-never land, and never really have a sense that this is as ruthless and vicious a place as any other city. I know that perspective, having been a reporter here looking at power and how it's manipulated. The movie business is a big part of this town but it's by no means the real power of this city. The people who wield that power are land rich and always have been. We deal with some of those people in the movie.

Q: *Was this an easier time for you than on AN OFFICER AND A GENTLEMAN?*

A: Yeah. . . it wasn't an easy shoot. . . no film is an easy shoot. But I produced this movie, it was my project from the beginning. Columbia, who picked the film up, has been an incredibly good place to make a film, completely supportive all the way down the line. They believed in the movie and have allowed me to make the movie that was in my head. If it works, great. And if not, I have no excuses.

F I L M O G R A P H Y

T A Y L O R   H A C K F O R D

b. December 3, 1944
THE IDOLMAKER United Artists, 1980
AN OFFICER AND A GENTLEMAN Paramount, 1982
AGAINST ALL ODDS Columbia, 1984
WHITE NIGHTS Columbia, 1985
CHUCK BERRY: HAIL! HAIL! ROCK 'N' ROLL! (FD) Universal, 1987
EVERYBODY'S ALL-AMERICAN Warner Bros., 1988
BOUND BY HONOR *BLOOD IN BLOOD OUT* Buena Vista, 1993
DOLORES CLAIBORNE Columbia, 1995
DEVIL'S ADVOCATE Warner Bros., 1997

$\mathcal{R}$ANDA $\mathcal{H}$AINES

Taste and intelligence are qualities often in short commodity in American filmmaking, so it's all the more reason to honor Randa Haines for incorporating them both into her body of work. I spoke with Haines very early in her career, after the ABC Theatre presentation of her honored television movie SOME-THING ABOUT AMELIA—which represented the first respectable effort in American film to come to grips with one of society's last taboos, incest—but before her first feature film, the sensitive CHILDREN OF A LESSER GOD, which would win an Academy Award for its star, Marlee Matlin.

Previous to SOMETHING ABOUT AMELIA, Haines had helmed two PBS films and episodes of such series as HILL STREET BLUES. Beginning her career as a New York stage actress, Haines moved into filmmaking first as a script supervisor and later as a writer before taking on the responsibilities of directing. She has since selected her projects with care and discrimination, taking on only three films since CHILDREN OF A LESSER GOD: THE DOCTOR and WRESTLING ERNEST HEMINGWAY, both of them incisive and excellently made, and the as yet unreleased (as of this writing) DANCE WITH ME. Sparse as her output may have been, it always gives the viewer reason to look forward to the next one.

MICHAEL SINGER: *Why did you decide to quit acting and go into film production?*

RANDA HAINES: My acting career was a long period of frustration. To be the ingenue in those days you had to be the blonde, petite, all-American girl. I just didn't fit into that at all, so the only parts I got were these poetic, abstract off-Broadway types who could be dark and mysterious-looking and taller than the leading man. I got a job acting at the School of Visual Arts where they hired actors to work with the directing students, and I found myself kind of moving to their side of the room. Around that time I got an acting interview for a tiny little picture, and again I was wrong for the part. But I did tell them that I was interested in learning about filmmaking, and they said, "Gee, we were just thinking about hiring our first employee." So they hired me. It was a very small company where I got to do everything. I answered the phones, opened the mail, cut the sound effects, bought the props, and was exposed to a wide variety of filmmaking situations. Business got slow and they were going to have to lay me off, so somebody I knew got a job on a low-budget feature and they needed a script supervisor. So off I went on this little film shot in the Catskills. I always found myself one step ahead of the director in figuring things out. After that, I got another job on a low-budget feature and I worked as a non-union production manager a little bit. But I specialized in script supervision, got into the union and did that for almost ten years. About six years into working as a script supervisor, I began making suggestions very discreetly to the directors I was working with. Then I began to want to say those things out loud to see if it would work for me. People were always coming up to me and saying, "You should be a director." I'd say, "Okay. . . how do we do it?" I couldn't figure out a way to make it happen.

Q: *This was still at a time when women directors were few and far between?*

A: Yes, I had never met one or even heard of one. Also, very few people moved up from crew positions to directing. But somewhere in those years I heard about the Directing Workshop for Women at the American Film Institute. The first year just about everybody in that program was a movie star, so I didn't think it was a real strong possibility. But somebody convinced me to apply. I wrote a letter describing the situation that I was in—a major support element of a lot of directors, but never getting a chance to say things out loud. I think I wrote a very passionate letter, and somehow I slipped in as a token unknown among many Oscar-winning classmates. Within two weeks of being notified, I packed up my life and moved to L.A., with my script supervisor bank account in my hand. I said okay, let's roll the dice. The only way to make a move is to strike out, take a chance and go all the way. I came out and participated in that program, which at the time had no real instruction. It was just, "Here's a thousand dollars, here's some very inadequate videotape equipment, go do what you want to do." A thousand dollars, of course, just barely pays for the bagels in the morning. I knew that to get people to work for free you have to treat them really well and make them a part of something. I also saw that the equipment was inadequate and so I rented a lot more. I really invested my whole bank account in the project, figuring that it was my best shot.

Q: *And it turned out well?*

A: Yes, it turned out very professionally and also, it was a piece of material that was very difficult—a novel by Doris Lessing. Very internal, very challenging kind of material to dramatize. It impressed a lot of people and led to some writing work Family and other television shows. Then I wanted to make directing a full-time effort, and that's what I did for the next couple of years. It was that tape and that energy that led to my first job on public television.

Q: *Which was?*

A: UNDER THIS SKY, a 90-minute historical epic for $250,000. A suicide mission, something we could never have duplicated again. The luck in every moment of it, to manage to come in on that kind of budget. The film was set in 1860's Kansas and we shot it in Rhode Island in the middle of the winter. It doesn't look anything like Kansas, but somehow we made it work. One of the reviews said something about the "John Ford exteriors." How did I do that? Behind every tree there's a little New England cottage and a little lake, so we had to shoot at very low angles to avoid all that.

Q: *Do you think PBS was just about the only place at the time that would be willing to take a chance on you as, first of all, a neophyte director; and second of all, a woman director?*

A: I suppose. I know other people managed to get their foot in the door some other way, but that was the way that presented itself to me. They did want a woman to direct the film, so I think it was a very special circumstance. I was in a very narrow field of competitors, and when the executive producer saw the piece that I had done for the Directing Workshop for Women, she thought that it had exactly the feeling that she wanted.

Q: *You followed with another film for PBS in 1979?*

A: Yes, for the American Short Story series—THE JILTING OF GRANNY WEATHERALL, which was based on a Katherine Anne Porter story that I loved. When I read a script, what pulls me into it is not so much the genre or the subject matter, but if it's about people with complex psychological makeup who are involved with complicated relationships. THE JILTING OF GRANNY WEATHERALL was really about secrets of the heart. That's the kind of material that I really care about.

Q: *You never had any doubt that you were going to be successful, did you?*

A: Oh, that's not true. I have had my periods of doubt. I've never said to myself, "I'm a woman, I can't do that," but just gone ahead and done it anyway. I think that's actually something I like about myself, because I'm always questioning and always driving myself crazy. But at the same time, that's never stopped me from doing things. But careerwise, after doing UNDER THIS SKY and THE JILTING OF GRANNY WEATHERALL, I came back to L.A. with the latter, which was a much better selling tool for me than the first one because of the nature of the material. And then two years went by in which I did not work. During those two years there was a lot of doubt.

Q: *You were between a rock and a hard place. You wanted to work but couldn't take a step back to do anything else but direct. What does a person do during two years of not working?*

A: I was always busy, somehow. Somehow I managed to sustain a real level of energy and commitment despite this parallel of exhaustion and a feeling of my spirit cracking. Maybe if my tastes were different it all would have happened more easily. I don't regret any of that time now because the kind of work I've done since has been the kind of work I wanted to do. And the job that I finally got was the créme de la créme of television, Hill Street Blues. Mostly, what you encounter in trying to make these breaks from one plateau to the next is that people—though they may respect your abilities—don't have the imagination or the faith or the ability to take the leap, that if you've done X kind of films you could also do Y kind of films. Mostly they say, "Gee, we love your film, but there's no chicken in it. Our film stars a chicken, and we don't think you can direct a chicken." So here was Hill Street Blues, as far away as you could get from THE JILTING OF GRANNY WEATHERALL, with this huge cast, enormous pace, action, a visual style that was light years away from the other film. And here were a group of people who said, "gee, here's someone with talent. . . we bet she could adapt to our style and do our show." I just sat down and made a study of the show, looked at its style, got a feeling for it, hung around the set to get to know the actors a little bit, went in and did it. And it worked out very well. In three years I did four Hill Streets.

Q: *During that period, did you find that you were accepted on the set as a woman director, or were there still barriers?*

A: Well, I think I have always tried to put blinders on a little bit about that. If you feel people aren't responding to you on the set because you didn't do your home-work, or because they don't like the way you're shooting, or because you're not giving actors enough direction, you can take their responses as feedback and work on those problems. But if you feel that they're not working for you because you're a woman, what can you do about that? When I look back on it I know there might have been a couple of incidents, but there were really very few, even in taking my blinders off.

Q: *Was SOMETHING ABOUT AMELIA a project that you developed or was it something that was brought to you?*

A: It was developed by a woman named Deborah Aal, a wonderful, talented person who was then working for Leonard Goldberg. The project was her idea and it took her about 2 1/2 years to get it developed. She was one of the people whom I met during the two years I didn't work. She filed me away in her mind and now, years later, she had this project and I came back into her thoughts. In the mean-time, I had moved way ahead from where I had been, so it all worked out. When the script was sent to me, I was a little apprehensive—I thought that the material might have been exploitative and sensationalized. But by page two, I realized just how good the writing was. It was tense, so much complexity beneath the surface of the dialogue, unlike a lot of television where the characters talk directly about what's going on. So I called back right after I finished it and said—I know this sounds corny—"This is terrific and I'm the person to direct it."

Q: *Weren't you afraid that network pressures would force you in directions you didn't want to take?*

A: The quality of the script indicated to me that everyone knew this was a spe-cial project. Standards and Practices, of course, was very involved, but we never got frantic phone calls after dailies. We had no major problem. When the rough cut was finished they were incredibly enthusiastic.

Q: *You went into the film knowing that it was a special project. This was your first network movie, an ABC Theatre project and, of course, the theme was so delicate. Couldn't that have been overwhelming?*

A: Of course, one thinks about the big view. There was a lot of responsibility, but the bigger responsibility was to the story. It ultimately narrows down to just the one family depicted in the film. I wasn't telling the story of everyone in the world who was ever in such a situation. We could only talk in terms of this daugh-ter and this father and this family and this story. You can't direct it thinking that you're going to make the definitive film on incest in contemporary American life. You just try to make the story as truthful as it can possibly be, which is what you do with any story.

Q: *Were you at all apprehensive about casting Ted Danson as the father?*

A: No, I think we felt that it worked to our advantage. Everybody knows what the story is about tuning in, so there are already twenty thousand strikes against that character. Casting the character with an actor who everybody has warm feelings about—because of his role in Cheers—is a real advantage. I did not want the father to be a villain. I thought he was a much more complex character, and as much as the audience would be capable of, I wanted them to feel compassion for him. Whatever despicable things he has done, by his own actions he has destroyed his own life and lost everything that meant anything to him. Plus, I also knew that Ted Danson was a really wonderful actor and could bring much to the role.

Q: *Did you expect the incredible effect that SOMETHING ABOUT AMELIA had on the American public and press?*

A: No. I knew that we were going to have the hotline numbers at the end of the show, but I never really envisioned 60 million people watching the show in one night and tens of thousands of phone calls pouring in.

Q: *In essence, the film altered public perception of incest and helped remove the stigma from victims.*

A: Television has such incredible power and people working in it do not often acknowledge the responsibility they have. It can open people's eyes and affect their points of view. And some of the choices that were made on the show affected the way people look at incest—not just that they can acknowledge that it's there, but that they can look at it without the kind of horror that prevents them from acting.

Q: *Is television work behind you now?*

A: I want to work in features, and I'm developing CHILDREN OF A LESSER GOD and other projects, but I don't believe in closing any doors. The problem with having done SOMETHING ABOUT AMELIA is that projects like that come along every ten years in television. Other things have been offered to me that haven't interested me as much, not just because of the subject matter, but because of the way the stories are told. I haven't yet come across a script that has excited me as much as AMELIA but wherever you find the material and the opportunity to tell a story, that's where you'll tell it.

F I L M O G R A P H Y

R A N D A   H A I N E S

UNDER THIS SKY (TF) Red Cloud Productions/PBS, 1979

THE JILTING OF GRANNY WEATHERALL (TF) Learning in Focus/American Short Story, 1980

SOMETHING ABOUT AMELIA (TF) ☆ Leonard Goldberg Productions, 1984

ALFRED HITCHCOCK PRESENTS (TF) co-director with Steve DeJarnatt, Joel Oliansky & Fred Walton, Universal TV, 1985

CHILDREN OF A LESSER GOD Paramount, 1986

THE DOCTOR Buena Vista, 1991

WRESTLING ERNEST HEMINGWAY Warner Bros., 1993

DANCE WITH ME Columbia, 1998

$\mathcal{A}$MY $\mathcal{H}$ECKERLING

It's nice to note that having started her feature directing career helming FAST TIMES AT RIDGEMONT HIGH, a film that helped to define the the teenage landscape of the early 1980s, Heckerling then bookended it with the hugely successful CLUELESS, which did the same for the '90s. In the process, she helped put such performers as Sean Penn, Jennifer Jason Leigh and Alicia Silverstone on the movie map, and proved that films about and for teenagers could be smart, funny and sophisticated. Indeed, FAST TIMES was from a script by the then-barely-out-his-teens Cameron Crowe, who went on to write and direct his very own SAY ANYTHING, SINGLES and JERRY MAGUIRE, and CLUELESS was cleverly based on a source so high-toned as Jane Austen's Emma.

At the time of our conversation, Heckerling had also directed the affectionate gangster movie sendup JOHNNY DANGEROUSLY and the box office hit NATIONAL LAMPOON'S EUROPEAN VACATION, and was to follow three years later with LOOK WHO'S TALKING—which helped to revive John Travolta from his '80s doldrums—and its sequel. But it was really CLUELESS that reminded audiences and critics of just how bright a filmmaker Heckerling can be when she's at the top of her game.

MICHAEL SINGER: *You seem to be a comedy specialist. That's not easy. Where does the ability and desire to direct comedy come from?*

AMY HECKERLING: You can argue whether or not I have the ability, but the desire comes from. . . well, basically, left to my own devices, I will think of very morbid things all day. Really, I'm not kidding. When you work on a movie, you spend a year of your life going over and over the same stuff. It it's depressing, and you've already started out that way, you're in serious trouble. I mean, movies are a great diversion. They're a great way to go out and not think about what's troubling you when you're watching them. But for the people who are making them, they're a great way to not deal with the horrors of life if you're making silly, light, romantic, goofy comedies. I need to have my mind in a happier place.

Q: *I never expected to find Kafka posters hanging on your office walls.*

A: He's my hero. If I really knew how to express what I feel I would have been him. Every word he's written makes so much sense to me, I can't tell you. That's why I do NATIONAL LAMPOON'S EUROPEAN VACATION.

Q: *It's almost as if you are saying that if you didn't direct comedies, you might be making the most depressing movies in the world.*

A: Yeah. If I was saying what's on my mind it would be very black.

Q: *Do you think there's a way of making your comedies a little darker?*

A: Well, you can make black comedies, which are great when they are done well like DR. STRANGELOVE or THE LADYKILLERS things like that. They're not real popular at the moment. People tend to take things more literally than they used to. They're not laughing at the same things, you don't hear, "Oh, no, not another summer black comedy."

Q: *Is it that the audiences have actually become less sophisticated in the last twenty years, or is it just the nature of the times?*

A: The things that are truly depressing now can't possibly be made funny. There can't be anything funny about a nuclear disaster, fatal sexually transmitted disease. . . I don't see the humor in any of that.

Q: *So the only real alternative is to make movies that are the opposite of what you read in the headlines every day. What about drama? Will there be a point when you direct straight dramatic films?*

A: I'm developing a drama now for The Mount Company. But it's actually difficult to make dramatic feature films. Different media have sort of gravitated towards different subject matter. You can do things on AIDS and other serious subjects on television, and they do very well. . . sort of the "disease-of-the-week" shows. I just saw a fabulous TV movie with Liza Minnelli playing the mother of son with a debilitating disease. Here's a great actress doing a great performance. . . why isn't it a movie? Well, if it were a movie, I don't think people would watch it as much. That subject matter has sort of gravitated towards television.

Q: *Isn't that a weird reversal from the early days of television, when it was the silly alternative to serious features?*

A: Yes. Let's say someone today said, "Here, I wrote a script. It's called, SWEET SMELL OF SUCCESS." Brilliant. Do you think you could get that made today? It's scary.

Q: *Does all this frustrate you as a filmmaker?*

A: If I were a lot more intelligent and a lot more serious it would probably frustrate me. Things being what they are, I fit right in.

Q: *The dramatic sequences in FAST TIMES AT RIDGEMONT HIGH worked really well, but your next two films had no serious stuff at all. Would you like to infuse your upcoming films with more dramatic material?*

A: I was very lucky to get that project. It was a wonderful script, and I related to it a great deal. After that, though, they weren't knocking down my door saying, "Here are more great scripts!" They were saying, "Oh, here are all the other high school pictures, here are all the loss of virginity pictures, here are all the preppy movies." And I didn't relate to any of that, nor did I want to spend the rest of my life dealing with the bad teacher, the girl who gets pregnant, the loss of innocence, etc. I wanted to do something different. I thought the script of JOHNNY DANGEROUSLY was very funny. It was pure satire of something that nobody remembers. I think that was the main problem, because all the actors and writers did great jobs. But we were definitely satirizing something. . . I mean, unless you watch 1930s movies on TV at night, people don't remember. Somebody told me that during a screening they were sitting next to Brian De Palma, who had just done SCARFACE—and he was in hysterics. If you studied those movies, you know what we were doing.

Q: *I appreciated the fact that you were trying to emulate the one-take, everybody-in-the-shot technique of the 1930s films. I sort of wish you had been able to shoot JOHNNY DANGEROUSLY in black-and-white.*

A: The producer wanted to, and I thought it was a great idea, and then the more I thought about it, the more I observed myself as a television watcher—flipping through channels, and sort of flipping by the black and white shows realizing that kids today are constantly bombarded by the video machine colors. What I wanted to achieve was the colored-in look of 1930's color films, almost unfinished. You can't really do that, though, unless you do it computerized —which would have cost an arm-and-a-leg. That's what I was going for, and now that JOHNNY DANGEROUSLY is on TV, I get to play around with the dials and mess around with the colors. There are a lot of things we could have done with that movie that would have made it less popular, but better.

Q: *How did Amy Heckerling come to the movies, or how did the movies come to Amy Heckerling?*

A: I can tell you exactly how it happened. . . I used to watch movies constantly on television when I was real little. I was madly in love with James Cagney—this is pre-school—and when I saw ANGELS WITH DIRTY FACES, Cagney was walking to the electric chair. Now I never understood what was going on in those movies, I just knew I loved them. I knew something bad was happening because of the music, so I started crying and crying. My mother told me that Cagney was going to the chair because he was a bad guy, and he was going to die. I didn't know what that was, so my mother explained dying to me. It seemed pretty horrible, but then my mother told me that he wasn't really going to die, because he was in a movie. Well, it just all seemed to click then! That was the way to beat it! I could see James Cagney die a million times, but he was always there. This year I didn't believe it really happened. I kept expecting Cagney to get up.

Q: *Having your name on movies does seem to give you a certain immortality.*

A: I was in a car accident right after I finished my AFI movie. We had sent the film into the lab, and the lab sent it back saying they couldn't read the edge-code numbers from the negative. So my assistant editor and I went through every piece of film, tracking down the trims and finding what the edge-codes were. We finally finished—the last thing that had to be done on the movie. It was sent to the lab again. To celebrate, we went to see MEAN STREETS and A CLOCKWORK OR-ANGE for the five billionth time, and on the way back I was broadsided by a drunk driver. There was the whole thing—the yellow light and all that stuff—and what went through my mind right then was, "Well, at least I got the film into the lab." So it's not going to save you from anything, obviously, but something about it pulls you forward.

Q: *How did you turn your dream of directing into a reality?*

A: I had made an AFI student film starring Glynnis O'Connor, and because she was so wonderful, it made me look good. I got an agent, and the agent got me development deals. . . I wrote something that I loved a lot called MY KIND OF GUY. It was going to be made by Warner Bros., and it went into turnaround. Then it went into turnaround at Universal. Then it went to MGM and they really were going to make it. I was casting, finding locations, building the sets, getting costumes and the crew together. Every single thing on that movie was planned. And then the actor's strike hit, when there wasn't one single thing left for me to do. For the rest of the summer they told me to keep working, because they really were going to do it. I knew every single color that everyone was going to wear against every wall in every frame, because I had nothing to do all summer except plan it during the strike. Then they dropped it. From this storybook career, all of a sudden it was this horrible thing. That day I read about four lifeguards getting cancer from stuff that had been dumped in Santa Monica, and I thought, "Okay. . . losing a film isn't that bad. Start all over again." Then I wrote something completely wacky and silly, and while that was happening, Art Linson offered me FAST TIMES. There I was, a young person directing a feature movie with a lot of wonderful actors, and it was back to the storybook career again. Then you do another two movies, and it feels like the whole world is against you, and it's back to "the horror, the horror" again. But after having a baby, it doesn't matter what the critics say, what the executives say, what a bunch of agents at the hottest agency say about me. I'm doing it because I like it. When I stop liking it then I'll do something else. It's always going to be good and bad and ugly, but that's not the point of it. The point is the same reason you get up in the morning and call your girlfriend in the Bronx and say, "Let's play cut-out dolls."

Q: *So, in a way, you're still playing cut-out dolls.*

A: Yeah. Except now they make millions of dollars.

F I L M O G R A P H Y

A M Y   H E C K E R L I N G

b. May 7, 1954 - Bronx, New York
FAST TIMES AT RIDGEMONT HIGH Universal, 1982
JOHNNY DANGEROUSLY 20th Century Fox, 1984
NATIONAL LAMPOON'S EUROPEAN VACATION Warner Bros., 1985
LOOK WHO'S TALKING TriStar, 1989
LOOK WHO'S TALKING TOO TriStar, 1990
CLUELESS Paramount, 1995

STEPHEN $\mathcal{H}$EREK

If I may be permitted a comparison, it's a high compliment to say that Stephen Herek is the Robert Stevenson of our time. . . . that is, the legitimate heir to a throne that sat vacant for many years after the demise of the man who directed the Walt Disney Company's finest live-action features, among them OLD YELLER, DARBY O'GILL AND THE LITTLE PEOPLE, KIDNAPPED, THE ABSENT-MINDED PROFESSOR, MARY POPPINS, THAT DARN CAT, THE LOVE BUG and BEDKNOBS AND BROOMSTICKS. Herek was charged by the new Disney organization to helm such A-list family features as THE MIGHTY DUCKS, THE THREE MUSKETEERS, MR. HOLLAND'S OPUS and 101 DALMATIANS, and the filmmaker emerged with flying colors (and considerable box office) each time.

But I spoke with Herek before he was even certain that he would cut it as a studio director, because it was after the shooting but before the release of BILL AND TED'S EXCELLENT ADVENTURE. . . which of course now qualifies as a pop culture classic, thanks to Herek's deft filming of the boisterously witty Chris Matheson and Ed Solomon screenplay, which set the stage for the later WAYNE'S WORLD, BEAVIS AND BUTT-HEAD and other odes to adolescent dimwits. Herek had directed the 1985 nasty-things-from-outer-space opus CRITTERS, which tickled audiences with its freshness and humor in a genre which even then had been pretty well wrung dry.

At the time of writing, Herek had just completed another big-time Disney feature, THE HOLY MAN, starring Eddie Murphy.

MICHAEL SINGER: *Were you a certified movie buff growing up?*

STEPHEN HEREK: No, I was actually more of a jock. In fact, I wanted to be a professional baseball player. In high school I did very well at the sport and got some scholarship offers. I played some semi-pro ball, in fact. But my father was in the military, and we got transferred from the places where I got all my scholarship offers. We eventually settled in Texas, and I went to the University Of Texas at Austin, where I actually played for a semester. But I didn't make the traveling squad, which devastated me. What is life without baseball? So I decided that I would get into radio, television or film geared to sports broadcasting so that I could still be around athletics. Well, during that time, I took my very first film course and that's when the bug hit me. I knew that I wanted to make movies.

Q: *What aspect of filmmaking interested you the most at first?*

A: I studied with Edward Dmytryk at U.T. Editing was his first love, and that's what turned me on. I liked cutting films. I would work all night long, and either shoot my own film or work on somebody else's. I eventually wanted to be a director, but I wanted to get there through the editing. So after I got out of college I came out to Hollywood with my wife, who I met at the school. Not very long after that I got my first job, working for Roger Corman. I was an apprentice editor on a show called SLUMBER PARTY MASSACRE, then apprenticed for another production group on O'HARA'S WIFE. I want back to Corman as an assistant editor on ANDROID, then SPACE RAIDERS. I kept getting more jobs as an assistant editor for three years. Eventually, I got bored. It was nice money, but the job was like being a file clerk, so eventually I got a job cutting trailers and T.V. spots for New World. It dawned on me one day that the stuff I was working on was pretty bad, and I figured that I could do just as well or better. A friend of mine that I met working on CITY LIMITS was a would-be script writer named Brian Muir who had written CRITTERS and just had it sitting in his drawer. I loved the title and read the script, which I thought was real interesting. I asked if I could do a rewrite on it, and Brian said no problem. He liked what I had done. When we wrote the draft of CRITTERS, GREMLINS was about to come out, so we registered it right away—because we figured that we were going to get in trouble for ripping off GREMLINS, when in fact Brian had written the first draft of CRITTERS before anyone even heard of GREMLINS.

Q: *So you got CRITTERS financed by New Line Cinema and were suddenly a movie director. How did you feel when you walked onto the set the first day?*

A: It was one of the most surreal moments I've ever had in my life. I have to admit that I had been very, very nervous before shooting started. Four weeks before we started I wasn't eating much. I couldn't sleep. I wasn't sure I was going to be able to do it. Then the day of reckoning actually came, and I decided to equate directing to coaching a baseball team. That's sort of how I philosophized the whole thing in my mind. So I figured, okay, I'm the coach of this team. All of a sudden, it was the very first rehearsal, and immediately everybody's attention came to me. They were waiting for me to utter my first words as a director. I don't remember exactly what I said, but I did say something and people started doing something. That day is really a blur now.

Q: *I assume, though, that you had done all your homework in advance of that first day.*

A: One thing that I feel is really imperative in moviemaking is prep time. We storyboarded about 80 percent of CRITTERS and shot-listed the entire film, so I pretty much knew what I wanted to do. Whether anyone else had a clue of what was going into the camera, at least I knew what was happening.

Q: Did you also storyboard extensively when you shot BILL AND TED?

A: Well, CRITTERS and BILL AND TED are two different kinds of animals. One thing about CRITTERS was that it was a very finite cast—there wasn't a whole lot of casting involved. Everything was very categorized. You could do things relatively expediently, whereas in BILL AND TED. . . first of all, we had a movie that is really driven by two guys on the screen one hundred percent of the time, and we couldn't afford to get a Michael J. Fox. Actually, we didn't want a Michael J. Fox. We wanted two fresh faces, and we got them in Keanu Reeves and Alex Winter. We had to cast the historical characters to come up with people who continued from page 19 looked somewhat like Abraham Lincoln, Joan of Arc, Napoleon and the others. We had about a twelve week prep period on BILL AND TED, and at least five of them were just in the casting area, so I storyboarded only the special effects or any sequences that were action-oriented. That was okay, because BILL AND TED is more driven by dialogue than CRITTERS was.

Q: After CRITTERS was released and well-received, did you suddenly become "bankable"?

A: Actually, I think I was more of a curiosity. I guess I was like the flavor of the month, because everybody wanted to meet me. I locked onto the agent that I've got now, then went on a studio tour meeting just about everybody. I did get more scripts, but it wasn't a big deluge. I read about people who all of a sudden get about a hundred scripts a week, but it wasn't like that at all. The attention was very nice, but I think people really did view me more as a curiosity. Maybe I under-estimating it. I don't really know.

Q: The screenplay of BILL AND TED was considered a very hot property. How did it find its way to you?

A: It was really was interesting. Interscope actually optioned it, and then they found a home for it at Warner Bros. I had no idea what the picture was when they sent it to me. They actually had another director for BILL AND TED, but they wanted to meet me anyway in case something did not work out. And it actually happened a week later that as things often happen in Hollywood, the director did drop off the project for one reason or another. So we made a deal with Warner Bros., but it was a frustrating six months. It was the first time I'd ever had to deal with development. I thought that when you got a script and committed to it, a couple of months later you were out there directing it. But Warner Bros. was being hit very hard by the failure of a couple of youth comedies, and they decided to go with their main staples, like the Clint Eastwood movies—they just didn't want to put twelve million dollars into what they categorized as a youth comedy. So we started talking about doing it non-union as a pickup, but Warner Bros. wouldn't do it that way either. I knew that Interscope was getting frustrated, and I was getting frustrated. My contract was expiring, and I told them that I had to make movies to make money, and if they weren't going to make BILL AND TED, I had to find another movie to direct. Interscope really had a lot of faith in the project, and they ended up forcing it into turnaround at Warner Bros. and immediately all the other studios wanted to make it—but everybody was turned away by the price tag for what they considered to be about a ten or twelve million dollar film. De Laurentiis, however, said that they could make films nonunion, and we decided to go with them to shoot BILL AND TED less expensively but with all the other production values intact.

Q: *The story of BILL AND TED is very offbeat and very funny, but seems to require a careful sensibility. It must have been a challenge to preserve what read so well on paper.*

A: Well it was, because there were a lot of ways you could have gone directing it. You could have gone into a very wild, crazy kind of thing, real Mondo Bizarro. But I opted for walking the line between Mondo Bizzaro and reality. In a way, the characters of Bill and Ted are just like you and me, only they're not. I needed to have the audience empathize with them if you watch these guys you've got to like them. Basically, we went after the "puppy dog effect"—that Bill and Ted were basically these exuberant, lovable retrievers just happy to go and catch a stick thrown at them. They have a wide-open attitude toward life, but they also take absolutely everything in stride.

Q: *Keanu Reeves and Alex Winter both have solid acting credits behind them, but how did you decide on them?*

A: I think my casting director went through six or seven hundred kids. I myself saw about three hundred of them, but Keanu and Alex were just by far and away head and shoulders above anyone else.

Q: *What were the challenges of creating other times and places in the film's time-travel sequences? Did you take a realistic or cartoonish approach?*

A: I wanted to create worlds which you think are real—so when we go back in time we feel they are really in medieval England, or 18th century Austria. I wanted it to be as close to reality as possible. The Monty Python films are a good example of what I was going for, because they went to great pains to make everything look realistic even though the events going on are hilarious and ridiculous.

Q: *Ed Solomon and Chris Matheson, who wrote BILL AND TED, were on location for the entire duration of shooting. Isn't that unusual?*

A: Yes, but Chris and Ed want to be filmmakers themselves and this was their first script that was produced. They really had a desire to observe the filmmaking process. At first I had a little bit of trepidation in that you have enough creative ideas on the set and more—especially from the guys who wrote the script—might just be too many shots in the pot. But we talked a little bit, and they were aware of that. Chris and Ed stayed pretty much in the background on the set, but it really came in handy a few times when either a line wasn't right or there was something wrong with the action. We could actually call on their services, and they were very willing to write something on the spot and help us out of a jam. Usually it worked incredibly well. In one sequence, due to budgetary requirements, we moved an important scene from an auditorium into a classroom. After shooting it, it became obvious that it was just not as effective as it should have been. This was a climactic sequence, and just by virtue of being in one room, it made the scene seem small and stagnant. We immediately talked with DEG, and they understood our problem and supported putting it back into the auditorium. Immediately, within two days, Chris and Ed had a whole new scene written! It was great.

Q: *Sounds like you had the kind of creative collaborations between director and writers which happens all too rarely in this business.*

A: I think it depends on egos. Really, for me it's a kick. I love watching movies, and just the idea of making them is really a thrill to me. So it's not just a director's movie, it's not just an actor's movie, it's a collaborative effort, and when everybody's working together, it's much like a football or baseball team. But when all the wheels are working, you have a team that's unstoppable—and that's pretty much the atmosphere that I try to generate. . . a kind of creative atmosphere where there's no bad idea. . . it's just that we're looking for the right idea. To me, it's my job to sift through and find the one that I feel works for my vision and the overall vision of what the movie should be. I don't think writers get enough credit. When a movie works, usually it's the director who gets all the credit. Very rarely does a writer ever get credit, and that's just not right. On the other hand, sometimes if a movie's bad, the director won't get panned and the writer will, which seems kind of odd.

Q: *Do you think that directorial technique is instinctive? Because you had a background as an editor and not a director, but somehow you knew what to do when you walked onto the set of* CRITTERS.

A: In a way it is instinctive, but I don't really know. I can't intellectualize it. You feel that something will work, and you do it. Sometimes it does, sometimes it doesn't. But that's where you make your money. . . when you're sitting on the set with thousands of dollars being spent

F I L M O G R A P H Y

S T E P H E N   H E R E K

b. November 10, 1958 - San Antonio, Texas
CRITTERS New Line Cinema, 1985
BILL & TED'S EXCELLENT ADVENTURE Orion, 1989
THE GIFTED ONE (TF) Richard Rothstein Productions/NBC Productions, 1989
DON'T TELL MOM THE BABYSITTER'S DEAD Warner Bros., 1991
THE MIGHTY DUCKS Buena Vista, 1992
THE THREE MUSKETEERS Buena Vista, 1993
MR. HOLLAND'S OPUS Buena Vista, 1995
101 DALMATIANS Buena Vista, 1996
THE HOLY MAN Buena Vista, 1998

$\mathcal{W}$ALTER $\mathcal{H}$ILL

If unpredictability was the key to success, than nobody would be bigger than Walter Hill, one of American film's most gloriously, infuriatingly and sometimes irritatingly mercurial directors. He's also, in that same vein, a true original, stubbornly going down his own road, with a body of work ranging from the downright personal to the overtly commercial. His best work—among them such odd pieces as HARD TIMES, THE DRIVER, THE WARRIORS, THE LONG RIDERS, SOUTHERN COMFORT, JOHNNY HANDSOME and most recently, the underseen triumverate GERONIMO: AN AMERICAN LEGEND, WILD BILL and LAST MAN STANDING—reveals a man awash with a keen sense of American history and mythology, noting that the two are often interchangeable. His exercises in popular moviemaking—such as the massively successful 48 HRS. and its inevitable sequel, ANOTHER 48 HRS.—are no less well made, but inevitably less interesting, because there's less of the the Walter Hill whose work veers towards noir surrealism, thick atmospherics and a streak of stylistic individuality. It should be interesting to see what happens when Hill tackles science fiction for the first time, with his most recent project, SUPERNOVA.

Hill, a native of Long Beach, California, originally aimed at becoming a cartoonist, then a journalist, finally entering film as a second assistant director. Before taking hold of directing reins, Hill warmed up by writing or co-writing such films as HICKEY AND BOGGS, THE GETAWAY (the Peckinpah version) and THE DROWNING POOL, all foreshadowing his later work. Considering his often tough-as-nails films, when I interviewed Hill in the Paramount Pictures commissary—he was shooting ANOTHER 48 HRS. at the time—I was surprised to find a man of quiet mien, free of macho posturing, and have never heard a negative word of his on-set manner from anyone who has worked with him. I've also been pleased to see Hill turning back to more personal subject matter since then, and to hell with the fact that box office response to his last three films has been disappointing. He's a man still carving his own niche in the studio system, a difficult enough accomplishment for any American filmmaker in the '90s.

MICHAEL SINGER: It seems to me that the reasons people become directors now are different than what they were 30 or 40 years ago.

WALTER HILL: I think there are a lot of people now who become directors because they're very committed to bringing certain projects to fruition rather than going into it as a career. If someone became a director in the old days, it was a career, a profession, and if you didn't get into it at a fairly early age, chances were you weren't going to become a director at all. Now there are a lot of people who become directors when they are in their forties. That didn't happen very much back then.

Q: It seems that now, if you're only a screenwriter rather than a hyphenate, you only have half a career.

A: That's unfortunate. I think screenwriting is a craft, a calling. The idea that you have somehow fallen short of the mark if you don't become a director seems silly to me, because an awful lot of people by temperament or talent are not cut out to be directors. The fact that you write doesn't guarantee that you can direct, any more than the fact that you can direct means you can write. There are people that are good at both, of course.

Q: When you segued from writing to directing, had that been the goal all along or did an opportunity just present itself to you?

A: I had a rather strange beginning in that my first real work was as a writer and then I became an assistant director and then I became a writer again and then I became a director. But I think I always really wanted to become a director. My own writing was pointed in that direction. I don't mean that to contradict my first remarks, but I think in my case it was true. I never really thought of myself, in that sense, as a writer. I think of myself as a director who writes. And early on I thought of myself as someone who probably was going to be a director but was writing to make a living. One of the reasons I like to work with writers is that I think they help you test your ideas. I don't like to write alone and then direct what I write, although I've done that. People often ask me, "Don't you want to write originals and then direct them?" I've done that and I don't want to anymore. I'd much rather work with other writers. It's a lot more fun. You have the excitement of being part of a conspiracy.

Q: I understand that you like to do a lot of writing on the set during production.

A: Yeah, I rewrite as I go, constantly. I think I know the film and the characters better as the picture goes on. I'm not one to think that if you write it, it's the same truth three or six months later. Making pictures is a process, at least the way I do it. You get the script and then you shoot the film and then you cut the film. In a sense, it's all writing. In another sense, it's all filmmaking. And the old joke is the truth—the final rewrites are in the editing room. Movies are always looking for something that plays, which is not necessarily the same thing as literary truth. You can construct something that is quite right on the page, but doesn't play. And filmmakers are always going to be pushing everything toward what plays.

Q: *You have a great feeling for rural America in movies like HARD TIMES, SOUTHERN COMFORT and THE LONG RIDERS. On the other hand, you're known for urban actioners like 48 HRS., THE DRIVER and RED HEAT. Do you like spending a lot of time in places outside Los Angeles to soak up atmosphere and ideas?*

A: I've traveled a lot. . . and I'm sick of traveling. Basically, I like to sit home and read. I don't like going out very much at all. I don't mind going out on a picture. But I think that atmosphere you mention comes out of your dream life. I grew up in the sticks, and I think I approached urban living with a sense of wonder. I like things with rural settings, but I think that generally those pictures aren't very commercial anymore. One has to adapt.

Q: *Do you feel that you've been forced to adapt as a filmmaker in any way?*

A: I think I'm a good example of somebody who would have been very happy in the studio system 30, 40, 50 years ago. I'd have probably made westerns. They don't make those very much anymore.

Q: *You made THE LONG RIDERS, which was a "real" western, and EXTREME PREJU-DICE, which was a contemporary western. Some have suggested that most of your films have a western sensibility.*

A: It's interesting to speculate on the decline of the western. I think the single biggest factor is that Americans are no longer in touch or care a lot about their agrarian past, which is a way of saying that they've lost a sense of their own history. I think it's also true that westerns were done to death on television, which exhausted the genre.

Q: *I think TV is still doing them to death with those "hunks-in-buckskin" sort of shows.*

A: I haven't seen them. The other thing you have to say about the westerns is that of all the motion picture genres, they were the most subject to parody. Once that begins to happen, it's a lot more difficult for the audience to take them seriously. The large audiences want very much to believe in the drama. Parody appeals to intellectuals, but on the whole it doesn't appeal to larger audiences. However, I don't think westerns are irreversibly gone. They'll never be what they were as an industry staple, but I think occasionally somebody will make one and have no better or worse a chance for success than any other period movie. If you've got one with the right story and cast, it could work very well. I think one of the sad things is that we've not only lost westerns, but period movies as well.

Q: *Period movies are still a staple in Eastern Europe, or at least were until the recent developments.*

A: I think a lot of that has to do with the social conditions in those countries. I think there's a greater nostalgia for the past over there than we have in America, and for good reason. I think the great majority of Americans are not imbued with a sense of nostalgia for their own history. Again, we're talking in very big generalities. The truth is, if you write a good book about some aspect of America's past, there's a great chance for commercial success. But to make a commercially successful motion picture, you have to get a much larger audience than you need to get a best-seller.

Q: *If you had your druthers, would you be working a lot more on period pieces than contemporary, urban action films?*

A: I don't know. You want to do a variety of films. I don't want to sound like I'm unhappy with my lot. I'm really mainly interested in the characters of the stories I have done. Therefore, I'd rather do a contemporary drama with characters I'm interested in than I would a nostalgic rural piece with characters that don't particularly interest me.

Q: *Your newest film, ANOTHER 48 HRS., is a follow-up to a smash hit you made a few years ago. One of your stars, Eddie Murphy, is in very different circumstances now than when you worked with him the first time. He's achieved superstardom, and has also directed as well. Has the dynamic changed between you on this shoot?*

A: People ask me, "How has Eddie changed?" I find Eddie to be exactly the same. . . except he's a lot more so. Whatever tendencies he had in the past, he's just more so now. But working with him has been exactly the same. We get in, rehearse the scene, work until we decide we like it, and we shoot it. We worked out the character of Reggie Hammond in the last one. The biggest difference between shooting the last one and this one is that Eddie, Nick Nolte and myself feel that we know the characters this time. We're more confident about how the characters would react to the situation. So in that sense, it's changed a bit. I've never made a sequel before. I suppose the nicest thing about a sequel is that you know the characters already. The most difficult thing about this sequel. . . I don't think it's unfair to say that 48 HRS. has been a much imitated movie. I wonder occasionally how much ground is left. Some of the imitations are good films, but you wonder how much ground they've used up. There's only so much land to stand on.

Q: *How do you find that additional square foot of ground that hasn't been covered yet?*

A: I don't know that we have. You'd better ask me that next year. I think it' s a good story. But what the film is really about is an exploration of the personalities of the two main characters—set in a bizarre, comic, violent world. It's certainly not realistic, but it's informed by a certain kind of street truth. That's the basis of the humor. I think the characters are necessarily softer in this one than they were in the original. A lot of the antagonism in the first movie worked at a very direct racial level. To put them back in that framework would mean that each character had learned nothing from the first experience. It would be a denial of the first movie, which I think would be unfair. So as I've uncharitably put it, a lot of this movie is like a husband and wife fighting with each other. They fight like they mean it, but at the same time you know they're going to kiss and make up.

Q: *Were you at all reluctant to take ANOTHER 48 HRS. on, because it is a sequel?*

A: Yeah, I was. Paramount had asked me a number of times over the years to get into it. It didn't appeal to me. But Eddie called me and said he'd very much like to do another one, and thought there was room to do another one, could we sit down and talk about it? Then he called Nick and Nick called me, and said we ought to do it. Eddie and I worked out a story which I liked, and thought, what the hell. I also like working with my friends, and I count both Eddie and Nick as my friends. I think having fun while you make a motion picture is important.

Q: *You said before that you would have been happy in the old studio system, and you're the first director I've ever interviewed who ever said that. . . except for George Sidney and Gene Kelly, who did work in that system and seemed to enjoy it.*

A: Well, I think I felt that a little stronger a few years ago than I do now, to be frank. I'll tell you why. I like the work, to stage and shoot for a living. I have a good time making motion pictures on the whole, even with all the problems that go with it. I think the most frustrating thing about the business—less so now than a few years ago—is the business, the negotiating, the deals. You're always going to meetings. What I like about my understanding of the old studio system is that they made lots of movies, and you just went to work. Nowadays, so often you spend more time getting a deal on a movie set up than you do on the movie itself. I think that was truer five years ago and certainly truer ten years ago than now. There's a more positive attitude now about making films, and what underlies it is their profitability. I think it's much easier to be a young director now than ten or fifteen years ago when I was first starting, because there's more product.

Q: *Here's the Walter Hill stereotype: two-fisted action director in the classic mode. Are you comfortable with that?*

A: I just say 'oh shit, throw me in the briar patch'. I don't think anyone wants to be thought of as just an action director, but I also think there's a long and honorable tradition in Hollywood with action directors. You hope you can make your own contribution. Historically, action directors in Hollywood have been thought of as being on the back porch. But listen, that's not exactly the fate of the Boat People. There are a lot of things in the world that are a lot tougher. I like doing action films. The definitions are always a little funny because what is violent to one person is action to someone else. If you say, "You wanna go out and see a violent movie?," most people would say no. If you say, "You wanna go out and see an action movie?," most people say yes. In dealing with physical violence, sometimes I've presented it in a very tough and harsh way. At times I've presented it in a way that's palatable for general entertainment. What I find remarkable is that if you film violence in a way that' s totally light and doesn't really deal with physical consequences, everybody' s quite happy with you. If you actually show how tough and hard it can be, everybody gets mad at you. The moralists jump all over you, when I would have thought they would be unhappy about the reverse. These are among the many things about the world that puzzle me.

Q: *What else puzzles you?*

A: When somebody transcends the genre, they're no longer considered action directors. Among many other things, SEVEN SAMURAI is an action movie. The fact that it is a very great film doesn't mean that it is not an action film. I find it a little off-putting that when somebody does it very well, there's a perception that it's no longer an action movie. The problem isn't making action films. . . it's whether or not you make good movies or bad movies.

People assume I like action movies. I don't particularly like them. If anything, I'm probably a harsher critic of action films than other genres. I like romantic comedies very much, dramas as well. George Cukor was one of my favorite directors. He was an admirable director not because of the kind of films he made, but because he made them so well. That's what directing is all about, not selecting high-toned subjects. I think that in Hollywood and in film criticism, movies are quite often judged by their intentions rather than their execution and the ability of the filmmaker to execute them. If noble intentions were what made a good film, then it would be very easy to get to heaven. It's not that simple.

Q: JOHNNY HANDSOME *was probably the most controversial of all your films. It won its avid supporters and incredible detractors, dividing people very strongly. Were you glad that it did?*

A: I think that's always a pretty good sign that something's going on. I didn't think it was a safe film to make when I was shooting it. The foreign reception has been quite good, but I think that' s not unexpected. Whether it would work for an American audience was always problematic. I frankly never thought it would, given what it was, because it was a film that was certainly not a feel-good movie. I liked it as a piece of work.

Q: *How do reviews affect you?*

A: I did a film many years ago called THE DRIVER. It got a very poor critical reception in New York. It got good reviews in London, Rome, Tokyo, Stockholm. Then people say "Too bad the critics didn't like your movie." I never quite know what to say. The critics in New York didn't like it, but the world's a bigger place than that. Still, as an American, it probably is more important what's coming out of New York. I had a movie a few years ago, RED HEAT. It did pretty well at the domestic box-office, but not as well as we hoped it was going to do. It was big foreign. It was a very big seller on cassette. Did the movie do poorly, medium or well? We're into a much less parochial market now than we were 15 years ago. The idea that you're going to judge a film's success or failure on its domestic box-office revenue or its reception by New York film critics is simply wrong.

Q: *Why do you think that grip has loosened?*

A: Most of it is economics. The world is a lot closer, whether it's the electronic revolution or the intellectual-political currents in Europe, America or Asia. We're all holding hands and standing next to each other in closer ways than before. I think, to a tremendous degree, the events in Eastern Europe last year had to do with the communications revolution and the fact that you can't hide the truth of how life is in the West. It created enormous dissatisfaction. It's hard to have a system work when nobody wants to live there.

Q: *Are there any films you would choose from your body of work that stands as the quintessential Walter Hill picture?*

A: Every film you do is an aspect of your personality. I don't analyze my movies. I don't see them after I'm done with them. I think that's counter productive. It's much better to go on to the next story.

Q: *What about the critics and reviews?*

A: There's a quote from Samuel Johnson—which I'll probably get wrong—"The author comes unasked into the arena seeking his fortune at the hazard of disgrace." The idea that you weren't rolling the dice when you took the job is simply naive. I've gotten a lot of good reviews in my life and I've had my share of scorchers. No complaints. I've had a good ride. I think I'm about halfway there. I'm going to keep doing it. Criticism is quite important to keep you honest. It's unfortunate

that so much of it is written by second-raters, but an awful lot of films are made by second-raters, so what the hell. First and foremost, one should be a good professional. I think that there inevitably comes a time when they take away your uniform. Directors are a lot like ballplayers. But very few of them go gracefully.

F I L M O G R A P H Y

W A L T E R   H I L L
b. January 10, 1942 - Long Beach, California
HARD TIMES Columbia, 1975
THE DRIVER 20th Century-Fox, 1978
THE WARRIORS Paramount, 1979
THE LONG RIDERS United Artists, 1980
SOUTHERN COMFORT 20th Century-Fox, 1981
48 HRS. Paramount, 1982
STREETS OF FIRE Universal, 1984
BREWSTER'S MILLIONS Universal, 1985
CROSSROADS Columbia, 1986
EXTREME PREJUDICE TriStar, 1987
RED HEAT TriStar, 1988
JOHNNY HANDSOME TriStar, 1989
ANOTHER 48 HRS. Paramount, 1990
TRESPASS Universal, 1992
GERONIMO: AN AMERICAN LEGEND Columbia, 1993
WILD BILL MGM-UA, 1995
LAST MAN STANDING New Line Cinema, 1996
SUPERNOVA MGM Distribution Co., 1998

$\mathcal{A}$RTHUR $\mathcal{H}$ILLER

An apt indication of just how long Arthur Hiller has been making movies is to realize that one of his best features—THE OUT-OF-TOWNERS, which starred Jack Lemmon and Sandy Dennis—is now being remade by a different director, Peter Segal, with Steve Martin and Goldie Hawn! In fact, Hiller helmed his first film 41 years before this writing, and has worked in virtually every genre (okay, no Westerns yet) since, over the course of directing 32 features. That's 31 if you discount AN ALAN SMITHEE FILM - BURN HOLLYWOOD BURN, from which Hiller removed his name and utilized the DGA-approved pseudonym of. . . well. . . Alan Smithee, thereby creating one of the most tragicomic conundrums in motion picture history.

A listing of Hiller's films brings forth some truly impressive credits—his two collaborations with Paddy Chayefsky on THE AMERICANIZATION OF EMILY and THE HOSPITAL; the Neil Simon-scripted THE OUT-OF-TOWNERS and PLAZA SUITE; POPI, the charming urban comedy/drama which was one of Alan Arkin's best roles (in what would now be considered a politically incorrect performance as a Puerto Rican father struggling to raise his two small sons in New York City); the hugely successful LOVE STORY, perhaps the world's most imitated film, for which he received an Academy Academy nomination; the very popular late 1970s comedies SILVER STREAK and THE IN-LAWS; and THE LONELY GUY, still one of Steve Martin's best vehicles.

Working in a tradition of craftsmanship and respect for what he calls the "blueprint" of the screenplay, Hiller has had his share of misses as well, as Hiller himself discusses within vis a vis MAN OF LA MANCHA. But this warm, delightful man—a former president of the Academy of Motion Picture Arts and Sciences in addition to his non-stop work behind the camera—can certainly look back without anger on a fascinating career.

MICHAEL SINGER: *You've worked in a great range of genres, excluding horror or science fiction films. . .*

ARTHUR HILLER: No, that's my uncomfortable genre.

Q: *Well, you seem to be holding out very nicely on the human front. Whether comedies or dramas, the human element seems to be primary in your films. Is that what drew you to filmmaking in the first place?*

A: Yes, no question, in the sense that I came to film from television and I came to television from radio. My work in radio was originally as a director of a public affairs program. When I first started, I was working on talk shows. Because of my interest in drama and my love of theatre, I started to do social dramas on radio dealing with civic or social issues. That came from my interest in people. I'm a great believer in the affirmation of the human spirit.

Q: *TEACHERS ends with such an affirmation.*

A: Yes, and that message has been in a few films that I've done. That you have to be in there fighting. It's not enough to see a problem. Once you realize what the problem is you have to try and do something about it. At the end of HOSPITAL, there's a phrase that says, "You've got to piss right smack into the wind." Also, in a sense, MAN OF LA MANCHA bears the same message.

Q: *POPI, as well. . .*

A: Yes, the struggle of this man to raise his kids, as he said, "To be high in their shoes." It could easily have just been a film about the ghetto, but it wasn't. It was about coming out of the ghetto mentality, to think of themselves as being able to do more.

Q: *You've worked with some great writers, and you have been referred to as a writer's director. I don't know if that's the right phrase. . .*

A: The phrase I use is that I drop to my knees in front of the good writer. I feel that they get less credit than they deserve, in films at least. I'm terribly dependent on a good writer.

Q: *Would you be more comfortable being described as an interpreter rather than an auteur?*

A: I really don't like either of those phrases.

Q: *Well, I do think of you as working in the time-honored tradition of a William Wyler or Lewis Milestone. . .*

A: I guess my favorites come from that tradition. . . David Lean and Fred Zinnemann. Sometimes people ask me if I have a style. And I think back and ask, what style does Lean have? Well, his style is excellence, that's all. He does each picture in the best way to bring that material to the screen. It just depends on what the material needs to best present it. For instance, in TEACHERS, there were more cuts than in any film I've ever done. It just lent itself to lots of cuts. A lot of other films, like HOSPITAL, could have had six pages in one shot. And yet, it's constantly in motion with a lot of movement and that semi-documentary feel.

Q: *Do you work closely with writers during production?*

A: It doesn't happen very often. By the time you get to production, the writer feels that he or she has done the work and is spending a lot of time with minimal results. They're happy to let you go ahead and do it. My life would be easiest if the writers were on the set all the time, because a picture changes. All those creative juices come together, and out of it comes something new and different. It grows and shapes itself just by nature of the actors' contributions, or backgrounds. And those changes, if the writer is there, can be helped in the right directions. And even if there aren't any changes, at least the writer is aware why you have made certain changes and what prompted them.

Q: *You went from radio to television to features. What are the best avenues to directing these days, in your opinion?*

A: I think the film schools are good. By the same token, if young film students come in to see me for advice, I ask if they've ever made a film. If they say no, I forget about them. Because if they really want to be a director, then somehow they've gotten ahold of an 8mm camera and shot 10 minutes somewhere. That's a good way to learn. I remember judging a student film festival one year. I saw a film by a nine-year-old that showed inventiveness and thought about what he was doing. Now it's true also that that particular student had a teacher who was interested in film and excited the kids. But I feel if they show that kind of interest, that kind of desire, than that's the way to learn. You learn in film school, you learn by observing on a set. Also, you have to be lucky. You really do. I'm not saying that you don't have to be good. But if you're in the right place at the right time, you're going to get the chance that twenty other people who are equally talented don't get.

Q: *I have a two part question for you. A, what were you thinking about when you were nine-years-old, and B, what was your lucky break?*

A: Well, I can't remember what I was thinking about when I was nine. I was loving theatre already. My parents had started a little theatre group in Edmonton, Canada, where we lived. And when I was eight or nine years old, I was helping to paint the sets or do whatever a child that age could do. I think my interest deep down was always the theatre, but when I finished high school, through a series of circumstances. . . there was a professor from the University of Ohio who was up at the University of Alberta, where I was a student, who was teaching teachers how to teach drama. And he taught them by putting them in a play. They had to play all the parts, build the sets, do the costumes, find the props. He was short a couple of actors, so he went to the high school drama teacher and he asked who the best actors were. I ended up playing Donald, the Black servant, in YOU CAN'T TAKE IT WITH YOU. And from that, I was offered a drama scholarship at the University of Ohio! Well, at that time I just said no, because acting was what you did on weekends. . . it was not what you did as a life's work. Then off I went to World War II, came back and studied psychology at the university. One day, as I studied, I realized that what I was really interested in was communication. So I walked into the headquarters of the Canadian Broadcasting Corporation, up to the information desk and said, "Who do I see about a job?" They asked what kind of a job, so I said, "Well, I want to be a director." The receptionist told me to call Mr. Doyle, who was the manager of the network. I said fine, went home, phoned Mr. Doyle. His secretary said the name was Boyle, not Doyle, and what did I want to see him about? I told her, and she said, "Well, you can't see him. But you can see his associate, Mr. Palmer." So I went to see Palmer and told him that I wanted to be a director, mentioning that I was completing a Master's Degree and needed residence, and preferred to work there. He took me to meet the supervisor of public affairs, and we had what I thought was a very pleasant hour-and-a-half conversation. Well, later I realized that he was pumping me. How do I feel about this particular issue, how do I feel about this social problem, what do I read, etc. And he suggested that I apply for a job that he had available. I joined 64 other people, and three weeks later I was working. He was looking for somebody with a social science background and some experience in radio. I had worked during the summertime as an announcer in a small station where I lived. So the luck part was there. When I walked up to that desk, suppose the receptionist had said to me, "Why don't you go to the personnel office?" I could still be sitting there waiting my turn! Fortunately, she told me to call Mr. Doyle. The series of events just go together.

Q: *That social thread has wound itself down throughout your career.*

A: I wish it had stayed there a little more. I've let it slip away a little. If I had my preference, I would be doing that all the time. But I like making movies and you can't always incorporate that.

Q: *Your strongest films have had those very powerful social concerns, though.* THE AMERICANIZATION OF EMILY, *for example.*

A: My favorite. But you see, again, you're talking about the writer. Paddy Chayefsky. As I've often said, the only genius I've worked with. It's phenomenal. You couldn't go wrong with Paddy's material. I might have had some disagreements with Paddy. We had an argument on HOSPITAL where he was so angry with me he went into his office and didn't come out for four hours. Two days later he walked by when I was on the set, said, "You were right," and just kept walking. Basically, when he spoke I listened. When a genius speaks you pay attention. But I'm a big boy. When I disagreed, I disagreed. When you direct you have to go with your feelings. That doesn't mean you shouldn't take advice, it doesn't mean you shouldn't listen, but your feelings have to come through. If not, it won't be your film.

Q: *You've been involved with a couple of fairly well publicized shoots where you've had serious dashes with other important personnel. How do you get through it?*

A: I don't know. Sometimes you wonder how you get through. If you have a feeling of responsibility, a respect for your fellow creative artists and the other people who are working. . . if you take on a project, you should give what you're supposed to give to that project. You can't give up. And that's what keeps you going.

Q: *How personally do you take criticism of your films?*

A: It hurts. I've often said that when you start a picture, you're all gung ho and ready to gamble and take big chances because you believe in it. The closer it gets to the release of that picture, the more you want it to succeed, the more you care, and if the milkman says he didn't like a scene, you go into panic. You just want everybody to love it.

Q: *If the milkman does tell you he didn't like a scene, or worse than that, several critics and a couple of studio executives tell you they don't like your picture, how do you get the strength and courage to get back at it again?*

A: It's hard. It does affect you and it does hurt. When I did MAN OF LA MANCHA, I had very high hopes. We felt very strongly that we had done something special and wonderful. It was adequately received and did good business, but not what I thought was going to happen. That threw me into a depression for about eight months, and I didn't work because I thought it was my fault. Here I had a play that was famous around the world, a terrific cast, United Artists was very supportive—so I could only blame myself. It took about eight months for me to figure out that MAN OF LA MANCHA was a play that shouldn't have been adapted for film. When you're in a darkened theatre with a surrealist set, and Don Quixote says, "That's not a kitchen scullery maid, that's a princess," you make the change in your head. But when Sophia Loren is standing there twenty feet tall on a 70mm screen, it's too real. You put too much pressure on the actor to make you believe what's going on.

Q: *Some of your most successful films have been comedies—THE OUT-OF-TOWNERS, SILVER STREAK, THE IN-LAWS—is it harder directing comedy?*

A: I guess it must be in the sense there are obviously fewer good comedy directors than any other genre, and yet I don't feel that. If you get food actors with a comedy sense, your life is very easy. In other words, you're not playing for the laugh. You're playing an honest character in an honest situation, and because they have that good comedy sense, it just brings it to the humor quite naturally.

Q: *You seem to never stop working. Do you live for movies?*

A: Yes. I love making movies.

Q: *Do you feel somewhat incomplete if you're not directing?*

A: I do. My favorite time is the shooting time. I've been trying desperately not to work for a couple of months, but it's very hard.

F I L M O G R A P H Y

A R T H U R   H I L L E R

b. November 22, 1923 - Edmonton, Alberta, Canada
THE CARELESS YEARS United Artists, 1957
THE MIRACLE OF THE WHITE STALLIONS Buena Vista, 1963
THE WHEELER DEALERS MGM, 1963
THE AMERICANIZATION OF EMILY MGM, 1964
PROMISE HER ANYTHING Paramount, 1966
PENELOPE MGM, 1966
TOBRUK Universal, 1967
THE TIGER MAKES OUT Columbia, 1967
POPI United Artists, 1969
THE OUT-OF-TOWNERS Paramount, 1970
LOVE STORY ★ Paramount, 1970
PLAZA SUITE Paramount, 1971
THE HOSPITAL United Artists, 1971
MAN OF LA MANCHA United Artists, 1972, Italian-U.S.
THE CRAZY WORLD OF JULIUS VROODER 20th Century-Fox, 1974
THE MAN IN THE GLASS BOOTH American Film Theatre, 1975
W.C. FIELDS AND ME Universal, 1976
SILVER STREAK 20th Century-Fox, 1975
THE IN-LAWS Columbia, 1979
NIGHTWING Columbia, 1979
MAKING LOVE 20th Century-Fox, 1982
AUTHOR! AUTHOR! 20th Century-Fox, 1982
ROMANTIC COMEDY MGM/UA, 1983
THE LONELY GUY Universal, 1984
TEACHERS MGM/UA, 1984
OUTRAGEOUS FORTUNE Buena Vista, 1987
SEE NO EVIL, HEAR NO EVIL TriStar, 1989
TAKING CARE OF BUSINESS Buena Vista, 1990
MARRIED TO IT Orion, 1991
THE BABE Universal, 1992
AN ALAN SMITHEE FILM - BURN HOLLYWOOD BURN released under pseudonym of Alan
    Smithee, Buena Vista, 1997

$\mathcal{N}$OËL $\mathcal{H}$OWARD

Director, second unit director, technical advisor, continuity artist, stuntman, author, painter, illustrator, raconteur. . . the life and fabulous times of the late Noël Howard were committed to print with his glorious memoir, Hollywood on the Nile, which specifically focused on his experiences with Howard Hawks and William Faulkner as they attempted to re-create ancient Egypt for LAND OF THE PHAROAHS in the mid 1950s. Written in French and published in France to wide acclaim, the book unfortunately remains unseen in the United States.

When I met with Mr. Howard in the West Hollywood aerie that he shared with wife Keline, he was already debilitated from the illness that would take his life the following year, speaking with difficulty through a brace bolted to his jaw. He was, nevertheless, full of charm, enthusiasm and joie de vivre as he recounted his amazing life and career. While it's true that Howard remains unknown to most American audiences—and even to the better part of the American industry—he was hugely appreciated by those who both had the privilege of working with him, or even knowing him. When I bid my final farewell to Mr. Howard at his funeral service, I was surrounded by the likes of Gene Kelly, Louis Jourdan, author/critic Todd McCarthy and many others who came to pay tribute to a not-so-unsung hero.

Born on Christmas Day, 1920, in Paris—the son of American sculptor Cecil Howard and his French wife—Noël Howard studied painting, served as a U.S. night-fighter pilot during World War II, and then entered movies for the rest of his life. The list of films on which he worked in various capacities—with such directors as David Lean, Lewis Milestone, Anatole Litvak, Victor Fleming, Nicholas Ray, Billy Wilder, Gene Kelly, Jules Dassin, Vincente Minnelli and, of course, Howard Hawks—include such titles as LAWRENCE OF ARABIA, THE SPIRIT OF ST. LOUIS, LOVE IN THE AFTERNOON, GIGI, JOAN OF ARC, DECISION BEFORE DAWN, LES MISERABLES, KING OF KINGS and 55 DAYS AT PEKING.

In addition to Hollywood on the Nile, Howard also authored and illustrated a series of charming French children's books. This was a remarkable man, and his interview provided extraordinary insight into the work of one whom, while often serving the visions of other filmmakers, never sacrificed his own. The poignancy of the interview is best revealed with his final quote, indicating an acceptance of his mortality and yet the desire to direct one more movie of his own.

Alas, it was not to be. But what a life he lived. . . and what a story he told. . .

MICHAEL SINGER: *You were an artist in Paris, and the son of an artist as well. How did you fall into filmmaking? Did it happen by accident?*

NOËL HOWARD: It happened quite by accident. I was in New York, just out of the Army in 1946, and I met Ingrid Bergman through Alain Bernheim. Ingrid was about to do Maxwell Anderson's JOAN OF LORRAINE on the stage. She invited me to a cocktail party, at which there were two gentlemen from Hollywood. One was Victor Fleming, who had come to see Ingrid about making JOAN OF ARC, the screen version of the play; the other was Richard Day, the famous art director. Over a few scotches, Richard Day said that he didn't have time to go to France and look at the color of the stones and the shapes of the roofs, and was very sorry about that. I suggested that there was some pretty good stuff at the Cloisters, a medieval-style museum in Upper Manhattan. He asked me if I was working at the moment, and I told him I was freelancing. He said, "How would you like to go the Cloisters and do some color samples of stone assembles and rooftops—paint them?"

Well, I worked my brush off on the project, and Day liked them very much. Then Victor Fleming asked, "How would you like to come to Hollywood?" I said, "What for?" He said that he needed someone who could do research as technical advisor, because he took it for granted that since I was born and went to school in France, I knew everything there was to know about Joan of Arc! The next day I took my toothbrush and Packard convertible and went to Hollywood.

Q: *How was life in Hollywood in the late 1940s?*

A: Well, the Bernheim brothers had introduced me to Gene Kelly, and every Sunday we'd go to his house on Rodeo-he still lives there—and play volleyball on cement courts. One day Gene mentioned that he was going to do THE THREE MUSKETEERS at MGM. Since I had studied fencing in France and was working at the studio at that time, they gave me a screen test. I didn't get the part. I had one sentence to speak in the test, but people with French accents usually have lisps, and the line was, "Sheathe your swords, gentlemen. You're under arrest!" Well, I was spitting all over the camera. Finally, instead of playing that one part for two or three days, I was hired as a stuntman and worked every day for fourteen weeks. I complained that I didn't ride a horse. But they said, "We don't pay you for riding a horse—we pay you to fall off!"

Q: *So you fell off horses for a while?*

A: If I didn't fall off, they pushed me! It was a hundred bucks extra to fall off a horse. But then, the man who really changed my career was Lewis Milestone. I fell in love with him immediately. He was one of the few directors at that time who used continuity artists. He was doing LES MISERABLES for Zanuck and, although Fox had their own continuity artist, Milestone wanted me to double as artist and technical advisor, because LES MISERABLES is, obviously, a French story. I was with Milestone on the set all the time and learned a hell of a lot. After LES MISERABLES, Milestone and I went to France to do Marlon Brando's first picture, but it never worked out. Milly and I remained friends forever. Unfortunately, I never worked with him again. I was supposed to work with him on MUTINY ON THE BOUNTY, but I was busy someplace else. Now, there was another important man in my life who lived and worked mostly out of Europe, and that was Anatole Litvak. I did four pictures with him.

Q: *You soon became known as a crack second unit director. Is that a great first step to becoming a full-fledged director?*

A: Here's the trouble. . . . I was offered second unit directorships all the time. Sensational way to learn. An opportunity to work with the greatest directors. But, after a while, you are branded "second unit director," and that is the kiss of death. When I tried to move on to being a director on my own, I was branded second unit. You can handle extras, but they never think you can handle anything else. I should have turned jobs down and fought until I was considered a director. But I could never resist the temptation. I mean, when Sam Spiegel calls and says, "LAWRENCE OF ARABIA and David Lean," who am I to turn that down?

Q: *How much independent creativity can a second unit director ever really have?*

A: A lot more than people think. On 55 DAYS AT PEKING, Nick Ray had a heart attack two weeks into shooting. So the two second unit directors, Andrew Marton and I, finished the picture. In one scene I have two thousand extras. It's at night. I've got Charlton Heston, Ava Gardner, David Niven. I don't have a script. Samuel Bronston's writers have, "the battle takes place" in the script. I'm exaggerating, but not by much. So I have to devise how the foreign legion troops win the battle against the Chinese Boxers. I drew up a storyboard and asked the writers for dialogue, but they had already written the screenplay, gotten paid and that was that for their contribution. So, I'm on the set, and suddenly there arrive three important guests of Mr. Bronston— distributors from all over the world—and they're waiting to see some of the shooting. Bronston came up to me and said, "Shoot, shoot, shoot." I said, "I'm not ready. There's no film in the camera." Bronston said, "It doesn't matter. I've got people here. They've got to see us working." I finally got some filming done—Bronston and his guests were happy, so they went away. Later on, exhausted, I was hiding behind the set with a piece of paper and a pencil, working on the scene. Suddenly I heard this deep voice behind me saying, "Fucking business hasn't changed much, has it?" I turned around, and it was Orson Welles. I said, "Look, wise guy. I know this has happened to you. For chrissakes, sit down and help me." So we sat down, worked out the scene, and that is what I shot. Bronston had brought Welles to Spain to talk about him playing a cameo role in the film, but it never worked out.

Q: *Although you shot longer than Nicholas Ray on 55 DAYS AT PEKING, he retained sole directorial credit?*

A: I wanted to make his picture. I would consult with him in the hospital every day.

Q: LAWRENCE OF ARABIA *was a project that was considerably bigger than* 55 DAYS AT PEKING. *You were one of two second unit directors listed on the credits, along with Andre Smagghe. How did you get involved in the film?*

A: Sam Spiegel sent for me in Paris and said that he wanted me to direct second unit. I said, "Second unit for David Lean? You must be joking!". . . because David Lean never worked with a second unit. Spiegel said, "No, I'm the boss here. I want a second unit, we'll have a second unit." Then he went on to explain what he expected of me—there was to be no camera, and my job as second unit director was just to rehearse everything for David. So I turned it down. Why should I do my conception of a scene, which Lean was bound to hate? And if the scene was good, and filmed that way, then why am I not Sir Noël Howard? It was ridiculous. Spiegel wanted a good organizer, which I'm not. I suggested Andre Smagghe, who was a good organizer, to Spiegel. Smagghe never shot one foot of film, never was anywhere near a camera. He went to Jordan and then left. For some reason, Spiegel gave his screen credit for second unit above my own credit. But I'm the only man who shot one foot of film besides David Lean on LAWRENCE OF ARABIA.

Q: *Obviously, Spiegel eventually hired you as a real second unit director. How did David Lean react to your arrival when you joined the production?*

A: I arrived in Jordan, and the whole unit was aboard Sam Spiegel's yacht-which was like a small Queen Mary for a production meeting. David stood up and said, "Gentlemen, I'll be very brief The reason we're all gathered here today is because Sam is trying to force a second unit on me. I want you to know that I loathe second units, and I'll do everything in my power to prevent the bastards from shooting one fucking foot of fucking film." He sat down. Then I got up and started walking off the ship. David called me over and said, "Look, nothing personal. It's nothing against you, just the principle of the thing. Stick around and we'll talk later." We spoke, and I told Lean that I had read the film's screenplay during the night. There was a scene where the camels were walking in the snow. I asked Lean, "How are you going to do this with a first unit? Are you going to take Peter O'Toole, Omar Sharif, Alec Guinness, the entire company and wait for the snow to come down? I can take three camels, three doubles, ten guys, a camera, a few prop and special effects men, and sit on top of that mountain and stay there for six months, if necessary, until it snows!" David said, "You're right." And that's how it started. I took the camels in the snow, shot the footage. . . and the son-of-a-bitch cut it out of the picture!

Q: *So you ultimately wound up getting along fairly well with Sir David?*

A: Yes. There were some rough times, though. He liked me personally, but hated the idea of a second unit director.

Q: *I'd like to ask you briefly about the three films you did personally direct. They were very diverse in subject matter. The first was an epic about Marco Polo which was a co-production of about five countries. The second was a French film starring rock-and-roll star Johnny Hallyday. And the third was made in Mexico and co-directed by François Reichenbach. First of all, how did you get involved with* MARCO THE MAGNIFICENT *?*

A: Raoul Levy was a fabulous man—until he committed suicide. He was a great con artist, but I loved him. I think the film business needs people like that. Now, he had this Marco Polo thing planned and didn't know how to go about it. He never had a screenplay. He hired all kinds of two-bit writers—about twelve of them. Levy talked me into it. I figured, what the hell. I had nothing else to do at the time. I did my best, that's all I can say, but it was impossible to make a good film under those circumstances. The casting was wrong. . . everything was wrong.., and we filmed it in Yugoslavia, which was agony in those days.

Q: *What about DOU VIENS TO JOHNNY, the rock-and-roll movie?*

A: A similar situation. I was out of work, out of money and figured that it would be a good film for kids. Making a movie with Johnny Hallyday in France was like making a movie with Elvis Presley in the States. And the kids loved it. It did very well.

Q: *Was the film you directed with Reichenbach, DON'T YOU HEAR THE DOGS BARK?, a documentary?*

A: No. I wrote the screenplay, and it was translated into Spanish by Carlos Fuentes. I got along fine with him. I didn't get along with François at all. No way. He's impossible.

Q: *I'd like to ask you for some quick impressions of directors you've worked with. You can be as honest, or as dishonest, as you want to be. . . Billy Wilder?*

A: I love him. He's my ideal. He was fun to work with, a Lubitsch of his time. I would work with him for nothing. I still see quite a bit of him. Professionally, he's one of best. Lewis Milestone, as I said, will always retain a tremendous spot in my heart.

Q: *I think that between ALL QUIET ON THE WESTERN FRONT, A WALK IN THE SUN, THE NORTH STAR, PORK CHOP HILL and some others, Milestone made the best war films of all time.*

A: You remember the ending with the butterfly in ALL QUIET ON THE WESTERN FRONT? Nobody did things like that in 1930, but Milly did! Another great war film that I happened to work on was DECISION BEFORE DAWN, which Anatole Litvak directed.

Q: *Of course, you've written an entire book about your experiences working with Howard Hawks and William Faulkner on LAND OF THE PHAROAHS, but tell me, how was it working with Hawks?*

A: Superb. . . superb. Hawks was a very bizarre man he was the biggest mythomaniac who ever lived. Fabulous! He would tell you story like the time he was at the airport in Oklahoma and there was an announcement on the loudspeaker saying that Mr. Howard Hawks was wanted by the control tower, because the pilot of TWA Flight 306 had just had a heart attack, and they wondered if Mr. Hawks would mind flying the plane to Los Angeles. Hawks would tell you this, in front of five people! Amazing!

Q: *Did he tell these stories knowing that everyone knew they were just stories, but enjoyed them anyway?*

A: I think that after a while, he believed them himself. But he was a marvelous, charming man.

Q: Vincente Minnelli.

A: Minnelli was very nice, very efficient, very artistic, very clever, but too nervous for me. He communicated his tension. I did some great stuff for him, though. I shot dialogue scenes for him with Maurice Chevalier and Louis Jourdan in Paris streets filled with horse-drawn vehicles for GIGI.

Q: You also worked on one of Robert Siodmak's last films, CUSTER OF THE WEST.

A: I did all the battle scenes. Siodmak was getting on a bit, you know, but we got along fine. The only person I didn't get on with was Phil Yordan, who produced and wrote the picture. I must have read 150 books on Custer. I told Siodmak that Custer was obviously one of the true bastards of history, and it was about time someone made a picture showing him that way. But Yordan said no, for all the American kids he was a hero, and that's the way he would be depicted in this movie. Well, CUSTER OF THE WEST did no business, and immediately thereafter, Arthur Penn came out with LITTLE BIG MAN, which was a huge success, and did paint a portrait of Custer as the biggest son-of-a-bitch of all time.

Q: You worked in Spain more than any other country. Was that by choice?

A: Everybody loved making pictures in Spain in those years, and I loved working there.

Q: Do you have a favorite picture that you worked on?

A: LAWRENCE OF ARABIA. Every day on the set I knew that it was going to be a classic. And it is. But I worked on a lot of unbelievable crap, believe me.

Q: How did you get along with Nicholas Ray on KING OF KINGS and 55 DAYS AT PEKING?

A: He was very intense and drinking too much, but I loved him dearly.

Q: Do you have any projects now that you're working on?

A: I've been working on a story for roughly thirty years. I want to do this picture and die. I mean, I'm in no hurry, but. . . It's very difficult, though, to raise the money. I would shoot it in Australia and America, and a little bit in Paris.

F I L M O G R A P H Y

N O Ë L   H O W A R D

b. December 25, 1920

d. 1987

THE HAPPY ROAD   co-director with Gene Kelly, MGM, 1957

MARCO THE MAGNIFICENT   co-director with Denys de la Patelliere & Christian-Jaque, MGM, 1966, French-Afghanistani-Egyptian-Italian-Yugoslavian

D'OU VIENS TO JOHNNY   Hoche Productions, French

DON'T YOU HEAR THE DOGS BARK? (FD)   co-director with Francois Reichenbach, 1975, Mexican-French

$\mathcal{H}$ ARRY $\mathcal{H}$ URWITZ

It was one of the saddest telephone calls that I ever received, when Sam Hurwitz and his mother Joy informed me that father and husband, Harry, had passed away. The shock could not have been greater. Only a few weeks before Harry had tracked me down by telephone, while I was on a remote location in Mississippi, to eagerly find out the exact publication date of the edition of my directors guide that featured the inteview we had done together a few months before. He sounded like his usual chipper, youthful self, bursting with excitement over a typically offbeat project called REMAKE, and quite thrilled that he had just received a verbal commitment from Johnny Depp to appear in the cast. Harry made brief mention of some medical problem. . . perhaps I should have been paying more attention, but he had never discussed it before.

In the all-too-brief time that I got to know Harry, his vivaciousness, honesty and articulate conversation—not to mention his adoration of cinema—completely won me over. His death was absolutely devastating, partially because I couldn't believe that Harry would no longer be there to shake the gates of Hollywood with his usual iconoclastic fervor. Harry Hurwitz was a man who cheerfully admitted that he was a struggler and something of an outsider. He actually found his greatest success in the art world, where his paintings and other works wound up in the permanent collections of such mighty institutions as the Metropolitan Museum of Art in New York, the National Gallery of Art in Washington, D.C., the Philadelphia Museum of Art, the New York University Art Collection, and more, including various private collections. Beginning his career as a professor of film and drawing, teaching at New York University, Cooper Union and the Parsons School of Design, among others, Hurwitz always wanted to make movies.

Harry led several lives as a movie director, beginning with the more personal films he was determined to make. His 1970 cult classic THE PROJECTIONIST was one of that year's most critically acclaimed films, influenced by Hurwitz's own inner life and the films of Charlie Chaplin, a lifelong obsession for the filmmaker. Other Hurwitz films on the subject of films were THE ETERNAL TRAMP, his examination of Chaplin's immortal character; the fictitious THE COMEBACK

TRAIL; and the vastly enjoyable "mockumentary" THAT'S ADEQUATE!, which premiered at the Sundance Film Festival. As a director-for-hire, Hurwitz specialized in such moderately-budgeted comedies and thrillers as SAFARI 3000, THE ROSEBUD BEACH HOTEL and FLESHTONE. And as his intentionally sleazy *nom-de-cinema* Harry Tampa, Hurwitz shepherded such soft-core romps as FAIRY TALES, AUDITIONS and NOCTURNA. Whatever it took to keep making movies Harry was there with a knowing wink and a smile.

Meanwhile, Harry also wrote several screenplays, including the original draft of what became UNDER THE RAINBOW (he was not pleased with the film that resulted from it).

REMAKE was to be a return to the tradition of THE PROJECTIONIST, a personal and gloriously surrealistic riff on his favorite subject, the movies. In my most sentimental moments, I'd like to think that in the next world, Harry got to direct REMAKE after all, probably convincing The Little Tramp himself into making a guest appearance.

Having known Harry Hurwitz, I wouldn't be the least bit surprised!

MICHAEL SINGER: *You've described yourself as "a filmmaker who never really made it" in the industry. You won't hear many directors referring to themselves quite so honestly.*

HARRY HURWITZ: Well, making movies was always my agenda, not making "it." Making "it" involves a lot of sacrifice and compromise, but I'm a filmmaker and a painter, and that was my life, that was my passion. I always managed to make every painting I ever wanted to make, and I made every movie I ever wanted to make. . . except for the one that I hope to do next. And the point of making it in the industry. . . I made my first five features without even being in the industry. I worked out of New York. I was making my living as a college professor, so I didn't even look to my art for financial sustenance. First of all, we're living in a culture that doesn't even dignify the artist. The artist has to teach, or have another job. I never heard of a proctologist who had to teach all week so he could practice proctology on the weekend. And as a filmmaker, I began with the same spirit that I did as a painter. Then, I got to see that I could make more money by joining the industry than by teaching. In other words, I realized that I'd rather make bad movies than do good teaching. The movies that I do for myself I manage to do once every five years. I write it, I direct it, I cut it, I produce it. And it's not an ego thing. It's just that I wouldn't have anybody come in and paint the red in my painting. It's a complete work, and good or bad, I stand behind it. Whereas to make a living, I am now a writer and director for hire, in which I'm perfectly prepared to compromise. I feel very comfortable joining a system which, by the way, I revere. There's always been a perverse marriage between art and industry, going back to Michelangelo and the Pope. My heroes are Chaplin, Griffith, Welles, Hawks, Kubrick, Hitchcock, Lubitsch, and they all worked within the system.

Q: *Now, when you say that you've made every film that you've wanted to make, does that exclude some of the films that you have made?*

A: No! I've made some awful films, but they've been for other people. They're films that I either didn't write or that I didn't write and produce. On every movie that I wanted to make for myself, I went out and raised the money and made the movie, and had nobody to answer to. There was no question of the final cut anymore than I would have somebody else put the finishing touches on a painting. But on movies that I've done for hire, I'm a good collaborator and good team player.

Q: *Yet you had a big influence on some notable students who went on to have good careers.*

A: Well, I didn't say I was a bad teacher. I just felt resentful not being able to make a living in my chosen profession. In other words, I had to work in another field in order to support my family and myself and put a roof over our heads and pay for the rent. And it turned out that I did have an influence on some students who went on make movies, like Joe Dante, Jonathan Kaplan and Jon Davison, and perhaps others I don't know about.

Q: *I understand that it was Joe Dante who said that there was a little bit of Harry Hurwitz in every film he's made.*

A: What he told me was, there's a little bit of THE PROJECTIONIST in every movie he's ever made. That film had an impact on him. But you know, I taught painting, drawing, film history and film aesthetics. I never taught anyone how to make a movie.

Q: *How did you become a professor at the age of twenty-five?*

A: I already had two one-man shows in New York as a painter and printmaker, and had my work in the permanent collections of the Metropolitan Museum of Art, the National Art Gallery in Washington and the Philadelphia Museum of Fine Art. So I had this very impressive background as a painter, not as a filmmaker, and my first teaching jobs were in drawing, painting and design. Basically the job was always about how much money I could make in the shortest period of time so I could do my real job, which was making movies and painting pictures.

Q: *Were you a film buff as a child?*

A: As a child I was not only a film buff, but films saved my life. I was one of those kids who lived in movie theatres. The safest place in the world was the darkness of that theatre. My teachers and parents couldn't find me because I was in the dark. I could fall into that big screen and literally leave reality. Because there is no reality in film. People talk about "realistic" films, but all art is a lie. All art is an abstraction of reality. "Real" is when you've had your last dream and you open your eyes and wake up. Movies are very much like dreams because you see them in the dark.

Q: *What kind of films did you like most?*

A: I loved all kinds of movies. In fact, I think it was Welles who said, "There's no such thing as a bad movie. The fact that they move is miraculous." The only movies I don't like are pretentious movies. And also, anybody who actually makes a movie, to me, is a hero. Everybody talks about making movies, wanting to make movies—they write screenplays, they develop, they talk, they try to raise money, they almost make a movie. But to me, one of the great achievements on this planet is those people who actually went and got a film in the can. I think they should get medals for actually finishing a movie. And that's why my motto has always been "Make that movie." I used to teach my students that. Go out and do it. If you can't raise the money from a studio, raise the money from dentists. If you can't do that, borrow money and use your credit card. If you can't do that, do it on the cuff any way you can. If you can't make it for $10-million, make it for $1-million. If you can't make it for $1-million, shoot it in 16mm and do it for $350,000. I haven't made my movies the easy way. It's been a hard life, and that's why I've been kind of a maverick, because it was more important to make the movie than to make the money or to "make it." I'm still trying to figure out what "it" is, because it's so fickle, so fleeting and so intangible. And I'm a happy man. At this stage of my life, I feel absolutely fulfilled. I feel rich and famous. . . in my own life. Because my priorities have not only to do with my art, but also my family. I don't let other people identify me, I certainly don't let the industry identify me, and I don't identify myself as a filmmaker or as an artist. I'm trying to be a complete person, and at the end of it all, I think I'll feel pretty good. I'll just say that I did most of the things I wanted to do, and I have three kids that I feel blessed having had, and I'm married to a woman who is so supportive and wonderful that she enriches my life. I'm a happy man.

Q: *Your films have taken you around the world, yes? You actually directed two films in Africa.*

A: I just finished a picture in Africa called FLESHTONE, and I got to do a film for hire that I directed for United Artists called SAFARI 3000, which was the worst script I ever read, and had the best time making because I brought my three boys and my then-fiancee, now wife, to Africa. It's a great thing for a father to be able to say, "Hey kids, I'm pulling you out of school so we can go to Africa to make a movie." I got to go to Beijing for the first American film festival that was mounted by the Museum of Modern Art, and I was honored that my film, THE PROJECTIONIST, was chosen as one of twenty, from BIRTH OF A NATION to the present, to be shown there. And I got to see that film in a theatre filled with 3,000 Chinese who laughed in the right places.

Q: *If your filmography could be converted into a charted heartbeat, there would be serious fibrillation.*

A: Oh yeah. And don't forget the stuff I did under another name.

Q: *You mean the immortal Harry Tampa?*

A: Harry Tampa's a legend in his own slime. You know, I did those awful disco vampire movies and used another name, but I had a great time. Everyone knew who Harry Tampa really was, but I used the other name because it was my way of saying look, I really know the difference. There's a place for this and a place for that. In life, there are some people that you give your total integrity to, your good friends and your family and your mate. Then there are people that you give a little integrity to, and those are the associates you have. Then there are some people that you don't have any problem lying to, because you don't give a shit. And that's how it is with film. There are movies that I'm uncompromising about, and there are movies when I say let's go play and have a good time and I'll give you what you want.

Q: When you're on set as Harry Tampa, are you actually a different person than when you're Harry Hurwitz?

A: No. I try to make the best movie and find the little gems and pearls that I can slip into these films. What happens is, I'm constantly betrayed by my conviction as an artist. Basically, on the highest level, you try to achieve excellence. That's what the ascent of man is about, people trying to achieve excellence and enriching the world. But you've got to make a buck. Rembrandt was a scoundrel. He used to sign his students' paintings and sell them. I'm not one of those guys who say that you must be the pure artist only and I don't think I'm that pure. I know I have skills I can sell, that I'm really good at, that doesn't involve my soul and my heart. And on the other hand, I'm not embarrassed to use the word "art." Film is an art. It's also the film industry. Again, that perverse marriage is what always comes together. It's impossible to make any kind of art without dealing with technology. The painter has to buy the paint and the canvas, and once the picture's finished you have to sell it. What are you going to do, put it in your closet? So there's a great schizo thing going on in even the purest of artists. You know, Van Gogh was dying to sell his paintings. He craved acceptance. You don't paint for yourself, and you don't make movies for yourself. You make movies for an imaginary audience that's going to sit there and be moved by what you make. Movies are probably one of the most emotional experiences we have in life outside of the real moments of our lives. When do you ever cry or laugh or tremble in fear or get as sexually or romantically aroused in any other artificial situation other than in a movie theatre, when you just become a blithering idiot? And it's wonderful, it's thrilling. You know, it's not so much fun in real life to have a guy with a chainsaw chase you.

Q: I don't know. It could be interesting.

A: You never know in Los Angeles. This is a great town for. . .

Q: . . . Blithering idiots?

A: It's a great town for blithering idiots and inspired geniuses. It's a great town for movie stars and serial killers. It's a great town for a lot of things, but it's not a city. That's always been its problem. L.A. thinks it's a city, but it's not. The only important thing about L.A. is Hollywood, which doesn't really exist. Hollywood was probably the great American cultural gift to the 20th century and it doesn't really exist in physical space because it's in Culver City, it's in the Valley. . . you know, I think Paramount's the only legitimately Hollywood-based studio. And of course, Chaplin was based in Hollywood. L.A. is lucky because it has Hollywood.

Q: THE PROJECTIONIST is your most famous and heralded film, and I think it holds up beautifully. I actually find it to be a rather spooky movie, just as I think silent movies are spooky.

A: Well, by seeing old movies you're seeing dead people, right?

Q: Yes. You're watching ghosts.

A: Right. Not only that, you're seeing them in black and white. And in THE PROJECTIONIST, the fantasy episodes were in black and white and the "real-life" episodes were in color. Somebody once said that there were no really great movie stars in color. It sounds like a glib statement, but if you think about it, those were huge, glowing black and white images made out of light and dark, shadows being projected by light being pushed through various densities of emulsion on a piece of acetate and projected onto a screen. Color film has the color of skin, so people in color are more real. They're not gods and goddesses, like the stars we see in black and white.

Q: There's a loss of that dreamlike quality in color.

A: Yes. The old films are haunting. They're spooky because you're taken back to a time that never really existed. We're not talking about old documentaries, but dramatic films, which were abstractions of reality. It was all fictional and dream-like and idealized. What amazes me was how cinematically literate the people of the 1930s and '40s were. They really understood the language of the movies. I mean, they could listen to Noel Coward and actually enjoy it. And we're not talking about New York and sophisticated cities, we're talking about all across the country. Today film viewers are more narcissistic and they just want to see their own culture reflected. They're not interested in sitting through dialogue. . . they want it fast. It's a result, I guess, of McDonalds and MTV. But in the old days, I'm amazed that pictures like TROUBLE IN PARADISE were successful. I'm amazed that Ernst Lubitsch was a successful director. He made very sophisticated, urbane comedies.

Q: Why your lifelong obsession with Charlie Chaplin? I mean, it seems redundant to ask somebody why they love Chaplin. The whole world loves Chaplin.

A: Well, you said the key word, which is "lifelong." The first movie I ever saw was a little Chaplin short. My parents took me to Coney Island, where they had a theatre that only showed Chaplin shorts. Then I saw the reissue of THE GOLD RUSH when I was four-and-a-half years old, and all through my life this incredible character of The Tramp kept appearing and impacting on me in a new way during each age. One of my first films was about Chaplin, THE ETERNAL TRAMP, narrated by Gloria Swanson, which was not so much about the man as about the character he made famous. I think that The Tramp is one of the most extraordinary fictional inventions. He's as profound as Hamlet or Don Quixote. Chaplin didn't make comedies. He made these incredible films that dealt with so many things on so many levels.

Chaplin was so easily identifiable by the average person, who understood what it was like to be alienated, to be the outsider, not to get the girl, to be hard up for money. And also, Chaplin was one of the greatest actors of all time. Laurence Olivier said that Chaplin was the greatest actor in movies. Chaplin was a comic and a tragic actor at the same time, because he dealt with that thin line between pathos and humor. And he drew his comedy out of the deprivation of his childhood. His whole screen persona was based on his deprived childhood, when he was always hungry. Food is always an issue in his movies—eating his shoe in THE GOLD RUSH, the Dance of the Rolls, eating the confetti as spaghetti in CITY LIGHTS. Chaplin's body of work was the most autobiographical, I think, of any filmmaker's work. If you look at it it's encoded, always reliving and recreating his childhood and trying to make it come out right through that character. I don't know anything, really, about Chaplin the man, and I'm not really interested. But I believe the character he created was so profound and moved me emotionally all my life. It was a lifelong love affair with this character that I must have identified with through my own sense of alienation, loneliness, rejection. Because I was one of those kids who didn't play ball and got beat up a lot. But I found pleasure sitting in the movie theatres, or at home drawing pictures.

Q: Hence, THE PROJECTIONIST is. . .

A: . . . Is me. Of course. It's a metaphorical image of myself. And the nature of the film is really about the daily bombardment of ideas and ideologies and feelings and thoughts that we go through, so the whole picture is about fragmentation. Our lives are made up of little serials. You drop one thing, you go to another, you're juggling 40 different parts of your life: the emotional part, the political part, the moral part. We're constantly being tempted, we're constantly being bombarded, so that's why THE PROJECTIONIST is full of commercials, superhero serials. It's this fragmenting of time, which is what our days are like.

Q: One of your more recent films, THAT'S ADEQUATE, was a very funny celebration of well-intentioned schlock.

A: It's a "mockumentary" about a fictitious studio called Adequate Pictures, the worst studio in Hollywood, celebrating its 60th anniversary. Their motto is, "An idea that's appealing is worth stealing." It's an affectionate satire of the studio system, but I just used this schlock studio because it's so extreme. It's just a crazy look at our preposterous, insane industry.

Q: Let's face it, no matter how much of a business or an industry this is, what it always comes down to is that guy on the set with some idea in his brain that he's trying to turn into "reality." I'm always amazed when I go to production meetings, and whatever is down on that sheet of paper called the script, they're going to make happen by hook or by crook.

A: Let's put it this way.., if screenplays were written in stone, then you would go to the theatre, be handed a script, sit down in the dark, the lights would come up and someone would say "Now turn to page one." The screenplay is just a point of departure. You gotta make a movie! An unfilmed screenplay is a dead thing. It's an architect's blueprint. I love improvisation, but I also have a great reverence for directors who literally follow a screenplay like Hitchcock. But the crafting of a screenplay has to be flexible as well. Even Shakespeare is altered on the stage. In the end, film is not a literary medium. People think that movies have a close kinship with literature and painting, but no. . . it's with music, because it's an art form that exists in time. It starts now and ends an hour-and-a-half later, like a piece of music. It exists in rhythms so that you can put together little pieces of time strung together. When you have three shots creating a whole new emotion, even though they have nothing to do with each other individually, it's like taking three notes and making a chord out of it. That's why music is the only other art that was ever necessary to film. There never were silent films. . . they were always accompanied by music. The sound film made it seem more real. Color made it seem more real. The more technologically proficient we get, the more we lose that fantasy element. On the other hand, the vicariousness of the experience is now greater than ever. I think it's all wonderful.

I still go to the movies like a 12-year-old. I pay money and give them my brain and say "hold it at the box office, I'll get it on the way out." I go in and I'm willing to believe what anybody tells me. . . unless they're pretentious and they're liars. It's like going to a party. The one you don't want to deal with is the one who's phony and really isn't talking straight. But any kind of movie that makes me feel something is a good movie. . . because that's what it's all about!

F I L M O G R A P H Y

H A R R Y   H U R W I T Z

b. January 28, 1938 - New York, New York
d. 1995

THE ETERNAL TRAMP   *CHAPLINESQUE, MY LIFE AND HARD TIMES* (FD)   Maglan Films, 1964

THE PROJECTIONIST   Maron Films Limited, 1971

THE COMEBACK TRAIL   Dynamite Entertainment/Rearguard Productions, 1971

RICHARD   co-director with Lorees Yerby, Billings, 1972

FAIRY TALES   directed under pseudonym of Harry Tampa, 1978

AUDITIONS   directed under pseudonym of Harry Tampa, Charles Band Productions, 1978

NOCTURNA   directed under pseudonym of Harry Tampa, Compass International, 1979

SAFARI 3000   United Artists, 1982

THE ROSEBUD BEACH HOTEL   Almi Pictures, 1985

THAT'S ADEQUATE   South Gate Entertainment, 1988

FLESHTONE   Prism Pictures, 1994

$\mathcal{N}$ORMAN $\mathcal{J}$EWISON

Considering the fact that he's enjoyed one of the longest and most successful careers of any big studio director, Norman Jewison still describes himself as an independent filmmaker. Certainly, there's a school full of moviemaking neophytes, studying at the Canadian Film Centre in Toronto—which Jewison founded and actively heads—who would agree with that self-assessment. Jewison has always enjoyed stirring the pot, and whether hot or cold, it's always bubbling.

The Canadian-born Jewison began his career as an actor and theatre director before winning fame and Emmys as one of television's finest musical and variety show specialists. His feature career was launched by Universal in the early 1960s, and Jewison was on a one way journey to Rock Hudson/Doris Day light comedy hell before he grabbed the gears, pulled them in the opposite direction, and made a dramatic killing with THE CINCINNATI KID, which he inherited after Sam Peckinpah was fired from the project. His next film—THE RUSSIANS ARE COMING THE RUSSIANS ARE COMING—returned Jewison to the world of comedy, but with a difference: it had real political and satirical bite.

Since then, Jewison has directed important and influential films with regularity, several of which (including the above mentioned) have become bonafide classics. IN THE HEAT OF THE NIGHT, a powerful look at race relations couched in an intriguing murder mystery, won the Academy Award for Best Picture of 1967 and an Oscar for its leading man, Rod Steiger. THE THOMAS CROWN AFFAIR was unafraid of its leading characters' utter amorality (there's been much talk of a remake). Following GAILY, GAILY, a charming and underrated film based on Ben Hecht's ribald memoirs of his life as a young reporter in Chicago, the TV musical specialist finally directed a big-screen musical—FIDDLER ON THE ROOF—which even The New Yorker's relentlessly tough Pauline Kael called the most powerful movie musical ever made. Miraculously, Jewison wrenched the musical away from its stagebound roots and created one of the most purely cinematic of all such adaptations. It was also a runaway smash hit at the box office.

Jewison's films have always reflected his highly personal tastes, from biblical rock opera (JESUS CHRIST SUPERSTAR) to futuristic corporate dominance

(ROLLERBALL, also scheduled for a remake), labor movements (F.I.S.T.) to examining our legal system (. . . AND JUSTICE FOR ALL). Jewison won praise for two screen versions of highly respected plays, A SOLDIER'S STORY and AGNES OF GOD. And the rhapsodic New York romance of MOONSTRUCK won tremendous acclaim and yet more Oscars.

Jewison's most recent four films have continued in this eclectic mode—the legacy of Vietnam (IN COUNTRY), Reagan-era greed and lust (OTHER PEOPLE'S MONEY) and two charming and underseen returns to whimsical light comedy (ONLY YOU and BOGUS).

Meanwhile, Jewison's company, Yorktown Productions, has continued its adventurous support of new filmmakers and risky filmmaking on both sides of the border, true to the spirit of his own remarkable career.

MICHAEL SINGER: *One of the things that has always interested me about you are your directorial roots. Lots of filmmakers emerged from 1950s television, but most of them—like Sidney Lumet, John Frankenheimer and Franklin J. Schaffner—directed live and taped drama. On the other hand, you were a musical and variety show specialist, and that area didn't produce many feature directors.*

NORMAN JEWISON: No, I guess not, although Bob Fosse also came from this background. When I came to the United States in 1959, my first assignment for CBS was The Hit Parade. And after that, I got kind of pigeonholed into musicals. But musical variety was my forte at that time. In those days there were a lot of variety shows on TV, and what I found interesting and exciting about it was the fact that they required a tremendous amount of creative input from everybody involved. In other words, we were the only shows that started out with a blank page, and we filled that blank page every week. Each week it was a whole different canvas. There was a great amount of creativity under pressure. Then I moved into specials, which allowed me two to three months to prepare the one hour with Harry Belafonte, or the hour-and-a-half with Jackie Gleason. I did do some dramatic shows, but you're right, most of my important credits in live television were in the musical field.

Q: *How did you finally break into features?*

A: I came into film inadvertently with 40 POUNDS OF TROUBLE in 1962. I was doing a Judy Garland special in Los Angeles, and was talked into directing the picture by Tony Curtis and his producer, Stan Marguiles. They had had some recent success with another television director named Robert Mulligan, and at that time, in the evolution of American film, there was a tremendous exodus of television directors into feature filmmaking.

Q: *It's hard to imagine all these years and so many films later how you felt that first day on the set of* 40 POUNDS OF TROUBLE.

A: Oh, I was lost. Totally lost. First of all, I had only one camera, and like all TV directors, I was used to multiple cameras. The cinematographer was Joe McDonald, and he was very patient with me. When he saw what I was doing, he explained to me that I had to adapt to the new form. But that's true, I think of all television directors who made that move—Sidney Lumet, Mike Nichols, everybody.

Q: *So it was kind of a learn-as-you-go situation?*

A: All directors kind of know what they want, because they see the film in their mind when they're working on the screenplay with the writer, and when they're planning the shots at home. In those days, we used to shoot a lot of the films on studio lots, so I had my floor plans. I was still working and plotting my scenes much like I would for the theatre or television without the fourth wall. Then when I went in and realized I was in a room with four walls, the crew would look at me and say "Which wall do you want us to take out?" It was difficult, but a real learning experience, and I was lucky enough to have people who helped and guided me. And for some reason, Tony Curtis had total confidence in me. If it wasn't for Tony Curtis, I really don't think I would have become a film director.

Q: *That was a Universal picture. Did you become a contract director for them at that time?*

A: I guess they liked the rushes of 40 POUNDS OF TROUBLE, because they put me under contract. I did four pictures for Universal in a row during the early to mid 1960s.

Q: *For some time you were their best young romantic comedy director.*

A: I think it was because of my experience with variety shows and comedy for TV. You see, directors get pigeonholed the same as actors and writers. But I finally made the break with THE CINCINNATI KID, which was for MGM rather than Universal.

Q: *Was that a conscious decision? Did you feel that if you didn't move into something more serious, you would never be considered a "real" filmmaker?*

A: Good comedy is just as difficult to do as good drama. In other words, I don't see any difference between comedy and drama, because everything has to be real and believable on the screen. It's the situation that changes. In a comedy it's a humorous situation, whereas in a dramatic film it's a serious situation. But the acting and the approach to the material should be honest and believable. Essentially, the only difference I can possibly think of is timing. I'm a great believer that timing is everything in films, and in life itself for that matter. I wasn't conscious of being pigeonholed as a comedy director as much as I was very much attracted to the Richard Jessup book on which THE CINCINNATI KID was based. The whole challenge was trying to make an interesting film about card playing, which essentially is uncinematic. I was challenged by the material and the excitement of working with that cast—Steve McQueen, Edward G. Robinson, Tuesday Weld, Karl Malden and Joan Blondell.

Q: *You took over that picture after the original director, Sam Peckinpah, left the project?*

A: Yes, it was offered to me by the producer, Marty Ransohoff, after Peckinpah had been removed after two weeks of shooting. The movie was originally being made in black-and-white, but I decided to shoot it in color instead.

Q: Why did you make that decision?

A: You needed color in order to shoot the card games, because color has everything to do with cards. How would you tell the difference between diamonds and hearts and spades and clubs?

Q: THE CINCINNATI KID was a pretty radical switch from the light romantic comedies you were known for, and you went into it under difficult circumstances.

A: It was a tough picture to do at that time, but again, I was very lucky to have the confidence of the actors. I was very rebellious in those days, and very insistent that I get the film that I saw in my mind on the screen. And they were very different days. . . directors weren't as powerful then as they are today.

Q: It was not yet an auteurist medium.

A: No way. It was still very much a studio controlled situation.

Q: Your next picture was THE RUSSIANS ARE COMING THE RUSSIANS ARE COMING, which really began your reputation as something of an iconoclast. You made a movie which humanized the Soviets during those pre-Perestroika, pre-Glasnost days.

A: That's what attracted me to the project. There was a tremendous anti-Communist feeling running through America at that time, which was actually advantageous to our story. The screenplay was written by William Rose, an expatriate American living on the island of Jersey who wrote some wonderful Ealing Studios comedies in England and IT'S A MAD, MAD, MAD, MAD WORLD for Stanley Kramer. Of all the films I've made, THE RUSSIANS ARE COMING was the one that caused the most controversy, not only during its filming, but when it was released. There were a lot of demonstrations against the film, because the McCarthy committee had done its work well in the '50s, and this continued into the' 60s. Curiously enough, the words "communist" and "capitalist" are never mentioned in the script. It was the first film about detente, and when it was finally released, it had its first screening in Washington for Hubert Humphrey, then the Vice President of the United States, and a glitterati of politicians and senators and Supreme Court judges and congressmen. All the foreign ambassadors were invited, and of course, the Russians and all the Soviet Bloc didn't come. When the Russians heard that the film wasn't damaging to them, they requested a print. . . which disappeared for quite some time. Apparently, it was shipped in a diplomatic pouch to the Soviet ambassador to the United Kingdom, who then sent it to the Soviet ambassador to France, who then sent it to the Kremlin. We had a tough time getting that print back, but as a result, I was one of the first western directors to be invited to Moscow. This was in 1966, during the height of the Cold War.

Q: Did they show the film publicly?

A: No. The film was not shown publicly, but it was shown to an audience of over 2,000 people at the Soviet Filmworkers Union, which was a great thrill for me. The Russians were just totally blown away by the idea that anyone would be allowed to make a film like that. I think they always thought from then on that I was some kind of Canadian pinko working in Hollywood. THE RUSSIANS ARE COMING was the only film I've made that's written up in the Congressional Record.

Q: I was 14-years-old when the movie was released, and I was convinced that THE RUS-SIANS ARE COMING was the key to peace between the United States and the Soviet Union. You have a way of making movies that are not overtly political, and yet make highly salient points about the human condition.

A: The whole purpose of a documentary filmmaker, I guess, is to dispense information. I think the purpose of a feature filmmaker is to make an entertaining movie about the human condition. And if you use film as a social vehicle for propaganda, it usually becomes boring, and the audience becomes suspicious. They realize that the characters are making speeches from a very specific point of view. IN THE HEAT OF THE NIGHT was about tolerance and respect based upon humanity and not racial judgment. Well, again, timing. IN THE HEAT OF THE NIGHT came along in 1967, possibly the peak of the Civil Rights movement in America. But when the film was released, I was convinced that it was going to be the victim of a white backlash. I did not think that it was going to capture the imagination of the filmgoing audience like it did. Now here we are in 1992, and there's a television series on the air called In The Heat of The Night, which is based on the movie. So they're essentially telling the same story more than 20 years later.

Q: Although some of your films have been filled with action—I think particularly of IN THE HEAT OF THE NIGHT, THE THOMAS CROWN AFFAIR and ROLLERBALL—you've never been thought of as an action director.

A: I'm more excited about conflict of characters than I am with endless reels of mindless action. As a matter of fact, ROLLERBALL was a film about the exploitation of violence in sports for the entertainment of the masses, something which I find to be obscene. Therefore, my films have a tendency to deal with words and music blended together into a story which hopefully has a raison d'être. You've got to have a good story. And if along the way that story is about something that expresses my private fears or private joys, then I become passionately involved. And it doesn't matter to me if the story's been told before. I don't consider myself a cerebral filmmaker. I'm always looking for a very basic, emotional approach to a scene. I don't think my films are too complex.

Q: But some of them are visually very complex, particularly THE THOMAS CROWN AF-FAIR, JESUS CHRIST SUPERSTAR and especially FIDDLER ON THE ROOF, which is visually and conceptually an extremely ambitious film.

A: FIDDLER ON THE ROOF was a big job. We spent almost two-and-a-half years making that film. It was a long, long, arduous process. I tried to take audiences into the reality of Sholom Aleichem, because I felt it was important to deal not only with a story about the breaking down of traditions, but a story that also dealt with pain and hardship and persecution. I wanted audiences to really feel the power of racial hatred. There's a moment toward the end of the first part of the fill when the Russian bullies attack the wedding party. They rip open some pillows which were meant as wedding gifts, and these goose feathers fly through the air like snow. This came from a conversation I had an old couple at a Russian kibbutz in Israel. They remembered this image from a pogrom that they witnessed as children in a Ukrainian village. There are just certain images that come into your mind when making a film, and the more research one does the better.

Q: You have a reputation as an actor's director, and the number of Oscar wins or nominations the stars of your films have received attests to that. You began as an actor yourself, which I imagine enables you to sympathize with them more than other filmmakers.

A: I like actors very much. I think they're intelligent, sensitive people, who are always out there alone. It's tough sometimes. When the words aren't right and the weather isn't right and your costume isn't right, it can be very lonely. You're the one that's up there on the screen, and you're the one that's going to take the blame if it doesn't work.

Q: Do you improvise on the set?

A: Sometimes. I think I improvise when I feel there's a need for something else in the screenplay that isn't written down. This usually comes when you're shoot-ing a film in continuity and you feel the rhythms of the piece. It's much more difficult to improvise if you're shooting totally out of sequence because you've lost the rhythms of your storyline. I try to shoot my pictures as much in continuity as possible because they change as you're making them. They grow and they breathe. They're living things. This family of people gather together at a point in their lives on a distant location far from their homes. They grow as the film is being made, and certain aspects of the story perhaps become more important than they appeared to be when the film began. Smaller parts start to become bigger, because a certain character becomes more important or the actor brings to the story a different accent. It's like an orchestration. . . all of a sudden the woodwinds take over and the brass punctuation becomes more dissonant than you thought. So there are times to improvise, but I'm a great believer in the screen-play. I spend a great deal of time with the screenwriter be fore I start a picture, and I like to feel that the screenplay is as good as we can make it. But I must say that some of them get better as you film them, and some of them deteriorate.

Q: You've been quoted as saying that you were rebellious early in your career. Have you changed?

A: I like to think I'm still rebellious. I still admire rebels. I don' t think there' s a part of any democratic society that shouldn't be challenged. I've always felt that I'm a loner, not a joiner. I don't know where that comes from, but I think it's true of most filmmakers. The good ones, I think, believe in something specific, and that's what they make films about. As I said, my films are fairly basic and simple to understand. I think it's my job to allow everyone to relate to the story and experi-ence the same feelings that the characters have in the story. And maybe, just maybe, it may have some relevance to their own lives. That's the trick, but when it happens, it's always a magical experience. A few films stay with you forever, and it's almost impossible to explain why. So those are the moments we're all looking for, I guess.

Q: And you're still looking for them?

A: Oh, always. Because as Willy Wyler once told me, "Kid. . . it's all over when your legs give out."

F I L M O G R A P H Y

N O R M A N   J E W I S O N

b. July 21, 1926 - Toronto, Canada

40 POUNDS OF TROUBLE Universal, 1962
THE THRILL OF IT ALL Universal, 1963
SEND ME NO FLOWERS Universal, 1964
THE ART OF LOVE Universal, 1965
THE CINCINNATI KID MGM, 1965
THE RUSSIANS ARE COMING THE RUSSIANS ARE COMING United Artists, 1966
IN THE HEAT OF THE NIGHT ★ United Artists, 1967
THE THOMAS CROWN AFFAIR United Artists, 1968
GAILY, GAILY United Artists, 1969
FIDDLER ON THE ROOF ★ United Artists, 1971
JESUS CHRIST SUPERSTAR Universal, 1973
ROLLERBALL United Artists, 1975
F.I.S.T. United Artists, 1978
. . . AND JUSTICE FOR ALL Columbia, 1979
BEST FRIENDS Warner Bros., 1982
A SOLDIER'S STORY Columbia, 1984
AGNES OF GOD Columbia, 1985
MOONSTRUCK ★ MGM/UA, 1987
IN COUNTRY Warner Bros., 1989
OTHER PEOPLE'S MONEY Warner Bros., 1991
ONLY YOU TriStar, 1994
BOGUS Warner Bros., 1996

$\mathcal{P}$HIL $\mathcal{J}$OANOU

The problem with being a *wunderkind*, Phil Joanou might tell you, is trying to fulfill the expectations of those who stuck the unsolicited label on you in the first place—and having the right, every once in a while, to not fully succeed.

Plucked from the University of Southern California film school by no less a personage than Steven Spielberg, who placed the young filmmaker under his powerful wings, Joanou then faced the task of building a career and body of work on his own two feet. Following THREE O'CLOCK HIGH, a coming-of-age comedy which gave Joanou the opportunity to flex his cinematic muscles, the director then made the rock documentary U2 RATTLE & HUM, hired by the Irish band to chronicle their *Joshua Tree* tour. Then Joanou stepped westward to New York, where he made his best film, the dark urban tragedy STATE OF GRACE, with Sean Penn, Gary Oldman and Ed Harris. Next, taking another unexpected turn, Joanou shot the CBS-TV documentary *Age 7 in America*.

Joanou's subsequent work has, unquestionably, been mixed. He was one of the directors of the provocative, Oliver Stone-produced mini-series WILD PALMS, but his two most recent features—FINAL ANALYSIS and HEAVEN'S PRISONERS—failed to win either audience or critical acceptance.

Which brings us right back to the first issue. Perhaps Joanou was rushed under the spotlight without having the opportunity to organically grow film-by-film, as so many directors do. And perhaps now, the fading of that glare will finally permit this naturally talented filmmaker to, as he indicates in the following interview, become a "completely three-dimensional, fully-developed, mature filmmaker. . . "

In fact, his most recent project promises just that. Entitled ENTROPY, the film takes as its subject a young filmmaker (portrayed by Stephen Dorff), and the personal travails he encounters while shooting a documentary about U2. And whatever kind of creative riff on reality ENTROPY wil turn out to be, this promises to give Joanou a remarkable opportunity to tell the story of his personal journey in the most intimate way.

MICHAEL SINGER: *You're very discriminating about your projects, and yet you stuck with FINAL ANALYSIS for quite some time before it actually went before the cameras. Why did you want to make this movie?*

PHIL JOANOU: The reason I stayed involved with FINAL ANALYSIS over a three-year period prior to production was that I felt Wesley Strick had written a very strong narrative, and one of the things I miss in films today is a good story. Wesley had a very unique narrative with interesting characters, and the idea of just telling this story the best way possible was an interesting challenge. THREE O'CLOCK HIGH had a very simple narrative; RATTLE & HUM was a documentary with no narrative; and STATE OF GRACE was character-driven rather than narrative-driven. So FINAL ANALYSIS was really the first film I've attempted to undertake with a truly strong driving narrative. When you read the scripts that are out there today, you realize that finding a good narrative is unique. To Wesley's credit, he formulated a powerful set-up and payoff. This was one of the best scripts I read.

Q: *Were you conscious of making a distinctively noir genre film when you were directing FINAL ANALYSIS?*

A: I think that when I first got involved with the project it was probably more film noir than the result on the screen. It was originally set in New York and the vision was somewhat darker, which we adjusted when the film moved to San Francisco. The idea of making a noir piece was ultimately rejected in favor of making a psychological thriller. I think it falls firmly into the "cat and mouse" mind game concept, and hopefully, that's the fun of the movie. As far as referencing to other films of the genre, I decided to eject them in making FINAL ANALYSIS to service the narrative as written by Wesley. It will be interesting to see if people ultimately find references that I have not consciously made. This film, I hope, has a certain style and tone of its own that isn't directly related to any other specific film or even the genre itself.

Q: *For somebody who came of age at a time when auteurism was really the name of the game—specially with film school graduates—saying that you put your style in the service of a writer strikes me as surprising.*

A: I don't see myself as an auteur and I don't really believe in the auteur theory. There are very few filmmakers alive today who to me truly exemplify that theory. . . perhaps Woody Allen, Stanley Kubrick, Martin Scorsese, Steven Spielberg, Bernardo Bertolucci. But I don't believe in it for myself. I try to do very much like what I think Billy Wilder did. He was incredibly diverse in the kinds of movies he could make, from SOME LIKE IT HOT to DOUBLE INDEMNITY, or STALAG 17 to SUNSET BOULEVARD. He always served the narrative. And so did many, many directors of that era. I try to find my directorial cues from the material, so the style in which I've shot FINAL ANALYSIS is totally different from the style in which I shot STATE OF GRACE, which was totally different from THREE O'CLOCK HIGH. The script dictates the style and tone. Directing is really an interpretive job unless one has written the script. What I'm ultimately doing is interpreting a piece of material, much like the actor interprets a character. Some directors are given more credit for being in control of their projects, which is in my opinion due to their stylistic choices and a consistency in their material. If one makes only comedies throughout a career, eventually there are similarities from film to film, which one sees as a pattern of that director's work although every single one of those films may have been written by somebody else.

Q: Ultimately, has the "Phil Joanou, Spielberg protégé" label hurt rather than helped you?

A: I'm not really bothered by that too much. What it does, though, is create unfair and false expectations, particularly when one is compared to maybe the most successful director in the history of the medium. Certainly, it was a huge compliment to be asked by Steven to work with him back during Amazing Stories, to be brought into his company and taught a great deal by him about film and the business. But now I'm 29 years old and still trying to discover for myself what kind of filmmaker I am. . . and I don't know what that is. I don't have a firm grasp of my own self-image as a filmmaker, so I'm still learning and growing and discovering things about myself as I make films. . . hopefully making them well enough to continue to make them while I grow. I don't see myself as a completely three-dimensional, fully-developed, mature filmmaker yet. FINAL ANALYSIS is only my third narrative feature. John Ford made something like 40 narrative features before he made STAGECOACH! I'll never make 40 features in my lifetime. . . it's physically impossible today. To me, the verdict on filmmakers is brought about much too soon today. I'm just trying to make the best movies I can, grow as much as I can during the making of each film, and then through the process, discover what I like, which will then affect my next decision in terms of what kinds of films I want to be involved with. So, I'm not worried about labels, whether it's being labeled a Spielberg protégé or anything else. What I'm worried about and concerned with is consistently growing and moving forward so that I can become a better filmmaker on each film, and hopefully, down the road, have an even better grasp of my medium.

Q: Do you think that filmmakers today are hindered by the labeling and stereotyping that seems to exist not just in the press, but also within the industry?

A: Absolutely, but to some degree that's our fault. Because what one tends to do is fall back on one's strengths, and that's only human. We say "that worked well last time, so why not try it again?," and it's also human nature for the public and press and industry to label you. Oh, he makes thrillers, but doesn't do so well with romance. So if you make six romances in a row and then want to make an aggressive drama, people are nervous about it. Even an incredibly successful director sometimes has difficulty making films that are out of their pattern. And by creating patterns, we label ourselves. Which is one of the reasons why I have not tried to create a pattern. . . although there's a downside to that too. Without a pattern, people don't know who you are and then don't know what to call you. I personally would rather confuse people and try to grow through working in different genres of film, rather than end up being stuck in one of them.

Q: You've worked squarely within the studio system, and yet at the same time there's still a perception of you as being a little bit on the fringe.

A: I've never attempted to ingratiate myself into the system. Though I've maintained certain relationships, I haven't tried to become part of the system per se. How do you maintain who you are when you become part of the system, or a cog in the machinery? When I started out with Steven, it was quite expected of me to do a Steven Spielberg-like production, although THREE O'CLOCK HIGH was a small, non-star movie that really should have been a television film. It was really an exercise in style and getting my feet wet in film production. Then the industry expected me to graduate to a medium-sized Hollywood picture. Instead, I went out and did a documentary on a rock and roll band that was financed by the band itself. From there, I went and did a dark New York tragedy, which I think surprised people. I think I've kept people guessing. And by keeping the industry and the press guessing, it's kept me unpredictable. My own agents send me the broadest spectrum of scripts imaginable, because even they don't know what I'm suddenly going to want to do. It's not a plan. . . it's just the way it's worked out.

Q: *You're well respected by the actors you've worked with, and on the set, you seem less of a technocrat and more interested in plot and performance.*

A: The most exciting part of filmmaking for me is working with the actors. . . probably that comes from the fact that I originally wanted to act myself, and to some degree I'm a frustrated actor. I love watching actors discover the character. . . I love watching them create. To me, it's the side that I can't control. I can only help, and then allow it to happen and put it on screen. The area that I probably put the most effort into is working with the actors, because I've laid out the technical side prior to shooting the film. I've broken down the script, decided on the visual style with the director of photography and art director, and try to shoot the picture in a way that will create an editorial rhythm. Well-designed films come out almost every week of the year from Hollywood, but films with strong stories and performances come out less often, and to me that's the real challenge. The fact is, you can turn on MTV or even watch a number of well-made commercials on television, and they'll all look as good as any feature film. To me that is no longer an area that is crucial to making good films, because it's a given. The wild cards—the elements that differentiate good films from not-so-good films—are performance and story. And they're also the only two things that one can never change once the film is done. You can never change what your cast brings to your film, and you can never change the core of the script that you shot, even with re-shoots. I think Milos Forman could have shot ONE FLEW OVER THE CUCKOO'S NEST on Super 8mm with the same cast and the same script and made just as good a film. Because the story and the characters and the actors were so brilliant, the film transcended technique.

Q: *One thing that's always intrigued me is when a director creates a lasting professional relationship with the same cinematographer. If you will, discuss Jordan Cronenweth, who's shot your last three films.*

A: I think Jordan is truly—and I don't use this word often—a genius at what he does. He's one of the two or three greatest cinematographers working in the world today. He's a risk-taker who has an incredible eye. To this day, I don't truly understand exactly how Jordan creates what ends up on the screen, even though I'm standing right next to him on the set. He has a unique visual style that's not similar to any other cinematographer I can think of. There's also a sense of film history to Jordan—he's been in the business for a long time, operating on films like BUTCH CASSIDY AND THE SUNDANCE KID and IN COLD BLOOD, then shooting BLADE RUNNER, working with Coppola on PEGGY SUE GOT MARRIED and

GARDENS OF STONE, as well as Ken Russell on ALTERED STATES and Jonathan Demme on CITIZENS BAND and STOP MAKING SENSE. Also, I love Jordan's versatility. When you work with him, there's not the sense that you're going to get the same look he did on his last three pictures. Like myself, he tries to adapt the visual style to the material. I find him a calming and stabilizing presence, and I'd love to make every film for the rest of my career with him.

Q: *You once said that pre-production is like packing, and shooting is the vacation.*

A: I'll always feel that way. No matter what goes on during pre-production, I feel the most comfortable and satisfied when I'm shooting. Probably the one regret that I have is that I wasn't a director in the 1930s and '40s, when I could have made three movies a year and 50 or 60 in my career. I would be at my best doing a great volume of work, and having been lucky enough within that volume to make a few very good movies. I don't like the Olympic athlete quality of making movies these days. In other words, directors today get a shot every two to four years to go out and run the race, like an Olympic athlete. I'd much rather be on the Lakers and play a hundred games a year. I remember, after I finished shooting THREE O'CLOCK HIGH, Steven said to me "Well, so that's it, it's over." And I said, "Well. . . I've still got to edit the film." But he said, "No, it's over. You can edit, you can do whatever you want. . . but in those hundred cans of negative sitting in a vault somewhere lies your film. You can edit, but you've already made the big decisions. You've chosen the granite. . . now you can sculpt."

Q: *So you're ready for another block of granite?*

A: Absolutely. . . bring it on!

F I L M O G R A P H Y

P H I L   J O A N O U
b. November 20, 1961
THREE O'CLOCK HIGH Universal, 1987
U2 RATTLE AND HUM (FCD) Paramount, 1988
STATE OF GRACE Orion, 1990
FINAL ANALYSIS Warner Bros., 1992
WILD PALMS (MS) co-director with Peter Hewitt, Kathryn Bigelow & Keith Gordon, Ixtlan
    Corporation/Greengrass Productions, 1993
HEAVEN'S PRISONERS New Line Cinema, 1996
ENTROPY Tribeca Productions/Phoenician Films, 1998

$\mathcal{R}$OLAND $\mathcal{J}$OFFÉ

Roland Joffé took such a critical pounding in the aftermath of his version of THE SCARLET LETTER, starring Demi Moore, that it's well worth reminding everyone that nearly every director has been entitled to a flop. Making matters even more difficult for Joffé was that his first two features—THE KILLING FIELDS and THE MISSION—were so spectacularly received, winning him Academy Award nominations for his work on both. Set against vast and stunning backdrops (the Khmer Rouge destruction of Cambodia in the former and the Spanish-Portuguese domination of 18th Century South America in the latter), both films retained dramatic intimacy and historical urgency. Along with his later (and underrated) CITY OF JOY, these features were impassionated and compassionate renderings of man's boundless capacity or nobility and cruelty, all informed with an exquisite sense of pure cinema.

In other words, THE KILLING FIELDS and THE MISSION were tough acts to follow, which is a partial explanation of the lukewarm responses that were afforded to FAT MAN AND LITTLE BOY (the story of the Atomic Bomb's development) and CITY OF JOY, and the much chillier reaction to THE SCARLET LETTER.

At this writing, it remained to be seen how Joffé's most recent film, the satirical GOODBYE, LOVER, would fare artistically and perhaps even more promising, the French company Gaumont announced that the director would helm a film called VATEL, a story of a chef working under King Louis XIV, starring Gerard Depardieu.

MICHAEL SINGER: *Both* THE KILLING FIELDS *and* THE MISSION *are enhanced not only by historical perspective, but also by a marked spirituality. If you'll pardon the expression, you seem to be a director with a mission.*

ROLAND JOFFÉ: Well, you make it sound more serious than it is. Simply, I feel that if I'm going to commit time to something, it's because I want to learn. So I pick subjects that ask questions, and I can't help but grow involved with them. And if one's standpoint is not to adopt a superior, critical point of view, but to enable people to experience incidents, to be engaged emotionally in moral dilemmas, to make connections, then a degree of passion must emerge. It's to do with how you see a film. I don't see films as a commodity, but as a response to living, not only as an object to be marketed. Film is not breakfast cereal; the same thing in different packets. Film is something that has to engage me on every level.

Q: *There's a large measure of compassion in your films, not just for the "good guys," but for the villains as well.*

A: I do feel it. I feel compassionate towards people who are so bound up in the moment that they may be doing things that run counter to their intentions that with hindsight they will regret. John Donne put it succinctly: "no man is an island." Of course, it's pretty easy to be compassionate on film. Whether I'm compassionate in life, I'm not so sure. I mean, I've been stopped by traffic cops on the street and not felt compassionate at all!

Q: *The physical backdrop of your films seems to play an immensely important part. One can't extricate the characters from their surroundings, nor the events that are occurring.*

A: I've always felt that if I'd been brighter, I'd have been an anthropologist. I'm fascinated by the way that people are their environment. The extraordinary thing to me about being a human being is that we're part of nature, and yet it is also our nature not to want to be a part of nature. Our consciousness drives us towards change, it drives us towards seeking to alter our environment. And yet, we are our environment. So, I try to take a holistic view and understand the complex connections that make up reality. What fascinates me about this age, scientifically, is that a holistic view of science and nature is gradually becoming current. We still view the world using the old Cartesian mechanical model. But it's more accurate to try and understand the world using a biological model that shows the organic, rather than the mechanical relationships, of people and things and ideas. Film is a wonderful medium for expressing these subtle, volatile relationships as part of a story. The Khmer Rouge, for instance, took their style from their country, its history and the constraints of their culture. If they'd not been Cambodian they would have been different. No idea is so pure that it can remain uncolored by the environment in which it is expressed. I remember once in Germany looking at some early Brecht films, being surprised that the images he used to express his idea of the perfection of a socialist Germany could have come out of the camera of one of Hitler's propagandists. There were blonde girls and boys with wonderfully muscular bodies and perfect breasts and thighs rowing on lakes. . . that fascinated me. I began to realize just how much we are all prisoners of our culture and our times.

Q: *You obviously have an avid fascination for history.*

A: I talked to an American critic once who said to me, "Well, I just can't get interested in history." And I replied, "Listen, I've got to tell you. . . if you are seriously telling me this as a critic, then you must be doing a poor job for your public." And he said, "What do you mean?" And I replied, "Well, let me put it another way. Do you have a son?" And he said, "Yes, I do." And I said, "Are you proud of him?" And he said, "Yes, I am." And I said, "Is he proud of you?" And he said, "Yes, I think he is actually." And I said, "Of course, you are his history. Your father was your history." History is crucial because it suggests where we came from, where we are, and where we may be headed. To deny the importance of history, is to deny the future. He may as well release his son into traffic in a blindfold.

Q: *I don't mean to push you into a corner, but is seems to me that your films are intrinsically religious. There seems to be a sense, particularly in THE MISSION, that man has to be answerable to something larger than himself, and that something larger demands that we treat each other as human beings.*

A: Well, I think that's true, but I'm actually an awed atheist. I look up at the night sky and can't explain what I see. It's magnificent beyond my understanding. But on the other hand, in terms of human beings, I think the measure of man is mankind. Each individual man is worth more than himself, because he stands for all of mankind. The glorious and hard thing about being a human being is that we can't accomplish anything without others. Our measure is the rest of humanity, and in that sense, each one of us signifies much more than just one set of bones encased in flesh.

Q: *What impressed me about both THE KILLING FIELDS and THE MISSION was how death was never trivialized. Even when the bad guys die, we are not encouraged to cheer. It made me think about the whole nature of adventure movies—which are essentially films in which people die violent deaths while rousing music plays on the soundtrack.*

A: To me the point of an adventure film is survival. But I'm not so sure that's what an action film is today. In America—and I say this as an outsider—there is discomfort about death that probably doesn't exist in other parts of the world. Maybe this has to do with the fact that this is an enormous country that's been built on an ethos of achievement. There's always more space to use, more land to colonize, more ground to irrigate, more corn to grow. . . and that's come to mean that Americans feel that somehow potentiality should go on forever. And this is confronted with the reality that one's potential as a human being is limited to 75 years, or 100, if you're lucky. And that's very difficult to take. People are irritated with themselves because physically, they can't match the ethos that drives the country. And that makes them very uncomfortable about death, and they begin to atavistically revel in it. Conversely, it may be that every death in fantasy affirms the spectator's life, in fact.

Q: *Let's talk about your history in film. What got you started?*

A: I found myself at a loose end after university—I had studied English and drama. Many went into the drama department because that's where the attractive girls were. . . again, the influence of the mundane on decisions. Then, to find enough money to subsist on, I ran a little theatre group in Leicester which toured around and improvised plays in schools. The kids I met were remarkable and I learned a whole lot about the world. I felt that the theatre had a lot to say, so I went down to the National and, with Frank Dunlop started the Young Vic. But I was beginning to find that the moments I really treasured were those in rehearsal when an actor was discovering for the first time. I always wanted to be in film as a child, but it seemed an unattainable goal in England at that time. But I began to feel that I was in the wrong medium being in theatre, and that my creative home would have to be in film. I was invited to do some television and jumped at the chance. I actually went up to a commercial company and started on the floor, did a news program and some documentaries. I had some problems doing documentaries, because I felt that the camera and the crew were, in essence, manipulative. I decided that I wanted to work with actors in a way that created a real world through imagination rather than muscling in on the lives of ordinary people. That led me to struggle to create a heightened reality. So there's sort of been a line to my career, although the initial start was accidental.

Q: *Documentary-like realism has continued in your feature films, though. Your television film,* THE SPONGERS, *looked and sounded almost like a documentary.*

A: Oh, yes, and that was intentional. In fact, some people did actually phone the BBC and ask how we had the cheek to have filmed a suicide. Certainly, the intention was to make people feel that we had snuck in with a camera and they were watching life unfold. And I've always enjoyed that.

Q: *Both* THE KILLING FIELDS *and* THE MISSION *are realistic and stylized at the same time. Do you purposely inject documentary style into your films, or is it more or less a subconscious carryover from your early filmmaking days?*

A: No, I do it consciously, and I play with it in the sense that sometimes you can find an exquisite tension between something that's set up in a very documentary way and then shot cinematically. The tension between the two can be moving. For example, the evacuation of Phnom Penh in THE KILLING FIELDS—I set that up as realistically as I could, but the camera move with the rising track was choreographed deliberately with music. I played music when we shot it—not the music used in the movie, but a temp track to find a rhythm for the camera. People thought that we used hand-held cameras in THE KILLING FIELDS, but we always used tracks because we couldn't get the precision we wanted hand-held. The evacuation scene with the helicopters was choreographed with infinite precision.

Q: *That scene was almost balletic. It all seemed to be done in one continuous shot. How did you accomplish that?*

A: Well, I wanted it to have a continuous flow. When we shot that scene, we had to film half of it in Bangkok where we could only use small helicopters. And then we couldn't resume shooting the scene until we went to San Diego, where the large Sea Stallion helicopters were available. We then cut the two sections together. I had to choreograph the first sequence of tracking shots with the small helicopters to fit the second sequence of tracking shots with the big helicopters. It involved everything I love about filmmaking.

Q: *For their expensive look, both* THE KILLING FIELDS *and* THE MISSION *were relatively moderate in budget. How do you manage to shoot so economically?*

A: The studio system here can be very top-heavy, and a lot of money never gets on the screen. My rule is to get the money on the screen. I think it's a healthy rule, too, because if we can keep making films reasonably economically, we'll be able to justify films that depart from the usual formula. We can't dominate the market, but if we can make a reasonable return in it, it won't dominate us. I've always known that film economics are really important. Every financial decision is artistic and vice-versa, so I'd like to know how much everything costs. I guess that's my theatre training. If you can make imagination happen with six-pence, it's better than making it happen with thirty pounds.

Q: Do you think that directors who come up through the British system are more prepared to become feature filmmakers than their American counterparts? Because it seems that most British directors start at the bottom and learn every aspect of filmmaking before they get behind the camera, whereas here a lot of neophytes make directing deals on the basis of other talents, like writing or cinematography.

A: The directors that I have the most respect for, whether American or British, have all knocked about a bit. Yes, it can take a long time for us to direct a feature in England, and that gives us a certain strength. Directors who make it very, very quickly, may then take a dip. But that dip is likely to be just part of the learning process. So it evens out. The problem with our work is that we have to learn in public and under pressure—that's hard on us all.

Q: On the touchy subject of message films, when I spoke with Stanley Kramer for this book, we discussed his getting knocked around a bit by critics for tackling the big issues. You have, in some quarters, been accused of the same thing. How do you respond?

A: Well, let me put it this way—when critics go to see films, they suffer from the delusion that they look at the films. The truth of the matter is that the films look at them. A critic who has a narrow spectrum of knowledge, narrow expectations will write reviews that reflect that. It would take an awful lot of critics to put me off dealing with issues. And unless one stays only with fashionable viewpoints, one will unearth surprising prejudices. I think that's par for the course.

Q: Do you think there's a certain cowardice in the industry today, avoiding issue-oriented films?

A: Well, there has to be a balance, I think, between the role of film as entertainment and the possibility of entertainment not excluding content. Absence of thought, and an obsession with sensation is probably a sign of decay. But there are a variety of films and like paintings in a gallery, different styles and intentions can be complimentary and enriching. The problem comes when commercial decisions are overriding, because then nobody's free anymore. But the studios have the sense to see that there are many ways of skinning a cat, and that even if lighter-than-air films seem more likely to be commercially successful than issue films, in the studio's broad spectrum there is room for both. . . and the one audience can help to build the other. Interestingly, the critics often muddle this issue by taking a film's financial success to be the only measure of its achievement, and I'm not only referring to the Wall Street Journal.

Q: Do you see yourself making films in a lighter vein the future?

A: I've got a couple of comedies that I really would like to make, but they are also about something. I guess I just have a questioning nature, and I think I'd be silly to pretend that I haven't.

F I L M O G R A P H Y

R O L A N D   J O F F É

b. November 17, 1945 - London, England
THE LEGION HALL BOMBING (TF) BBC, 1978, British
THE SPONGERS (TF) BBC, 1978, British
NO, MAMA, NO (TF) Thames TV, 1979, British
U.K. (TF) BBC, 1981, British
THE KILLING FIELDS ★ Warner Bros., 1984, British
THE MISSION ★ Warner Bros., 1986, British
FAT MAN AND LITTLE BOY Paramount, 1989
CITY OF JOY TriStar, 1992, British-French
THE SCARLET LETTER Buena Vista, 1995
GOODBYE, LOVER Warner Bros., 1998

GENE KELLY

It was probably the most nerve-wracked that I had ever been before an interview, but then again, this wasn't just any subject. It was Gene Kelly, who was not just a movie star and star director, but a legend in his own time, and mine. But the gentleman who answered the door of his Beverly Hills home that day in 1988, immediately making me feel at home, wasn't a butler or aide. It was Gene Kelly himself, putting me at ease in a role that hundreds, or even thousands had done before me over his amazing career in show business. . . the interviewer, trying to get the job done.

I had no desire to hear an unreeling of Kelly's Greatest Hits (that would have taken much too long anyway), just to discuss his work as a film director. And this he did, with charm and a crystalline memory, for a little less than an hour before politely asking me "Do you have enough?," and thanking me for my interest.

As if I didn't share that interest with millions of others around the world. For in addition to his status as the most energetic, charming and athletic musical comedy star in movie history, Kelly had also been one of the genre's most revolutionary directors. With Stanley Donen, he co-directed three bonafide classics—ON THE TOWN, SINGIN' IN THE RAIN and IT'S ALWAYS FAIR WEATHER. He also conceived, choreographed and directed INVITATION TO THE DANCE, which further advanced the art of the musical dance film, and helmed the gigantic HELLO, DOLLY!, which converted virtually the entire backlot of 20th Century-Fox into New York at the turn of the century. Kelly's non-musical directorial credits included THE HAPPY ROAD, GIGOT and A GUIDE FOR THE MARRIED MAN.

In addition to his full-time directing, Kelly choreographed, for other directors, COVER GIRL, ANCHORS AWEIGH, THE PIRATE, TAKE ME OUT TO THE BALL GAME, AN AMERICAN IN PARIS and BRIGADOON—starring, of course, in each of them. Kelly, who was honored with the American Film Institute's Lifetime Achievement Award, changed the way we look at film and the way we think about dancing. His passing in 1996 was a real loss to the world, and it's impossible for me to pass that house in Beverly Hills without thinking of the unforgettable hour I spent with one of the greatest talents the film world has ever known.

MICHAEL SINGER: *You were the most successful musical comedy star in the world, and yet you decided to become a film director as well. Why?*

GENE KELLY: I just felt that to have dances shot in a specific way and then handed over to an editor was a first step toward losing what you had done, and there's only so much cutting in the camera that one can do.

Q: *Was that the way you controlled how one of your dance scenes would look on screen?*

A: Yes. You go up to a certain point and cut, so the editor is forced to go into the angle of the next shot. But to have real control over your own work, its a good thing to shoot it yourself. There was no ego involved. It was all tied up with the dancing. When I got out of the Navy after World War II, I wrote a little storyline idea and showed it to Stanley Donen, and we sold it to MGM.

Q: *So when the time came for you and Donen to do* ON THE TOWN. . .

A: I was more than ready, but I never prided myself that I could jump in front of the camera and direct a whole picture alone. I've often had someone to work with me behind the camera, and it just happened that I was lucky enough to have Stanley working with me on our first picture as co-directors.

Q: *How did you and Donen meet?*

A: Stanley had been in PALJOEY with me on Broadway, and also worked with me in BEST FOOT FORWARD. He turned out to be one of the best things that happened to me professionally. As you know, we co-directed three pictures together. Then we finally got Stanley to do his own pictures, which was a blessing, I think, for the cinema in general.

Q: *There were a lot of talented musical film directors working at MGM at that time.*

A: Well, Vincente Minnelli was there, Charles Walters was there, Stanley was there. The underrated fellow was Chuck Walters, who did such great work—and all the other performers will tell you the same thing, although he wasn't the big name the rest seemed to be. At MGM, we worked on a lot of pictures that we didn't take credit for. Chuck always seemed to be in line if somebody broke a leg, or went away, or whatever. They'd call on Chuck, and he'd finish a number. He did a lot of that. I did a lot of that. We didn't beg for a credit, For example, I finished the choreography of LES GIRLS when Jack Cole became ill, but I never asked for credit. In the old studio days everyone in the family knew who was doing what.

Q: *That camaraderie and lack of ego seems inconceivable in today's business of tortured billing negotiations.*

A: I think we liked working together. And I think we did have camaraderie. But everything wasn't easy. We always had to deal with the different personalities and creative instincts of each individual. But we sat down and talked everything out.

Q: *You helped set in motion one of the first great revolutions in the art of musical film by filming on real locations in New York City for ON THE TOWN in 1949. Did you have to fight with the studio for that?*

A: Oh, yes. We had to fight very hard, but the good thing for me was having Stanley by my side, because together we were able to convince them.

Q: ON THE TOWN *was a big hit on Broadway. How did you become involved in the film version?*

A: I saw it while I was still in the Navy, and was back in New York on leave to visit my wife and child. I went to see ON THE TOWN, and here was this play set in New York City with about 24 chorus people representing blacks and Japanese and whites and Hispanics—the whole melting pot. I thought, what a perfect movie this would make. You go out into the real streets of New York and shoot the city! So I phoned Arthur Freed, and he said that MGM owned the rights to the play. I told him that I wanted to make it as soon as I got out of the service, but it just never worked out. I found out later that Louis B. Mayer had gone to see it and didn't like the melting pot idea. He thought, oh, we can't put that on the screen—all these people touching and dancing with each other. The tenor of the times just frightened him, so that stayed it. And every month I'd go up and make a Ciceronian speech on how and why ON THE TOWN should be made as a film. Meanwhile, when I was still in the Navy, I had gone out to the Brooklyn Navy Yard to shoot some footage of the USS Ben Franklin and some of its crew who lived in the New York area. And because I had my uniform on, I could knock at anybody's door and ask them if they could let me in to shoot. So they would say, yeah, come in, and I would sit in the living room, point the camera out the window and steal all the shots I needed. We would have extras or actors out on the street. A member of the crew would wave a white handkerchief and I would start shooting—but no one else out there except the actors, extras and crew would know that a movie was being made! I tried to explain to MGM what I had done a few years before with Navy filming. We could hide the camera and get all the shots we needed on city streets. But they didn't believe it. They thought you needed fifty policeman surrounding the crew.

Q: *But you eventually convinced them. How did you actually go about filming on New York streets without being mobbed?*

A: Well, by using very similar techniques to those when I did the film for the Navy. We hired Yellow Cabs for the cast and a station wagon for the crew. We put Frank Sinatra on the floor of one of the taxis so that no one could see him, because that was the height of the Sinatra mania among the young women. Then we picked out places where we could steal the shot. First we filmed on top of the Radio City building and shot 360 degrees of New York with me, Frank and Julie Munshin singing. We hired about a dozen extras and stole every shot the Brooklyn Bridge, Brooklyn Navy Yard. . . that was a real ship coming in at the beginning of the movie. . . I got permission from the Navy because I was one of their boys. We also stole the stuff on Mott Street and Grant's Tomb. We'd jump out of the Yellow Cab, a crew member would wave the white handkerchief, and before anybody could see us we'd ride horses through Central Park, or walk down through Grant's Tomb and get the shot. Nobody knew we were there. We did it all with stopwatch timing. We didn't have playbacks. It was an exciting thing to do, and very primitive now.

Q: It looks great, though. I think many films—WEST SIDE STORY, in particular—owe a tremendous debt to the location filming in ON THE TOWN. When people saw the film in theatres, were they delighted by the location footage?

A: We had the biggest crowd at Radio City Music Hall for weeks. At one time, I had a picture that MGM took of the waiting line snaking down Sixth Avenue, Fifth Avenue, 52nd Street, down 51st Street and around like a big snake. People liked the film. It was new, but perhaps the feel of the picture now is dated.

Q: I really don't think so, except perhaps the obvious differences between what was shot on location and what was shot in the studio back in Hollywood.

A: What was good about the studio shooting was that we had to invent things that tied in with what we did in New York. The use of color, I think, was very original. . . shooting against a red background, or the simplicity of the sailor's white uniform and the girl in a black leotard against a red background. There was something stark about it. If you ever see that again, turn off the color on the set and you'll see what I mean. The use of color was very good in that film, and as exciting as the New York shots were to us, we did several other things in the studio that worked as well.

Q: Your next film as co-director with Stanley Donen, SINGIN' IN THE RAIN, is now generally acknowledged as one the best, or even the best, musical in movie history. But when you were filming, was there any sense on the set that you were doing something so historical, that something was clicking better than usual?

A: We felt that way on every picture. But I didn't think that 35 years later I'd be sitting talking to somebody about it. You see, Stanley, Betty (Comden), Adolph (Green) and I thought musicals were a real, legitimate art form. We were as serious as Monet was about painting. But we never said, "Now this one will last!"
If I had to guess in that period of time which picture would last, I would have picked something like AN AMERICAN IN PARIS, or THE PIRATE or even ON THE TOWN. We just did our best on every picture. But we didn't foresee the impact of television. I know that if I had foreseen it, I wouldn't have gone to all the trouble of shooting INVITATION TO THE DANCE so that people could see that there were more dancers in the world except for five or six of us out in Hollywood. That's why I did the picture. But if television were as popular then, it would have been a whole different picture. No sense of dedicating six months or a year of your life to say, "Look at all these great dancers—they don't sing and they don't act. They just dance." INVITATION TO THE DANCE was an homage to the dancers of the world. But nowadays, I can turn on the set and look at great dancing every few weeks. But you couldn't then. The only people the world knew were the few of us in Hollywood.

Q: INVITATION TO THE DANCE was such a remarkable project, and so radically ahead of its time—stories told completely in dance. I know that you filmed it in 1953, but MGM held onto it and didn't release it until 1957.

A: They didn't know what to do with it. Of course, they thought I was a little nutty, and then they got enthused after the first ballet was finished shooting. Then they cut the third ballet, which was based on popular songs. I just had a piano track, and the singers were gong to be Sinatra, Garland, etc.—great singers but it never saw the light of day. I did that ballet because I realized that an hour and a half of straight dancing was going to be too long for an audience. I wanted to either put that ballet in the middle or the end. Funny, but that's now been done a few years ago by Twyla Tharp for Baryshnikov. . . Sinatra songs. That was the whole idea, but MGM thought it was nonsense. I replaced it with a live-action/cartoon ballet, which people seemed to like. INVITATION TO THE DANCE wasn't a great picture, but it had some very good things.

Q: *Well, you were making a very serious statement with the film, a conscious effort to introduce serious dance to general audiences.*

A: It was a *beau geste.* I thought I was very lucky to be where I was, and I wanted to share it with a lot of dancers who wouldn't normally be in movies because they weren't actors.

Q: *Replacing the popular song ballet reminds me that an enormous amount of fiddling went on in those days with musicals, with entire numbers being cut—sometimes after the first or second sneak previews.*

A: It's very true. It was almost a credo at MGM. Dore Schary called the upstairs executives "the college of cardinals." They went to a premiere, and decided what should stay and what should go. But we would overshoot and overdo, for those very purposes. There wasn't so much fiddling around by cutting a minute here and a minute there as removing whole numbers. And the number that always seemed to go was the leading man's ballad. I got stuck in things like COVER GIRL where I had to sing, Long Ago and Far Away, but usually I'd throw the ballads to Judy or Frank or whomever. But the ballad was always the first to go, and this happened in ON THE TOWN when some of Leonard Bemstein's most beautiful music was thrown out, including Sinatra singing Lonely Town. In AN AMERICAN IN PARIS there was one too many love songs. Georges Guetary had a love song, and I had a love song, and we both said "I love you" a couple of times—so both those numbers went. Instead of being light and frothy and lovely, they got ponderous.

Q: *In Hugh Fordin's book about Arthur Freed and the great MGM musicals, The World of Entertainment, there is an extremely grim account of the filming of IT'S ALWAYS FAIR WEATHER. In Fordin's book, neither you nor Donen nor anyone else seemed to have anything good to say about the picture, either the experience of shooting it or the results. I find that very hard to believe considering the film's classic status.*

A: That book is false on practically every other page. The only mistake we made on that picture was that we all believed CinemaScope to be the answer to our prayers. We shot it in perfect CinemaScope style. The whole story is about three guys and much of the film is framed sectionally. The trouble is that now when the film is shown on television, they pan and scan all over the place, and that careful framing is completely lost. But if you saw that picture in a theatre on a CinemaScope screen, I think you'd be amazed.

Q: *The camera loves you, and you seem to love the camera as well, because you directed some of the most elegant sequences I've ever seen. . . just seemingly effortless. The camera always seemed to know where to go—it was very mobile in your films.*

A: If there is ease to what you see in the camerawork, it's because of the hard work behind it. I planned every little step of the way. Then if on the stage something special happened, or one of the actors had a great idea, I'd throw it all out. But there's a lot of blood, sweat and tears in making a camera move. The other thing is that, looking back on it, something happened to me in my own experience. I was always a man of the theatre. I never learned how to do a close-up. It was always better in the long shot. I always marveled at how fellows from the stage like Spencer Tracy and Marlon Brando walk right in front of the camera and do an entire 75 millimeter close-up. I don't know whether you can learn that. I never tried, but I didn't think about it very much. I was always thinking about the songs and dances, the stage stuff, because that was interesting—the dance. Nobody around here seemed to be interested in it as film. A great dancer like Fred Astaire would say, "Don't cut me in half, that's all," and the camera just followed him around. He was like Chaplin—they always stayed in full figure. I'm not of the school that keeps jumping in and cutting, and one of the reasons is not a disagreement with some very fine directors and choreographers of that school, but because in the days when we came out of the studio system, we didn't have the power to say, "Do this." So to shoot it in one take or a few takes and cut in the camera was better.

Q: *I am fascinated by this notion of cutting in the camera.*

A: I had this discussion long ago with John Ford, and he said that he cut in the camera as well. A lot of us did, including Minnelli. We didn't bother much cutting to close-ups. The camera was there. It was a flow and that was it.

Q: *Do you have a favorite MGM musical of those years?*

A: My favorite musical is, I think, MEET ME IN ST. LOUIS. Minnelli and his actors, crew, cinematographer, were all so perfect. It was no accident. It was hard, beautiful work. That is a picture that is seamless, touching, marvelous—the wedding of song and story.

Q: *Of course, one can describe SINGIN' IN THE RAIN with the same superlatives. It's so effortless in the final form that I can barely believe that you were all doing the usual sweating and straining.*

A: Let me assure you that Stanley Donen and I were in this very room that you and I are sitting in now, working out every shot of that film.

Q: *You also directed a number of nonmusical films, including a charmer called THE HAPPY ROAD. Last year I interviewed the late Noël Howard, who I know worked with you on that.*

A: The whole idea of making THE HAPPY ROAD was that television had just come in and everybody was worried. They were saying that they couldn't make huge pictures anymore, and it was true. I had a reputation that every picture I participated in as director, choreographer, dancer or whatever cost a lot of money. So my determination was to show everyone in the business that I could do a nice, small-budget picture in Europe. And we did. The production values of THE HAPPY

ROAD are immense, and everybody wondered how we were able to do it on that small a budget. Well, one of the reasons was Noël Howard, because he knew France and filmmaking like the back of his hand. The year we made THE HAPPY ROAD was a very tough one for me—I was going through a divorce and my father had died—and without Noël's help I don't think that picture would have any quality. It's a sweet little picture.

Q: *What are your feelings about the new generation of young movie-makers?*

A: I see some very good young people who know how to use the camera. Whether they learned it in a film school or somewhere else, it doesn't matter. They know it. I think we're going to pass this hurdle of making films for seven year-olds. The kids often years ago who were looking at those things are ten years older now, so I am very bullish and optimistic about the future.

Q: *What do you think the chances are for a revival of the classic screen musical?*

A: Well, you need the performers who can do it. The good news is that our friend Mikhail Baryshnikov is going to do a musical with Herb Ross that is not about ballet. That's a big breakthrough, because others will follow. But we do need the Donald O'Connors, Fred Astaires, Dan Daileys and so forth. You can't really fake musicals. You can dub in a voice, but you can't dub in a dance. They've done it in a few films, and I was shocked that people didn't get wise to it. People want to see personalities who perform. Baryshnikov is the best example nowadays. He can play a role and he is believable, and of course he's a great dancer to begin with. He's not only a charmer, but the best talent that's walked over the hill in many, many years. In classical dance he's just super, and the fact that he wants to explore other milieu is unusual. There are not many guys who want to do the kind of exploring that a lot us did in the 1930s. But there will be other guys coming along as well. When you think of all the wonderful dancers that we've seen in movies who can play comedy. . . now, Fred and myself, we were pretty good at comedy. And Dan Dailey was far better than we were—he was just marvelous. But the fellow who was not only a great dancer but also a great clown was Donald O'Connor.

Q: *Do you think the musical theatre will still be the best breeding ground for new talent?*

A: Certainly. It has to be. And the good thing is that it's going to happen in the colleges and universities. Every once in awhile I get a tape of a musical done in a university or college, whether it's one of my musicals or somebody else's, and they do them pretty well. Let me reiterate—a musical needs *performance*. You can take a writer, a director, a cameraman and pretty much get a lot of actors and actresses and put them in there with a script, but in a musical, they have to *perform*. They have to have this particular kind of talent which transcends the limits of the two dimensional screen. It's very hard to do. There are a lot of live performers who have never been able to get up on a two-dimensional screen. They just go flat, like a painted image. I think Orson Welles said it best—"The camera loves some people." They can say hello and be interesting on screen. If they said hello on stage, you couldn't hear them in the back row. It's a mystery. I'm thinking now of all the fine actors I've known. . . the camera gets on them and they're not half as good as a person with half their talent or half their experience.

Q: One of the most wonderful things about your films and persona is that you're rediscovered and intensely enjoyed by younger audiences.

A: Yes, young people still write me letters. I get more letters now than I did when I was a movie star, and they talk about my old films as if they were just discovered. Little girls write me mash notes! They think my movies were made last year. The students who are coming out of every college and want to go into film all write letters and rediscover our films. A lot of this is technological, because they're looking at the stuff in their own homes on videocassette recorders. It's a whole new era.

F I L M O G R A P H Y

GENE KELLY
(Eugene Curran Kelly)
b. August 23, 1912 - Pittsburgh, Pennsylvania
d. 1996
ON THE TOWN   co-director with Stanley Donen, MGM, 1949
SINGIN' IN THE RAIN   co-director with Stanley Donen, MGM, 1952
IT'S ALWAYS FAIR WEATHER   co-director with Stanley Donen, MGM, 1955
INVITATION TO THE DANCE   MGM, 1956
THE HAPPY ROAD   co-director with Noel Howard, MGM, 1957
THE TUNNEL OF LOVE   MGM, 1958
GIGOT   20th Century-Fox, 1962
A GUIDE FOR THE MARRIED MAN   20th Century-Fox, 1967
HELLO, DOLLY!   20th Century-Fox, 1969
THE CHEYENNE SOCIAL CLUB   National General, 1970
THAT'S ENTERTAINMENT, PART 2 (FD)   co-director with Jack Haley, Jr., MGM/United Artists,
   1976

IRVIN $\mathcal{K}$ERSHNER

By any conventional standards, Irvin Kershner has had one of the most unconventional careers of any Hollywood filmmakers. Completely unpredictable, he's been responsible for such striking, independent-minded features as THE HOODLUM PRIEST, THE LUCK OF GINGER COFFEY, A FINE MADNESS, THE FLIM-FLAM MAN and LOVING—all of them small gems which scrutinized the human condition with humor and poignancy. On a larger scale, Kershner was responsible for RETURN OF A MAN CALLED HORSE, a sequel vastly superior to the original; NEVER SAY NEVER AGAIN, Sean Connery's return to the role of James Bond (Connery had previously starred for Kershner in 1966's A FINE MADNESS, one of the first films to break his Bondian mold during the period in which he was best known for playing the suave superspy), and perhaps most notably, was charged by George Lucas with the task of directing THE EMPIRE STRIKES BACK. . . the second in the STAR WARS trilogy, and considered by many to be the richest and most visually and emotionally complex of the three.

And what's where the frustration sets in. In this remarkable interview, Kershner discusses with great thoughtfulness and clarity his feelings regarding the depiction of on-screen violence. At that time, as the reader will discover within, he was planning to direct a film entitled THE WHITE CROW, in which Robert Duvall was to portray Nazi mass murderer Adolf Eichmann. Unfortunately, this project never got off the ground, and instead, Kershner made ROBOCOP 2, which was savaged by the critics for the very excesses that he rails against in this interview. Perhaps this is an indication of how some filmmakers, in order to keep working, are sometimes forced to toil on projects which are inappropriate to their sensibilities.

Kershner's all-encompassing background in the arts, including painting, graphic design, still photography and music, laid the groundwork for his surefootedness as a director. He began to work in features only after learning to become a complete moviemaker with 300 documentaries shot around the world. In addition to his considerable work in features, Kershner has also done some excellent work for television, receiving Emmy Award nominations for both RAID

ON ENTEBBE and TRAVELING MAN, and helming the pilot episode of Steven Spielberg's elaborate underwater science fiction program, SEAQUEST DSV.

An inspiration to the generation of filmmakers that suceeded his own, Kershner was cast by one admirer, Martin Scorsese, as Zebedee in THE LAST TEMPTATION OF CHRIST. And after encountering Kershner's biblical mien and stentorian voice in person, one can certainly understand why.

MICHAEL SINGER: *What fascinates me about your career is that I can't make clear connections between your films in terms of subject matter or stylistic consistency. You just seem to be a complete filmmaker, whatever the project.*

IRVIN KERSHNER: I've been accused of not having a point of view because of it, but actually it's by design. I can't understand how people can have the same point of view year after year. There are scripts that I've worked on and then put aside for three or four years. Then people come back and say, "Hey, we'd like to make that film." I re-read the script and say, "I don't see it that way anymore, I don't believe it anymore, that belongs to some other time, place and sensibility. I don't want to make it." People expect you to be consistent but I think that's very uncreative. The creative process has to do with inconsistency. I don't see how you can have art without ambiguity.

Q: *The film industry seems to expect formulas and exactitudes.*

A: It looks for last year's successes, repeated this year so you can't recognize that it's a repeat. That's what's called "commercial." It's safe. Machine-made products do work and you see them all the time. TOP GUN was a total machine-made product. It was a wonderful job, very commercial, and very sound filmmaking. But I don't think it had anything to do with film as a humanizing media, which is what I think it should be—something which makes you feel for other people. It gives you an experience that you can't have in your real life. You can commit incest, you can murder, you can steal millions of dollars, you can punch out your enemies—and it's all done through other characters. That's what I call the humanizing element. You don't have to do it with your own life. You can experience it through the dramatic form. And as a result, I think film releases tensions.

Q: *Well, one common thread which does run through all your films is the thread of recognizable humanity, which is one reason why THE EMPIRE STRIKES BACK is usually thought of as the best of the STAR WARS trilogy. Even your one television movie, RAID ON ENTEBBE, had unusual emotional impact.*

A: It had a special problem, in that we were dealing with Jews—who everyone agrees, especially Jews themselves, are emotional to the point of sentimentality. We had a big job with RAID ON ENTEBBE, because we could not allow the drama to become sentimental. We needed to maintain a certain element of truth. In fact, I pushed the actors over the edge towards a certain coldness. I said, "Hold it in, don't let it show, feel it, but don't exploit it." If you look at RAID ON ENTEBBE closely, you'll see that there's a certain reserve to the people—they know they're in great danger, and there's nothing they can do to get out. But they have a certain dignity. I call it "post-Holocaust awareness."

Q: *I understand that you're now preparing a film which deals with the Holocaust.*

A: Yes. It's called THE WHITE CROW, with Glenn Close and Robert Duvall, and we'll be shooting it in Argentina, New York and Israel. It's not so much a film about the Holocaust as it is about responsibility. Robert Duvall plays Adolf Eichmann, a man who was a "good soldier," who was "only following orders." I had in mind Colonel Oliver North, Poindexter, some of the people who worked for Nixon, and what the Army propagates. An order is given and you're supposed to carry it out. Well, what if it's an order that in your mind is a crime against humanity? What if it's an unjustified bit of violence you're asked to do? Do you have a right to say it's unjustified? What would have happened if during World War I, the soldiers in the trenches said, "Walt a minute, this is ridiculous. They're sending us in against machine guns. We'll be wiped out just so we can gain three feet of earth." A lot of men would have lived, maybe. So you have to investigate. Who gives the orders? I think the most important thing is to question everything. Maybe it's my Zen training, but I believe that everything should be scrutinized. As the Jews say, "You're supposed to question everything but the existence of God."

Q: *So you're concerned with making films which have the audacity to induce the audience to think?*

A: I think you learn a great deal through films. . . about yourself, because you are feeling through characters who are in trouble, and you see how they solve them. You see how characters react to each other. I think that's how you learn. You have a more profound experience if there's art element of truth in the psychology of the character. If it's strictly melodrama, then I don't think you learn very much. Then I think it's what we call pure entertainment, although I think the greatest entertainment is also an insightful learning experience. Not that I'm didactic about this. . . when I saw GONE WITH THE WIND, I learned a hell of a lot about the Civil War. I also learned about how men and women act with each other. It enhanced my life. On the other hand, there are so many films that I see that I wish I hadn't gone to, because I don't want to have the memory in my unconscious. I don't want to see severed limbs floating around, bullet holes ripping people apart, people screaming in pain. I'll see it if it's a war documentary, but I've yet to see any war film that depicts violence in battle as it really is. I was in the war and I've seen it happen and believe me, men don't die that easily-they scream and holler and carry on and weep and know they're dying and it's a pitiful, terrible, horrible thing. In the phony pictures that we've come to expect through TV and film, the bad guy catches a bullet and he's dead. It just isn't right.

Q: *It occurs to me that you've never treated violence lightly in your films, even though some of them have required a good deal of it. Haven't you ever wanted to make a war film to set the record straight?*

A: No, because nobody would go to see it.

Q: *Are there any war films that you admire?*

A: Stanley Kubrick's last film, FULL METAL JACKET. Because when that Vietnamese girl was dying at the end of the film, you saw the awareness of death in her eyes. She wanted to die. The whole film was based on that moment, but the worst violence was what occurred afterwards, when one moment the Matthew

Modine character shoots her, and the next moment he's marching with his fellow Marines and they're singing. He's unaffected by what has happened, and that's the worst violence of all—the violence of the soul. To kill and just forget about it, not even to think about it. You're just singing a song. Terrible.

Q: *Kubrick's point seemed to be that such dehumanization is the worst result of any war or military training.*

A: You can do anything to people as long as you dehumanize them.

Q: *You did make one film which directly addressed genocide, and that was RETURN OF A MAN CALLED HORSE, which I thought was a much more serious effort than the first film.*

A: I did the second film because I was supposed to do the first one, but National Genera/couldn't make up its mind so I went and did LOVING for Columbia instead. I wasn't happy with the first MAN CALLED HORSE, which I thought was fragmented and sentimental. When the chance came to do the second one, even though the script was a comic book story, I said I wanted to do it. It was a lot of hard work trying to get the script to work, and to do justice to the Indians in the process. I did a lot of research in Sioux country. I went to Rosebud, attended different festivals, met some medicine men, read dozens of books. The genocide you mention of the white man against the Indians took many forms. One way was to destroy the religious life of the Indians, who couldn't understand how the white man walked into a little building for an hour on Sunday and called himself religious. Another way was to destroy the buffalo. The white man felt that if they could wipe out the buffalo, the Indians would just disappear, because so much of their sustenance came from those animals. I felt a great respect for the Plains Indians, what they were and how they treated each other and the courage that they had.

Q: *Some of your most notable films were small and very offbeat, like A FINE MADNESS, which featured Sean Connery in his first big studio non-Bond role after he had started the series.*

A: I did make some small pictures. THE HOODLUM PRIEST was a bit of a statement against capital punishment, which I still do not believe in. Then I made THE LUCK OF GINGER COFFEY in Canada with Robert Shaw, which was a wonderful experience. Another film I liked very much was THE FLIM-FLAM MAN, with George C. Scott. It didn't make it commercially, but it has a lot of fans.

Q: *As does LOVING, which has really become a cult classic. I find an interesting parallel between A FINE MADNESS in the 60s and UP THE SANDBOX in the 70s, because you took huge commercial stars and cast them in films that were utterly unconventional.*

A: Well, Barbra wanted to make UP THE SANDBOX and I said that I didn't know if audiences were going to want to see her in it. But she said, "Look, I don't care if it doesn't make any money. I want to play an ordinary person, a real person, a woman, a mother, a wife." She did and I thought she was great. When the picture came out, some of the critics loved it and some thought it was a bore. But I got a letter from Sam Peckinpah, of all people, who wrote "I just saw UP THE SAND-BOX and think it's an absolutely stunning picture." Would you believe that Sam Peckinpah said that about a woman's lib movie? You see, we tend to categorize people.

Q: You began your career directing very low budget films. . .

A: No, I started out making documentaries—I did 300 of them, all over the world, before I ever got into features.

Q: Were these documentaries for television?

A: No, first I worked for USC, the World Health Organization, the United Nations, UNESCO, and then finally did a three-year television program called "Confidential File." I directed, photographed and edited all these films, and had only one assistant. I would make one documentary a week, and that's how I learned about directing before I ever did a feature fill. I put millions of feet through a camera before I ever walked onto the set of STAKEOUT ON DOPE STREET, which was my first film.

Q: I'm sure that Roger Corman was delighted that he had a young director who already knew the ropes.

A: Corman had little to do with it. He simply put up a few dollars, and that was it. When the picture was finished, he went out and sold it. He had something to do with the title, though. I wanted to call it A NIGHT ON THE RAINBOW, which is what happens to a dope addict—he gets all the dope he needs and has a night on the rainbow. But Roger wanted to call it STAKEOUT ON DOPE STREET, and I'll never forgive him for that. I love him though. . . he's helped more people than anybody in this business.

Q: Incredible to think how many directors started out on Corman pictures.

A: He's done a great job, and not because of any altruistic motives. That's why I like him. He says, "Come and work cheap for me. If you learn, fine. If you don't, get out and sell insurance."

Q: What happened after you finished STAKEOUT?

A: I got a contract from Warner Bros. for seven years, but I left after a year—I didn't want to make any of the films they wanted me to do. I then made a little picture for Paramount called THE YOUNG CAPTIVES, which cost $190,000. They did very well on it, and then I made THE HOODLUM PRIEST. But it was very hard, because I never felt that I was part of the establishment. I didn't call in the favor of stars, I went to few parties. In fact, George Lucas said something interesting when he asked me to do THE EMPIRE STRIKES BACK. I said, "George, why do you want me?"—because I knew that Fox was asking him to find a young director, and I'm not that young anymore—and George said, "Because you know everything a director's supposed to know, but you're not Hollywood." I asked him to let me think about it, because I wasn't sure that I wanted to do the follow-up to the most successful film ever made up to that time. I talked some more with George, and he was totally honest. He said, "Remember, it will be years of work." It ended up being almost three years of intense labor. Finally, I said okay, but I had to have a lot of freedom. That was fine with him, so I sat down with George and Larry Kasdan and we worked on the script for three months. Larry was great. We all threw ideas into the pot and molded the story. Then I went to England and began storyboarding. George stayed in California and never interfered. We had wonderful communication, and I shot the picture in six months to the day. There were only two weeks of outdoor shooting in Norway, where it was 26 below zero on the first day of shooting. The rest of the time, I never left the studio. Everything was done indoors. There were 64 huge, killer sets that had to be lit and prepared for special effects. The production was a nightmare of logistics, but I really loved it. All the actors were involved and helpful.

Q: *The obvious question would have to be what in your directing background, as extensive as it was, could possibly have prepared you for the immensity of such a project?*

A: I learned on EMPIRE. I learned by doing it, and that's the greatest way to learn. I remembered what George said at the beginning of production—"Remember, nothing's going to work"—and he was right. Every day was a challenge. There were times when everybody got sick and everything was falling apart. Every weekend I had to lay out the shots for the next week, because I never had a chance to see the sets—they weren't finished until I walked on them the night before or the morning I was to shoot. The moment we finished shooting on a set it was gone. Boom. A huge, complicated set would just disappear because they had to build the next one. I'd walk on the set and my feet would stick to the wet paint. . . 64 sets built on seven stages.

Q: *How in the world do you keep a consistent tone shooting under those conditions for six months?*

A: Because I had been an editor and a cameraman myself. Had I not had that experience, I couldn't have done it. And George was able to keep a consistent tone because he's a great editor and knows what story he wants to tell.

Q: *I clearly feel that EMPIRE was the best of the trilogy, because the characters were deepened and the story was darkened. How did you view your creative task when you took on the film?*

A: THE EMPIRE STRIKES BACK was the second of a three-act play. I couldn't have an upbeat action ending, because a second act never does. I was aware that I was making an advertisement for the third act. I had to do it by humanizing the characters and keeping their problems hanging in the balance so you'd want to follow them into the next act.

Q: *Did you have an interest in science fiction films or literature before you directed EMPIRE?*

A: No, I didn't know anything about it then, and I still don't read science fiction books. What I did research, though, were fairytales. . . because if you look at it closely, the trilogy is a fairytale and not science fiction.

Q: *And you found the darkness that is at the heart of most fairytales.*

A: All fairytales are dark. You don't have sentimental fairytales. That only happens when they rewrite them for children.

Q: *Did you think you were running a risk by making the film too dark?*

A: No, the quality of a melodrama depends on the power of the antagonist. And we had two great antagonists in Darth Vader and the Emperor.

Q: Why didn't you direct RETURN OF THE JEDI?

A: I would have liked to, but at the time, I didn't encourage it because it would have meant another three years on one film.

Q: Yet, your next project was also a huge undertaking—NEVER SAY NEVER AGAIN, which returned Sean Connery to James Bond.

A: We shot the film in five countries. You know, there's one scene where Sean and Kim Basinger are on a horse galloping across the parapet of a castle, which is really two castles in the south of France cut together. Then they jump off the parapet into the water. For the approximate 20 seconds of screen time, we shot the castle in France; the jump was in Spain, the landing was done in the Bahamas, the underwater shots were filmed in Florida and the miniature was done in America.

Q: You have homes in both America and England. Is it important for you as an artist to keep yourself away from Hollywood for much of the time?

A: I've found traveling to be very important, but now I've been overstimulated, so I'm writing and planning and I'm going to do some teaching. My ideas flow when I'm with young people, and I like very much the idea of giving something back.

Q: Speaking of which, how did it come to pass that Irvin Kershner, director, was cast by Martin Scorsese to play Zebedee, an ancient Israelite, in THE LAST TEMPTATION OF CHRIST?

A: I was in New York City about five years ago visiting the casting agent Cis Corman, who's a friend of mine. At the time, Scorsese was supposed to do LAST TEMPTATION for Paramount with Aidan Quinn starring. He came into the office and said, "Hey, I've got a great idea. I want you to play Zebedee in my film." He took me into the next room and shot a test with me and Aidan, then called me back a couple of days later for another reading. I didn't hear a thing for weeks, and about a month later I got a telegram telling me that I'd been cast and they'd contact my agent. Then I got yet another telegram a month later telling me that the film had been canceled. That was the end of it for years until I got another telegram from Scorsese telling me to get on a plane and come to Morocco. I shot in a Berber village for nine days. It was tough, but I loved watching Scorsese work.

Q: So what is Irvin Kershner's opinion, as a director, of Irvin Kershner, the actor?

A: It's terribly difficult to watch yourself on screen. I looked up there and saw a stranger. I didn't think it was me. I would have liked to have done more with the character, and been freer, but people tell me it's okay. I can understand why actors get so discouraged when they see themselves up on the screen. You feel you could have done it better.

Q: But I thought you created a wonderful, angry biblical character. How much of you is in Zebedee?

A: Zebedee is angry, he's furious. I don't think of myself as angry anymore, although I think I was for a long time. People change. That's why I don't believe in consistency, which brings us back to the beginning of our conversation. The consistent person is usually the dull person. What we need in this business are some great moguls and great producers, people who aren't afraid to take a chance and try out new things. The business of filmmaking has become so commercial. I think it's a shame the way the studio system has gone, because it was calculated to train people, keep people working, actors and directors and craftsmen. Well, that machine is gone now. And in this country we don't have the filmmaking atmosphere that exists in Europe. When Ingmar Bergman or Federico Fellini decide to make a new film, all their people show up. Why? Because there's such a thing as loyalty. You might be making less money, you might have to wait three months for work, but they will show up because it's important to make that film with that director. And I think that kind of loyalty is so necessary. Film is an expression. You're not documenting scenery, you're revealing the human heart. The greatest landscape in film is the human face. Well, something has happened in our time and it's only profit that seems to count, not what the film says or what it can do for people. We are living in a time of moral indifference. . . but I think it will change.

F I L M O G R A P H Y

I R V I N   K E R S H N E R
b. April 29, 1923 - Philadelphia, Pennsylvania
STAKEOUT ON DOPE STREET Warner Bros., 1958
THE YOUNG CAPTIVES Paramount, 1959
THE HOODLUM PRIEST United Artists, 1961
A FACE IN THE RAIN Embassy, 1963
THE LUCK OF GINGER COFFEY Continental, 1964, Canadian
A FINE MADNESS Warner Bros., 1966
THE FLIM-FLAM MAN 20th Century-Fox, 1967
LOVING Columbia, 1970
UP THE SANDBOX National General, 1972
S*P*Y*S 20th Century-Fox, 1974, British-U.S.
THE RETURN OF A MAN CALLED HORSE United Artists, 1976
RAIN ON ENTEBBE (TF) ☆ Edgar J. Scherick Associates/20th Century-Fox TV, 1977
EYES OF LAURA MARS Columbia, 1978
THE EMPIRE STRIKES BACK 20th Century-Fox, 1980
NEVER SAY NEVER AGAIN Warner Bros., 1983
TRAVELING MAN (CTF) ☆ HBO Pictures, 1989
ROBOCOP 2 Orion, 1990
SEAQUEST DSV (TF) Amblin TV/Universal TV, 1993

STANLEY $\mathcal{K}$RAMER

In the pre-auteur days of Hollywood, when directors' names meant about as much to general audiences as the grips' and gaffers', Stanley Kramer was instantly recognizable and identifiable with quality and topicality. Working his way up the movie ladder as a researcher, film editor, writer and associate producer, Kramer formed his own independent production company after World War II military service. Unafraid from the start of taking on ambitious projects and "big issue" films, Kramer produced such classics as CHAMPION, HOME OF THE BRAVE, THE MEN, CYRANO DE BERGERAC, HIGH NOON, THE WILD ONE and THE CAINE MUTINY. In the mid-1950s, he began directing, and with his third film—the iconoclastic racial drama THE DEFIANT ONES—Kramer established a credo of technical excellence and social provocation.

Working outside of the studio system, Kramer was able to tackle a wide variety of such sensitive topics as nuclear holocaust (ON THE BEACH), fundamentalist Christianity vs. scientific fact (INHERIT THE WIND), German guilt and retribution (JUDGMENT AT NUREMBERG and SHIP OF FOOLS), black/white relationships (GUESS WHO'S COMING TO DINNER and the Kramer-produced PRESSURE POINT), Sixties student rebellion (R.P.M.) and nature vs. human nature (BLESS THE BEASTS AND CHILDREN). His one great comedy epic, IT'S A MAD, MAD, MAD, MAD WORLD, was a trenchant and very contemporary commentary on man's endless greed, couched in a star-studded Cinerama spectacular. Kramer was honored with three Best Director Academy Award nominations and received a special Oscar, the Irving Thalberg Award, in 1961.

When I met with Kramer, he was in vibrant health and spirits, having recently moved back to Los Angeles after a sojourn in Seattle, where he was active in both media and education. He was developing several projects, among them CHERNOBYL, the story of the Soviet nuclear power plant disaster, and POLONAISE, which chronicled the life of Polish Solidarity leader Lech Walesa. Unfortunately, David Puttnam's unceremonious departure from Columbia Pictures doomed the former, and the latter also never left the ground. Sadly, Kramer's last feature is still THE RUNNER STUMBLES (1979), as the twin devils of ageism and ignorance struck him from the New Hollywood's list of employable filmmakers.

But there's now, thankfully, a healthy backlash to an elitist critical consensus which marked Kramer as the classic Hollywood kneejerk liberal. Anyone insightful enough to see Stanley Kramer in proper perspective would note him as a revolutionary force in Hollywood who utilized both his power and his talents to present troubling issues through films which nevertheless refused to sacrifice their appeal to a mass audience. As we approach the millennium in our jaded, cynical states, it's nearly impossible to recall the shockwaves that rolled through the audiences as they watched Sidney Poitier kiss Katharine Houghton in GUESS WHO'S COMING TO DINNER. This may seem like a limp gesture from the hindsight of our times, but at that moment, it was a taboo-breaker almost as amazing as watching Marlon Brando, Maria Schneider and that stick of butter in LAST TANGO IN PARIS five years later. However, between 1967, when DINNER was released, and 1972, when LAST TANGO appeared, there was a little matter called the Vietnam War and all the socio-political tremors that resulted from it. Kramer was always at the edge in more innocent times, reminding everyone that it was a less than innocent world that surrounded them.

MICHAEL SINGER: *Why did you leave Hollywood in the first place, and why did you decide to return?*

STANLEY KRAMER: Well, I was away for about six years or so, and the reason I left is that I felt that after being reasonably progressive for many years, maybe I had fallen half a step behind. And I thought that by getting out I could find some answers. Well, I didn't find any answers in the time I was gone. I wrote a column for the Seattle Times and hosted a television show and taught at the university, but I was just asking more questions. Now, if the mark of an educated man is to be able to ask the right questions but not necessarily to provide the answers, than I am highly educated. But that doesn't make it any more satisfying. Eventually, though, I did feel that somehow—in all the things I was feeling and the questions I was asking—there was still a place for me in Hollywood.

Q: *When you returned to L.A., did you already have the Chernobyl project in hand, or were you approached with it afterwards?*

A: No, I didn't have it in mind at all when I came back. One of the reasons that David Puttnam talked with me about the project is that he had been in the Soviet Union and they had talked about trying to work out some cooperative deal—not a co-production, mind you, but a cooperative idea. The Chernobyl film is one of three that I've been working on, and it's just taking time to develop. We've got a Soviet writer on it who's doing a treatment, which won't be due for quite a bit. And then an American writer will take over, and then we need to lay the plans for where we're going to shoot it, how we' re going to shoot, where to blow the top off the nuclear plant. . . and that's going to take time.

Q: *This Chernobyl project seems to make sense for you to work on, because you've had an association with the Soviet Union that considerably predates anyone else in Hollywood.*

A: I can remember the first time they had a sizable delegation of Americans at the Moscow Film Festival—there were about twenty people—and they brought us on stage before they showed the American film entry. I think that year I was the first American juror they'd ever had. At any rate, all twenty of us were up there. . . and they were very nice to everybody. . . but when I was introduced they had a staged demonstration! Everybody rose and applauded. And all of the American delegation was looking at me as though I was the leader of the American Communist Party. It was rather strange and embarrassing, but it was due to the fact that they had seen so many films that I had made. They were at that time pirated, actually, because they never paid to buy them. And maybe I was considered somewhat critical of the American way because of the films I had made, although they were not intended that way. Now, isn't it amazing that all of the writers and directors and poets and painters who talked with me so intimately 25 years ago about what they dreamed of and what they wanted have got it in some part now? I just returned from a visit to the Soviet Union and I think that glasnost is real. I don't think that it's just politics. Implementation, of course, is something else. I won't comment on that. . . we'll see.

Q: *Being looked upon as something of a radical and a maverick in the film industry is nothing new to you, though. When people talk about your films as being socially conscious they have to look back on not only the films you directed, but produced as well, such as* HOME OF THE BRAVE *and* THE MEN.

A: Well, there's a certain amount of timing involved in terms of being socially conscious. I can point out to you my experiences with Lieutenant Calley. I attended his court-martial and had the rights to the whole story of My Lai, but I couldn't get that financed for love or money. I ended up doing a special on television about the court-martial just to get it out of my system. But they would not finance a film about Vietnam at that time.

Q: *Is there any chance of that project being revived now because of the current plethora of Vietnam films?*

A: I think it's too late. This was the definitive story about Vietnam, about one man—the only man—ever to be convicted of an atrocity in Vietnam. One lieutenant for us all.

Q: *The story still remains to be told.*

A: Well, the story still remains to be told certainly from the Vietnamese standpoint. But look, somebody had to break the line. And they finally did, because you couldn't touch a Vietnam story for years.

Q: *But you were breaking the lines all over the place throughout your career.*

A: That's probably a dangerous statement. . . at least for *me* to make. . . it's alright if *you* make it. My own feeling is that I grew up in the Roosevelt years of great social change, which seemed to me to be the road to drama, real drama. You felt there was drama in these issues, why wouldn't people go for that? But sometimes you were in for a surprise. I produced a story about paraplegic war veterans called THE MEN, and Radio City Music Hall bought the film. . .

Q: . . . Starring an unknown young actor named Marlon Brando. . .

A: The Music Hall booked it, and wouldn't you know that the first week we opened, the war in Korea broke out and nobody wanted to go see it. It's all timing sometimes.

Q: I want to go back to something you said before. . . that you felt you had gotten a half step behind the rest of Hollywood. Did you really feel that way or was that a case of you starting to believe your own press? Because it seemed at that time you were really taking it on the chin from certain film critics.

A: First of all, I understand critics. Critics never really bothered me—they may have hurt the grosses of my films, but they never bothered me personally, because I did not take myself too seriously. I took the job seriously, but not myself. And my standards for what I wanted to achieve with those films was much higher than what the critics imagined, so to me, all of those films fell short anyway. That's a true evaluation. And falling short, I never was disappointed with the reviews. I always wanted to get good reviews, but then I sometimes got wonderful reviews and the pictures didn't do business anyway. I remember standing outside the Leicester Square Theatre in London with a handful of reviews that I could have written myself on INHERIT THE WIND. And nobody came. And nobody came all over the world when that film was released. Later, as a new generation discovered it on television, it became a minor classic. How can you tell? It's very dangerous to say you're ahead of your time—because you're not. You have great pretension when you make a film about something, and it had better measure up or you're very vulnerable.

Q: You never turned away from issues, though.

A: I didn't turn away—I embraced them. The National Rifle Association took me apart on BLESS THE BEASTS AND CHILDREN. They said I was a "Bambi-ist," which was Gun Magazine phraseology for people who anthropomorphize animals so they can't shoot them. I was the Anti-Christ on INHERIT THE WIND because in the movie Spencer Tracy says that the Bible is a book—a good book, but not the only book. That was murderous to them. Then the films about the blacks and the reactions from both sides. . . James Baldwin said that I didn't understand the black soul. Well, I'm not black! I tried, and nobody else was trying. I got as close as I could get from my viewpoint. It's wonderful to achieve some modicum of success in terms of people reacting to what you do. And when they don't react to a highly controversial piece of material, when you go to a preview and realize, "My God, this is cottage cheese!"—it's brutal.

Q: Did the "cottage cheese" reaction happen very often?

A: It happened. . . most notably when I took a dip into musical fantasy on a movie called THE 5,000 FINGERS OF DR. T.

Q: A classic!

A: Yeah. . . Now he says it's a classic! But my God, half the audience got up and left after Fifteen minutes at the first preview. It wasn't what I wanted it to be. It was created by Dr. Seuss, who wrote the script, and we worked very hard. I didn't direct it, but I certainly supervised it and dreamed it, and it never got to where I wanted.

Some of the music did, but it never came off to reach out and gather in that great audience out there. It was philosophical and intellectual and surrealist.

Q: *I think we can safely acknowledge that that film was considerably ahead of its time.*

A: I won't acknowledge it. I did films of the time as I felt them, thought them, dreamed them, and my feeling is—and it is an absolutely irrefutable position-that if a film is good enough it will triumph over all those adversities, including being ahead of its time. And if it isn't, it's going to have a rough road. Well, I had a rough road a lot of times.

Q: *It seems like each film you made won you enemies on one ground or another.*

A: Yeah, but it brought together a lot of people too. You know a person by your enemies, I guess. The idea was to bring the enemies out into the open. But I have a feeling that no film ever really changes anyone's opinion. I think if two people come out of a theatre in Kansas City, and one says to the other "I never thought of it that way before"—that's the most you can expect. You don't change their opinions. . . you provoke a certain chain of thinking. And that's a lot, it seems to me. You may plant a seed, but I don't think you change anyone's opinion.

Q: *You've worked with a lot of great actors. Any favorites you care to talk about?*

A: I had the good fortune to have in my life a man named Spencer Tracy. The audience could identify with Tracy—he was Mr. Everyman. Now, in GUESS WHO'S COMING TO DINNER, since his character objected to the marriage of the black man and his white daughter, I tried to put into Tracy's mouth all of the things that the audience sitting in the theatre would be thinking. And he stated them—"do you know what this is going to be like. . . this isn't going to be easy because you know what people are going to think. . . what about your children. . . ?" and all the rest. And then when his character switches, when he says "If you're in love, no matter what anybody thinks, get married—screw all those people"—the audience says "yeah, right," and goes with that emotionally. I wish I could tell you that I knew in advance that the film was going to reach out to so many people, but I didn't. Too many haven't, and I thought they would. But GUESS WHO'S COMING TO DINNER captured what people were thinking and what they were really feeling. I loaded the deck, of course I had Katharine Hepburn and Spencer Tracy and Sidney Poitier. And sometimes there were objections—why did I have to make the black man so personable, so intelligent, so educated? Well, it was because I was trying to make the point that since Poitier's character had all those qualities, if there was an objection to him marrying a white woman, it could only be because he was black!

Q: *You produced for almost ten years before you started directing. But was directing always in your game plan?*

A: Oh, it was. I always was schooled, from the time I was a writer and film editor, to be a director. But I became a producer because the producer is the boss—it was the only way I could get off the ground. And when I went to a lettuce grower—as good a source for film financing as anybody— he asked me a very key question. . . "well, who are you?" Well, I wasn't anybody. It's very hard to describe who you are when you're not really anybody and you haven't done anything. But I was a dreamer. So I told the lettuce grower, "Who am I? I'm the fellow who's got the ideas, that's who!"

Q: *You took the independent route almost your entire career, avoiding the studio system as much as possible. Do you think you could have made the films you were doing if you had stayed within the studios?*

A: Maybe. It depends upon wielding power and where the power structure is. If you're in a major studio set-up and your last one was a big hit, you tell them "this one is going to go, this is it," and they say, "well, he was right the last time!" It's all a matter of power. Independently, I had to go out and promote each film, so that made a difference. And maybe it was more provocative or exciting.

Q: *I've always thought of you as a director with an invisible technique. You never threw fancy camera angles in the audience's face.*

A: Oh, yes I did! In JUDGMENT AT NUREMBERG, for example, I did 360 degree turns with the camera. The whole crew was carrying all of the equipment with them so that when they came around they wouldn't be photographing them-selves. I think that it depends on the situation—any place where technique or angles or camera dominates the whole situation, there's something wrong from my standpoint. I always felt that I was dealing with characters and ideas, and that's what interested me the most. Whatever is called technique or style has to be varied according to what you're doing.

Q: *Speaking of technical virtuosity, SHIP OF FOOLS seemed to use an extraordinary rear projection system for the illusion of the ship—which was, I know, a studio set—being at sea.*

A: We never went to sea at all. That wasn't rear projection, but Paramount's VistaVision-sized screen—a giant process screen. They were extremely well done and gave me great control, because we built the ship on stage and there it was. The technique was buried. We were doing a story about people, after all, and sometimes it was hard to keep it all under control. After all, Katherine Anne Por-ter wrote a book called SHIP OF FOOLS which was several hundred pages long. It would have been a six hour movie if we had done it all. And here we were with a two-and-a-half hour movie with dozens of characters, and it took a lot of editing and welding together of many incidents to keep it all cohesive. I needed to work in those controlled circumstances.

Q: *There's been a lot of talk about restoring the original three-hour roadshow version of* IT'S A MAD, MAD, MAD, MAD WORLD.

A: Yeah, there's a group that's formed itself into a whole army who want to restore it, and I don't know where to get the film for restoration. There were some arbitrary cuts made to establish time limits after the roadshow run, and the roadshow itself didn't have some of the scenes about which they're talking, which were in the original script and were shot. But I can't even remember, after all these years, if I edited them out or if somebody else did. Those were the days when the Directors Guild was trying frantically to prevent those kinds of cuts. In those days we knew about those things and tried to protest, but it never got anywhere because the distributor was in charge of the film.

Q: Do you share this group's passion for restoring MAD, MAD WORLD?

A: I am passionate about it, but having lived with the reality of it for so many years, I know how difficult it is to find these pieces of film (Most of the cuts were found, and a restored version of IT'S A MAD, MAD, MAD, MAD WORLD was distributed on videotape and laserdisc by MGM/UA Home Video. -MS)

Q: Are you also involved in the battle against colorization? You made several beautiful black and white films—I cringe to think of watching THE DEFIANT ONES or SHIP OF FOOLS in color.

A: Well, I'm involved as a participant on the board of the Directors Guild of America. I can look at it very objectively. If you tried to put color into ON THE BEACH, what would you do—make the radioactive dust purple?!

F I L M O G R A P H Y

S T A N L E Y   K R A M E R

b. September 29, 1913 - New York, New York
NOT AS A STRANGER United Artists, 1955
THE PRIDE AND THE PASSION United Artists, 1957
THE DEFIANT ONES ★ United Artists, 1958
ON THE BEACH United Artists, 1959
INHERIT THE WIND United Artists, 1960
JUDGMENT AT NUREMBERG ★ United Artists, 1961
IT'S A MAD, MAD, MAD, MAD WORLD United Artists, 1963
SHIP OF FOOLS Columbia, 1965
GUESS WHO'S COMING TO DINNER ★ Columbia, 1967
THE SECRET OF SANTA VITTORIA United Artists, 1969
R.P.M.* Columbia, 1970
BLESS THE BEASTS & CHILDREN Columbia, 1971
OKLAHOMA CRUDE Columbia, 1973
THE DOMINO PRINCIPLE Avco Embassy, 1977
THE RUNNER STUMBLES 20th Century-Fox, 1979

$\mathcal{M}$ARY $\mathcal{L}$AMBERT

Heaven forbid we should get politically or socially relevant here, but there's a simple, nagging fact that just won't go away—if you're a woman who makes movies in Hollywood, no matter how successfully, you're still going to have a tougher time getting work than your male counterparts.

We present for your consideration the case of Mary Lambert. After graduating with a painting degree from the Rhode Island School of Design, the Arkansas native became an award-winning director of short films and commercials. . . and then launched her pioneering work in rock videos. If you watched your MTV in the '80s (and who didn't?) and boogied down to Madonna's "Like A Virgin," "Material Girl" and "Like A Prayer"; Sting's "We'll Be Together Tonight"; Janet Jackson's "Nasty Boys" and "Control"; or Mick Jagger's "Say You Will" and "Throwaway," you were hearing their music but watching Mary Lambert's impressive imagery.

In 1986, Lambert made her feature directorial debut with SIESTA, a highly-acclaimed and controversial drama featuring a terrific cast that included Ellen Barkin, Jodie Foster, Julian Sands, Gabriel Byrne, Martin Sheen and Grace Jones. The film, which divided critics and outraged some, has become something of a cult favorite. So it came as a big surprise when Lambert's next feature assignment was the decidedly commercial adaptation of Stephen King's PET SEMATARY in 1989. The irony, of course, was that the film grossed more than a hundred million dollars, which is about $99.5 million more than SIESTA took in at the box office. That same year, Lambert received a CableACE Award nomination for her direction of "Collection Completed," an episode of HBO's popular *Tales From The Crypt*.

Needless to say, Lambert was besieged with offers from all Hollywood, right? Well, she might have been if her name was Martin Lambert, perhaps. But another two years went by before she got behind the camera again, returning to a more serious mode with Turner Entertainment's GRAND ISLE, based on a Kate Chopin novella and starring Kelly McGillis, Adrian Pasdar, Ellen Burstyn, Glenne Headly and Julian Sands.

Since then, Lambert directed PET SEMATARY II, the inevitable sequel to her big Paramount hit, as well as DRAGSTRIP GIRL, her entry in Showtime's retro-'50s REBEL HIGHWAY series, and the telefeature FACE OF EVIL. For 1998 release is CLUBLAND, which is hopefully a return to a more independent format. When I spoke with Lambert, she was on location for PET SEMATARY II, and offered no apologies for her foray back into blatant commercialism. It may not be the way it should be, but it's the way it is. . . until changes *really* come.

MICHAEL SINGER: *Forgive me for making you a symbol of sorts, but your career does seem to emblemize both the triumphs and travails of women filmmakers. It seems that no matter how much success comes, the struggle for work and basic respect goes on.*

MARY LAMBERT: I couldn't agree with you more. I've thought about it a lot. Women don't seem to get much recognition professionally from the press, or from their peers. I mean, women have been directing since the earliest part of this century. Dorothy Arzner made 17 movies with all the major stars of her day. Women just don't get recognition for what they do. And what's more, women don't give other women recognition either.

Q: *That's a very interesting point. Fact is, there are a lot of women producers and production executives, who seem no more eager to give women directors a break than their male peers.*

A: Well, some women have fought so hard for what they've got that it sometimes makes it tough for them to want to share the goods.

Q: *You've gone from prestigious rock videos to a highly experimental first feature SIESTA then to PET SEMATARY, which was hugely commercial, back to a "small" film with GRAND ISLE, and now you're shooting PET SEMATARY II. Would it be fair to say that your career possibly due to the reasons we've been discussing has been a little schizophrenic?*

A: I've heard that comment more than once. I'm not sure that it reflects conscious decisions that I've made. I want to have a career, and I want to do pictures that reach a public. I want to do work that has commercial viability. But there are some connections between all of my work that may not be immediately apparent. PET SEMATARY may be a very different movie from SIESTA, but I thoroughly enjoyed making it. There's a mysticism in Stephen King's work that I find very appealing.

Q: *Which explains, I suppose, why you've chosen to direct the sequel. . . not to mention the fact that the first film grossed over $100-million.*

A: Well, it's a gig. To be honest, GRAND ISLE is completed but doesn't have a distributor yet. You wait for your last project to propel you into the next one. But on a more positive note, as I said before, I really liked making the first PET SEMATARY, and on this one, I've been able to have more input into the script and therefore guide the project in a much more personal way.

Q: *Which does indicate some gaining of power within the studio system, which is not a waging of war for power's sake, but rather for art's sake. I guess this is a battle you've been fighting from the beginning of your feature career.*

A: It's a battle that can't be quit. You have to gain the authority to do what you want to do.

Q: Does this battle ever exhaust you?

A: It does right now. We're shooting 17 hours a day with two units shooting simultaneously, working with the editors, going to dailies. But there is something more exhausting than this. . . and that's trying to make a project happen. There's nothing more exhausting than putting time and effort into something that never happens. You always have to have that faith that it will all work out, that it could happen.

Q: Do you find though, that when you finally get back behind the camera after a period of attempting to get things going, that it re-energizes you for the next several years?

A: Oh yes. I'm convinced now that everything I want to do is going to happen. I'm convinced that I'm going to get it all worked out for myself.

Q: Looking back to the beginning of your career. . . like many others who found themselves swerving into filmmaking, you originally studied art. Did you become interested in making films at that time?

A: Yes, I became interested in film when I was attending the Rhode Island School of Design. Painting was in a really fallow period back then. . . people were calling anything a painting. I started to regard filmmaking as another way of doing a painting, an extension of that interest in conceptual art. It was a real revelation.

Q: The short film that you co-directed—RAPID EYE MOVEMENTS—as well as SIESTA and several of your rock videos, were highly experimental and very idealistic in their approach to free-form filmmaking.

A: That's true. I approached SIESTA in a completely idealistic manner. I knew that it would cause problems in the marketplace. I knew that its non-linear structure would confuse or even outrage some people. After all, linear structure in American films is a religion. . . a basic tenet. . . a dogma. I was bending that form, and it really divided people.

Q: But shaking people up is exciting and important, isn't it?

A: I guess so. . . and one thing that's certainly true is that I had no ulterior motive in making a movie that radical.

Q: Is it fair to say, though, that you do have an ulterior motive in making both PET SEMATARY movies?

A: Yeah, that's probably accurate. But there's a certain style that you can bring to genre films that's legitimate and fun. And I want to prove that. I can make movies for the public, which I already succeeded in doing with the first PET SEMATARY. I can do commercial work, and I enjoy commercial work. I don't want to limit the kinds of films I can or want to direct. I can have it both ways.

Q: In the way that people have of sexually stereotyping filmmakers, a lot of critics were shocked by how graphic the first PET SEMATARY was, as if a "woman's touch" would soften a horror film. It was a really tough movie.

A: I enjoyed that! I mean, anyone with a clear understanding of the world knows that it's often not pretty. Nature itself is not soft. You know, the mother lion will ferociously defend her cubs. And as for women taking an easier approach, it's important to remind people that matriarchies are some of the toughest societies on earth, and female deities and goddesses are some of the most fearsome.

Q: *So you don't mind being a bit scary?*

A: I have a lot to offer. . . my own point of view, and my own way of making movies. I don't mind being scary at all, but there's no reason for the industry—or anyone—to be frightened of a woman who just wants to keep directing.

F I L M O G R A P H Y

M A R Y   L A M B E R T

b. Arkansas
SIESTA   Lorimar, 1987, British
PET SEMATARY   Paramount, 1989
GRAND ISLE   Kelly McGillis Productions/Turner Pictures, 1991
PET SEMATARY II   Paramount, 1992
REBEL HIGHWAY: DRAGSTRIP GIRL (CTF)   Drive-In Classics Cinema/Showtime, 1994
FACE OF EVIL (TF)   Larry Thompson Entertainment CBS, 1996
CLUBLAND Gitlin Productions/Intrepid Entertainment, 1998

$\mathcal{B}$ARRY $\mathcal{L}$EVINSON

Barry Levinson is an "A-list" director with a difference. His films project rigorous intelligence, respect for the audience and unpredictability of both content and style that nearly always results in work of lasting import. His films can roughly be divided between the intimate, personal, alternately hilarious and touching reflections on life in his home city of Baltimore (DINER, TIN MEN, AVALON) and forays into a wide range of topics and backgrounds, whether the mythology of the Great American Pastime (THE NATURAL), Victorian special effects-driven fantasy (YOUNG SHERLOCK HOLMES), the humor and horror of an American "police action" (GOOD MORNING, VIETNAM), the tenuous relationship between a Sammy Glick-like young businessman and his autistic brother (the multiple Academy Award-winning RAIN MAN), a starstruck, visionary gangster (BUGSY), dangerous sexual politics (DISCLOSURE), an epic New York street story (SLEEPERS) or, most recently, an outrageous political satire (WAG THE DOG) shot nearly back-to-back with a cerebral science fiction thriller that went decidedly against the grain (SPHERE).

In other words, Levinson has always gone where the story has taken him, and that includes his medium-altering contributions to television, both network (HOMICIDE) or cable (OZ). Curiously enough, very little in Levinson's background would indicate his future in film. The son of a Baltimore businessman, as a young man Levinson did everything from selling encyclopaedias to used cars to part-time work in a TV station before packing his bags for Los Angeles and acting lessons. His first appearances were as a stand-up comic, and then a highly successful career as a writer, first on TV, and then for Mel Brooks on both SILENT MOVIE and HIGH ANXIETY. With his then-collaborator Valerie Curtin, Levinson also wrote such diverse screenplays for other filmmakers as . . . AND JUSTICE FOR ALL, INSIDE MOVES, BEST FRIENDS and UNFAITHFULLY YOURS, before trying his own hand with his own very personal script of DINER.

The results, it can honestly be said, are now classic, and were tremendously influential. Perched somewhere between an independent and mainstream film, DINER reveled in a naturalistic approach to story, dialogue and performance (it was the starmaking vehicle for nearly every main player, including Kevin Bacon, Mickey Rourke, Ellen Barkin, Daniel Stern, Paul Reiser and Steve Guttenberg) which has trickled down into dozens of imitative films, TV shows and even commercials. Levinson has managed to continue keeping one foot firmly planted in the personal (a new Baltimore-based film is promised in the near future), with the other following whatever leads suit his considerable imagination and range.

MICHAEL SINGER: *You shot your last two films, WAG THE DOG and SPHERE, nearly back-to-back. One was decidedly uncommercial, the other, it would seem, much more likely to be embraced. And yet, WAG THE DOG was the more successful of the two. Did that take you by surprise?*

BARRY LEVINSON: I was very pleasantly surprised that WAG did as well as it did, because satire is not a genre that really works well in America. I think you can count on your hand the number of political satires that have been made. So you're playing in a territory that has been very tough terrain. So yes, I was pleased that we were able to do some good business. I wouldn't have guessed it.

Q: *On the other hand, although you tried to refresh and subvert the science fiction genre with SPHERE, the reviews seemed mean-spirited.*

A: Well, I never understand that. I would understand it more if you just played the game, but sometimes if you're kind of reaching for something else—whether you ultimately succeed or not—you wouldn't assume to be treated with any kind of anger. But I think they assumed that I'm not supposed to be able to make those kinds of movies, and Dustin Hoffman isn't supposed to be in those type of films.

Q: *But in fact, you've worked in several genres: comedy, satire, drama, fantasy, suspense. When you go from project to project, what are you looking for?*

A: There are two sides to it. One is, if you're just reading, it's whatever catches your interest, holds it, and rattles around in your head in some way that doesn't let go, to the point where you say 'Oh, well, I've got to pursue this.' It's not like I'm looking for a particular agenda, it's simply the ideas you connect with. Now, in terms of what you might call the more personal films—the ones set in Baltimore, like DINER, TIN MEN and AVALON—those are self-generated. They are purely, internally generated. So it's two different ways of working, and I never decide which is when.

Some people deal with their careers in a much more calculated way, in terms of the image they want to present, and how they want to be perceived. That's all well and good, because packaging is obviously important in this world. I basically have just sort of gone wherever the hell something has gotten my attention, and then everything will fall wherever it falls. And when the dust clears, you take a look at your career, and you see what it is in retrospect. But it's the process, the examination of ideas and characters that you're pursuing, and stories that you want to tell. It's just purely the passion of it. When it's all said and done, who the hell knows? Reflection is less interesting to me than the pursuit.

Q: *Your films seem to take in the unpredictability of human nature, and generally go in unexpected directions, whatever genre they're in.*

A: I just like anything that's really about character, and that can reveal moments to us as an audience. I think that's always something that you make room for.

Q: *Individual scenes in your films often seem to have an immediate, almost improvisational quality. Do you ever allow your actors to improvise within the context of the scripted scenes?*

A: What I will do in any given scene, knowing what we need to accomplish, knowing and understanding the characters, is to find out what else can be added or what else can be said. What other moments can come about, if we were to explore the scene. In that respect, I've always improvised, only in the sense of testing the material. Whether the script is mine or another writer's, have we explored all of the boundaries of it? You can't simply say 'Alright, we're gonna make it all up, and it's gonna be wonderful.' Because that's not the way to work. But you do challenge the dialogue at all times, I think. So therefore, if the moment is right and an actor does something that's not exactly there in the script, it might open the door to something else that you need to explore, another moment, another beat.

Q: *You're known for developing relationships with certain actors which last through several films, including four collaborations with Dustin Hoffman, and two each with Robin Williams and Robert De Niro. What is it about working with them, for example, that makes it fun for you and creatively profitable?*

A: I just always enjoy actors who are always adventurous. It's always interesting, and the worst thing that happens is that you try something that doesn't quite work. It's only film, but there's always the possibility that we may discover a great moment. I love to work with actors like that, because at all times you're on the high wire.

Q: *Was directing always a goal for you, from your days of stand-up comedy and then screenwriting?*

A: No. If I were to think back, I would never have thought that I would have been a director or, for that matter, I never would have thought that I've have been a screenwriter. I never would have thought I would have been a comedy writer before that. All of those things sort of came step by step. At first, I started to write sketches, and I thought, 'Oh, I'd like to write something longer than a sketch.' Then I wrote a half-hour script, and said that I'd like to try something longer and more complex than that, which led to the next thing, and ventually to a screenplay.

And then, from writing the screenplay to saying, 'Well, what happens if I directed that screenplay?' I didn't start out with any pre-conceived ideas. They just sort of evolved naturally out of taking these various steps.

Q: *Had you directed anything at all before* DINER? *A television episode? A short film?*

A: No, I hadn't. I hadn't been planning it. I will say that I learned a lot during the period of time I worked with Mel Brooks as a writer, being around the set when he was directing, and then during the editing process. It was all very helpful to me, even though he has a specific style that he works in that ultimately I would say is very different from what I had in mind. But at least I saw the process. As I watched Mel work, I would wonder, 'Gee, I wonder what would happen if you did this, or how about if you did that?'

You know, what if and what if and what if. And then your brain begins to compute and begin to see certain things you would try. When I directed DINER, I tried to do those things I was curious about as a style. It's not like you're conscious of a style, though. But you begin to find a technique that works for you.

Q: Which for you was. . .

A: Which for me was to find a rather naturalistic way to put characters in motion, how they talk and interact with each other, as if everybody was making things up. I thought that was interesting. And I always wanted the camera to serve the piece. I never wanted the camera to get in front, to the point where we notice the shots and how it's all done, as opposed to the work itself. I never wanted the camera to become the star. I always think that the camera needs to be totally motivated by what is taking place in the scene. And any time that I can spot what the camera's doing in front of it all, would throw me out of whack. I wanted to be buried in the material.

Q: However, you made a tremendous stylistic leap from the naturalism of DINER to the grandiosity and romanticism of THE NATURAL.

A: It's funny. I wasn't even aware of it. But filming that kind of larger than life, mythical story kind of established, in retrospect, a film language. It's been mimicked in other movies and TV shows and commercials. But at the time, it just seemed correct for the story we were telling, and had never really been seen before. It was like stepping up to the plate and being a little bold, just like the character of Roy Hobbs that Robert Redford played in the movie. And being a little over the top was part of the humor of it all. When Glenn Close stands up, and because of the hat that she's wearing, and the way the sunlight is falling in late afternoon, almost looks as if she glows. . . I mean, that's kind of funny. It's a serious enough moment so that we can appreciate it and find the humor at the same time, as opposed to just making it campy. There needed to be dignified extravagance.

Q: Looking at your body of work, it strikes me as being very American in both locale and subject matter, with the exception of YOUNG SHERLOCK HOLMES. Is that a conscious choice?

A: No, but you're right. They are all very American themes and characters, and I like dealing with times in our history.

Q: Actually, with AVALON, THE NATURAL, BUGSY, GOOD MORNING, VIETNAM and SLEEPERS—all of them period pieces—we can almost track the story of 20th century America through the prism of your movies.

A: [laughs] I suppose that's true, but it really wasn't intentional.

Q: A great many writers, producers and directors who started in television have left it forever after they've achieved success in features. But you've stayed with it in a big way, changing the territory in the process with programs like HOMICIDE and OZ.

A: It just seemed appropriate. It's all about the material, and where they're best suited. So when HOMICIDE came along as an idea to develop as a feature, I thought it was better suited as a television series, to explore the subject on a weekly basis. And it turned out that HOMICIDE was perfect for television. OZ is pretty out there in exploring men in prison, and that was more appropriate for cable television.

Q: *What have been the personal high points of your career?*

A: It's hard to say. But obviously, getting a chance to do DINER as a writer/ director was great. I mean, the idea that you sit down and type 'Fade In - Baltimore'. . . and all of a sudden, somebody gives you money and you go to Baltimore. . . that was a great moment. And then, after the movie was finished, the studio was so down on it, saying that it was a worthless piece of junk that shouldn't even be released. That's obviously a *down* moment. . .

Q: *And all on the same movie!*

A: And then, all of a sudden, six weeks later, we ended up in one theatre in New York City, and suddenly it was time for celebrating. I went from the opportunity of directing DINER, which was thrilling, and then all of a sudden it was a piece of garbage in the eyes of the studio, and all of a sudden it's wonderful. You're up, down, all over the place.

Q: *And you've been on the roller coaster ever since.*

A: Since day one.

Q: *Have things become even crazier in dealing with the pressures of making movies since DINER?*

A: It's gotten more difficult in that as soon as the first weekend grosses became publicized, the second that the opening of a film was literally like rolling the dice on one weekend, the movie business changed forever. It's become much, much harder for individual expression to be part of the business. The fact is, some of the movies that were made upon a time are much more difficult to make now, because you can't feed the machinery the same way. It's a whole other game, you know? The movie as a piece of merchandising. What are the video possibilities, what are the ancillary markets, what about the action figures. . . all of these things are part of the business now. And it just makes everything that much harder.

Q: *Does that have anything to do with your move from Los Angeles to Northern California? Do you have more spiritual space to work in now?*

A: I think so. I think just the fact that you're not so immersed in it full time, all the time, is very beneficial to the creative process.

Q: *What's next? I've been hearing of everything from a Bobby Darin biography to a property about the 1906 San Francisco earthquake.*

A: I just wrote a fourth installment of the Baltimore movies.

Q: *Is this a follow-up to DINER?*

A: No. They all sort of go to different places, but in some ways interlock with one another. They're not sequels or prequels, but pieces of time in a particular location.

F I L M O G R A P H Y

BARRY LEVINSON

b. 1942 - Baltimore, Maryland
DINER   MGM/United Artists, 1982
THE NATURAL   TriStar, 1984
YOUNG SHERLOCK HOLMES   Paramount, 1985
TIN MEN   Buena Vista, 1987
GOOD MORNING, VIETNAM   Buena Vista, 1987
RAIN MAN ★★   MGM/UA, 1988
AVALON   TriStar, 1990
BUGSY ★   TriStar, 1991
TOYS   20th Century Fox, 1992
JIMMY HOLLYWOOD   Paramount, 1994
DISCLOSURE   Warner Bros., 1994
SLEEPERS   Warner Bros., 1996
WAG THE DOG   New Line Cinema, 1997
SPHERE   Warner Bros., 1998

$\mathcal{G}$ARRY $\mathcal{M}$ARSHALL

When THE FLAMINGO KID appeared, a few conspicuous eyebrows were raised in the motion picture industry. The surprise was that the praised serio-comic story of a Brooklyn teenager's getting of wisdom in the early 1960s was directed by Garry Marshall, who for 20 years had reigned as televison's most successful purveyor of popular comedy, having created such quintessential sitcoms as *Happy Days, Laverne and Shirley* and *Mork and Mindy*.

But when I met with the effortlessly hilarious, New York-accented Marshall, the best was yet to come. Following the middling reaction to OVERBOARD the following year, Marshall enjoyed his greatest successes with BEACHES and then the monster hit PRETTY WOMAN, which made a star of Julia Roberts and re-invented Richard Gere. His subsequent output has been decidedly mixed, but Marshall's strength remains his eye for small but significant human details, and ear for clever and often ringingly funny dialogue. Most recently, he helmed THE OTHER SISTER for Touchstone Pictures, starring Juliette Lewis and Diane Keaton.

If you've seen him on-screen, occasionally gracing such films as Albert Brooks' LOST IN AMERICA and his sister Penny Marshall's JUMPIN' JACK FLASH, it's easy to see how Garry Marshall's Bronx sensibilities made such headway in Hollywood.

MICHAEL SINGER: *You seem to be intent on giving comedy a human face in your feature films.*

GARRY MARSHALL: I'm trying to do comedy that has a little more depth to it, what I like to call an emotional comedy on the serious side.

Q: THE FLAMINGO KID *surprised a lot of critics who didn't expect such a serious film from Garry Marshall. And* NOTHING IN COMMON *certainly continues this style. It's a contrast to much of the work you did in television. Why did you move into features after twenty years of being the number one producer, writer, creator and director of* TV *comedy?*

A: Well, that's the reason. I was in television too long. I had done it for twenty years. I had done over a thousand situation comedies—that was the only type of show that interested me in television—and I had just done it for such a long time that I was no longer fighting scared. Tennessee Williams once said, "Security is a form of death"—not a happy man, Tennessee, you understand. . . he said a lot of things that depressed everyone around him—but every once in a while he said something I liked. To go into another field where I had to learn everything from the bottom up was very exciting. What I learned from television which helped me in filmmaking was discipline and not to be self-indulgent. There's no time for that in television. That's why people like Ron Howard, Rob Reiner, Jim Brooks and Penny Marshall basically bring pictures in on-budget. . . we're trained that way. But I was just a little too complacent, and television was no longer challenging in the particular arena I was in. The type of films I'm doing come as a little bit of a shock to some people. They always wrote nice things, but in a backhanded way. One man who wrote that I was the "Dean of Dreck", the "Chairman of Cheap", the "Champion of Cotton Candy Pop Art", went on to say how shocked he was that I did a wonderful picture like NOTHING IN COMMON that had depth, emotion and intelligence. Another man wrote that after NOTHING IN COMMON we must call Garry Marshall one of the most intelligent American filmmakers, which is very depressing, because this is the same man who gave us Laverne and Shirley. I do things that I like to see and that please me. Comedy is my tool, and how crazy the comedy or how serious the comedy or how emotional the comedy is up to me and the story. I think that my approach is not to do what everybody else is doing. In television I tried to do things that were counter to what went on. I had done The Odd Couple, a wonderful and very intelligent show. Prior to that, I had worked with Carl Reiner on The Dick Van Dyke Show. But then I noticed that a lot of people were doing those types of shows, and there was an opening for another type of program. Nostalgia was becoming popular in those days, but all of it was serious. So I made a comedy nostalgia program called Happy Days. There hadn't been one of those on since I Remember Mama. Then I also saw that there was a wave of shows featuring bright young women, all of whom had wonderful jobs, lovely clothes and looked like Mary Tyler Moore, because there were no blue collar girls on television at all. I also noticed that there was no physical comedy on anymore since Lucy left, so I gave Laverne and Shirley some of that stuff. With Mork and Mindy, I found somebody who had to be on television because nobody had ever seen a man work like this Robin Williams. Sometimes I built a show around a unique talent. I haven't done a movie that way yet, but I might. They did it with Prince in PURPLE RAIN and it worked. Then they let him take charge, and it went right into the toilet. . . He made himself purple! NOTHING IN COMMON to me was kind of a different approach to what I was doing in Happy Days, which was a fantasy of family life. NOTHING IN COMMON, when I first read it, struck me as the way a family really is. And I thought that the reality of the family on the big screen, even though there was humor in it, would make a good dramatic film. So, I haven't gone into film and suddenly gotten very serious—I'm just trying to do what other people are not doing. I saw that everybody was making teenage crazy films where kids are irreverent and all the adults are idiots. That's why I did THE FLAMINGO KID. Everybody said, "How can you make gin rummy interesting to teenagers? What a stupid idea, Garry." But with Michael Phillips, and the writer, Neal Marshall, I felt we could make it interesting because it was part of an emotional story about family. I thought it was off the beaten path. It's what we used to call "counterprogramming" in television, and I guess it's "counter-filmmaking" in movies. When I read NOTHING IN COMMON, I thought it had a great story finally a film that grownups and young people could both enjoy. Of course, my luck runs quite comical, because I did THE FLAMINGO KID, a picture about a beach club in the summer that they released at Christmastime. I did NOTHING IN COMMON, a grown-up story that they released in the dead of summer with all the kid pictures. So marketing is not my best luck, but what the heck, I was thrilled to be allowed to make those films. With YOUNG DOCTORS IN LOVE, I more or less paid my dues in filmmaking. I showed them I could put a joke on the big screen and not lose eighty million dollars. After that, they let me make these other stories and I truly hope they will continue—my, what a long answer to such a short question.

Q: Was NOTHING IN COMMON *a film that you developed from the start, or was it a completed screenplay that came to you?*

A: All three of the films that I've done were scripts brought to me that were already completed. None of the films I've made so far were initiated by me as a writer. But on the other hand, I know they don't hire me because I'm a director who knows all the lenses so perfectly, or can shoot crazy from a helicopter or will dabble with pastels. They usually hire me because they feel I can work with actors and also that I can rewrite as we go along. I like to work with opposites. With Matt Dillon in THE FLAMINGO KID, I was taking a basically dramatic actor and trying to make him do the comedy turns. With Tom Hanks in NOTHING IN COMMON, it was totally the opposite—I was taking a fine comic actor and stretching him to make him do more emotional turns. I get involved, as I said, with blood ties. . . I like family stories. We have a lot of choices in the 1980s. . . if you want a new nose, you can get a new nose. . . if you don't like your hair, choose some new hair. . . one of the few choices we don't have is who our parents are. We come into the world, somebody says, "Here's your mama, there's your father, there's your sister, there's your brother he's going to beat you up everyday," and you say, "No, I don't want them." You have no choice. That's who you get. So because you have no choice, it brings about a lot of anger, a lot of hate, a lot of love, a lot of conflict. And that's what I find interesting.

Q: *One of the nice things about your films is that even the unsympathetic characters emerge as understandable human beings.*

A: I think you've got to do things that aren't totally predictable to the audience, and what I try to do is take characters up roads and then turn them where the audience might not expect they're going. This sometimes throws the audience for a minute, but in the long run they seem to appreciate it. I also truly have to get up in the morning and believe that human beings are basically good, and the human condition is a positive thing. I also tried to show in NOTHING IN COM-MON that people who might be a little bit silly are also sensitive. Again, that's part of it—to make characters that are full-fledged. And actors like to play those roles. A lot of times in films and television you only have time to make stick-like characters, because you're so busy doing other things. A lot of films today spend too much time on special effects, wonderful chases, terrific visuals. . . there just isn't time to develop characters. I feel that you need the time to develop them. . . but you can't do it quickly. I figure that you watch television for free, but people who go to the movies pay at least six bucks to get into the theatre. They should have a full evening. So I try to do a full movie. I must say that the critics have given me some of the best reviews I've ever gotten for NOTHING IN COMMON, but I feel that THE FLAMINGO KID was a far more polished film. It was smooth, whereas NOTHING IN COMMON is a little bumpy. I had a lot of good actors and a lot of stories to tell. I didn't have the time to really perfect it.

Q: Was this a case of Tri-Star rushing it into release?

A: NOTHING IN COMMON was projected for Christmas. Then they moved it to the fall, but then they previewed the picture for an audience. Now, for twenty years I did TV in front of a live audience, so I know their sounds—their silences, their coughing, their "aahs," their "oohs," their laughter, their non-laughter—and during the previews of NOTHING IN COMMON, to the shock of Tri-Star, it played dynamite not only for adults, but also for 18 to 24 year olds. Tri-Star felt that the competition for grown-up films wasn't so bad in the summer, and decided to take a chance. So they rushed it out, and I felt that I could have used a few more weeks to work on it.

Q: You seem to make the kinds of films that you would want to see.

A: Well, when it comes to humor, there's a lot of different kinds. And what's popular in our society today is meanspirited humor. I've never been very comfortable with that kind of comedy. I try for gentle hilarity. I like very gentle comedy that is very funny and about people.

Q: How much anti-TV criticism have you had to put up with since going into features, and how do you deal with it?

A: Whatever I've done I'm basically proud off As I said, I did over a thousand situation comedies. I can't look you in the eye and say that every one of those episodes was brilliant and perfect. Some were perfect. Some were good. Some were pretty good. Some were a little embarrassing—but every piece I've tried to make professional. I've never been ashamed of anything I've done. However, people often don't take comedy seriously. Woody Allen said that comedy isn't better than drama, but it's harder to do. He's absolutely right. Comedy is hard to do. Some people will always put you down for doing a certain kind of comedy. When the reviews of NOTHING IN COMMON came out, a friend of mine called and said, "You know, the reviews are so good that it's now safe to mention your television credits!"

Q: The advertising agency office scenes in NOTHING IN COMMON had a very improvisational feel to them. Did you encourage the actors to improvise?

A: To me, if you do pure improvisation, everybody goes right to sleep. However, we did guided improvisation. We gave the actors room to ad lib, but everybody knew where they were going.

Q: The session where Tom Hanks and his staff created the airline ad campaign had a jazzy intensity.

A: The pitching of the ad campaign was totally from my comedy sitcom days where ten writers and I would sit in a room and throw ideas around. In the same vein, I was always impressed by the movie BLOW-UP. The story came to a stop at one point, and David Hemmings started to develop pictures. They showed the exact process of what a photographer goes through to develop pictures. I was shocked by that, because usually you don't see a person just doing his exact job in the movies. And I found that the audience was not bored. That's what I copied in NOTHING IN COMMON. I decided that I would show the audience the exact process of making an ad campaign. In the original script, the presentation of the commercial campaign was not so precise. There was a montage with music over it, and suddenly Hanks' character says, "We got it." I said no, that we were going to actually do it in detail. We brought it off, strictly because the actors did a good job with no tricks.

Q: *What about your own acting appearances? Is this something you take seriously?*

A: At one time I was a night club comic, a musician, a journalist, an athlete, a publicist, a critic. . . I used to review movies and plays that I didn't go to because I couldn't afford to. I used to review them from other people's reviews. That's why if I get a bad review I say they probably didn't see the picture. I like performing, but I wasn't very good at it. I was great in the Army, though. I was All World Army Comic. They gave me a plaque. I felt I could entertain men with machine-guns stuck in foxholes very well. A captive audience I could put away. But anybody who paid money—no good. So I gave it up, and would act occasionally in my own TV shows when anybody got sick, or I played with my own jazz band in the program. Every once in a while, somebody will ask me to do a favor. When I'm there on the job I take it seriously, but when I leave I really don't worry about it. I hope I did well for that person directing, not for me. It's not quite what I do for a living, so it's okay and I'll do the best I can.

Q: *What is it about the Marshall clan that made you all so funny and talented?*

A: In the neighborhood we grew up in—the Bronx—you only had a few choices. You were either an athlete or a gangster, or you were funny. There really weren't a lot of other choices, except for the guys who were into clothes. Out of my block came Calvin Klein and Ralph Lauren. Truth! And Ralph Lauren's name was Blackie Lipschitz, but that's a whole other story. But other than a few guys like that, you were either funny, an athlete, or you beat people up. A lot of great writers came out of DeWill Clinton High School—Robert Klein, Neil Simon, Paddy Chayefsky. It was our way of defense. Another factor is that all three of us got our senses of humor from our mother. She was truly the funniest lady on the block. She always made us laugh. My father had sense, logic. . . he was a business-man. My mother taught us, at very early ages, to cultivate friendships with people who were funny. Because then we would have joy and laughter and our lives would be happier. We all grew up surrounded by the sound of laughter. I look at life with a bend, so I always think I'll have comedy in my work.

F I L M O G R A P H Y

G A R R Y   M A R S H A L L
(Garry Marscharelli)
b. November 13, 1934 - New York, New York
YOUNG DOCTORS IN LOVE   20th Century-Fox, 1982
THE FLAMINGO KID   20th Century Fox, 1984
NOTHING IN COMMON   TriStar, 1986
OVERBOARD   MGM/UA, 1987
BEACHES   Buena Vista, 1988
PRETTY WOMAN   Buena Vista, 1990
FRANKIE AND JOHNNY   Paramount, 1991
EXIT TO EDEN   Savoy Pictures, 1994
DEAR GOD   Paramount, 1996
THE OTHER SISTER Buena Vista, 1998

$\mathcal{M}$IRA $\mathcal{N}$AIR

When I spoke with Indian-born, Harvard-educated director Mira Nair following the release of her fine first feature, SALAAM BOMBAY!, I could only have hoped that her future wouldn't be clouded by the challenges faced by any female director, let alone one from a far country attempting to base in the United States. Thankfully, she's continued to work ever since consistently and without sacrificing the insights into other cultures. . . and the clashes which often ensue within and around them.

SALAAM BOMBAY!, which won the *Palme* D'Or at the 1988 Cannes Film Festival and was nominated in the Best Foreign Film category in that year's Academy Awards, was a film at once solidly in the Western neo-realist tradition and entirely Asian—as befitted the woman who directed it. Breaking with the flamboyant traditions of commercial Indian filmmaking, Nair first discovered motion pictures as a tool of artisic and social expression while studying at Harvard. Previously a stage actress, she took camera in hand and made four documentaries between 1979 and 1987, one of which, INDIA CABARET, won prizes at the American Film Festival and Global Film Festival. These films laid the stylistic groundwork for the splendid naturalism of SALAAM BOMBAY!, Nair's first dramatic film. The street urchins who populated the film's tawdry environs—portrayed by Dickensian non-professionals plucked by Nair and her associates from local Bombay neighborhoods—meshed seamlessly with the more experienced screen actors, creating a screen canvas at once tough, sweet and as a familiar as American inner cities.

And in fact, Nair turned her attention to American landscapes—albeit those populated by foreign inhabitants—in her next two films, MISSISSIPPI MASALA and THE PEREZ FAMILY. The former, chronicling an interracial romance between a man and a woman of two different minorities (Denzel Washington and Sarita Choudhury), plied its themes of cultural alienation and the healing reconciliation of love with considerable skill and insight; the latter, a comedy-drama set amidst the Cuban community of Florida, was hit-and-miss with the critics, but displayed considerable visual energy. Nair returned to her native land for KAMA

SUTRA: A TALE OF LOVE, the last word in exotic eroticism, stunningly shot on Indian backdrops with stupendously beautiful performers.

She then returned to the American South for the Showtime cable movie, MY OWN COUNTRY, chronicling an Indian-born doctor's grappling with the early impact of AIDS in Tennessee.

MICHAEL SINGER: SALAAM BOMBAY! *is a complete stylistic break from commercial Indian filmmaking, and seems to be more in the neo-realist tradition of Satyajit Ray. What in your background led you to this kind of filmmaking?*

MIRA NAIR: You know, I'm not like many directors who say they made their first film when they were eight years old with their Super 8mm camera. I'm quite uneducated about cinema. I discovered cinema as a means of entertainment, and then personal expression, when I was 20 years old and going to Harvard. The path I've taken to cinema is not a typical path for Indians to take. I actually came to film as a stage actress, influenced more by people like Peter Brook, Jerzy Grotowski and Jules Chaikin than, say, OKLAHOMA!.

Q: *What happened at Harvard that got you interested in film?*

A: I took a course in photography, which was very compelling but not for my personality. I stumbled from that into documentary filmmaking, which was what Harvard offered at the time. My teacher was Albert Cassetti, a very rigorous man who introduced me to films by Chris Marker and people like that, which was a base for my education. But I've never really watched films day after day. . . I've just followed my nose, really.

Q: *What was it about documentary filmmaking that captured your imagination?*

A: It encompassed all my interests of theatre, working with people, capturing the inexplicability of everyday life, its arbitrariness, the contradictions of what we are. Since 1979 I've made four documentaries, all based on India, which really is where my inspiration has come from. I guess you have to work from what you know—which is not to say that I've lived like the street kids in SALAAM BOMBAY!—but on a general level, being Indian myself, it's something I can smell and feel. Incidentally, I saw my first Satyajit Ray talk when I was here in the States, not in India.

Q: SALAAM BOMBAY! *is shot in a style which seems directed more toward American and European audiences than Indian.*

A: I must say, though, in conceiving SALAAM BOMBAY! and writing it with Sooni Taraporevala, our intention was to make this primarily for Indians. I'm as much at home in New York now as I am in India, but I feel very strongly that India's commercial cinema caters to the lowest common denominator in an audience. They insist that's what an audience wants, and I just don't accept that. I don't underestimate Indians. The economy of SALAAM BOMBAY! is definitely the way I think cinema ought to be used. I see that as cinematic power. . . what is cinematic versus what is literary. It's like subliminal advertising. . . if I show you an image for ten seconds, you get a lot more from it than if I keep repeating it for ten minutes. I think this is the power of cinema—you can just get to the point very quickly. In

SALAAM BOMBAY! we were meshing 54 characters, six major subplots, and at the same time trying to distill it into a very simple narrative balance that also had a complexity to it-which is what life is like in Bombay itself.

Q: *I cannot even begin to imagine the problems you must have had shooting on the streets of Bombay and controlling the action.*

A: Well, it was grueling. I come from documentaries, where the whole crew is one person with a camera and one person with a sound recorder. That's what my terrain was. But I made SALAAM BOMBAY! as fiction because I wanted more control over expression and nuance and drama and gesture and storytelling. . . at the same time, wanting it to be like the best of my documentaries.

Q: *Had some of your SALAAM BOMBAY! crew worked on documentaries as well?*

A: Only my camerawoman, Sandi Sissel. She worked on the MOTHER TERESA documentary, and was also a camera operator for Robby Muller. Now she's shooting some of "The Wonder Years" television episodes.

Q: *SALAAM BOMBAY! was very beautiful to look at because of the way the fantastic colors of the neighborhood were captured, even though the milieu is often sordid as well.*

A: It was partially the production design too. That is the color of the red light district in Bombay. Somebody was telling me, as a criticism of the film, that it's too beautiful. I asked them if they had been to India, and of course they hadn't. I told them that beauty is relative. My mother, who is an upper middle class Indian, would think that those colors were totally lurid.

Q: *You shot on all practical locations in the red light district—the challenges must have been monumental.*

A: It's true that a lot of people told me it was impossible to shoot in certain places. Maybe it's madness, but I refused to take no for an answer. I would not surround myself with people who would constantly tell me it was impossible. I'd just keep going. My attitude also came from working under very difficult conditions as a documentary filmmaker. At any given moment in SALAAM BOMBAY! we had an average of 500 to sometimes 5000 people to control. The way we did it was. . . there were no hard and fast rules of what people's jobs were on the set. Nobody sat on their ass—very actor, every kid, every gofer, every technical person had to control crowds if he or she were not working in front of or behind the camera. I cast most of the crowds in the film from real neighborhood people. I wanted no professional extras, because the beauty and richness of the Bombay streets lie in the eccentricity of its idiosyncratic characters, and the film is filled with people like that. That helped in controlling the crowds, but it was very difficult and often very tricky.

Q: *After a time, did the denizens of the district in which you were shooting start treating you all like friends?*

A: Well, I had to go in front of a union of 16 madames from the red light area and tell them about the story of the film before they gave me their blessing. And I had made some connections there from my last film, INDIA CABARET, which was about strippers in Bombay.

Q: Do you find yourself attracted to films that deal with the lower strata of society?

A: It's not something that I've intellectualized about. But the fact is, I feel that people who are considered marginal in a society are pretty inspirational. To my mind, they are survivors who don't just survive miserably, but with an enormous amount of resilience, dignity, humor, and sometimes, flamboyance. I feel that the children in SALAAM BOMBAY! not just the kids in the film but children of the streets everywhere—have that spirit. That's what grabbed me. . .not the fact that it's so obviously a hard life for them, but that they live with this resourcefulness and just keep going on.

Q: Even though your film is set in a specifically Indian milieu, it's been compared to other films which deal with downtrodden children in other countries—Mexico's LOS OLVIDADOS, Brazil's PIXOTE, even France's THE 400 BLOWS.

A: I say that the film could have easily been called SALAAM BRONX! Unwanted children are a universally wasted potential. They are always talked down to, never respected as human beings, especially street kids. As you can see, even on a technical level, the kids in SALAAM BOMBAY!, who had never acted before, have this special gift.

Q: I understand that you and an associate named Barry John trained the street children as actors in a special workshop.

A: The workshop was a total experiment. Barry John had never worked with street kids before, but he had a great gift with children. We scouted certain areas in the Bombay inner city and rented a hall in a church, very close to where we were going to film. We talked to a number of kids on the street for about two weeks about this workshop, purposely quite vague about what it was all leading to. In the first two days, 130 children showed up and we auditioned them down to 24 kids, and worked with them for six weeks—nine hours a day, six days a week. . . pretty rigorous, but also a lot of fun. We were not like guilty liberals. We had a job to do, and the deal was, if you join us, you stick with us. We never gave the kids the illusion that we would be their mothers. We were always level and straight with them. We told them that if they wanted to come with us on this voyage of discovery, they had to stay with us right to the end.

Q: I understand that the children gave nicknames to the people on the crew, including you.

A: The nickname they gave me was Tough Sister, which they call me even till now. My husband, Mitch Epstein, was the co-producer and production designer on the film, and they called him Hot and Spicy Uncle. . . in their language, "Mitch" sounds like a word for "chili." And we had a huge boom man who they called Child of an Elephant. They have great imagination.

Q: Did you have a problem coordinating the acting styles of the professionals in the cast with the less trained children?

A: The professional actors had to be part of our workshop as well, because the children had to become used to them before we started shooting. It was very helpful, because they were able to explain acting to the children.

Q: *You avoid pointing fingers or making clear political statements in the movie about who's to blame for the condition of the street kids in Bombay.*

A: I think it is very myopic, or unrealistic, to point a finger at one person or one institution. I have no grandiose notion as to who we should ascribe blame to. The point is that finally, it's about your own backyard. At the Cannes Festival, somebody said to me, "How do you feel about these terrible things happening in India today with these children you portray in your film. . . ?" And I told her that I had seen, among children and older people on the Bowery and in the Bronx, a kind of aloneness that I have not yet seen in India—where even the most miserable are somehow bound in a tradition and society of their own. I'm not comparing anything. . . but just talking about the fact that these problems exist everywhere. For me to just neatly tie it up and say, "Okay, it's the Indian government screwing up," is totally simplistic. It's not that we don't ascribe blame. . . I think by revealing the kind of gray areas in Bombay, it is clear that it is an indictment of the system, of the government and of people who have chosen to be numb and blind to truth. That's a way of surviving in India, Mexico and everywhere else.

Q: *You said before that you choose to make films about what you know. Will your next feature also deal with India?*

A: I'm making my next film outside India in the golden language, English. But it's about an Indian family living in Uganda which is expelled by Idi Amin in the 1970s. It will be based partly in Africa and partly in the American South.

Q: *Is this based on any family experience?*

A: No, it's nothing personal. . . just an original idea born out of a lot of reading I've done.

Q: *Tell me about your own family background. I know that you were born in Orissa. . .*

A: That's a fairly remote state in eastern India, about 300 miles south of Calcutta on the coast. When I was born and raised there, it was fairly backward and remote by any standards.

Q: *So how does it happen that a young woman from a backward part of India in a traditional society came to become an independent film director?*

A: Actually, we were not so traditional. My father was in the civil service, and he was from the north. India is a very regional place. Orissa was an enchanting place to grow up, but nothing happened there and you would have to invent things. You really had to rely on your imagination.

Q: *And is that where the artist begins to develop?*

A: I think so. I think it helps, rather than always being given packaged things to look at or do. My childhood was extremely simple.

Q: *It's interesting that although you're from a middle class background, the subject matter of your documentaries and SALAAM BOMBAY! are from the lower strata.*

A: Well, I hasten to add that Sooni Taraporevala, who co-wrote the screenplay and conceived the film with me, is a native of Bombay and really sees it from the kids' point of view. But a lot of our material came from two months of solid documentary research, hanging out and talking with kids. A lot of the stories in SALAAM BOMBAY!, even though they're tied together by imagination and organic development of character, came from real lives.

Q: *Do you still keep in touch with your young star, Shafiq Syed, and the other children who were in the movie?*

A: My assistant director, Dinaz Stafford—also a native of Bombay—is a child psychologist who worked full time with the kids since we started, and her attitude is an extension of what we did in the workshop. . . which means that we told the kids that we weren't there to reform them, we weren't missionaries, they had to tell us what they wanted in their lives and we would try to make that happen. So after the movie was over, five of the kids returned home to their villages, and four are going to school—which is a very big deal, because it's tough to get through the bureaucratic paperwork to send a street kid to school. One kid is artistically inclined and he now teaches sculpture to blind children. Three of the older kids work as messengers in the film company that invested in SALAAM BOMBAY! Shafiq and two other kids recently worked on a play with Barry John in Delhi. But we've organized the Salaam Bombay Trust, which is a non-profit organization that will try and raise money for two learning centers for street children—one in Bombay and one in Delhi. These will be places that cater to the specific needs of these children, exploring their potential. There are many places in India that will give a kid a meal, a bath or a bed, but there really aren't any that will work with that child and develop his talents. Again, I have no illusions. . . I want to make my new movie, I'm a filmmaker. . . but it's just that this film has gotten a strong reaction. There are a lot of people out there who work with kids, and it's a way of marrying what the film was and what it was saying. SALAAM BOMBAY! was created by the kids, and they think it's their movie. And it's great to have that continue.

F I L M O G R A P H Y

M I R A   N A I R
b. 1957 - Bhubaneswar, Orissa, India
JAMA MASJID STREET JOURNAL (FD)   Mirabai Films, 1979
SO FAR FROM INDIA (FD)   Mirabai Films, 1982
INDIA CABARET (FD)   Mirabai Films, 1985
CHILDREN OF A DESIRED SEX (FD)   Mirabai Films, 1987
SALAAM BOMBAY!   Cinecom, 1988, Indian-British-French
MISSISSIPPI MASALA   The Samuel Goldwyn Company, 1991, U.S.-British
THE PEREZ FAMILY   The Samuel Goldwyn Company, 1995
KAMA SUTRA: A TALE OF LOVE   Trimark Pictures, 1996, British-Italian-Spanish-French-
    Japanese-Indian
MY OWN COUNTRY (CTF) Maintitles Pictures/Showtime, 1998

$\mathcal{G}$ REGORY $\mathcal{N}$ AVA

A film of poetry, magic and moving social drama, EL NORTE opened a door to a world rarely explored in such depth—the Indian culture of Latin America—as it depicted the heartrending journey to the U.S. of a Guatemalan brother and sister fleeing political oppression in their own land, and finding tragedy in the new one. Critically praised, an official U.S. entry to the 1984 Cannes Film Festival, and the most successful Spanish language film ever released north of the border (EL NORTE was bilingual, with Indian dialects and English also spoken), it was directed by Gregory Nava.

That EL NORTE still stands as Nava's best work is not to negate his subsequent studio-affiliated efforts, in which some compromise betwen the independent and commercial roads are inevitable. In fact, 1995's MY FAMILY, MI FAMILIA was a heartening comeback from the disappointment of 1988's A TIME OF DESTINY. Both were epics of family conflict and reconciliation, but MY FAMILY, MI FAMILIA was imbued with much of the inner fire that so illuminated EL NORTE.

Continuing to chronicle the Latin American experience, Nava's most recent release—SELENA—was unquestionably his most mainstream effort, the story of the slain Tejana music queen unapologetically based on the classic models of the Hollywood biopic, but made with sincerity and heart. Presumably continuing in this mode, Nava then turned his attention to another popular singer gone before his time, the African-American rock/soul pioneer, Frankie Lymon, in WHY DO FOOLS FALL IN LOVE?

MICHAEL SINGER: *What in your background prepared you for a career as a film director?*

GREGORY NAVA: I grew up in a generation that very much loved the movies, and I did as well. From a very early age I was interested in getting ahold of my parents' movie camera and making movies. My relatives are Mexican on my father's side and Basque on my mother's side. The Basque side of the family has always taken hundreds of pictures going way back. And they got into home movies very early on, back to 1939. I look at these old single-strip color home movies, and they have a magical quality. Someone once said that one day, home movies are going to be studied like folk art. My brother was also interested in film, so he and I got together to make our first film—the history of the world. We started with a grand theme, and everything has been downhill ever since. But my brother didn't really like it too much, so I bought his camera and started making my own films. I started going to a theatre which opened in San Diego called the Unicorn. Since San Diego had not been hit too much by the wave of European films, they went through almost an entire backlog of the classics of both foreign and American cinema on double bills that would change every week. I saw all these movies by Bergman, Resnais, Godard, John Ford, Hitchcock, Satyajit Ray, Akira Kurosawa, Sergei Eisenstein. I was in ninth or tenth grade at the time.

Q: Did you study film in school?

A: Yes, I went to the UCLA film school. The first 16mm film that I made there was titled THE JOURNAL OF DIEGO RODRIGUEZ SILVA, which was loosely based on the life of Garcia Lorca. It was a half-hour long and in black and white. I filmed it in Mexico all by myself, and found out something very important—you must do extraordinary things with very limited means if you're going to accomplish anything at all. If you're going to find anything, or do anything, or impress anybody or achieve what you want to achieve, you are going to be expected to do miracles. People said, "Why don't you shoot it here and use some adobe buildings around Los Angeles." But having been to Mexico, I knew that if I tried to shoot that story in Los Angeles it would look like junk. I could have a big crew and better equipment, but it wouldn't look as good. And who cares what's behind the camera? The only thing that matters is what's in front of the camera. It's better to go down to Mexico with a Bolex and shoot in Guanajuato and get something really extraordinary. DIEGO RODRIGUEZ was a tremendously successful student film—it won the National Student Film Festival Award for best dramatic film of the year in 1972. When people watch student films at UCLA at the end of a term, they watch them for an entire week, from eight in the morning till eight at night for five days straight. All the films look like Los Angeles because they've all been shot here. So when DIEGO RODRIGUEZ was shown, it looked amazing because it had been shot somewhere else. Latin America is a magnificent place, and Central Mexico is incredible. Those billowing clouds and fantastic landscapes and extraordinary cities with mindboggling architecture. The only thing people look at when they see a movie is what you have put in front of the lens.

Q: Did you study anything else at UCLA besides film to round out your education?

A: My feeling is that everything is relevant to film. I took a tremendous number of courses outside the film department. One year, in addition to my film course, I took Mayan Archaeology. Pre-Columbian civilization, with my background, has been a lifelong interest. And many of the more striking visual concepts in EL NORTE began to develop from studying Mayan archaeology and civilization at UCLA at a time when a lot of film students thought I was nuts for doing that. The best visual ideas I ever have for films come not from other filmmaking or from other cinematography, but from painting and studying the arts of other societies and other cultures. In essence painting is particularly inspiring because you have—up to a certain period in history—the greatest minds of the world applying themselves to executing what in films is only one frame.

Q: *So the success of* DIEGO RODRIGUEZ *inspired you to pursue full-length filmmaking?*

A: Right. The reaction to DIEGO RODRIGUEZ confirmed the ideas I had while making it. When I came to make my first very low-budget feature, which was about a wandering scholar in the Middle Ages, we shot it in Segovia, Spain.

Q: *This was* THE CONFESSIONS OF AMANS?

A: Yes. It was 88 minutes long and shot in 1973, but it wasn't finished until 1976 because we needed more money, which we finally got with a grant from the American Film Institute. Even though it won the Best First Feature Prize at the Chicago Film Festival in 1976, there was a very big lull between THE CONFESSIONS OF AMANS and EL NORTE. It was very well reviewed, but nothing really happened. So at that point, Anna and I got an agent and started writing screenplays. Then, Anna was able to raise the budget to direct THE HAUNTING OF M, for which I did the cinematography.

Q: *In terms of what you said before about being influenced by art, did this continue with your work on* THE HAUNTING OF M?.

A: For THE CONFESSIONS OF AMANS, I took all my visual cues from medieval art—the way the space is organized and the way compositions are envisioned. I didn't want to make a film which looked at the middle ages from our perspective, which is the way they're generally done. I wanted to make a film as though it had been conceived by a medieval mind. This was a real breakthrough in terms of our visual style, which we then extended in THE HAUNTING OF M. Just to give you an example, when you look at medieval painting and you see portraits of people, they are never portrayed—or rarely—in a three-quarter or frontal view. Most of the portraits are in profile. So in THE CONFESSIONS OF AMANS, I used a tremendous number of profile close-ups. I fell in love with them. I also used a lot of them in shooting THE HAUNTING OF M and EL NORTE. It is a very striking and magnificent way of looking at the human face. It is also true of Mayan art that the face is conceived of in profile, so again, when I was designing the visuals for EL NORTE, I wanted to make a film truly Mayan in its visual conception. Again, I believe very strongly in looking outside film to find new visual ideas and concepts. But when you find new ways to express them, you always have to take your key from the story. For me, the visual research that goes into a film is very important. I've become a strong advocate of storyboarding a film, that is, figuring all the shots and cinematic concepts before going in to shoot it. That's not to say that you don't change things in the course of shooting, but the clearer you are on what your concepts are going to be for each scene, the more remarkable your film can be. It's very hard to be brilliant five minutes before you shoot-so many things are happening. One thing in EL NORTE that many people have commented on is the transition between the sequence in which Enrique is killing the soldier, to a shot of the father's decapitated head, to the shot of the full moon, to a full frame shot of the funeral drum. That's a classic case of something which can only be figured out with storyboards before the shooting starts.

Q: *Can you tell me how you collaborate with Anna [Thomas] on her projects and vice versa?*

A: Working on THE HAUNTING OF M with Anna was very important for me. We work very, very well together. That film was Anna's vision. I feel I contributed to it and enhanced it. I always tried to key on her feelings about what she was trying to express. Our movies are so much better because Anna and I worked on them together. There's so much of her in EL NORTE. It is probably one of the greatest producing efforts in the history of film. She's also a fantastic director, and that's the avenue she wants to pursue.

Q: *I know from talking with Anna that filming EL NORTE was an incredibly challenging experience.*

A: What we had to do to capture this film, to really tell it. . . well, there's nothing in the world that looks like the Mayan highlands. We had to shoot it there. We had to find that world. It's hard to get there and it's dangerous, but nothing else was going to give us that look. We shot in Chiapas, Central Mexico, the Mexican-U.S. border, San Diego, Los Angeles. Two different countries with essentially two completely different casts and crews on over a hundred locations. There were over eighty speaking parts, a two hour and twenty minute film with 139 scenes with the kind of budget that we had. I mean, what an unbelievable job of producing Anna did!

Q: *What about the origins of the film?*

A: I mentioned that my family is Mexican on my father's side and Basque on my mother's. The Basque side emigrated to Southern California in the 1890's, and I have a lot of relatives from my father's side in Tijuana. So they're both settled on the border. The inspiration for EL NORTE comes from my experiences as a kid on the border. I speak Spanish, and as a child I wondered who lives in those "lost cities" across the border. A child can't explain this incredible cultural contrast. There's no natural border there. Nowhere else in the world do the first and third world share a common border as do the United States and Mexico. It's an image not only of the Americas, but of what's happening in the world. There's no place where the movement of the third world into the first is more graphic and more on the line than the border at Tijuana.

Q: *I remember the first time I drove from Los Angeles to Tijuana, coming down the freeway and suddenly seeing hills crowded with small, odd-colored buildings and church steeples. I realized that from a freeway in the United States I was looking at another world.*

A: You're absolutely right. Visually, it's an astonishing transition. That world has always been very important to me. From an early age, I traveled a lot in Mexico. To a certain extent, EL NORTE came from a need and a desire to deal with that part of me. Latin America is going through an epic period in its history. It's a world where the dream is as real as reality. That's the first thing that strikes you when you go there. I've always been interested in dreams and dream technique. That really started for me when I was a sophomore in high school and visited Central Mexico with my parents, leaving the border areas for the first time. On that particular trip I started reading the dream realist literature of Latin America—Carlos Fuentes, Gabriel Garcia Marquez, Vargas Llosa, Borges. And most of all, in talking about EL NORTE, the Guatemalan writer Miguel Angel Asturias.

Q: *That doesn't surprise me. A few days after seeing* EL NORTE *for the first time, I saw a performance of Asturias' play* Soluna *at UCLA, which dealt with so many of the same themes. At the time I was glad that I had been introduced to Guatemalan folkloric and mystical themes by* EL NORTE, *which helped me to understand the play.*

A: Well, everybody who sees EL NORTE talks about the influence from Gabriel Garcia Marquez. Of course, I do love his books and they're a real inspiration, but the real central inspiration for EL NORTE in terms of dream realism is Asturias, who was the first of that group to win a Nobel Prize. The dream realism that you find in the literature and life of Latin America is so amazing. What I wanted to do was make this film about Latin America from a Latin American point of view, which is part of me as well. And to tell it in a dream realist way, because if you do that, you capture all the richness and complexities of the culture. You can't tell this story in a neo-realist way. That may be fine for Italy after the war, but those styles developed to deal-rightly so—with those people's problems at that point in history. When people heard that a film was being made about Latin American social problems, they thought it would be neo-realist or a docudrama, but that's wrong for EL NORTE. It misses the half of the story that's going to make everything else make sense, especially when you're dealing with Indian people—that's the way they think. They don't make any distinction between their waking life and their dreaming life. It's a style and a way of doing films that I'm going to continue, because I think that it's something to work at breaking down the false barrier that exists between people's waking and dreaming lives. And certainly, film is the medium that has traditionally been thought of as doing that, isn't it? People talk about Hollywood as a "dream factory." And going to a movie is like dreaming—the lights get dark and the images come up before you like a dream. The relationship between the dream and cinema is fascinating. It affects and touches the audience deeply, and I think in that realm we find the true power of cinema. In that realm we find the essence of drama itself. I wanted to make a film that would be a cultural journey: telling the story of all the Americas. I wanted it to refer back to the pre-Columbian era, and also to the future, to the way the Americas are changing.

F I L M O G R A P H Y

G R E G O R Y   N A V A

b. April 10, 1949 - San Diego, California
THE CONFESSIONS OF AMANS   Independent Productions, 1976
EL NORTE   Cinecom/Island Alive, 1984
A TIME OF DESTINY   Columbia, 1988
MY FAMILY, MI FAMILIA   New Line Cinema, 1995
SELENA   Warner Bros., 1997
WHY DO FOOLS FALL IN LOVE? Warner Bros., 1998

$\mathcal{R}$ONALD $\mathcal{N}$EAME

A one-man treasure chest of British and American film, and self-described "jack of all trades," Ronald Neame has worked for, with and above some of the most distinguished names on both sides of the Atlantic. Previously allied with such luminaries as David Lean, Noel Coward, Anthony Havelock-Allan and Alec Guinness, Neame is himelf a three-time Academy Award nominee. Cineguild, the partnership formed in 1943 between Neame, Lean and Havelock-Allan, was responsible for such truly immortal classics as BLITHE SPIRIT, BRIEF ENCOUN-TER, GREAT EXPECTATIONS and OLIVER TWIST.

The son of famed actress Ivy Close and early filmmaker Elwin Neame, he worked his way up the ladder of British film in a classic manner, joining British International Pictures at Elstree Studios as a messenger boy. Like his father, Neame was attracted to the power of the visual image, and he became an assistant cameraman. Auspiciously, his first assignment in that capacity was on Alfred Hitchcock's BLACKMAIL in 1929. Ascending to the cinematographer ranks five years later, Neame's magnificent black and white work was demonstrated in such films as MAJOR BARBARA and David Lean's IN WHICH WE SERVE (co-directed by Noel Coward), THIS HAPPY BREED and BLITHE SPIRIT, contributing to the latter two as a screenwriter as well.

As a director, Neame has been responsible for 23 motion pictures since 1947, with such classics among them as THE HORSE'S MOUTH and TUNES OF GLORY (both of which continued Neame's association with Alec Guinness that began in his Cineguild days) and THE PRIME OF MISS JEAN BRODIE. And there have been solid entertainments in several genres, including THE MAN WHO NEVER WAS, ESCAPE FROM ZAHRAIN, I COULD GO ON SINGING, THE CHALK GARDEN, MISTER MOSES, GAMBIT, SCROOGE, HOPSCOTCH, FIRST MONDAY IN OCTOBER and one of his biggest hits, THE POSEIDON ADVENTURE, which pre-dated TITANIC's watery adventures by 25 years.

Neame's most recent feature was the sly British comedy FOREIGN BODY (1986), and since then he's devoted himself to teaching the craft in which he's so nobly served for seven decades. This reprinted interview with Neame, which first appeared in the second edition of *Film Directors: A Complete Guide*, will finally correct a 15-year-old embarrassment. . . a scrambling of the text due to the last-second revisions of a somewhat inebriated typesetter. Mr. Neame, we finally got it right!

MICHAEL SINGER: *Considering your parentage, you really qualify as a child of the industry, can't you?*

RONALD NEAME: I think so. My mother, Ivy Close, was an actress. And my father, Elwin Neame, became a director, cinematographer—everything. It's rather a romantic story in a way. My father was a very successful London photographer. He had a reputation for photographing all the beautiful girls. If a family had a lovely daughter they always sent her to my father to be photographed. And in 1910, the Daily Mirror—which is a London tabloid—decided to hold a world beauty competition, to find the "most beautiful girl in the world." They asked my father if he would photograph the twenty-five finalists in this competition. One of them was my mother. Of course, she won the competition, and my father married her. She was immediately offered a film contract, with Walter West Productions. So I was really, like Judy Garland—who was born in a trunk—born on a set practically.

Q: *When did you know for certain that like your parents, you were going to follow into films? Or had you ever considered doing anything else?*

A: Well, when I was 12 years old, my father was killed in a motor accident. And since he was a one-man business—by that I mean everybody went to him to be photographed—when he was dead there was nothing. The money ran out because he didn't believe in insurance, so I had to go out to work. My uncle got me a job with the Anglo-Persian Oil Company. I became an office boy there at 14, but I didn't really enjoy it. And my mother, who was still acting a little bit, knew the studio manager at British International Pictures at Elstree Studios. So I left the Anglo-Persian Oil Company and went to work at Elstree Studios as a messenger boy. Now, you see, it's extraordinary how things change so much. Because my greatest ambition at that time was to be a very good assistant cameraman. That was my total ambition, really. And it always puzzles me when young men come in to see me about a job, and the first thing they say is, "Well, of course I'm going to direct." I would never have had the aspirations of ever becoming a chief camera-man, let alone a director. I mean, it just wouldn't enter my head. I got six pounds a week. . . oh, not to begin with—I started with two pounds-ten. When I became assistant cameraman, I worked for a man called Claude Friese-Greene. Now, we in England claim that William Friese-Greene invented the motion picture. Here, they claim Edison of course, and in France they claim Lumière. But I suspect they were all on to it, really, about the same time. But as far as we were concerned it was William, and I worked for his son. Claude drank very heavily. He would start drinking at about ten in the morning, and I had to take over doing quite a bit of lighting for the picture, and then he'd sort of pull himself together and take over again. But it was wonderful in a way for me, because I got the opportunity to learn all about lighting without any of the responsibilities. Then one day poor Friese-Greene collapsed on the set and had to be taken to the hospital. The studio management—more out of meanness than anything else, since they didn't want to train another cameraman—asked if I thought I would be able to carry on. What

I didn't know about lighting could fill volumes, but at that age—I was 21 at that time—I thought, well, I could do anything. And so I finished the picture, which was called DRAKE OF ENGLAND. Then I was offered a picture called INVITATION TO THE WALTZ. And from then on I became a cameraman, photographing quota quickies. You know about quota quickies? To protect the industry from American pictures, a certain percentage of screen time had to go to British films. The American companies were very clever. What they did was make their own British pictures. They were five thousand feet long and had to be made in a week. I worked for 20th Century-Fox. What happened was that 20th Century-Fox would engage a British producer and tell him, "We will give you six thousand pounds for a five thousand foot film." The producer would then make the film for five thousand pounds, which is a pound a foot, and he would then take the other thousand for himself as the producer. The movies were real stinkers, but they gave one tremendous training. Not only for people like myself, but performers like James Mason, Glynis Johns and Jessica Tandy as well. A lot of people who are now stars played in those quotas for nothing.

Q: *I suppose the pressures also forced a certain creativity to come up with something interesting and acceptable for so little time and money.*

A: Well, it's extraordinary to see how proud we became of them, because it was not a question of "Have we made one of the best pictures?" Of course we hadn't. But our criteria was, "For one week's work, that was pretty bloody good." By law, the theatres only had to show them once a day. So they would put them on at the West End Theatre, or the Plaza, at 10:30 in the morning whilst the cleaners were cleaning the theatre, and then they wouldn't put it back on again. So nobody saw them.

Q: *People think of film being more business than art in this day and age, but with the quotas, it sounds like that's only what they were.*

A: It was a pure ruse to get around the laws. Now, there were a few good British picture being made at the time. A producer named Gabriel Pascal was directing quotas, but he always went over budget, even on those. And it came to the point where he had wooed George Bernard Shaw—how I don't know—to give him all his properties for nothing. And when he was about to do MAJOR BARBARA, he had a terrible row with Freddie Young, who was the senior cameraman. I'd been doing second unit work in a steel factory in Newcastle with David Lean directing my unit. And David said, "You know, Ronnie, Freddie's leaving the picture. You ought to photograph it." Gabby told me to do some tests with Wendy Hiller, and I made her look so good that they gave me the picture.

Q: *Did you also shoot* PYGMALION?

A: No, but I'm always being given credit for it. Harry Stradling photographed it.

Q: *I didn't know he was English.*

A: He wasn't. He came over to England. At that time, all the big pictures in England, particularly those that had American financing, would only use American cameramen. We British cameramen, at that time, were considered to be just junior boys and not very good.

Q: *That's certainly changed over the years.*

A: The war changed that, because all the American cameraman had to go back to American to do their thing and we young British characters got the opportunity. It was in the wartime that I became a top cameraman. Later, I trained people like Oswald Morris. See, Ozzie was my number boy when I was a focus puller. Then he was my focus puller when I was an operating cameraman. Then he was my operator when I was a lighting cameraman. And when I became a producer, I gave Ozzie his first lighting job.

Q: *In those years, all the top names in the British industry seemed to know each, work together, learn together and teach together. Does that explain the uniformly excellent work that began pouring out of England in the early 1940's, which continued until, say, the mid-1960's when things started to slide?*

A: They started to go wrong before then, really. But we were a very small community, very small indeed. Most of us grew up together. And also, we had this wonderful character named Arthur Rank, who gave us complete and utter freedom. For example, I came to Amenca for the first time in 1945. Arthur Rank sent me over to take a look at all the American stages and studios and to see what we needed in England to re-equip after the war, because we didn't even have Mole Richardson lights. I got an arrogant notion in my head that I could make a picture that would please American audiences. So when I went back, I said to David Lean, who was then an editor, "How about you direct a picture and I'll produce it?" And he said, "That would be wonderful. What shall we make?" So together we found GREAT EXPECTATIONS. I went to Arthur Rank and said, "Arthur, David and I want to make GREAT EXPECTATIONS" and he said, "Okay, how much?" We said, "Three hundred and fifty thousand pounds," and he said, "Okay, go away and make it." And that was it. That applied to all those pictures—nobody saw any rushes or had anything to say. We had our freedom

Q: *How closely did* OLIVER TWIST *follow the completion of* GREAT EXPECTATIONS?

A: About a year.

Q: *Was the same creative unit used?*

A: Yes and no. In the case of GREAT EXPECTATIONS, David and I did the screenplay ourselves. And indeed, we took screenplay credit, which I suppose was fair enough, but I still think it was Charles Dickens.

Q: *You tackled Dickens again in the musical* SCROOGE.

A: Yes. Well, that was brought to me pretty well complete. I had just walked away from a picture with Darryl F. Zanuck, and was in the clear when Leslie Bricusse and Gordon Stulberg, who was then head of Cinema Center Films, asked me if I would do it. Then I got Albert Finney interested. It wasn't bad. . . I enjoyed it. I would have liked to have made another musical, but I never have since, although we nearly got THE FANTASTICKS off the ground last year. You know, it's difficult to get anything off the ground these days. The pictures that I like best, the pictures that I enjoyed the most of my own work were THE HORSE'S MOUTH and TUNES OF GLORY. Now, they were made by sheer pieces of luck. There was a man in New York called Robert Dowling who was a multi-millionaire and whose corporation at that time owned the Empire State Building, the Carlyle Hotel and several other properties. He had been wooed by Alexander Korda to come into partnership. They financed a four picture deal with Alec Guinness, but in the middle of it Korda died. So there were two pictures left with Alec Guinness that Robert Dowling owned. Now, Dowling had gotten United Artists out of a big financial problem and had gone onto their Board of Directors. Guinness and I got together on THE HORSE'S MOUTH and went to Dowling with it. He pretty well insisted that United Artists finance it. Well, when we had a preview of THE HORSE'S MOUTH in New York, and it was a big success, Arthur Krim said to me "Ronnie, I don't know how you made that picture from that script." I said "Well I'll tell you, Arthur. That picture was that script. It's just that you didn't know how to read it." And I think that one of the sad things is that people don't know how to read scripts. A lot of lovely things get turned down because readers read them for the company. . . turned down and never seen by anyone else. It's only the most obvious scripts, it seems to me, that people understand. They understand car chases, explosions, buildings falling down, people being stabbed to death, people being screwed all over the place. . . but I don't think they can read anything that's subtle. They say to me, "Ronnie, why aren't you making films as good as those that you used to make?" I don't think that I've slipped. I think it's simply that I cannot get good material going.

Q: Have you had some frustrating experiences over the past few years with properties that you've tried to activate?

A: Yes, indeed I have. I've got two now, both of which I think could make very nice small pictures. But it should be with an unknown cast—in the case of one it's two 17-year-old girls. You know, they'll say, "Get Brooke Shields and you can do it." It's a bit disheartening and of course, the thing is that fortunately—because of a bad picture of mine called THE POSEIDON ADVENTURE—I've made sufficient money that I don't have to worry about paying the rent. It tends to make you a little more choosy. I think, to hell with it, why should I make this? Sometimes you can be wrong. I didn't want to make THE POSEIDON ADVENTURE. I did my best to get out of that almost until the day we started shooting. And then when Gordon Stulberg phoned me in England six months later and said, "This film's going to make more money than all the rest of your films put together," I said, "You're out of your mind, Gordon."

Q: When did you start making films in America?

A: The first film I made in America I only made half of. I was longing to come to Hollywood and make a picture, and I was offered a terrible thing called THE SEVENTH SIN that MGM was making with Eleanor Parker. There was a big change of management going on at MGM, the whole place was in turmoil, and I found myself in the middle of it. I also found that my rushes were being seen before I saw them. I got into a terrible state and began to really lose control, and the fact that the material was so poor didn't help. After four or five weeks, I could see that the studio was unhappy, I was unhappy, everybody was unhappy. My agent at that time said, "Ronnie, you've taken enough of this. You should resign, pack up." Well, I knew that this was a kind of way of him saying, "Better leave, because if you don't they're going to ask you to." So I left the picture and Vincente Minnelli took it over. I thought that was the end of my career. I was absolutely convinced that

that was it. And I remember going home that evening to the little house that I had rented on Miller Drive, very depressed. At about eight o'clock in the evening the telephone rang. I got on and the voice said, "Mr. Neame?. . . Yes?," I said. He said, "My name is George Cukor. I'm phoning you because I imagine you must be feeling a bit low this evening." I said, "Well, to be honest with you, I'm devastated." He said, "Well, that's why I'm phoning. Don't worry about it. I was the director taken off of GONE WITH THE WIND. And it won't make any difference to your career." I thought, what a wonderful thing to do. I didn't know that man, yet he went to the trouble to phone.

Q: *I have a feeling that you love actors, since your films have been filled with some great performances—I think of Guinness in THE HORSE'S MOUTH, John Mills and Guinness in TUNES OF GLORY, Maggie Smith in THE PRIME OF MISS JEAN BRODIE and Judy Garland in I CAN GO ON SINGING. That was her last film, wasn't it?*

A: Yes. We had a great love-hate relationship. When she was fond of me, which was half the time, she used to call me "Pussycat." When she disliked me, which was half the time, she would say, "Get that goddamned British Henry Hathaway off the set!" You know about Henry Hathaway? He was the great bully at that time.

Q: *Of all the actors you've worked with, whom did you enjoy the most?*

A: Well of course, enjoyment takes so many different forms, doesn't it? That's a difficult one to answer. I still think the greatest actor I've worked with is Alec Guinness. And I think I would have to say that I enjoyed working with Guinness more than anybody else. But for sheer fun and pleasure, I'd have to say Walter Matthau. He's such a funny man, never a dull moment when we're working together. He keeps the unit alive and full of fun when he's on the set. And I mean the right kind of fun. Who taught me the most? Guinness taught me a great deal about acting and actors. I was directing him in THE PROMOTER, which in English is called THE CARD. He got a bit difficult, a bit sulky over something and was being miserable. I asked him what was wrong. And he said, "Ronnie, would you like me to tell you something about actors that may help you as a director? Most so-called normal, ordinary human beings go through a period when they want to act. This period usually is between the ages of ten and fourteen. Little boys want to dress up as cowboys or Indians and go bang-bangbang. Little girls borrow their mother's dresses, put on their mother's makeup and flounce around the place. At the age of about fourteen and fifteen they grow up through this adolescent period and they become scientists, clerks, doctors, dentists, cab drivers, bus drivers, anything you like. But the actor and actress, in that part of their mind that wants to act, remains terminally and forever fourteen. Therefore, even though I may be much better read than you, I may be more intellectual than you, I may be more intelligent than you . . . the part of me that wants to act is still fourteen. And I want to be treated like that. I want to be encouraged. I want to be told, 'Well done, Alec.' But occasionally, I also have to be spanked. I also have to be cut down to size. I also have to be put in my place and told to behave myself. And if you can treat actors like that, Ronnie, you won't go far wrong." And it's absolutely true. The trouble is, it's not always easy to treat a highly intelligent man like Guinness as a 14-year old! Now, Noel Coward taught me a great deal, and of course I loved working with him—he's godfather to my son Christopher, by the way. Maggie Smith. . . I loved working with her because she's such a first-rate actress. I loved working with Judy Garland, but she could drive you around the bend. Albert Finney is wonderful. I didn't get along very well with Gene Hackman. I don't think I was the right kind of director for him. He didn't quite understand my Britishness, I suppose. He said "I'm used to somebody shouting."

Q: *I guess he should have gotten Henry Hathaway.*

A: Yes, I suppose so.

Q: *Your style of movie making can be described, if you'll permit me, as being old-fashioned in that one is rarely aware of overt technique. How would you characterize the difference between your style and that being used by most young filmmakers today?*

A: I belong to a school that said, "There is no camera." In other words, what you're seeing is happening, but there is no camera. So we tried to cover up any camera movements. Although my camera tracks all the time, and it's never still, I would cover up all those movements, disguise them. Now, what's happened in the present generation is that instead of it being "There is no camera," it's become "I am a camera." I, me, am the camera. Modern filmmaking has a different kind of realism. It's got a documentary realism. It's got the realism of having grabbed the moment, instead of the realism of my generation, which was very much rehearsed.

Q: *It's interesting to me that although you know and recognize the more contemporary style of filmmaking, you make a conscious decision to do it your own way. That seems to indicate a kind of purity.*

A: Well, I don't know. You see, Picasso—not that I would say any film director is like Picasso— came through the conventional, classical style of painting to what he finished up with. I would love to be able to change, but I've been so programmed that I can't.

FILMOGRAPHY

RONALD NEAME

b. April 23, 1911 - London, England
TAKE MY LIFE   Eagle Lion, 1947, British
THE GOLDEN SALAMANDER   Eagle Lion, 1950, British
THE PROMOTER   THE CARD   Universal, 1952, British
MAN WITH A MILLION   *THE MILLION POUND NOTE*   United Artists, 1954, British
THE MAN WHO NEVER WAS   20th Century-Fox, 1956, British
THE SEVENTH SIN   MGM, 1957
WINDOM'S WAY   Rank, 1958, British
THE HORSE'S MOUTH   United Artists, 1959, British
TUNES OF GLORY   Lopert, 1960, British
ESCAPE FROM ZAHRAIN   Paramount, 1962
I COULD GO ON SINGING   United Artists, 1963, British
THE CHALK GARDEN   Universal, 1964, British
MISTER MOSES   United Artists, 1965, British
A MAN COULD GET KILLED   co-directed with Cliff Owen, Universal, 1966
GAMBIT   Universal, 1966
THE PRIME OF MISS JEAN BRODIE   20th Century-Fox, 1969, British
SCROOGE   National General, 1970, British
THE POSEIDON ADVENTURE   20th Century-Fox, 1972
THE ODESSA FILE   Columbia, 1974, British-West German
METEOR   American International, 1979
HOPSCOTCH   Avco Embassy, 1980
FIRST MONDAY IN OCTOBER   Paramount, 1981
FOREIGN BODY   Orion, 1986, British

$\mathcal{P}$HILLIP $\mathcal{N}$OYCE

Since the time of this conversation, Phillip Noyce—a self-described directorial "chameleon"—slammed into the "A" list with such high-octane action epics as PATRIOT GAMES, CLEAR AND PRESENT DANGER and THE SAINT. Until that point, the Australian native had crossed a number of genre and stylistic borders with such homegrown product as NEWSFRONT, ECHOES TO PARADISE and the chilling suspenser DEAD CALM, which was the first film to expand his influence beyond U.S. arthouses (and made stateside stars of Sam Neill, Nicole Kidman and Billy Zane). And if anyone thinks that Noyce sacrificed art on the altar of big-budget American commercialism, as clearly seen in this interview, Noyce's fondest hope was always that it would be "totally impossible to categorize me, at least stylistically." In other words, he serves the material rather than the other way around.

A native of Griffith, a small town in New South Wales, Noyce studied at the Australian National Film School in the first year of its existence, and helped pioneer the renaissance of his country's movie industry in its mid-1970s heyday. And like many of his colleagues, when Hollywood called, Noyce listened. Since then, Noyce has enthusiastically and unapologetically embraced big-budget moviemaking with nary a backwards glance.

MICHAEL SINGER: *What do you want out of movies?*

PHILLIP NOYCE: Movies are for me a piece of life. It isn't a job, it's everything. You can't make them unless you're obsessed. They tend to take you over, like a spell. Even when you're on holiday you're not really on holiday, because the characters and story you're dealing with chases and catches you. Even when you're asleep, the tensions that are running through the film you're making are the tensions that enter your mind like spirits and trap you. They guide your dreams as much as they guide your waking. There's no escaping movies, and as I get older I realize I have a limited number of films that I can actually make. Ten years ago, I thought I was immortal and my total potential film output could be counted in the hundreds. Now I know that I might only make ten more films in my whole life.

So given the limit on how many films you can make, and the fact that films are your life, and the fact that I want to continually be challenged as a life goal and as a film goal, I guess I want to keep making different kinds of movies. Each film I make—I hope—will be very different from the last one. If anyone ever writes a summary of my work, I hope they call me a chameleon, because they'd find it totally impossible to categorize me, at least stylistically. Obviously, in the end because a film director is just a person in the end and even though they think they're god—certain obsessions come through even when you're trying to be different.

Q: *It's true that NEWSFRONT, HEATWAVE, ECHOES OF PARADISE, DEAD CALM, and BLIND FURY are all completely different. Some directors need to impress a very personal and recognizable style onto their films, but you seem to quite intentionally avoid that.*

A: Yes, I do. To make films, you can't escape the movie-making process. Therefore, it is your life. Each film, for the duration of a year or two or three, just takes you over. Everything else is subordinated to making the movie. So what you realize is that you want to keep having as many different life experiences as possible. I would just go crazy if I had to remake DEAD CALM over and over again, or NEWSFRONT, or any of them. I guess I'd like to be a cat, and in the ten more films that I will make have ten more lives, rather than the same life ten times over.

Q: *Some directors seem to keep making the same film, even if the subject matter is different.*

A: I feel that the subject of each movie dictates the style, the approach. There's not a technique or approach that you then adapt—the movie dictates how you treat it

Q: *Do you get upset when you see films that put the story in the service of style, rather than the other way around, which is how you seem to work?*

A: Absolutely. Finally, what I'd say in answer to your first question—what do I hope to get out of movies—is pre-eminently, a good time. I want to have fun. As long as I can keep doing that and people keep paying me to have fun, then I won't change the way I make movies. Eventually, maybe I'll run out of benefactors.

Q: *Has it mostly been fun so far?*

A: Always it's been fun. It's tough, but it's always fun. In part it comes from being an Australian and growing up in a country that had absolutely no film industry, where almost all films were imported. You would have been considered a madman to say that you were going to make a career as a film director. It wasn't something you could do even if you had the talent, because no one was making movies, and there were no potential opportunities to make them. I still feel it's some sort of incredible privilege to have the chance to direct films.

Q: *If there is a consistent thread in your films, it's atmosphere and the importance of the physical setting. Is that conscious?*

A: The only answer I can give is that I just respond to the material and the situation.

Q: *I suppose it's your response to the place where you happen to be shooting—whether it's the ocean in DEAD CALM or Thailand in ECHOES OF PARADISE.*

A: For me, sound plays a very important part in any film that I make. Atmosphere or sense of place is often created more strongly for the audience by the soundtrack than by the images. Sound goes directly from the ear to the heart. Images go from the eye, then they're decoded by the brain. Sound is the most piercing and direct emotional connection you can have with your audience. More than an image of heat, for example, the sound of cicadas can suggest you're in a tropical or very hot place. More than the lighting even, the right musical note or the right natural sound elements can suggest tension. My images have always been okay, but I don't see myself as an imagist. However, I've always been obsessed with soundtrack. I probably spend more time on sound than I do on image.

Q: *Were you always a sound fanatic, or was this something that began to develop when you started making films and discovered how important sound could be when matched with image? You started making experimental films when you were very young.*

A: It comes from an experimental film weekend conducted in Canberra, Australia's national capital. Two Australian experimental filmmakers, Arthur and Corinne Cantrill, were conducting the weekend. They had a lot of found footage, newsreel footage, offcuts from TV stations, that type of thing. They were encouraging us to take these bits, cut them together, then go and find a soundtrack and play the two on a doublehead projector. They also gave us some clear film and encouraged us to draw on it. So here we had a random image and clear film with some marks on it and sound elements. What I observed was that the same image could be altered to produce the absolute opposite emotional response from the audience just by changing the sound. It's sort of like that old theory of shot A plus shot B equals C, but shot B followed by shot A equals something else. There we had 80 people just fooling around with film, and there was a real naiveté and sense of experimentation about what we were doing. We had nothing to lose, and just tried anything. I guess that's when I first became aware of the power of sound in movies.

Q: *You were raised in a small town called Griffith. Did you fall in love with the movies there, or did you have to venture to Sydney?*

A: Falling in love with the idea of making movies was a two-stage process. First of all, it was falling in love with show business. That resulted from a fascination with the tent shows that came to town before television. In a small country town, the special day of the year for us was the show. It started as an agricultural show, where farmers used to show their produce, but vaudevillians would also come to town on that day. Eventually there would be 100 or more tent shows that would perform on the showgrounds of each country town. You would have the Roaring Twenties, the boxing troupe, the magicians, the twoheaded lady, the pygmies from Africa and so on. There was something about these traveling shows that caught my imagination. Every year my parents would give me one Australian pound, and my brother and I would put it underneath our pillows. The night before the show we would amuse each other with stories of which performances we were going to see based on what was there last year. Of course, they were always different. There were 100 shows, and a pound could only get you into ten of them. So once you ran out of money, there were only two ways to get in. One was to sneak under the tent, which I did a lot of. The other was to present yourself as a stooge. A stooge took part in the greatest show of all, which was outside of the tent—getting the people to pay their money to go inside. And the stooge had to be a local person who was known and could basically be made a fool of. I tried to get them to choose me as often as possible, which was a little easier than the others because I was taller than the rest.

Q: *I understand that you became quite an entrepreneur, raising money for your first short film by selling roles to your friends.*

A: It was a completely fallible idea. Unfortunately, the guy who had the most money. . . he was a doctor's son. . . was a rotten actor. He played the lead in that film, and he was terrible. But that taught me a director is very much dependent on his actors. A good performance is largely due to the right casting. The socialist bookshop owner was a bit of a capitalist, and he gave us the top floor of his shop for the cinema. So the people who came to the filmmakers' cinema had to pass through his bookshop, and inevitably they'd spend more money on books than admission to the cinema. This cinema ran every Sunday and people like Bruce Beresford, Peter Weir, George Miller, Paul Cox, Gillian Armstrong, myself and others would personally show their films there. None of us were making features yet, but would collect a program of films that were linked thematically or at least stylistically—or else a filmmaker would show his life work— and then we would talk after each film. There was a lot of interplay with the audience and the filmmakers in the audience. About 120 people would fit up there.

Q: *What happened in Australia during the early 1970s that allowed all of you to start making features?*

A: It was government intervention, purely and simply. The fertilizer that allowed us to bear flowers was much more complex. It was a time of great change, just like the flowering in the Spanish cinema since the overthrow of Franco. Australia had been ruled from 1949 to 1972 by one government, an extremely conservative government. And Australia was one of the most censored countries in the world, in terms of literature, film and art. In 1972, we elected a socialist democratic government, the Labour Party, the first nonconservative government for 23 years. With that government came the aspirations of a whole generation. The second factor was the Vietnam War. Our involvement ended in 1972 with Labour's election. The war had been for Australia, as it was for America, a traumatic experience. It taught us that we needed to think more independently about politics. There was also the factor of the post-war baby boomers, the first generation whose parents encouraged them to be frivolous and gave them the opportunity to do whatever they wanted. For Australians, this was perhaps the first generation which was given leisure time to devote to cultural activities. The result was an overnight film industry.

Q: *What's inevitably happened, of course, is that good Australian directors-having been discovered by the rest of the world, particularly Hollywood—have to some degree left their country to make films elsewhere. There was a fear that the Australian film industry was going to be destroyed by the success of its own filmmakers. Do you feel a need to keep a connection with Australia, while at the same time pursuing your career in the U.S?*

A: I can't think of any Australian director who actually maintains his principal home here in America. I don't know anyone who lives here full-time. When they come here, they come as outsiders. Obviously, their Australian identity is very important to them.

Q: Is the Australian government still supportive of the film industry, or have things changed from the early 1970s?

A: The government is still supportive, but one of the problems there is that you get sick of the system and want to break out of it. You see, every time a bureaucrat looks at the film industry, they want to change the rules by which the subsidy is administered. If you have to make films because of the government handout, you're subject to the whims of whoever is controlling that government. The only way out of that is to get real, and within our orbit the only reality is here in Hollywood. Hollywood is the most successful colonizer in the history of mankind. More successful than the Romans, because Hollywood has colonized the hearts and minds of all the world. Hollywood has developed such an amazing distribution system around the world that it always needs product to feed that system. The only way out of the whims of government control is to somehow take advantage of this machine, this octopus that has its tentacles stretched all over the world. Let this octopus sell your film—because it does it better than anyone else—and let the octopus finance your movie. That way, as long as you can keep supplying that machine with whatever it wants, it will keep allowing you to make movies. The only real criteria is the criteria of economics, ordinary supply and demand. This is a difficult mine field to negotiate, but it's a lot better and you know the rules, because unlike bureaucratic rules, they're consistent from generation to generation.

Q: Do you feel that the compromises you might have to make under the Hollywood system are less disturbing than those you make under the Australian system?

A: The thing I've learned—and I guess you'd have to be incredibly thickskinned if it didn't impress itself upon you—is the way Hollywood is connected to the audience. You can almost feel the connection when you talk to some of the people in Hollywood. I feel grateful that I have relative artistic independence in Australia, and that as an outsider I can look at what Hollywood has to teach a filmmaker about contact with an audience. For me, if I'm not in contact with that audience, then forget it. I may as well not be doing it. I'm not making films for me. I'm making films for them, wherever they are.

Q: When did the audience become more important to you than your own aesthetics in the transition from experimental to more commercial filmmaking?

A: It was actually through making films for television and experiencing the audience reaction to my feature HEATWAVE, which was a film that I made for myself. I remember sitting night after night in cinemas in Sydney when HEATWAVE opened, and I realized that I hadn't pressed the buttons with the audience. I hadn't connected with them. I'd mingle with the audience, and they didn't have the buzz that I meant them to have. It wasn't working. After that, I spent several years making television films, working with the Kennedy-Miller organization. And the turning point for me was a 10-hour mini-series which I co-wrote and co-directed called THE COWRA BREAKOUT. It has to do with the nature of the television medium and its relationships to the audience, which is so different from cinema. In the cinema, once you get them into the theatre, they're there. They're not going to leave unless you really upset them. In television, they've got multiple choice. Unless you reach out of the screen and grab hold of them in their seat and bolt them down, they'll leave you. So you have to involve a TV audience more and more as time goes on. Here I was, faced with writing and directing a ten-hour mini-series, which is like five feature films. We started out at a certain level of ratings, and we increased every half-hour over the ten hours. I spent two-and-a-half years on that project, and I thought "Now I've graduated. Now I know something about making a movie. Now I know something about telling a story." And even though it was television, we never thought of it as TV. TV was only the means by which we were delivering it to the audience. We were just telling a story. It's not TV, it's not cinema, it's just a story.

Q: *Television as a training ground for feature filmmaking is hotly debated in this country, because the networks tend to ground down any individuality of style on the part of the director.*

A: But this was a different sort of television. This was television where the sponsor and the network had bought the project from Kennedy-Miller on an idea and the next time they were involved was when they saw the finished project. We had total creative freedom to do anything in the world that we wanted to do. The network had no involvement in casting, scripting, editing or anything.

Q: *Is this system still working in Australia?*

A: Certainly at Kennedy-Miller, because that's the kind of deal they've had on every project they've done.

Q: *Does Kennedy-Miller use TV as a training ground for young directors?*

A: I think TV is used as an investigation into the nature of storytelling, as I've said before. As it happens, certain directors have then gone on to make feature films with Kennedy-Miller. Chris Noonan is now working on a feature. On the other hand, Ken Cameron made features and then went on to do TV with them. It's not so much a conscious decision to provide a training ground as it is something that grows out of working together.

Q: *There's no stigma in Australia of going from features to TV? Here that seems to be a problem for directors.*

A: No. We go from commercials to theatre to cinema to television.

F I L M O G R A P H Y

P H I L L I P   N O Y C E

b. 1950 - Griffith, New South Wales, Australia

BACKROADS   Cinema Ventures, 1978, Australian

NEWSFRONT   New Yorker, 1979, Australian

THE DISMISSAL (MS)   co-director with George Miller, George Ogilvie, Carl Schultz & John Power, 1983, Australian

·HEATWAVE   New Line Cinema, 1982, Australian

THE COWRA BREAKOUT (MS)   co-director with Chris Noonan, Kennedy-Miller Productions, 1985, Australian

PROMISES TO KEEP   Laughing Kookaburra Productions, 1986, Australian

ECHOES OF PARADISE   SHADOWS OF THE PEACOCK   Castle Hill Productions/Quartet Films, 1987, Australian

DEAD CALM   Warner Bros., 1989, Australian

BLIND FURY   TriStar, 1989

PATRIOT GAMES   Paramount, 1992

SLIVER   Paramount, 1993

CLEAR AND PRESENT DANGER   Paramount, 1994

THE SAINT   Paramount, 1997

$\mathcal{R}$OBERT $\mathcal{R}$ODRIGUEZ

By now, it's very clear that if your brand of cinema is high-octane, high-body count, off-the-edge and most definitely off-the-wall, then Robert Rodriguez is The Real Thing.

It all started when the then 24-year-old Rodriguez shot the wildly acclaimed EL MARIACHI for seven thousand bucks, so ridiculously cheap that it even defies jokey one-liners. Made as a throwaway for the Spanish-language video market, Rodriguez was astonished when Columbia Pictures bought it for remake purposes, and dumbfounded when they actually decided to release the original version. It is now something of a legend, its filming hilariously chroncled by Rodriguez himself in his book *Rebel Without A Crew*, which is a textbook for guerilla moviemakers.

The third eldest in an Austin, Texas family of ten, Rodriguez demonstrated an early interest in cartooning and filmmaking. While attending the University of Texas at Austin, he created a daily comic strip entitled "Los Hooligans," which ran for three years in the *Daily Texan* newspaper. Meanwhile, from childhood, Rodriguez shot nearly 30 short narrative movies, with borrowed video equipment and no money. An award-winning video anthology, AUSTIN STORIES, boosted Rodriguez into film school where he produced his first 16mm short.

This film, BEDHEAD, went on to win a significant number of awards in film festivals across the United States. High on its success during the summer break of 1991, Rodriguez wrote, short, sound-recorded, edited and directed EL MARIACHI. He produced with his childhood friend, Carlos Gallardo, who also starred in the title role as the Hombre Sin Nombre who unwittingly becomes involved in havoc, chaos and mayhem in a Mexican border town.

In-between the first EL MARIACHI and the second—entitled DESPERADO, shot in the same border town of Acuna but with an astonomical budget of five million dollars and Antonio Banderas in the leading role—Rodriguez directed ROAD RACERS, one of the most popular of Showtime's REBEL HIGHWAY series of homages to '50s American International teen sleaze flicks.

After bringing the apocalypse back to Acuna in DESPERADO, Rodriguez joined Quentin Tarantino, Allison Anders and Alexandre Rockwell for the omnibus FOUR ROOMS, before rocking and rolling again in the neck-chomping, boot-stomping, ass-kicking vampire comedy-thriller FROM DUSK TILL DAWN. Most recently, Rodriguez completed THE FACULTY, written by primo horrormeister Kevin Williamson, back home in Texas.

And while he doesn't make movies for seven thousand dollars anymore, it's doubtful if Rodriguez's sensibilities will ever have him sailing comfortably in the mainstream.

MICHAEL SINGER: *It's funny.* ROAD RACERS *was obviously the work of somebody who felt very affectionately toward those old American International teen movies that the Showtime series was based on, but you were too young to actually grow up with them. You must have discovered them all on video or TV runs.*

ROBERT RODRIGUEZ: Oh yeah. They sent me the tapes of the movies that we were remaking. In fact, they wouldn't send me ROAD RACERS because it was so terrible. I wanted to live up to the old posters, which said stuff like, "Some have to dance, some have to kill! Then you'd watch the movie and they were lame, you know? So it was like, we're going to do the poster beyond the poster. Make it as sordid and crazy as they promised, and then some.

Q: ROAD RACERS *was great fun, and one of the things that interested me is that I think your background as a cartoonist came out very strongly in the piece.*

A: Did it really? Why's that?

Q: *Because there was so much comical material that defied all logic as we know it, which is the cartoonist's hallmark.*

A: What in particular?

Q: *The skating rink scene, where our hero is greasing the floor by skating on his head? That's not necessarily the kind of thing one would normally see.*

A: Yeah, I guess you've got to kind of mix it together, because ideas for a strip or a movie can come kind of at the same time. We were just driving along, me and my cowriter, trying to come up with ideas—we had ten days to write the ROAD RACERS script, so we had to do it very quickly. We were taking a road trip from San Antonio to Mexico, and going through San Antonio, we saw an old skating rink and I just said, "Hey, we've got to get a skating rink scene in the movie", which leads to a rumble on roller skates—never thinking it'd actually make it into the movie. But when they give you free reign like that, we actually thought, well, it'd be a challenge to actually just try to pull it off in the time we have, with all the crazy shots we designed. We did, and it was fun.

Q: *There's a tradition of cartoonists who became filmmakers, and most of them became really, really good filmmakers.*

A: Really?

Q: David Lynch, Frank Tashlin, Tim Burton. . .

A: My earliest movies were actually cartoon movies. I would spend all day in school in the back of the class—because I wasn't very good in school—using the margins to do STAR WARS things, like, you know, little stick figures, and then, "Ssshhh", a light saber would come out, so if you flip it, you had a lot of room to have, like, spaceships going, and I'd spend hours doing that. And I'd show it to the students—you know, these paperback dictionaries—and they'd all laugh, and so I'd feel good because my grades were so low, it made me feel good about something about myself. But I never thought it would go anywhere. But then I got a video camera, and I'd make little claymation movies, and then movies with my brothers and sisters. Then I started a daily comic strip in Austin at the University of Texas. I had it for three years. A daily strip, so my drawing got much better, and you know, you're writing, and comic timing develops, I guess, just by practicing. You had to turn that thing every day or you wouldn't get paid, so those little eight bucks a day that I'd get doing that strip was what kept me practicing and made my drawings improve.

Q: *It seems that people who started either in animation or cartoons seem to have a much less limited notions of what they can do on film. Their visual sensibilities seem to be much expanded. Do you feel that you owe anything as a filmmaker to your background as a cartoonist?*

A: Sure, sure. Do I owe it to drawing?

Q: *Yeah.*

A: I think just because you don't even think about it, anything you visualize, you can immediately make concrete by drawing it. So, you feel like you can make any vision that you have in your head a reality, either on film or on video, or on paper. I think I get kind of the two mixed together, because there was stuff in ROAD RACERS that people asked, "how are you gonna do this?". . . Then I'd make a drawing of the actual contraption that I'd need them to build me so we could pull off that head slick, and I don't know, it just kind of goes hand in hand. And they'd see it and go, "oh, okay", and then they'd build it, and there you go. They make it and it works fine. So, you know, I think a lot of the ideas I get visually, just being able to put them down and show somebody else, to reaffirm what you have in your head, just goes a long way.

Q: *On the other hand, I don't get the impression from either* EL MARIACHI *or* ROAD RACERS *that you do a lot of storyboarding.*

A: [raises eyebrows] Why do you think that?

Q: *Because your films are very spontaneous.*

A: Everyone else thinks that I do storyboards for all the movies.

Q: *Well, I don't. So who's right?*

A: I used to. I used to early on for my short movies, but I didn't draw one frame for EL MARIACHI, because you usually do storyboards to show other people what you have in mind. But since I didn't have a crew on EL MARIACHI, why draw for myself? You see it in your head, and you know a lot of it's going to change on location—you're going to be very spontaneous—and I didn't need to draw it down because I was already watching it in my head. On ROAD RACERS I drew out the roller skating rink scene for the crew, very much stick figures and stuff. We had about 12 hours to shoot 52 setups for that scene, which was. . . impossible. A normal Hollywood movie will get through 15 or 20 setups if they're fast. To explain everything I needed to the crew would just take forever, because they would have told me that there was no way I could have gotten all those shots in one day.

Q: *What's your record for a number of setups in one day?*

A: On ROAD RACERS, 78 for a single camera. And it was because they were going to start cutting my scenes out. We had a 13 day shooting schedule, and we could have shot it easily in 13 days, but it would have looked like a cable movie. You know, the camera sitting in the corner. And that's not what I wanted. I wanted it to have some more setups to cut, because I love to edit. ROAD RACERS is a fast cars and rock'n'roll kind of movie—it's got to look like a really high octane chromium film—and I was so used to getting so many setups on EL MARIACHI, because I was basically doing everything by myself. That's why people thought EL MARIACHI looked more expensive than it was—because of the number of setups—and people in this town know that setups usually cost more.

Q: *To say that it looked more expensive than it was is an understatement, to say the least. It looked like a $2 million picture, if not more.*

A: I didn't know. To me, it looked alright. It was a little slow, but when I was making it, I thought, well, if I just had a little more time. Not necessarily money. . . just a little more time. Our camera got taken away after the 14th day.

Q: *So you're shooting schedule on EL MARIACHI was 14 days?*

A: Yeah. And the funny thing is that on ROAD RACERS we only had 13. So see, when I produce, I get more days out of my budget.

Q: *Yeah, but we're talking about a budget that was probably lower than most directors' cellular phone bills for a week.*

A: I know, I know. It's talking about two different things. One's making a movie for the sake of making a movie, and another is doing a job. I mean, you're getting paid, and you spend, and it's not your money. That was my money on EL MARIACHI, and you're more careful. You're paying for your own materials and you're just trying to make a film and learn from it. You're not going to turn it into a big production.

Q: *So when you finally do a movie that costs $10 million. . .*

A: Maybe I'll shoot it in nine days? I'm going to try and produce my next picture so that I can kind of put the money where it belongs. Everyone shoots differently, but for me, a lot of money can get wasted very easily.

Q: *But you're sort of at a crossroads now. You're about to do DESPERADO with a much higher budget. Like. . . maybe $3 million?*

A: Five, man.

Q: *Five. . . whoa.*

A: Well, you know, because we have some name actors, it goes quick. But it's going to look much more expensive than five. The whole idea is to put the money on the screen, and shoot 35mm and scope, but I want it small so I can run free. Because really, all it comes down to—no matter if you've got 100 people or two people on the crew—is the moment when you push the button and start shooting. That moment is what you're getting. The rest is just decoration. It doesn't need all the frills, because it's not that kind of a movie.

Q: *Do you actually worry about inevitably working on films with bigger budgets?*

A: I wouldn't do it right now. I think as time goes on and I start producing more of my own things and move up little by little, I'll be able to do something I never could have done if I hadn't done MARIACHI or ROAD RACERS first.

Q: *Is it true that when you made MARIACHI, you never conceived of it getting U.S. distribution?*

A: Oh, not at all. I would have shot it in English if I expected it to get released in the U.S. It was just a very plotted thing for me to do, because my short films had gotten to the point where they started winning festivals. You know, you've got to cultivate your talent. I mean, you can't just go take a class and think you're going to be a filmmaker. So when I saw my little movies starting to win festivals after so many years just shooting on home video, I thought, wow, I can actually make it in this business, even from Texas, if I was just able to get more practice telling feature-length stories. So the whole MARIACHI idea was to shoot three low-budget Spanish-language action movies so that if the movies were terrible, no one would ever see them. But I knew that I could shoot on 16mm, but edit on 3/4inch video at a local public access station. I could have a 3/4-inch master that I could sell to a Spanish distributor for the straight-to-video market. That way, I could keep the cost under $10,000 and make back maybe, you know, a profit of maybe another ten grand. That's why I kept the budget so low, because I could only sell it for so much. I figured I could learn sound, camera, lighting, feature stories and directing, all in one year on three small action movies. I'd have three features under my belt. You can't beat that. It's the best film school, because you make all your money back. So I knew that after that year, I would have a great demo reel. . . I'd just take the best scenes from the three movies. That's why EL MARIACHI ends the way it does. He becomes the Mariachi in the first movie, because then we were going to do something like THE ROAD WARRIOR and MAD MAX BEYOND THUNDERDOME after that, continue his story. Then, after those three, I'd try and get financing for a real independent American film to take to festivals and try and get noticed. I was in no hurry. I mean, I was 24 years old. I figured, take the time now to experiment freely—which is why you see MARIACHI with the sped-up shots—because I didn't think anyone was going to see it. No one rents Spanish action movies. Do you ever go to the Spanish video store and rent a movie?

Q: *Sometimes, actually.*

A: You do, really? They're pretty terrible, aren't they?

Q: They're the worst.

A: That's why we thought we couldn't lose. That was the whole plan. So when it got bought by Columbia, it was a surprise. But they bought it to remake because they liked the story. But then when the guys upstairs said "We like it the way it is, we want to release it the way it is," then it got funky, and I thought, whoa, that's really outrageous. A Spanish-language movie released in the States by a major studio? We made the Guinness Book of World Records for the lowest-budget movie ever released by a studio. So it wasn't anything conceivably planned at all.

Q: Were you freaked out at first?

A: Yeah, it was a gradual process, you know? First I got the agent out of it, which really blew me away because I thought it would take me. . . maybe the third film before I'd get a big agency like that to sign me up. And then they started sending it around as a sample of my work and I got deal off of it. Just off that same seven thousand dollar tape, you know—pop it in and watch it—and then Columbia bought it, so that freaked me out because I got much more money than I would have just selling to the Spanish video market—and then they wanted to release it, and it won festivals—and it was like, God, the movie wasn't that great! It was good, but I could do better if I just knew people were going to actually watch it. I would have put so much more work into it. There were so many times that I was just like, eh, it's hot. . . one take. . . let's get out of here.

Q: How many takes do you normally do?

A: The most takes we did on ROAD RACERS was five.

Q: So when you hear of a director doing more than 30 takes on a scene. . .

A: I can't relate to that at all. But if that works for him, you know, but that kind of just sucks the fun and energy out of what you can make happen. You know, maybe when I'm older, I'll be sitting in my hotel room watching via satellite what they're feeding in from the set. "Come on guys, more setups. You're moving too slow down there." You never know. It could get to that point. They already can sit in a trailer and watch what's going on. They don't even have to talk with anybody. That kind of takes the fun out of it for me. I might go into painting after that, or, you know, aluminum siding.

Q: Come to think of it, because of the budget, you wouldn't have used video assist on either film.

A: No, it's terrible. I tried it on ROAD RACERS. You just can't tell on that thing. It's all flickery—black and white, and fuzzy. I just prefer being behind the camera and looking through the lens, and being right there near the actors. It seems like you're making the movie that way. I can see why some directors forget to say "action" or "cut," because you don't feel like you're part of it anymore. You want to feel like you're making your picture, and not like some assembly line's doing it for you.

Q: What I loved about EL MARIACHI was that it was almost as if Sam Peckinpah had taken over a Rene Cardona, Jr. movie. It had a kind of glorious sleaziness about it. Very atmospheric. When you were growing up, did you watch a lot of "B" Mexican movies?

A: No, not really. I mean, I'd see some of the comedies and some of the pictures from the golden era. But I really got the idea to make EL MARIACHI when I was on the set of LIKE WATER FOR CHOCOLATE.

Q: *What town was it shot in?*

A: Acuna, across the border from Del Rio, Texas. There's nothing there, it's like a dust town, but for some reason all these movies are shooting there now. I used to shoot video movies with my friend Carlos Gallardo, who was working in production on LIKE WATER FOR CHOCOLATE, so I was shooting behind-the-scenes video and one of the production managers said, "Hey, why don't you come make one of these cheap Spanish action movies for us? We spent 30 grand on 'em." I said "Wow, 30 grand for those horrible things? Man, we can do much better than that, just me and my friend here." That's how we got the idea to do it, and capture the town and its atmosphere.

We did our homework, and rented some of those movies, and they were all shot in apartments. Really low budget, no atmosphere, and no action, even though they're called action movies. So Acuna turned into a whole backlot to shoot in and capture the energy they weren't capturing in those other low-budget movies. We didn't really see anything we were modeling EL MARIACHI after, except maybe THE ROAD WARRIOR or the Clint Eastwood Italian westerns, in that we would have a character created in the first movie and go on for two more. A complete genre picture. People wonder why my first picture isn't a personal kind of story—because I was just making an exploitation flick to get some practice. I didn't think it would end up winning prestigious film festivals. That just goes to show that no matter what, don't copy what the last success was. At the time SLACKER was coming out, and I could have gone and made one of those Austin-type movies. And here I was making a Mexican exploitation flick. And that ended up being what people wanted next. You never know. Just follow your own thing.

Q: *Did EL MARIACHI actually have a theatrical release in Mexico?*

A: Oh yeah. It got a lot of publicity, and did fairly well, but by the time the video came out, people had all heard about it and realized that it wasn't just another one of those Spanish action movies. It was a complete joke, because "Mariachi" means "guitar player." I figured that no one in the U.S. would ever see it, because no one goes and rents movies in the Spanish market. And no one in the Spanish market would see it, because no one would rent an action movie called THE GUITAR PLAYER. So I thought that no one would find it except the poor slob who, when all the other action movies are out, finally says, "Alright, I'll rent this one," and it has more action than the other ones—with titles like RABID DOG and DEATH BY FIRE—put together. That was the whole joke. But now it's gotten quite popular in Mexico on video.

Q: *Has that put you into contact with Mexican directors?*

A: Yeah. They're good guys, real nice guys. I'm glad they're doing well because they've just got their own nice demeanor about them, and yet, wild imaginations. We ought to do something together. Maybe an anthology centered around the Day of the Dead, something like that. It would be fun.

Q: Now you've have your foot on both sides of the border with EL MARIACHI and ROAD RACERS.

A: It's nice to have two sides, to be able to choose the best from your favorite parts of each culture is really wonderful. I'm a North American director, and a Latino director. It's nice to be able to distinguish yourself a little bit.

Q: And you have no problem distinguishing yourself that way?

A: No, not at all. I figure that's why I was born the way I was. It's great that DESPERADO will be the first decently budgeted Hollywood movie with a Latin hero in it. I mean, you never see that.

Q: How do you maintain your purity now, being out here in Los Angeles?

A: I don't live here. I live in Austin, Texas. I'm only out here because we're casting, but we're going to Mexico in a couple of weeks and I won't even be back here until editing time in late November.

Q: How long is your shooting schedule on DESPERADO?

A: Forty-two shooting days. Can you believe that?

Q: Shooting in Mexico versus shooting in the United States? Any difference for you?

A: God, like night and day? In the U.S., if you want to shoot, you can't just call the cops and say "Close up the street first. Oh, and by the way can we borrow your .45?" Down there we could. Or go into the jailhouse and say "Could you please move all the prisoners into this other cell so we can film in this one? In fact, do you want to play the jail guard in the movie?" You can't do that here.

Q: Have you become a local hero for a lot of tough guys across the border, like Coppola did here after he made THE GODFATHER?

A: Oh jeez, I don't know. I'm afraid to find out!

F I L M O G R A P H Y

R O B E R T   R O D R I G U E Z

b. July 20, 1968 Austin, Texas
EL MARIACHI   Columbia, 1992
REBEL HIGHWAY: ROADRACERS (CTF)   Drive-In Classics Cinema/Showtime, 1994
DESPERADO   Columbia, 1995
FOUR ROOMS   co-director with Quentin Tarantino, Allison Anders & Alexandre Rockwell,
   Miramax Films, 1995
FROM DUSK TILL DAWN   Dimension Films/Miramax, 1996
THE FACULTY   Dimension Films/Miramax, 1998

$\mathcal{M}$ICHAEL $\mathcal{S}$CHULTZ

For 25 years, Michael Schultz has been the quiet man of Black American filmmakers, a modest pioneer consistently employed in either features or television. Working from a background in classical theatre, Schultz's first two films were the independently produced dramas TOGETHER FOR DAYS and HONEYBABY, HONEYBABY. He then eased expertly into the funky urban settings of COOLEY HIGH and CAR WASH before directing Richard Pryor in two of his early starring features, GREASED LIGHTNING and WHICH WAY IS UP? The vilified SGT. PEPPER'S LONELY HEARTS CLUB (which Schultz unapologetically defends within) and SCAVENGER HUNT moved the director away from the ethnic arena, but he returned with BUSTING LOOSE, again starring Richard Pryor, CARBON COPY and two examples of his best work—both made for television— BENNY'S PLACE and FOR US, THE LIVING, the latter a deeply moving biography of martyred civil rights leader Medgar Evers.

I spoke with Schultz in 1985, after he completed filming of THE LAST DRAGON, and his work since has alternated between theatrical features (KRUSH GROOVE, DISORDERLIES, LIVIN' LARGE) and telefilms (TIMESTALKERS, DAYO and two of the better YOUNG INDIANA JONES entries, YOUNG INDIANA JONES AND THE HOLLYWOOD FOLLIES and YOUNG INDIANA JONES: TRAVELS WITH FATHER). No one—least of all the modest Schultz himself—would claim that his films are great and enduring works of art, but there's much to be said for a man who, without fanfare, has gone about his business as a working director of unpretentious Hollywood entertainments. Even so, one can feel Schultz's frustration in the following conversation as he notes that "Right now we're heading into what I call a real errant period of teen movies and blockbusters. Everything outside of that is very difficult to get produced." Indeed, every one of his features since speaking those words has been a youth-oriented comedy. He certainly called that one right. . .

MICHAEL SINGER: *There's been speculation that* THE LAST DRAGON *is anything from a kung fu movie to a fantasy film, but I have a feeling that it's neither of the two. I'm wondering if you once again return to an urban setting, which you seem quite comfortable with.*

MICHAEL SCHULTZ: The setting is New York City. It's a contemporary urban fairy tale. Or, if you will, a musical fantasy. It is called THE LAST DRAGON because the lead character, whose name is Leroy Greene, is a young kid who wants to be Bruce Lee. There is an element of kung fu in this movie, but it's not a kung fu movie. It's a movie about a young man who finds who he really is, finding himself through various trials, like the trials of Hercules. It's very contemporary and laced with music. I won't call it a musical, but much of the film is driven by the Motown beat. And it's a love story.

Q: *Are these all original songs, or did you use any Motown classics?*

A: No, it's all original music. We toyed with the idea of using at least one classic but discarded it because we want the film to have a totally fresh feel to it.

Q: *Music seems to play an important role in your films, particularly the constant underscoring of* CAR WASH. *You obviously love music. Do you actively seek projects that will allow use to make extensive use of music?*

A: Sometimes. It really depends on the subject matter. I seek projects first and foremost out of the subject matter, usually with a narrative line that has something that, I feel, is valuable to say. I do love music and it's fun to work with.

Q: SGT. PEPPER'S LONELY HEARTS CLUB BAND *was one of the last musicals in which people were actually singing to each other.*

A: It was a tremendously underrated film and will probably come back around again sometime. A lot of people loved it, but all of the critics, almost, roundly hated it.

Q: *How badly do you react to negative responses from the press? I see that you didn't waste much time getting onto another project after* SGT. PEPPER. *It was certainly not your* HEAVEN'S GATE.

A: Actually, I took a long rest, much longer than normal, because at that point I had directed four features back to back. So I turned down a lot of projects just because I wanted a normal life. . . watch my kids grow up a little bit. Then I thought, better get another project going because I'll forget how to do it! No, critics do not really affect me. I was outraged by some of the critical responses to that picture simply because a lot of them were personal attacks on [producer] Robert Stigwood rather than the picture itself. Other than that, the audience will determine. Critics hated FLASHDANCE, for example. One of the problems with SGT. PEPPER is that everybody had grown up to the music of The Beatles, and The Bee Gees did not fit their idea of successors to The Beatles. FLASHDANCE, though, had all original music so audiences had no such similar problems.

Q: *If you had to do it all over again, would you have done it differently? Or did you pretty much make the movie you wanted to make?*

A: I think I made the movie I wanted to make. Stigwood had a very strong story concept, but outside of that, I had tremendous freedom to do whatever I wanted.

But after the picture got out and we saw the audiences' responses, we noticed that the two segments that were the most successful, musically, were Earth, Wind and Fire's rendition of Got To Get You Into My Life and Billy Preston's Get Back. They brought the house down. And what was different was that we were being extremely faithful to how the music was produced with all the other songs except those two. Those two artists wanted to do it their way. If I had to do it all over again I'd have all new and individual interpretations of The Beatles' classics.

Q: *You're one of the very few filmmakers who makes films on Black subjects which are essentially serious, even if they're comedies like CARBON COPY. How important is this to you as a moviemaker?*

A: It is very important. When I came to Hollywood, my background and reputation were all heavy drama, political statements and very impactful material. I had never really delved into comedy. I've always felt that all material, whether comic or tragic—in order to have value—should relate to something that we're about, the way we hope the world should be. And when it comes to Black material, a significant part of the human family in this country has had no real representation in the media. I'd just like to add to the quality of life on all our pans, Black and White and everything in between. . . if there's a good story to be told.

Q: *Such as the story of Medgar Evers in FOR US, THE LIVING, which was a rare piece of cinematic Black history. I'm almost amazed that you got it made in the first place.*

A: It wasn't easy. The torch carrier for that project was Ken Rotcop, a very committed person who happened to be Jewish. He tried to get the project made for seven years. He would just not give up. He had met Medgar Evers' wife, a magnificent woman who had gone through the first of three brutal political assassinations in a very close timespan. Eventually, he got the Corporation for Public Broadcasting to put up some money for it. I was not the original director, by the way. They had come to me first, but I was busy directing another film, and they hired someone else. Then they had problems, so I agreed to come to the rescue because I thought it was the kind of material that the world needed to know more about.

Q: *You must be very glad now that you were able to do it.*

A: Oh yes, it was a terrific experience. We shot it in Atlanta. The city was extremely cooperative in giving us locations and helping us with extras. We shot it in 17 days at a killing pace.

Q: *Before THE LAST DRAGON, your previous two films were both for television. Are there certain projects which you think are best suited for TV, and that you would actually prefer to make for the small tube rather than the big screen? Or would you prefer to stay with features?*

A: It really doesn't make that much difference to me. Television requires tighter schedules and money, and that's the only thing that I don't like about it. That is counterbalanced by the fact that television offers more latitude in dealing with topical subjects that feature producers feel might be too soft for theatres. From my standpoint, it's all the same. You have heard stories of how difficult it was to get projects produced like TERMS OF ENDEARMENT or THE CHINA SYNDROME or ONE FLEW OVER THE CUCKOO'S NEST. Those kinds of projects, now today more than ever, studios feel are too soft for theatrical audiences in light of escapist, blockbuster competition. But it's all horse puckey. Right now we're heading into what I call a real errant period of teen movies and blockbusters. Everything outside of that is very difficult to get produced.

Q: *You seem to veer from very different kinds of projects in tone and sensibility. It's difficult to type you. How do you see yourself?.*

A: I consider this first ten-year period my development stage. I wanted to explore as much as I could—unfortunately, I couldn't get a shot at really dramatic material, so I decided to try as many kinds of films as I could so that I could learn as much as possible. I think I'm ready to move on now.

Q: *Do you hope to return in any way to your classical theatre roots?*

A: As far as film goes?

Q: *Or theatre.*

A: Definitely yes. I've been away from the theatre for too long. I shot THE LAST DRAGON in New York, so I was back in my milieu. I realized how much I miss doing theatre. One of my earlier goals—which I abandoned because I kept working so much—was to alternate one film and one play a year. Now I'd like to get back on track and start incorporating some theatre into my schedule. It would be great fun to have a live audience there. When theatre is good, it is unforgettable. And when it's bad. . . it's horrible.

F I L M O G R A P H Y

M I C H A E L   S C H U L T Z

b. November 10, 1938 - Milwaukee, Wisconsin

TOGETHER FOR DAYS   Olas, 1973

HONEYBABY, HONEYBABY   Kelly-Jordan, 1974

COOLEY HIGH   American International, 1975

CAR WASH   Universal, 1976

GREASED LIGHTNING   Warner Bros., 1977

WHICH WAY IS UP?   Universal, 1978

SGT. PEPPER'S LONELY HEARTS CLUB BAND   Universal, 1978

SCAVENGER HUNT   20th Century-Fox, 1979

CARBON COPY   Avco Embassy, 1981

BENNY'S PLACE (TF)   Titus Productions, 1982

FOR US, THE LIVING (TF)   Charles Fries Productions, 1983

THE JERK, TOO (TF)   40 Share Productions/Universal TV, 1984

BERRY GORDY'S THE LAST DRAGON   THE LAST DRAGON   TriStar, 1985

KRUSH GROOVE   Warner Bros., 1985

TIMESTALKERS (TF)   Fries Entertainment/Newland-Raynor Productions, 1987

DISORDERLIES   Warner Bros., 1987

THE SPIRIT (TF)   von Zerneck-Samuels Productions/Warner Bros. TV, 1987

ROCK 'N' ROLL MOM (TF)   Walt Disney TV, 1988

TARZAN IN MANHATTAN (TF)   American First Run Studios, 1989

JURY DUTY: THE COMEDY (TF)   Steve White Productions/Spectator Films, 1990

LIVIN' LARGE   The Samuel Goldwyn Company, 1991

DAYO (TF)   Steve White Productions, 1992

YOUNG INDIANA JONES AND THE HOLLYWOOD FOLLIES (CTF)   Lucasfilm/Amblin
   Entertainment/Paramount TV, 1994

YOUNG INDIANA JONES: TRAVELS WITH FATHER (CTF)   co-director with Deepa Mehta,
   Lucasfilm/Paramount TV/The Family Channel, 1996

$\mathcal{J}$OEL$\mathcal{S}$CHUMACHER

What a long, strange and wonderful trip it's been for Joel Schumacher, one of the industry's most sought-after directors. Schumacher's seamless technique, sensitive work with actors and lack of pretension have resulted in a numer of popular works of first-class Hollywood entertainment, including ST. ELMO'S FIRE, THE LOST BOYS, FLATLINERS, FALLING DOWN and two of the most successful adaptations of John Grisham bestsellers, THE CLIENT and A TIME TO KILL. He was also passed the baton of that great hunk of enduring American mythology as the director of both BATMAN FOREVER and BATMAN & ROBIN, and along with A TIME TO KILL, Schumacher had three successive films that broke $100 million at the domestic box office.

Most recently, Schumacher returned to the urban grunge that informed FALLING DOWN—considered by some to be his finest work—for 8mm, a dark thriller starring Nicolas Cage and Joaquin Phoenix.

In the classic tradition, the Schumacher molds his technique to the subject matter, but he's a master stylist who pays equal attention to his films' dramaturgy and aesthetics. Rigorously prepared and confident, Schumacher never shoots 10 takes if three will suffice, and although he loves to maintain an atmosphere of fun and fellowship on set (with the cast, crew and general public), has little tolerance for ineptitude or foolishness.

I speak from experience, having worked on four of Schumacher's films. . . the two BATMAN opuses, A TIME TO KILL and now, 8mm.

Joel Schumacher emerged from the excesses of the fashion world in the overheated '60s—during which time he made a name for himself as a designer and co-owner of a hugely popular New York City store called Paraphernalia—as a costume designer on such films as Frank Perry's PLAY IT AS IT LAYS, Herbert Ross' THE LAST OF SHEILA, Paul Mazursky's BLUME IN LOVE and Woody Allen's SLEEPER and INTERIORS. Schumacher's dogged determination to direct led him to discover his considerable talents as a screenwriter on SPARKLE and CAR WASH, both of which demonstrated his ability to deftly juggle ensemble stories and characters. He got his first directing breaks on the telefilms THE VIRGINIA HILL STORY and the much-acclaimed AMATEUR NIGHT AT THE DIXIE

BAR AND GRILL before making his feature debut on THE INCREDIBLE SHRINK-ING WOMAN. Schumacher's career was truly launched by the raucous D.C. CAB, and then the era-defining ST. ELMO'S FIRE (writing both films, the latter in collaboration with Carl Kurlander).

Following 8mm, the unstoppable Schumacher was barrelling right into his future projects, including his long-awaited screen version of the Broadway musical hit DREAMGIRLS. The following conversation took place during principal photography of BATMAN FOREVER inside a cavernous domed studio in Long Beach, California, a long way from the dreary streets of Long Island City, New York, where the story began. . .

MICHAEL SINGER: *You're a rare case in the history of film, in that never before has someone who began his career as a costume designer for motion pictures gone on to become a successful director. Did you always want to make movies?*

JOEL SCHUMACHER: Since I was seven-years-old. I grew up behind the Sunnyside Theatre in a poor neighborhood in Queens, Long Island City. I lived in that theatre. I was one of those kids who had to be dragged out of the theatre. When I was about nine, I built a marionette theatre, along with the sets, costumes and marionettes themselves. I wrote these little plays and performed them with the puppets. Looking back on them now, I realize that since I had seen no theatre, I think I was trying to make movies in my own way. So yes, I always wanted to make movies, and I really consider myself extremely fortunate to have realized that dream.

Q: *In essence, everything that you achieved before entering the movie business—design school, your boutique in New York, the costume and set designing—were just vehicles toward the goal of directing.*

A: But I didn't know that. You know, we were poor. My father died when I was four. My mother worked in a store selling dresses six days a week and three nights a week to support us. There were no film schools then, no film colony in New York. I needed to make a living, and I had a dream of supporting my mother, so I went to art school. I had a scholarship to the Parsons School of Design, and I did the windows at Henri Bendel at night to support myself through school. I made a hundred dollars a week.

Everybody said that I had a great eye and a lot of style, and that I should go into the fashion business. I majored in fashion design at art school, graduated in 1965, and opened my store, Paraphernalia, with two other people in September of that year. It became an overnight success, and I went from making a hundred dollars a week to $20,000 a year. But then Charles Revson, who owned Revlon, bought out my contract, and I was suddenly making $65,000 a year. I was only out of school for a few months, and all of my dreams of taking my mother out of her little apartment in Queens and giving her some privilege came true. But she died suddenly right at that moment, in October of '65. It very traumatic, because I had sort of done all that for her. And it was a strange period for me, because by this time I was smack dab in the middle of the entire beautiful people '60s madness of New York City at that time, and I was rapidly becoming a drug addict.

After my mother's death, I just plunged into it. And also, I really didn't like the fashion world. I really wanted to make movies and be part of that world.

So I stayed in and out of the fashion world through the late '60s. I did Halston's first collection with him, when he was designing clothes. I worked for Diana Vreeland at Vogue. I always worked with very interesting, exciting people, but I was really one of the casualties of the '60s in the sense that I just became hopelessly immersed in drugs, sex and rock and roll. None of my life made sense. I just kept getting offers in the fashion world, and I didn't want that. I didn't know how to get into the movie world. I didn't know what I was doing. I really crashed and burned. I was down to 130 pounds, I had lost five teeth, I owed $50,000 in debts. . . my brain and my body hadn't been connected for years. I finally got off hard drugs in 1970, and I'm sure you've heard many people describe it as really feeling like you've been born again. I had to piece my life together, start all over again.

I decided that I was going to try and work in the movie business, but I had destroyed my reputation, and people were right to flee from me because like all drug addicts, I was irresponsible, self-consumed and reckless. So my old boss at Bendel's, Geraldine Stutz, gave me a chance again. I went back to my old job, did the windows and rebuilt the store, attracting a lot of attention again. Of course, I was making $10,000 a year and I owed $50,000, $30,000 of which was to the Federal Government. It was a tough year. I went through about a year-and-a-half living on two dollars a day. It was quite an interesting experience. Then I started getting offers to do art direction and styling in commercials. I really needed the money, and it also gave me a chance to work near the camera for the first time. I worked with some of the great commercial directors: Howard Zieff, Steve Horn, Lear Levin. Then through a friend, I met Dominick Dunne, who's now a world-famous author but was then a producer. I talked him into giving me a two week trial period as a costume designer on an independent film he was producing called PLAY IT AS IT LAYS.

Q: Which Frank Perry directed.

A: Frank Perry was kind enough to give me the chance, but it was really Dominick who kind of hounded him into letting me do this. The movie was from a great book of Joan Didion's, and she and John Gregory Dunne wrote the screenplay. So I gave up my apartment, my job at Bendel's, my life in New York. I gave up everything, and came out to Los Angeles the Christmas of 1971.

Q: You obviously survived the two week trial.

A: I passed the two week trial, and then I did several other movies as costume designer. The fourth film was SLEEPER with Woody Allen, who was not getting along with the production designer. Woody was the first director that I had worked with who really encouraged me to step outside my department and make other contributions to the film. So I started working on some of the sets and production design with him. And he also encouraged me to be a director. He's still one of my greatest supporters.

Q: Did he encourage you to write as well?

A: Yes, and he still encourages me to take bigger and bigger risks. He also gave me a wonderful piece of advice, which I always tell young people who are starting out or are at film schools. When I told Woody I wanted to be a director, and he told me that he thought I would be some day I said that it seemed so far away. And he said, "Yeah, but take a good look at the business. There's a handful of geniuses touched by the gods. The rest of them. . . if they can do it, you can do it. And you can do it better." I always tell that to people who are starting out, because it's really true. I'm not one of the handful of geniuses touched by the gods. I'm just a hard-working director, and I really worked my way up to this position in the business. It can be done.

Q: Shortly thereafter, you started to write screenplays?

A: I knew that I was never going to be a director through the costume and production design route, but I saw writers getting the opportunity to direct some of their work. I was living in a $60-a-month apartment in Hollywood, I had a little car, and was paying off my debts. I sat down at the kitchen table and started to write a script. . . and it sold for $9,000 to Barry Diller and a wonderful woman named Deanne Barkley who worked for him. At the time they were doing movies at ABC, before Barry became the head of ABC. It didn't get made, but I sold it. So fueled with this triumph—and you can imagine how much selling something for $9,000 meant to me then—I wrote a feature on spec, SPARKLE. Well, that sold to Robert Stigwood and Warner Bros., and did get made. It's a small movie, but it was my first movie. It was Sam O'Steen's first feature as a director. It also introduced actors Lonette McKee, Irene Cara, Dorian Harewood and Philip Michael Thomas, and Curtis Mayfield did the wonderful score. It's become a cult movie, and I'm proud of it.

Q: It was also the first indication of how in tune you've always been the popular culture that surrounds you.

A: I'm from the streets of Long Island City. I am a pop culture sponge. When rock and roll happened, it happened to me. I remember when I used to sneak a radio under the covers late at night to listen to a program that Alan Freed used to host that played what was then known as "race records." These fantastic black singers were singing music that is now called rhythm and blues. I remember Elvis Presley's first television appearance. I grew up when all the songs were by Tony Bennett, Georgia Gibbs, Teresa Brewer, Patti Page and Doris Day. The music was all big band influenced. And then suddenly this whole other pure American pop culture art form happened. At the same time I was in the movie theatres where this other great pop culture phenomenon—the American movie—was happening to me. Fabulous movies with Marilyn Monroe, James Dean, Montgomery Cliff and Marlon Brando were being made then. And at the same time, just by accident, there was a tiny little theatre in our neighborhood called the "Center" that showed foreign films. So I was watching DeSica and Fellini and Renoir and Kurosawa. That's why I always say that I'm a pop culture sponge. It's just what I live and breathe.

Q: So in SPARKLE, your first script to be filmed, you married your fascination with both film and music.

A: Yes, but not thinking about it. I used to stand outside all night at the Brooklyn Paramount so we could be in at the 9:00 AM rock and roll show. That's what SPARKLE is all about. I just wrote about something I knew. Then I wrote CAR WASH, which was a big hit. So I was able to use my writing to direct television movies. The second one, AMATEUR NIGHT AT THE DIXIE BAR AND GRILL, won a lot of awards. I was hoping to do as much TV work as they would allow me, hoping to build that into some kind of feature career. I got offered features right after I did AMATEUR NIGHT. And I said yes to THE INCREDIBLE SHRINKING WOMAN because I thought with my background in costumes and sets that it would be fun to do. And I had also been a big fan of Lily Tomlin.

Q: *I've read of the raw terror that you felt at that time.*

A: Well, I truly did not know what I was doing. And you know, I will always be grateful to Ned Tanen—who was running Universal at that time—for giving me that break. What a courageous man. Because I didn't know what I was doing. It was a strange thing. I wanted to be a director ever since I was a child, I thought that it was my calling. So naturally, I thought that when I did my first feature it would be pure genius. And it wasn't. I was so ignorant and so desperately ungifted that it was a shock to me. I was very confused after SHRINKING WOMAN, even though it was relatively well-received. But I was so astounded by my own lack of talent that I didn't know what to do with the rest of my life. But then, Thom Mount and Bruce Berman—who were then both executives at Universal—called and offered me a small, inexpensive movie called D.C. CAB. I was going to leave the business, but I thought I would try and see if I could do a good job, and if I really enjoyed directing.

Q: *And it was a big commercial hit.*

A: Well, D.C. CAB certainly wasn't LAWRENCE OF ARABIA, but it was a step forward. It was received well, and did well at the box office.

Q: *Did it give you your confidence back?*

A: Well, I enjoyed the process. It was a modest movie, but better than the first one. Then I started getting offered wacky comedies, and I realized that if I wanted to make a better movie I'd probably have to create it for myself.
So with my assistant at the time, Carl Kurlander, we sat down and wrote ST. ELMO'S FIRE. I had lived in Georgetown for part of the shooting of D.C. CAB, and was fascinated with after-college life, because Georgetown is a small community that seems to be of, by and for 22 year-olds. When we made the movie in 1984, we were in the middle of the '80s yuppie madness. It was a period when young graduates had to have a 25-year-plan. They had to have the right car, the right clothes, the right everything. They had to know who they were marrying and how many children they were going to have. So I decided to make a film about how difficult the personal, social, sexual, political life was for these people, and also how difficult it is to stay with a group of friends. But in casting the movie and writing it I had no idea it would have the impact that it did, because I didn't realize that people would identify with it on such a strong basis.

Q: *Your life must have changed radically once again after the success of* ST. ELMO'S FIRE.

A: Well, it did. I started getting offered all the yuppie angst movies, but I felt like I had already covered that area. So Mark Canton, Bruce Berman (who had moved to Warner Bros.) and Dick Donner offered me THE LOST BOYS. I thought I was going to say no, because the characters were all children, and I didn't think I was the right director. I called everybody to tell them I didn't think it was for me, but everybody had gone to lunch. So I went out jogging, and while I was doing that I thought, wouldn't it be great if they were teenage vampires, like a band of gypsies, with rock and roll? Everyone liked the idea, so we made the film, and it was a hit. There were a lot of people who didn't think I was a real director until THE LOST BOYS, even with the success of ST. ELMO'S FIRE.

Q: *THE LOST BOYS was a very different project from what you had previously done. Obviously, you were trying to demonstrate your range. How did the industry react?*

A: I became the vampire horror director, but I was lucky to get offered COUSINS, a romantic comedy which was 180 degrees away from LOST BOYS. And then I made FLATLINERS, which was a great time. Then I was going off to do THE PHANTOM OF THE OPERA, and it got canceled because Andrew Lloyd Webber was divorcing Sarah Brightman, and it became part of the legal entanglements.

Q: *I know that its cancellation was a huge disappointment to you, but have you been able to divert any of your PHANTOM intentions into BATMAN FOREVER?*

A: Oh yes. In a way, BATMAN is a better PHANTOM.

Q: *DYING YOUNG followed FLATLINERS, which seems to have been a very risky project from the start.*

A: I'm proud of the movie, and I think Campbell Scott and Julia Roberts did an extraordinary job. But I'm not sure if I was the right director for that movie, and I'm not sure I did it for the right reasons. I had fallen in love with Julia Roberts on FLATLINERS. But you don't do a movie because you're crazy about the movie star. . . you do a movie because you're crazy about the movie. And I don't know if it's the movie I would necessarily have done if Julia hadn't asked me to do it. There's no answer. But then I really got lucky. Warners offered me FALLING DOWN. And then to top that luck, Michael Douglas said yes to playing the lead.

Q: *FALLING DOWN was a highly topical and controversial piece that really changed the way people perceived you as a filmmaker. Is that why you did it?*

A: I was pissed off at America. We were in bad shape, and I was angry. Everybody was angry. I think all the credit for FALLING DOWN goes to Ebbe Roe Smith, who wrote it, because it really hit a nerve. It was a tough movie to make. We were on the mean streets of L.A. before, during and after the riots. We were rocking and rolling on those streets.

Q: *What about THE CLIENT? It's not only been a great box office hit, but it won you the best personal notices of your career.*

A: It's all thanks to John Grisham. Listen, it wasn't a novel in search of a movie. . . it was a movie! From the minute that boy gets dragged into that car until the last goodbye on the airfield, it's a movie. And I got a great cast. I'm a very cast dependent director.

Q: *You seem to be a director who actually likes actors.*

A: Well, you know, if you're going to be a painter, you'd better love paint. You better love color. I have friends who are directors who tell me they hate actors. I don't know how they go to work every day. It would be so painful. I love actors. I like to see them shine. I want them to be at their best.

Q: How did you feel when Warner Bros. asked you to direct BATMAN FOREVER?

A: I was down in Memphis and New Orleans getting ready to do THE CLIENT when I was summoned to Burbank for a meeting with Bob Daly and Terry Semel. They were wonderful, and we had a great meeting, and I said that I would really love to do the movie only if Tim Burton wanted me to do it. And thankfully, he did.

Q: What do you bring to the project?

A: Well, Batman was created in 1939, which is the year I was born. I grew up on Batman comics. I found them to be darker, sexier, more fun and iconoclastic than other comics. The whole legend of Batman has dark elements, but the comics are also done in bold, colorful strokes. I'm trying to capture both of these elements, so that the audience will have a visual ride as well as an engaging story.

Q: Are you concerned about the inevitable comparisons with Tim Burton's two Batman films?

A: I think Tim did a wonderful job with the other movies, but to copy someone isn't really to flatter them. I think it was incumbent upon us to give our own version of the Batman legend, trying to incorporate some of the great things Tim started, but also to give it a fresh look. Most of all, I want people to enjoy themselves.

Q: You work in a wide range of genres, as if you never want to repeat yourself thematically or even cinematically.

A: I think that there are a lot of great directors who excel by doing a version of the same movie over and over again. But I think the only way that I can learn is by doing something new that challenges me. I feel if I grow as a man and as a director, then hopefully the audience will get a better movie. Not that I think it's necessary for the audience to know that I made it, because I don't think it's necessary for the audience to know the director's name. I think it's important for the movie to have an effect, that they just have an experience.

Q: You don't seem to separate yourself from the audience. Perhaps you're not all that different now than the kid who spent hours in the Sunnyside Theatre?

A: I hope not. Sitting there in the dark, I had such great experiences watching those movies. I still do. I still love to go to the movies. It's my favorite thing to do . . . next to making them. I was such a lonely, disconnected kid, and those movies I saw reached out to me. If I can make movies, and they reach out to other people in the darkness, then I don't feel so lonely and disconnected anymore. That's the real thrill. Not fame, not fortune, not any of that. I've been lucky that all my movies have found an audience. Maybe not blockbuster audiences, but large enough for all of the films to have been profitable and known. And it's very exciting to go to Tokyo or Sydney or Rome and meet strangers that know and have been touched by my films in some way. I consider myself a very privileged and lucky man. And my worst days are when I forget how lucky I really am.

F I L M O G R A P H Y

J O E L   S C H U M A C H E R

b. New York, New York
THE VIRGINIA HILL STORY (TF)   RSO Films, 1974
AMATEUR NIGHT AT THE DIXIE BAR & GRILL (TF)   Motown/Universal TV, 1979
THE INCREDIBLE SHRINKING WOMAN   Universal, 1981
D.C. CAB   Universal, 1983
ST. ELMO'S FIRE   Columbia, 1985
THE LOST BOYS   Warner Bros., 1987
COUSINS   Paramount, 1989
FLATLINERS   Columbia, 1990
DYING YOUNG   20th Century Fox, 1991
2000 MALIBU ROAD (TF)   Spelling TV/Fisher Entertainment/CGD Productions, 1992
FALLING DOWN   Warner Bros., 1993
THE CLIENT   Warner Bros., 1994
BATMAN FOREVER   Warner Bros., 1995
A TIME TO KILL   Warner Bros., 1996
BATMAN & ROBIN   Warner Bros., 1997
8mm   Columbia, 1998

$\mathcal{R}$IDLEY $\mathcal{S}$COTT

Without question one of the film's great visual stylists, Ridley Scott has walked no easy path since exiting the television commercial world to bestow his visions upon the big screen. THE DUELLISTS, with its painterly evocations of a past world, was Scott's debut film, leading to the alternately beautiful and terrifying visions of the future in the now-classic ALIEN and BLADE RUNNER, two of the most influential and stylistically imitated films of our time.

Along with Alan Parker, Adrian Lyne, his brother Tony Scott and others, Ridley Scott is a graduate of what was tantamount to film school for many British feature directors—TV commercials. Working within the less constrictive boundaries of European advertising, these filmmakers developed a way of telling stories in striking, often concise images. . . narrative through pictures rather than words. Perhaps that's why Scott has often been praised more for his imagery than dramaturgy, although it can be argued that if film is first and foremost a visual medium, than that's the appropriate way to go.

I spoke with Scott relatively early in his career—between the releases of BLADE RUNNER and LEGEND, a gorgeous fairy tale which had trouble finding an audience—and his output since has been interesting, to say the least. SOMEONE TO WATCH OVER ME and BLACK RAIN were both suitably stylish thrillers—the latter against a neon-lit Japanese backdrop which had previously influenced BLADE RUNNER's look. These were followed by a definitive change-of-pace, the iconoclastic THELMA & LOUISE, a feminist road trip into America's heartland that was a smash hit on all levels, bringing Scott an Academy Award nomination for Best Director, and winning an Oscar for screenwriter Callie Khouri.

After releasing his long-awaited director's cut of BLADE RUNNER—much to the relief and gratitude of its millions of fans—Scott then tackled the ambitious story of Christopher Columbus in 1492: CONQUEST OF PARADISE, which met with a chilly reception. Scott's most recent two films—the seabound coming-of-age drama WHITE SQUALL and the high-testosterone Demi Moore vehicle G.I. JANE—were both perceived as offbeat projects for Scott by fans anxious for him to return to the mistier climes of his imagination. This was promised in a projected screen version of Richard Matheson's science fiction classic

I AM LEGEND, but alas, just as this book was completed, Scott withdrew from the project.

MICHAEL SINGER: *You've made three films, one set in the past, two in the future. You don't seem to be terribly interested in the here and now, rather creating alternate worlds for the audience. Is that accurate?*

RIDLEY SCOTT: It's an accurate assessment almost coincidentally. I've got no intentions of locking myself into that pattern. I tend to be somebody who rather follows his nose along a route. I have had a route of being involved with science fiction movies, since BLADE RUNNER and ALIEN are science fiction or futuristic movies. It just fell that way. There was really no preconceived plan. I mean, I've got every intention, at some point in time when I've got this out of my system, of moving around to more contemporary material. But I think that nearly all the material I get locked into has a slightly exotic central core to it. And half the predicament is that the present day, the way I see it, isn't terribly interesting to me.

Q: *Your films have a very specific look to them, and it's as if you might have taken your visions somewhere else—on canvas, in sculpture or on a stage. Why film?*

A: I've often asked that question myself because film, most of the time, is a lot of aggravation. If I were a writer I think I would probably stay with that, because writing in its physical form is the simplest art form. You have a pad, a piece of paper, a quiet room, and you can create your world. And it doesn't cost anybody anything, right? That's why I don't bother as a writer. I couldn't do it. I can write, but not to the degree that I can write screenplays. I started off as a painter. I did seven years of art school and three and a half years as a painter. I found the painting process to be—at that particular time in my life—slightly directionless. I was standing there filling in a white canvas. . . to what purpose? The occupation was too lonely. I think I needed people, to communicate with people and be happy about my own creativity. I can't stand my own company, and writing and painting are both lonely occupations, and static occupations. Obviously, the excitement of the obvious elements of cinema—the movement, the color, the sound—is much more exciting. Other than film, I think what I'd like to have done was to play in a band, because a musician to me is instant adrenaline and instant pleasure. Films take eighteen months to two years to turn around. The instant pleasure happens after that eighteen months and that's only if I feel I've got the film right which usually occurs sometime just at the end of the dubbing. The dub has just glued the film together and I think, "God, that's interesting," or, "Oh my God, it doesn't work." That's the biggest moment of pleasure. A musician gets his pleasure every night.

Q: *It's an interesting analogy. Musicians play together in bands, and filmmakers work in grand collaborative efforts. Your collaborations with designers and cinematographers have always been interesting.*

A: Well, I don't ever try and pretend to be an expert in all fields. I know about quite a few which are involved in the film process—art direction, the way a film should look—and therefore I suppose I know a little bit about cinematography. I certainly know how it should look to me. But I prefer to collaborate, and therefore the whole thing becomes a much stronger and richer process. And that's why, certainly in the last three films, including LEGEND, I've involved artists, illustrators or painters at a very early stage to illustrate the general feeling of the film. And these are usually very, very elaborate pieces of artwork. I'm very curious to actually go through that process as well as try something which is just about people in a contemporary environment. That would be a different kind of challenge.

Q: *When you were a boy, did you derive more inspiration from watching movies or reading books?*

A: When I was a kid I was not the inveterate filmgoer, probably because of the part of the world I came from. Northern England isn't exactly big film buff territory, so I used to be a regular Saturday afternoon kid going in to see Hollywood movies and look at the great rolling credits at the beginning and end of the movie and wondering who did what. The thing I actually keyed into was the person called the art director. That was my first real long term connection with the idea that I might want to make films, because I think my strongest subject, early on, was painting.

Q: *I know that you had a project for a time called KNIGHTS. Were you ever influenced by the Matter of Britain—the Arthurian legends?*

A: I don't know what makes any individual really tick, or what makes them gravitate towards one facet or the other, whether you are a contemporary person or have an affinity for the past. There is no specific answer to that question. I think as I began working seriously in advertising and commercials, I just found that I sort of gravitated towards period pieces, whether Victorian or earlier. I found that in England, the opportunity for me to explore all those kinds of periods was vast. Frequently I would change an idea or concept. I wanted to get into films, and the film that I found myself getting into was a Napoleonic period piece called THE DUELLISTS. I was shooting where Eleanor of Acquitaine used to live as part of her domain, and therefore I was actually walking through the forests and the fields everyday that were essentially Arthurian-where you mix fact with mythology. And I sort of keyed in on that. When I was doing THE DUELLISTS, I had the idea that I'd like to do something with knights, which nobody had actually done properly for many years. So we started planning something, and I went into a very highbrow version of that, which was TRISTAN AND ISOLDE. We had it scripted, but I felt that at that particular time it was just too esoteric—I wouldn't dare go in and do something like that as a general audience movie. I was interested in Hollywood cinema. I was being totally blown away at that point by Francis Ford Coppola, George Lucas, Steven Spielberg, and I thought, what am I doing? Here I am planning a little, minuscule capsule. I like what they do. And now, five years later, I finally came up with a writer who had developed something. Immediate past attempts at what I'd call Arthurian material hadn't worked for me. I can elaborate on why I don't think they work, but I don't want to do that in case mine doesn't. But I think I've got it right. It's taken four or five years thinking, going from TRISTAN AND ISOLDE, vaguely messing around with a project called KNIGHTS, which again, was too on the nose, too historical. I was trying to put more mystical magic into it rather than a strict historical piece about crusaders in North Africa. You can't do dialogue like, "My liege" and, "My lord" for a contemporary audience. And so what we've now come to is the story for LEGEND. The final idea for LEGEND, in a funny kind of way, has taken twelve years. It's a compilation of various do's and don't's. It's a kind of combination of Cocteau's BEAUTY AND THE BEAST and Walt Disney. . .

Q: *That's quite a combination.*

A: . . . meet THE EXORCIST.

F I L M O G R A P H Y

R I D L E Y   S C O T T
b. 1939 - South Shields, Northumberland, England
THE DUELLISTS   Paramount, 1978, British
ALIEN   20th Century-Fox, 1979, U.S.-British
BLADE RUNNER   The Ladd Company/Warner Bros., 1982, U.S.-British
LEGEND   Universal, 1986, British
SOMEONE TO WATCH OVER ME   Columbia, 1987
BLACK RAIN   Paramount, 1989
THELMA & LOUISE ★   MGM-Pathe Communications, 1991
BLADE RUNNER: THE DIRECTOR'S CUT   Warner Bros., 1992, U.S.-British
1492: CONQUEST OF PARADISE   Paramount, 1992, British-Spanish-French
WHITE SQUALL   Buena Vista, 1996
G.I. JANE   Buena Vista, 1997

GEORGE SIDNEY

To a lot of film buffs, Technicolor was invented just for George Sidney. A total original, utterly unafraid of splashing vibrant palettes across the big screen with abandon, his name has become synonous with "movie musicals." For at MGM in the 1940s and '50s—where the musical was king—Sidney was one of the princes.

Imbued with tremendous enthusiasm and flamboyant visual flair, Sidney directed not only such great MGM tuners as ANCHORS AWEIGH, THE HARVEY GIRLS, ANNIE GET YOUR GUN and SHOW BOAT, but was also responsible for more serious dramas like CASS TIMBERLANE and THE RED DANUBE, as well as the fabulous period pieces THE THREE MUSKETEERS, SCARAMOUCHE and YOUNG BESS. Even after departing MGM for Columbia in the late 1950s, Sidney continued to create some of the screen's most durable entertainments—THE EDDY DUCHIN STORY, JEANNE EAGELS, PAL JOEY, BYE BYE BIRDIE, and at MGM once again in the early 1960s, VIVA LAS VEGAS!, a cult favorite which most Elvis fans agree was his strongest musical film.

Sidney was always an experimenter and an innovator. Note the dance duet between Gene Kelly and Jerry the animated mouse in ANCHORS AWEIGH. Note the split screens and occasional animated backdrops in BYE BYE BIRDIE. Note the incredible climactic swordfight between Stewart Granger and Mel Ferrer in SCARAMOUCHE that seems to last just about forever, every bit as choreographed as the most elaborate numbers in his musicals. Justifiably, he was honored in 1998 with the Directors Guild of America President's Award, befitting his place in this nation's motion picture history, and his enormous contributions to the DGA through the years.

Retired from directing since 1968's HALF A SIXPENCE (appropriately, his last film was also a big-scale musical), George Sidney has instead pursued the study of law, paleontology and still photography, and has traveled the world several times over. I chatted with Sidney in the studio of his Beverly Hills home, awash in thousands of photographs he's taken on movie sets and on his international journies, a living museum of a man who is himself a living monument to what made—and makes—Hollywood great.

MICHAEL SINGER: When you started in the film industry at MGM, you were a messenger boy, sound technician, film editor, assistant director, second unit director and short film director before receiving your first feature assignment. How old were you when MGM first hired you?

GEORGE SIDNEY: Fourteen.

Q: Was directing always your ultimate goal?

A: The first day I went to work in the studio, somebody asked, "What do you want to be?" I said, "I want to be a director." They said, "It's impossible. There are 360 departments and you have to spend three years in each department." I said, "I'm young. I'll die trying." I had a kind of WHAT MAKES SAMMY RUN attitude. I was just curious to know everything about everything, and I speeded things up by working day and night. There's no question that in those days, it was easier without the union problems. You weren't so constricted as you are today.

Q: The system itself would actually help an aspiring director to become that if he had the talent?

A: Yes, and what none of us really knew was that we were being watched. I thought I was out there doing this and doing that, stealing a little something here and moving it over there, and the day I became a director I had already worked everywhere. One day somebody told me that the screen test director had gone to play golf and there were three tests to be made. So I went down to Stage 21 and said, "I'm the director." They said, "Well, okay, go direct." And suddenly, I was a film director!

Q: But you paid your dues before you were handed your first feature assignment?

A: I started with short films, tests and second units—you were expected to do all kinds of things. I'd get an assignment to leave the studio at 4:30 in the morning to shoot the sun coming up in San Diego. I'd call back and say, "Sorry, the sun didn't come up—there was too much fog this morning," and they'd say, "Get it tomorrow." I once spent 30 days on the beach waiting for the damn sun to come up. Or maybe they needed a shot of a cute gopher coming up out of a hole. I was available. I gladly did it. In those days, many directors would work on a picture if help was needed.

Q: That was something Gene Kelly talked about when I spoke with him. . . the spirit of camaraderie that existed among the different MGM directors who would help each other out in a pinch.

A: Nobody thought of asking for credit. . . you never did that. They had a backup system at MGM. A director would start a picture, but they would send the script to another director and expect him to know what was being shot every day. They might call you at seven in the morning and say "Get your ass out here, so-and-so is sick." So you'd just go right to work and know what had to be shot. You'd work for a day or two, and then the regular director would come back.

Q: Sounds like a good, supportive atmosphere.

A: It was fun. There was a free spirit in those days. We directors used to show each other our pictures, sit together and talk. Now I doubt that any of this exists, because there's no studio system anymore. Victor Fleming, George Stevens, Harry Beaumont, John Ford, Leo McCarey. . . they were bigger than life. It will never be the same.

Q: And what about films themselves nowadays?

A: What's happened in recent times is that they've disenfranchised people over 65 years old. God forbid you have grey hair, you don't go to a movie theatre. Times are rough. Hell, you're not going to take your grandmother out to Westwood on a Saturday night unless she's a Marine captain. Also, the subject matter that's prevalent nowadays—and we're generalizing here, which is always dangerous, because there are still pictures that everybody wants to see—has nonetheless lost 50 percent of the audience. But I would say that within ten years it will be a different ball game. There'll be all kinds of pictures again, thanks to pay TV, which I think will be very healthy.

Q: I want to go back again to the beginning. . . you're most famous as a movie musical director. . . was music a passion of yours as a child?

A: Oh yes. From the time I was five years old my father owned four theatres and I used to climb up on the organ benches and learn to play. Then I started playing violin, clarinet, saxophone. I studied music vociferously, but one thing that I didn't do was go to school. I had no feeling for it. I used to go down and hang around Broadway all day, taking dancing lessons at Billy Pierce's and Chester Hale's. Then to contrast that, I used to learn to box and wrestle in the gymnasiums, like Philadelphia Jack O'Brien's and George Bothner's.

Q: Both of your parents were in show business?

A: My father owned theatres and my mother was one of the three Mooney Sisters.

Q: When you started directing movie musicals in the early 1940s, it was a very transitional period for those kinds of films—moving from threadbare plots with huge, Busby Berkeleyesque production numbers to a more integrated format. What were you and people like Vincente Minnelli, Charles Walters, Gene Kelly and Stanley Donen trying to do with musicals at MGM that made them so different?

A: I'm not a spokesman for my other colleagues, but I think we all felt pretty much the same way. We all went to work every day trying to make entertainment. That's all there was to it. We never thought of anything else. I wanted people to come in and see the pictures I made and enjoy themselves for a couple of hours. If you say that I'm an escapist, well, that's fine. That's my bid. We were out to make entertainment. . . and I think we did.

Q: These days, there are a lot of directors who walk onto a set in the morning and think to themselves, "Okay, today I'm going to make history." You and your colleagues did make history at MGM. . . were you aware of it at the time?

A: On this I think I can speak for Mike Curtiz, Walter Lang, Pop Leonard and all the rest. . . we never really thought of the 80 million people in the audience who were looking over our shoulders as we made movies in terms of a threat. Again, I just wanted to entertain them. I believed that all girls were pretty, all men were handsome, people wore nice clothes, and everyone sang and danced perfectly. Maybe it was all too perfect, but you have to remember the times. We came back from a brutal war. Everybody just went back to work. . . it was a time of prosperity and happiness. As filmmakers, we just held up a mirror to the public and tried to reflect what they were feeling. I think that of late, they've held up the mirror again and reflected some of the worst things in America—and I don't think that is necessarily entertainment. I'm completely against censorship of any kind, but there's a point where serf-imposed decency should take over.

Q: *You had an astonishingly vivid color palette, as if you thought to use Technicolor for everything it was worth in a time when most features were still being shot in black and white.*

A: Being a bad painter, I was always interested in color. And without getting artsy, I tried to have a specific color palette for each film. With THE HARVEY GIRLS, I tried to capture the sand colors of the Southwest. In SHOW BOAT, I was influenced by a pretty good French artist named Monet. There's a shot of Ava Gardner on the railing which is almost an exact duplicate of a Monet picture. In other words, I tried to make the color fit the realism or non-realism of whatever the setting was without making the audience too aware of it.

Q: *You never wanted to make your technique obvious to the viewer?*

A: Technique should be something you have in your back pocket. You rely on it, but you don't force it out and say, "Look how good my technique is." The talent should come through in a natural fashion.

Q: *What astonishes me about your films is that even the non-musicals—I think in particular of* SCARAMOUCHE—*have a distinct rhythm. The great climactic duel between Stewart Granger and Mel Ferrer is every bit as choreographed as any of your musical numbers.*

A: Well, I always thought that SCARAMOUCHE would have worked very well as a musical, what with its theatrical backdrop. I sometimes thought of staging it on Broadway first. But Mr. Mayer very wisely said that if it was a big hit on stage, we wouldn't get to film it for five or six years. And if it was a flop, nobody would want to see it made as a film. Wouldn't it be fun, though, to stage THE HARVEY GIRLS in Vegas or Reno and bring a real train right into the theatre?

Q: *You seem to enjoy doing things full-sized. The centerpiece of* SHOW BOAT *was the real thing, wasn't it?*

A: Yeah, and all we were worried about was whether or not it would actually float.

Q: *Among your innovations was the famous dance duet in* ANCHORS AWEIGH *between the live Gene Kelly and the animated Jerry the Mouse. . . a combination which predated* WHO FRAMED ROGER RABBIT *by some 44 years. Have you seen* ROGER RABBIT?

A: No, but I understand it's wonderful.

Q: *Did you enjoy directing your nonmusical films as much?*

A: I think I preferred the musicals, because I would actually operate the camera on those. But as you said before, I always had the feeling that the nonmusical films were musicals. . . I always directed from a rhythmic point of view. I always rehearsed those films with music playing on a phonograph. . . drove them crazy on THE THREE MUSKETEERS and SCARAMOUCHE.

Q: *Toward the latter part of your career, you made what most people consider to be Elvis Presley's best musical film, VIVA LAS VEGAS! Are there any memories of Elvis that you care to share?*

A: That's a nine-part question. I don't think people had the proper respect for his talent. For VIVA LAS VEGAS!, we rewrote the script in ten days and tried to put some flesh on the character Elvis was playing. And the combustion that developed on-screen between him and Ann Margret brought an excitement to the picture that was often lacking in his other movies. I enjoyed working with Elvis very much. I was possibly a bit of a shock to him, because I, like Elvis, often drove to work on my motorcycle. That threw him off somewhat. I wore boots and wild clothes and collected crazy automobiles, and I think he was able to relate to me perhaps a little better than some of his older directors.

Q: *It's interesting that VIVA LAS VEGAS! was released only one year after BYE BYE BIRDIE— one of your most popular musicals—because the character of Conrad Birdie was a very funny parody of Elvis. How did he respond to the movie?*

A: He saw both the show and the picture, and I think he liked them.

Q: *I hate to ask such a boring old question, but I have to. . . of all your films. . . do you have a personal favorite?*

A: No. Each picture is a love affair. You play all the parts on and off the screen, you have this whole wonderful, warm feeling. Then comes the wrap party, you say good-bye to everybody, you'll never forget each other. . . and two years later you run into somebody and you say, "Hey, didn't we make a picture together?" There are a few people who you remain friends with, but each picture has a life all its own. When you finish editing a picture, it's an awful problem to cut the cord. Usually they take a small team of horses and drag you out of the cutting room.

Q: *When you stopped directing, you were only 50 years old and still in the prime of your career. What happened?*

A: Well, there were a lot of other things that I wanted to do with my life. I told myself that I'd better just do them while I was still in the condition to enjoy myself.

Q: *So what have you been doing for the past 20 years?*

A: I've been very busy. I've been studying the prehistory of man at international universities and traveling all over the world. Right after I finished films I went to the University of Southern California Law Center and tried to find out what law is all about. They gave me a little piece of paper that says I qualify to know something about the law. I suppose I've been to just about every archaeology and paleontology site in the world trying to find out where this mad species called Man came from and trying to decide where he's going.

Q: *And you've kept your eye sharp with still photography?*

A: Well, I have about a million negatives that I've shot through the years. I have photographic shows, and put a lot of pictures on videos which I run, not publicly but privately. I shoot at the DGA functions and parties. This year I've done some book covers and author's photographs.

Q: *Can we hope to see another George Sidney film?*

A: I would like it unashamedly, if it was something I feel. They tell me things are different. They tell me audiences are different. Well, I don't think that audiences can be that immune to entertainment. . . but who knows. . . you just never know. I'd like to test the world.

F I L M O G R A P H Y

G E O R G E   S I D N E Y

b. October 4, 1916 - Long Island City, New York
FREE AND EASY   MGM, 1941
PACIFIC RENDEZVOUS   MGM, 1942
PILOT NO. 5   MGM, 1943
THOUSANDS CHEER   MGM, 1943
BATHING BEAUTY   MGM, 1944
ANCHORS AWEIGH   MGM, 1945
THE HARVEY GIRLS   MGM, 1946
HOLIDAY IN MEXICO   MGM, 1946
CASS TIMBERLANE   MGM, 1947
THE THREE MUSKETEERS   MGM, 1948
THE RED DANUBE   MGM, 1949
KEY TO THE CITY   MGM, 1950
ANNIE GET YOUR GUN   MGM, 1950
SHOW BOAT   MGM, 1951
SCARAMOUCHE   MGM, 1952
YOUNG BESS   MGM, 1953
KISS ME KATE   MGM, 1953
JUPITER'S DARLING   MGM, 1955
THE EDDY DUCHIN STORY   Columbia, 1956
JEANNE EAGELS   Columbia, 1957
PAL JOEY   Columbia, 1957
WHO WAS THAT LADY?   Columbia, 1960
PEPE   Columbia, 1960
BYE BYE BIRDIE   Columbia, 1963
A TICKLISH AFFAIR   MGM, 1963
VIVA LAS VEGAS!   MGM, 1964
THE SWINGER   Paramount, 1966
HALF A SIXPENCE   Paramount, 1968, British

STEVEN SODERBERGH

When *sex, lies, and videotape* became an international film festival favorite (winning, among other awards, the Grand Prix at Cannes) and a major critical and box office success in the United States, no one could have been more surprised than its young creator. As admitted in the following conversation, he remarkably gifted Steven Soderbergh wrote *sex, lies, and videotape* as an act of personal expiation rather than as a determined commercial venture, never dreaming that millions of moviegoers would so willingly hook into his moving and funny vision of alienation and salvation.

Sharpening his filmmaking skills with a series of self-financed shorts, Soderbergh brought the craft of a talented veteran to *sex, lies, and videotape*, his first feature. Quickly heralded as Hollywood's latest flavor of the month, Soderbergh quickly proved that his independent streak—which included re-siding in Virginia, some three thousand miles from Los Angeles—would not be compromised. (Indeed, this was a telephone interview from the West Coast to the East). He followed his debut with a series of progressively quirky films that included KAFKA, KING OF THE HILL, THE UNDERNEATH, SCHIZOPOLIS and GRAY'S ANATOMY, not one of them indicating that Soderbergh had any intention of "settling down." However, he finally lent his talents to a major studio for the accessible and brilliantly reviewed OUT OF SIGHT. It seems unlikely, however, that Soderbergh will abandon his beloved esoterica for the fleshpots of Babylon any time soon.

MICHAEL SINGER: *Have you been truly surprised by the commercial success of* sex, lies, and videotape?

STEVEN SODERBERGH: Well, when I finished the screenplay, I certainly felt it was the most aggressively non-commercial thing I had ever written. I had other pieces of original material, five other screenplays, that I felt were much more accessible and palatable. Of course, they hadn't gone anywhere either, but for different reasons. All of them were on a bigger scale, and people were reluctant to drop four or five million dollars on a first-time director. *sex, lies, and videotape* was written so much as an act of expulsion—I just had to get it out of my system—that I didn't really expect anybody to want to do it. I thought I would have to raise some money from friends and make it on the cheap for about $60,000.

Q: How was the film financed?

A: What happened was, Robert Newmyer, Nancy Tenenbaum and Morgan Mason [the producers of the film] all had connections that we ended up following. Bob Newmyer knew a gentleman named Larry Estes at RCA/Columbia, and he is the man who got the film made. He liked the script very much and just pushed it through. Nancy and Morgan, meanwhile, pursued connections that they had with Virgin Vision in the U.K. for foreign financing. RCA/Columbia came in for $1.2 million, and Virgin bought foreign rights for about half that figure. But our actual production budget was $1.2 million.

Q: It went a long way on-screen.

A: It did. The irony is that most of the money—even though the actors accepted well under what they normally got—went to actor's salaries. Which is why, when people say "Couldn't you have used more money?," I think the film would not have been any better with more money, and it may even have been worse. I don't know if the film that I originally thought about making for $60,000 in black and white and 16 millimeter would have been any worse. I think it would just have been very different.

Q: Although $1.2 million is a lot grander than $60,000, it's still a very small budget by feature standards. Do you think the budgetary restrictions helped to make sex, lies and videotape the film that it turned out to be?

A: Absolutely. I think that the film could have been harmed by attempts at opening it up, saying, "Well, we got more money, so let's try to stage more of it outside." I think ultimately that would have diluted it. In this case, the enforced restrictions were helpful.

Q: I assume that going the independent route, the film didn't have to go through the usual development hell.

A: Well, you're right in the sense that it didn't have to go through that kind of creation-by-committee process, which is rarely successful. Most of the changes that did occur were discussed with Nancy Tenenhaum over a period of months, and then of course, once the actors got involved. We had a week's worth of rehearsals before we started filming, and I made a lot of changes in the dialogue and incorporated ideas from the actors. The changes were very consistent, and always along the same lines.

Q: There was such a sense of the actors completely inhabiting their roles in the film.

A: I thought so, too. Obviously, in a film like this, rehearsal time is mandatory. I knew that we needed time, and I knew that ultimately it was important for the performances to be good, that each actor be able to bring something to their part. That was more important than them speaking every word that I wrote. I also think it's important, when you're directing your own script, to have a healthy disrespect for your own material. Ultimately, you have to sit there and make decisions while you're shooting, and I believe that actors have to sound natural. And if you're objective about it, if you have good actors and can tell them, "Look, if you're having trouble with the lines, just make them your own," then they will. It's idiotic not to take advantage of actors who have really good ideas.

Q: *It was a revelation to discover what a wonderful actress Andie MacDowell is.*

A: I felt lucky for the two of us, actually, when she came in to read. I felt lucky for me because I was going to look like a hero. I got to look smart simply because I recognized her talent. I felt the same way about Laura San Giacomo, who had never done any films. I'm so happy for Andie, because she had been getting a bum rap after they dubbed her voice in GREYSTOKE. Like a lot of actors, Andie needs to be comfortable. When she is comfortable, she can be amazingly unselfconscious. I did everything in my power to make sure she was comfortable, and I got everything I wanted from her performance.

Q: *The film struck an amazing chord in the public, almost as if a lot of us saw pieces of ourselves in not one, but all four of the protagonists. I don't know if that was your intention, because you often speak of how personal the film was to you.*

A: That's exactly why I've been so surprised by the success of the film. It did seem to me, in many ways, very fragmented, very internal, and reflected things that only I thought about at any great length. I may have just overestimated how unique I am. It turned out that everybody has these thoughts.

Q: *I recall reading that you wrote sex, lies, and videotape almost as an act of contrition.*

A: Yes, I was trying to get this thing out of my system. I'd been through a relationship that I really screwed up, and I thought for a long time. . . why did this happen. . . how did this happen? I guess my therapy was to turn it into art. So in many ways, once it was written, it had served its purpose. And since it had, in this odd way, there was less of a burning desire to get this film made than some of my other unproduced scripts.

Q: *Was there ever a point where you were almost afraid to put something so personal on film?*

A: There were a couple of times when I knew that the line was very, very fine, in the sense that it was either going to be very good or unbearably pretentious.

Q: *Do you feel that the film is, as so many critics have suggested, more European than American in style?*

A: Yes and no. I do things that seem more European than American in execution only because the film is paced in a way that many American films aren't. But the films that I kept in mind like FIVE EASY PIECES and THE LAST PICTURE SHOW—are films that I felt were incredibly well directed, that had the consistency of conception and execution. If you were looking at these films as a director, you saw that they were very wonderfully made, yet not flashy, and never called attention to themselves. It just always seemed like the camera was in the right place. That's the kind of thing I tried to keep in mind, and certainly those are two very American films.

Q: One thing that impressed me about sex, lies, and videotape was that it seemed to at the same time have an improvisational quality, and yet the camerawork was very careful and meticulous. I know that you were open to changes from the actors, but how prepared would you be with mapping out camera placement?

A: I really went seat-of-the-pants, because I knew that this was a performance movie. We'd come onto the set, block the scene-making whatever changes or improvements that we had made through all the various processes of rehearsal—and then I would decide where to put the camera. The camera always followed the actor, and so in that way we were able to easily accommodate any improvisation. At that point, the improvisation going on was extremely minor and would not really affect camera placement. It was really a matter of watching the actors go through a scene and finding the right tone.

Q: But the film never seemed static, even though most of it was shot indoors.

A: That was a tough one. I knew that I was going to have to keep the camera moving a decent amount to keep things going, but I didn't want it to move in a way that called attention to itself. I really wanted this feeling, or impression, of the camera floating toward something, both emotionally and visually.

Q: The film was shot far away from Hollywood, in Baton Rouge, Louisiana. Is that where you're from?

A: Mostly. I lived there longer than anyplace else, and that's where I started making films.

Q: Can you talk about your background in films? Where did you acquire the assurance you demonstrated in sex, lies, and videotape?

A: Well, I think the most important thing to address and especially people reading interviews with directors who are themselves aspiring directors—is that I've made a lot of short films, and have essentially done a lot of odd jobs, both in and out of the film business, to finance them—in the belief that they are the only real proving ground for feature filmmaking. On the other hand-and this is the key—they were never resume pieces. In my case, they were never shown, except to people who were interested to see my work. They were all very legitimate, very personal acts of expression. I was trying to develop my craft as a filmmaker and getting ideas onto the screen. The last three shorts that I made are every bit as complex, technically and conceptually, as sex, lies, and videotape— which is kind of distressing, because it makes me feel like I haven't really come that far since I got out of high school! The other important thing about financing your own short films is that you get a very clear understanding of what things cost. I did the budget for sex, lies and videotape with John Hardy, one of the producers. I did the first version, he did the second, and then we went back and forth adjusting every dollar in the budget so that we could get bang for our buck. I think it's going to be interesting to see if I'm able to apply the same "guerrilla filmmaking" mentality to a film that costs $5 or $10 million. In theory, if I made a film for $1.2 million that looks like $2.5 or 3 million, then I should be able to make a film for $9 or $10 million that looks like $15 million. I can't stand waste on a film.

Q: Some people suggest that you can learn how to direct by watching films.

A: Well, I think that's like a woman watching another woman giving birth it's just not the same thing. There's only one exception that I can think of off-hand, and that's Lawrence Kasdan, who hadn't directed anything before BODYHEAT. But if you're an inexperienced, insecure director, things can get bad quickly. If you've never directed anything before, you'll be up against a lot of things that will be confusing, frustrating and nerve-wracking. If you don't know what's important to deal with and what to let slide down your back, it's going to drive you nuts. It's not something I would wish on just anybody.

Q: When you walked onto the sex, lies, and videotape set that first day, did you have that confidence?

A: It was no big deal. I had a few more people on the crew than I was accustomed to, but not that many more. I knew the process, and it's the process of making a film that excites me, not the reward. So that's why, when people ask me if I'm afraid of getting swallowed up by Hollywood, I just answer that basically, the process is the same. It may involve more money, but you still have to tell a story in a series of images, and you have to shoot them one by one whether it's in Super 8-millimeter or 35-millimeter.

Q: You indicated before that you had some scripts that were more commercial than sex, lies, and videotape. Does this mean that you're not necessarily committed to alternative cinema?

A: Although I have an appreciation for specialty films, I don't want to make them for the rest of my life. There may be other films that I'll make that will fall into that category, but certainly not all of them. It just worked out with sex, lies and videotape that this particular script, this particular budget and these particular people came together. But I like a lot of different kinds of films, and I'll make a lot of different kinds of films if I'm able to.

F I L M O G R A P H Y

S T E V E N   S O D E R B E R G H

b. January 14, 1963 - Atlanta, Georgia
sex, lies, and videotape   Miramax Films, 1989
KAFKA   Miramax Films, 1991, U.S.-French
KING OF THE HILL   Gramercy Pictures, 1993
THE UNDERNEATH   Gramercy Pictures, 1995
SCHIZOPOLIS   Northern Arts Entertainment, 1996
GRAY'S ANATOMY (PF)   Northern Arts Entertainment, 1996, U.S.-British
OUT OF SIGHT   Universal, 1998

OLIVER STONE

My conversation with Oliver Stone took place at a Holiday Inn in Chinle, Arizona, within the borders of the Navajo Indian Reservation. The first week of principal photography on NATURAL BORN KILLERS had just been completed. All over the "Four Corners" region at that point in time, chaos ruled supreme as a mysterious respiratory illness (later identified as a Hantavirus) took its toll both on and off the Reservation. Hell was breaking loose. But filming progressed without delay on NATURAL BORN KILLERS, a satire about love, violence and the American media, which promised to become the most controversial film of a controversial career. . . and was, in spades.

I pretend no objectivity. I was working on the film as unit publicist, had already worked with Stone on HEAVEN AND EARTH (and would again on NIXON), and developed a working and personal relationship with him that explains the informal, what-the-hell nature of the discussion that follows.

Oliver has now directed 13 films: SEIZURE, THE HAND, SALVADOR, PLATOON, WALL STREET, TALK RADIO, BORN ON THE FOURTH OF JULY, THE DOORS, JFK, HEAVEN AND EARTH, NATURAL BORN KILLERS, NIXON and U-TURN. He co-wrote CONAN THE BARBARIAN, YEAR OF THE DRAGON, SALVADOR, WALL STREET, TALK RADIO, BORN ON THE FOURTH OF JULY, JFK, NATURAL BORN KILLERS and NIXON. He wrote MIDNIGHT EXPRESS, SCARFACE, PLATOON and HEAVEN AND EARTH.

Stone is not without his enemies. Many filmmakers have no enemies. They've never directed projects risky enough to win them. Stone has managed to delight and outrage, provoke and entertain. And two things are certain: he will not stop making the films he wants to make; and none of them will be "safe." What he has been, and continues to be, is ahead of his time, with all of the fame, notoriety, criticism and imitation coming with that particular territory. Stone is both evolutionary and revolutionary, incapable of dancing to anybody's tune but his own.

MICHAEL SINGER: *You work at a much faster clip—in terms of going from one project to another—then just about any other major filmmaker. You've released two films in one year, which is almost unheard of for an "A" director. You seem to be driven by a need to work.*

OLIVER STONE: There's a degree of anonymity in it. There's been a lot of pent-up impatience. For years, this is what I wanted to do, and I always knew it. And there was such a period of writing and obstacles, and it taught me a lot, too, about patience. But I feel that when you have a window, and you're in your stride, you should exercise. A horse is only good if it runs in daily practice.

Q: *Years ago, one of your colleagues told me that the only time he ever felt free was when he was on the set working. Do you share that sentiment?*

A: I think that's true, because you lose yourself. And sometimes in losing yourself, you find yourself again. And it becomes a bit narcotic. The need to re-design yourself and reevaluate yourself.

Q: *Sometimes I get the feeling that you think directing is a gift that was given to you for a certain period of time. I mean, you're going to be doing this forever and with the same intensity.*

A: Who says? It could disappear tomorrow.

Q: *You really think so?*

A: Yes. I could live somewhere else and do something else. . . or not do something. I've gone through a lot of different stages in my life, doing different things. I'm not sure who my real self is.

Q: *It's not as if you're playing it safe. You keep pushing in different directions. With NATURAL BORN KILLERS, you're heading into the realm, to some degree, of experimental filmmaking. You don't seem to be afraid.*

A: I have my own fears.

Q: *Which you explore on screen.*

A: Some of them I have.

Q: *Every time someone thinks your career and subject matters have settled in a comfortable direction, you take an unpredictable turn. With HEAVEN AND EARTH, some may feel that they're seeing—if you'll pardon the expression—a kinder and gentler Oliver Stone. That some of the rage is subdued through a story of spiritual enlightenment. But that was only one thing on your mind that you wanted to explore, because now with NBK, the rage is definitely back. Each one of your films examines its protagonists' spiritual odysseys, but those journeys can be gentle, or they can be brutal. . .*

A: I hope you don't mind if I don't answer any of your questions. I like to hear you rattle on.

Q: *Rattling is one of the things I do best. Anyway, at what point did you know that film was going to be the vehicle of your creative expression rather than just writing?*

A: During NYU. 1969 to '71. I felt the urge.

Q: Were there any inklings before then?

A: No. Not in film. I never thought it was available. The concept of film school just started to emerge in the late '60s, and the concept of getting the G.I. Bill to pay for going to school seemed attractive to me.

Q: What did film school do for you?

A: Basically, for me it was a period of discovery, coming off the war, going back into a domestic situation, going into an ego-ridden film school, crawling up the walls. Highly competitive, baboon cage environment, difficulty in obtaining materials, working very hard even then to make films. I made three films while I was there. I had a lot of ideas, and I loved Godard, who was my hero at that time. He was prolific, thinking of ideas, trying new ways of expressing them. Nothing was sacred. BREATHLESS inspired me deeply because it was done so cheaply in 16 millimeter (I think for about $60,000).

Add to that Antonioni and Fellini and Buñuel, who were also discoveries in film school. And then an increasing appreciation—at first not much but increasing appreciation of American films, going back to the '30s, '40s, '20s, and even admiring the films of our youth in the '50s. So I guess I'm saying that at that point of my life—and it still is—film was a dream. It was a delight to come away from Vietnam and get involved in something so creative and interesting, and in a sense avoiding the war and losing myself so I wouldn't think about all the demons in Vietnam. I tried to hide that stuff. I just wouldn't give in to it. Made films about it. It's probably all coming out now. I don't know if I did the right thing. I never thought it, I kind of suppressed it. And in a way, doing PLATOON and BORN ON THE FOURTH OF JULY so many years later was a wonderful opportunity to deal with that. Hanging out with Dale Dye, and all of those guys, really brought me back and helped me get through that process. And I think you can use film as a vehicle for having your own life. Sometimes you do it obliquely, like in NATURAL BORN KILLERS. I think I'm examining a part of myself that's very, very scary to me. . . very close to me. There's a lot of me in those characters. And that view of the world is a dark view. I admire Truffaut for having dealt so directly with his view. I admire any filmmaker. . . Louis Malle for example. . . who are so personalized in their view of the world.

And then there were the Americans. Kazan, Sturges, Stevens, Ford, Welles, Wyler, Fleming, Huston, etc. I'm reluctant to get into a catalog of names, because you always leave out people. I think that what you discover in film school is that there's a tradition of filmmaking. You're joining a tradition. I'm always torn between that and the pirate. . . the pirate and the traditionalist.

Q: Do you feel a sense of responsibility to that parade you're joining? Or ultimately is it only a responsibility to yourself and your own inclinations?

A: It's a bit of both. I don't think you're only responsible to yourself, although it can be true. But I think that sometimes you have to step back and give yourself a little pause from the subjectivity of your life and try to see the tradition. Understand where you are in the flow of time, and what your films are really saying and adding up to. I always felt when I did SALVADOR in '85, I made kind of a personal vow having been through so many setbacks, having things derailed—a lot of frustrations. I was doing a lot of writing, but it wasn't happening with my writing. I had much self-doubt about whether I really could write. But when I did SALVA-DOR, I thought that every time you go out and throw a stone, you should throw it as hard and as far as you can. It's only a moment in time, so make it good, because you may not get the other chance. Nature and time are crueler than any single human being I've known.

Q: *You do seem to have the audience at heart, but at the same time it doesn't restrict what you're trying to say and how you're trying to say it. Yet, one of the criticisms often leveled at your films is that they drive home their points too strongly, not giving the audience an opportunity to come to their own conclusions. You've actually been compared, both positively and negatively, to Frank Capra. Does that disturb you?*

A: Yes, it disturbs me, but it doesn't disturb me as much as it would if I was making movies and no one responded, and they had no audience. I think there's been so much categorizing about it, that it's really distorted from what it really is. And I just think that they should be watched as films. I think they're well-made films, very exciting. You don't have to buy it. You sit, you watch and share in the filmmaker's enthusiasm. Hopefully you share that point of view, but not necessarily. You just may not. You can't worry about that too much, because if you broaden yourself out too much, you become a publicist.

I think it's important to keep an ear. I worry about that—listening to people. You have to get out there in the streets with people, countries, places. You have to listen to the world. The more talking you do sometimes, the worse off you are.

Q: *I should remember that when I do interviews.*

A: I felt strongly about [John F.] Kennedy. And I obviously let a lot of my personal emotions get into JFK. Because I really felt the truth was faked. He'd been killed duplicitously, and the people of an older generation should have known better. They should have done something about it instead of sleeping in the closet. The generation of our fathers behaved like vipers. And they never sought to deal with it. They put it in the long bag of repression, as Robert Bly calls it. I guess I'm passionate about it, but I also see my own passion and I can detach from that more so than maybe I was, because there's a line at which an artist can become a politician. And then he should be a politician. I think the film helped open files. That's a thankless task.

What's being forgotten in this stampede of angry rhetoric over who shot Kennedy, or why, is the larger issue of how our government is run in secrecy, and how the secrets are really so distorted, so warped by this point in time—50 years of Cold War behavior. In my opinion, America has radically changed into a much more ghastly and darker empire. World War I is really the kernel of this century, and it echoes right up to Bosnia and Herzegovina now. It's like those ripples that will go for the next seven or eight years. It's going to be an interesting summing up of the 20th century.

I would also like to do comedies and have fun making films. We shot a scene the other day for NATURAL BORN KILLERS, a kind of Roger Corman homage. We went out in the desert, back seat of a car, a half-naked blonde with a gun, a guy with a shaved head looking right out of a '50s movie in a black leather jacket wheeling down the highway, pursued by a high-speed cop, firing bullets.

Q: When I was on the set that day, I thought, shit, I feel like I'm on the set of EAT MY DUST. In fact, NATURAL BORN KILLERS does have lots of comedic elements weaving in and out of the darkness. Some of the scarier stuff is comedic, and you seem to be having a lot of fun with it.

A: Is that good?

Q: I think so. It has to be, actually. If this thing were shot like IN COLD BLOOD. . .

A: Well, it could be shot like IN COLD BLOOD. It's a very scary movie in its origin and there's a definite movie there that is frightening. It could be well done.

Q: But then it becomes HENRY: PORTRAIT OF A SERIAL KILLER.

A: It could have been a great B-movie. It's a question of whether you do a B-movie or do you try and raise your sights and go A level on subject. And then you can blow that. . . all the B people want you to blow it. They love to say, "Oh, it could have been a great little movie." They always say that. There's a great little movie in there someplace. The cynics also always say the original was better. It's easy to criticize, easy to hate, hard to build. But in this case, we've got to look at all the levels of the movie. It could be a ridiculous movie. This is a total all-out gamble. Arizona, after one week of shooting. This is madness. This is chaos. This is a splendidly gothic road movie. Sam Peckinpah meets Kubrick. I enter these gates so humbly, but it's exciting to be in their trail. I don't care, whatever. But they rode that path well, and I'm taking my horse out.

Q: There are certainly elements of Peckinpah and Kubrick here, but you also seem to be getting back to the French New Wave filmmakers you loved so much at NYU.

A: I've always used black and white, and 16 millimeter.

Q: Yeah, sure, particularly in JFK, which incorporated the biggest pastiche of visual elements. A little blue period with a little cubist. But here it's being used more in the service of sleazy fun.

A: No. Wrong. Bing! The duck comes down from the ceiling. You lose.

Q: But certain scenes. . . like the Corman homage.

A: What is the moral. . . what is the message of this movie?

Q: Oh man. The demon's always out there. And inside of ourselves. We keep turning away from the demon. We think that if we ignore him, he'll go away. We won't face the insidious relationship between criminals and the media. We have these twin hydras. . .

A: Twin hydras? What are you talking about?

Q: The media. . . and murderers. They're linked. They always have been. Today it's TV which promotes their exploits. Five hundred years ago it was troubadours. But we were talking before about the direction this country has been taking. Has there been less of an awakening?

A: Walter Winchell is back.

Q: He always is. I was thinking of that great quote. It was Admiral Yamamoto of the Japanese Imperial Navy, and of course, it was the last line of dialogue from TORA! TORA! TORA!, which is the real reason I know it. After Pearl Harbor, he said, "I feel that all we have done is to awaken a sleeping giant, and fill him with a terrible resolve. I think America has become a sleeping giant once again. Morally, intellectually, politically. Do you think that things are being shoveled under again, that the tide has come in and is taking everything back with it?

A: Yes, I do. I think it goes into the collective unconscious. Therapy won't work, because it applies only to the conscious mind. Only deep immersion, hypnosis and meditation can affect us. It's fear. . . some boy in Louisiana shoots a Japanese guy at his doorstep. That's fear. There's a lot of fear out there. Fear is a very paralyzing emotion in our society. . . in many societies.

Q: *"Fear is the mind killer." Frank Herbert's DUNE. Or at least the movie version.*

A: Film is a means to liberate that fear, liberating all the psychic emotions that are buried in the long bag that we haul. Movies cut to the quick a lot sooner, the good movies. People know right away what's going on. That's why with JFK, many of us were worried about the multitude of information, that it would be confusing. But it worked out—I think that the average moviegoer is much more open than the traditional view of the moviegoer.

Q: *Well, both my 75-year-old mother and 11-year-old nephew understood everything in JFK.*

A: That's pretty amazing, because it's still confusing in some parts to me!

Q: *I'd like to ask you about your first two features.*

A: They were learning experiences, to put it kindly. I enjoyed making them. What did you think of them?

Q: *I never saw SEIZURE. THE HAND I liked very much.*

A: Really?

Q: *Yeah. It stayed with me.*

A: The mood of it bothers me so, because I feel like there's so much talking. I wanted to re-shoot parts of it. To watch your own films is nerve-wracking. It makes you. . . it shouldn't, I hope I'm getting beyond that. . . but it irritates you because you think of something you missed, and it hurts you to think of your ignorance. It makes you self-critical and self-doubting.

Q: *Do you feel that way about every one of your films?*

A: Yes. Absolutely. It's very difficult for me still.

Q: *Do you also ever feel that way after you film a scene? I don't ever see you going back to re-shoot something.*

A: I think I get bored sometimes. When it's done, I want to move on. My restless instinct wants to solve the whole crossword puzzle sometimes, and then go back and worry about the details later. I would reshoot. I mean, if you're happy, and you walked away 85 percent convinced that you were there, you can let it go. But then, it may not work and then you may have to re-shoot, if you need to re-shoot. Or you can cut the scene. Sometimes that's simpler.

Q: But the spontaneity of the moment seems to be important to you. I never see you work with storyboards, even in the most complex sequences.

A: I sometimes do boards. Things happen, though. I see the whole scene in my head, generally, in the writing or co-writing of it. I come in with a plan in my head, it's all drawn and imagined. And if you have it in your head, why do you have to write it down? The reason for writing it down, it seems to me, is sometimes you can get confused on the set. It's chaotic, and you might lose track. You've been on the sets. You'll see me look at the book. I sit in this quiet little black dome where I can think and remember the initial impulse, the original reason for the scene. Sometimes the obvious is confused in a war situation. It's the same thing in a movie situation. I often look up in amazement during a take at an actor or actress who has just said one of the lines that I didn't recognize from the script at all, because it sounded so new. I look up in amazement. . . was that in the script? And then my eyes go back down, and look at the script, and there's the line! And I can't believe it. That was in the script?!

Q: You must love those moments.

A: I love it when the actors surprise and transform the material in ways that you hadn't dreamed, and push it. An actor becomes your dance partner, takes what you mean and weaves, and something blossoms. I think that's magic. Part of the reason to make movies is to be in touch with those magic people—like a big circus caravan. We're in the Southwest right now like Barnum & Bailey—30 trucks, trailers, tents. We have a lot of different crafts and services people, technicians of all types, several hundred people in this journey.

Q: You've just talked about your work with actors. Your technique and the topicality of your films are often discussed, but less so your work with actors. Yet, each one of your leading players have arguably given the best performances of their careers in your films: James Woods and Jim Belushi in SALVADOR; Charlie Sheen, Tom Berenger and Willem Dafoe in PLATOON; Michael Douglas in WALL STREET; Tom Cruise in BORN ON THE FOURTH OF JULY; Val Kilmer in THE DOORS; Kevin Costner in JFK; Hiep Thi Le, Tommy Lee Jones and Joan Chen in HEAVEN AND EARTH. You like actors, don't you?

A: Most of them. For the very reasons I said above. They can transform the raw stuff of reality for me into something else. They need writers, though. I perform two different functions, you know, because I function as the on-set writer and I'm quite willing to change on the set, right away. Knowing where the material comes from and realizing the point of origin, and the text that you had, then the actors . . . because time has elapsed and you've had the rehearsal process, you've been able to talk the idea out with many collaborators. . . by the time you shoot, the actor has thought a lot about it. So there's the moment where often the magic hits, because through the preparation period, the knowledge has become more and more acute. And when the filming starts, the actor will move your argument, move your stroke.

Q: Have you always had a rehearsal period before the start of principal photography?

A: Always did rehearsals. I don't think they're necessarily the way you're going to shoot the scene, but they're certainly a loosening up. You have to relax the muscles. For NATURAL BORN KILLERS, Juliette Lewis had to practice guns, and get to know things that she needed to do in the role. It's a period of preparing. I don't think we get enough rehearsal. I don't like it when an actor doesn't want to rehearse. That's a bad signal right off the top.

Q: *Do you think it's an unwillingness to work. . . laziness. . . or thinking they have all the answers?*

A: Laziness. All my problems have been in that area. If I have a problem I'll know it at the start, and I'd rather not work with that actor. I'd rather do it then—lose the actor. I think it's important. Each actor is different. I think I've been successful with 80 percent of the actors I've worked with, but I do think I've failed with 20 percent. So you do your best with each person, and they help each other enormously, too, because once they understand the idea, the potpourri, they can help each other. Also, they can harm each other, it's true.

But essentially, I feel that often I've failed them. They didn't have the right material, I couldn't make it work, I couldn't solve the problem. So that happens, and you cut around it. I do take a lot of chances, in terms of getting large groups of people to work on an idea. On HEAVEN AND EARTH, I took 20, 30 Vietnamese oneliners, unknown actors, unknown people who never acted before, and gave them roles with dialogue.

Q: *Including the star, Hiep Thi Le, who carries the picture on her shoulders.*

A: . . . Her little shoulders. . .

Q: *. . . Like Vivien Leigh in GONE WITH THE WIND.*

A: Her four-foot-eleven shoulders.

Q: *Did your careful work with actors begin in film school? Was it something you were concerned with even then?*

A: No. I tried, but I don't think I was particularly good. John Cassavetes came to the school once, and he very much influenced us. I loved his technique. We studied that a little bit. We relaxed, we rehearsed, we improvised. Going to acting school helped me a lot, although I wasn't there long, and I wasn't a particularly good actor.

Q: *When did you go to acting school?*

A: Right away, in the '69-'71 period. I went to a Russian woman, Sonya Moore, and also to HB Studio. Also, some modern dance classes for movement purposes, freeing up the body.

Q: *This was all in New York?*

A: Yeah. And a couple of other places for a period of time. A little here and there, but it was not really my forte. I felt happier writing. I hated the criticism of being up on the stage. I didn't understand the Stanislavsky philosophy at that point in time. So I went through a bit of a trauma about that. To make a long story short, I think I learned about acting. I did a feature. I learned a lot from Michael Caine on THE HAND.

I've always been interested in people, I like people; and I enjoy being with people a lot. So it's a social function, too. The hard thing about being in the Hollywood profession is the deal. . . the deal and the money. . . it all seems to come between the work. Not being available for certain days, not wanting to do more than a week of rehearsal, having a schedule with other interests. It's always difficult, because you want to really merge and have your actors there. I think John Ford probably never issued a call sheet. He'd just have everyone show up at six o'clock in the morning and work together as a company.

Q: *Yet, unlike some of the great autocratic filmmakers of the past, like Ford, you're unusually open to other people's suggestions and input. It seems important to you to have people around who will not hesitate to put forth their own ideas.*

A: Yeah, I bounce off my ideas too. . . thank God for the people I've come to trust through time. It's wonderful. It's much more support than I've ever had before. I trust these people, they're wonderful partners. I can often deal with a situation just by looking into their eyes.

Q: *Like the telepathic relationship you have with Bob Richardson, your cinematographer?*

A: He's very attuned to what I want, very giving. There's also Victor Kempster [production designer], Dale Dye [military and action advisor], Clayton Townsend [producer], Richard Rutowski [associate producer/aide], Herb Gains [assistant director], Chris Centrella [key grip], my editors, David Brenner, Sally Menke, Hank Corwin; Bud Carr [music supervisor], Mike Minkler and Wylie Stateman [post-production sound technicians]. . . I trust these people a lot. It's built up in time. Sometimes I feel like I should just go out and start with a whole new look and feel. But I love working with these people. It's just fun.

Q: *Have you found that as your fame and notoriety have increased, some people have been too respectful? Has the price of success been a certain distance that people put between themselves and you?*

A: I've always felt distance. I think you live in the distance. I think you live in the abstract a lot. I think you do get cut off. I've tried to maintain contacts. I've tried. But sometimes a filmmaker's ordinary life is of no interest. It's just a series of comings and goings and fuckups and failures and disasters and successes. You know, filmmakers try to be happy too. Sometimes people don't forgive them, give them that right. They're just trying to live ordinary, fucked-up lives. Children. Wives. Lovers. Dying people. Hospitals, organizations, taxes. It's a huge amount of ordinary life. I think it's irrelevant how you live it. Totally. It has nothing to do with what you're doing. That's a separate thing.

Film is your liberation, it's your demon, it's your nemesis, it's everything. It's your life. And beyond that. . . you're in the service of that, that's what overrides everything, it smashes apart your ordinary problems. And unfortunately, it wrecks some lives. Filmmakers are often wounded people stumbling around and unhappy. But that's irrelevant. Whether you're happy or unhappy, it's totally irrelevant to the demon. . . not the demon, the "d-a-e-m-o-n." You're the slave of that.

Napoleon once said something like, I set aside everything. My happiness, my family, my life, for my Destiny. So he's in bondage. I think Bergman and Kurosawa are. I think all artists and tyrants and political leaders are.

Q: Then with the perfect freedom also comes a perfect bondage.

A: It's serving the daemon. And that's a hard taskmaster.

F I L M O G R A P H Y

O L I V E R   S T O N E

b. September 15, 1946 - New York, New York
SEIZURE   Cinerama Releasing Corporation, 1974, Canadian
THE HAND   Orion/Warner Bros., 1981
SALVADOR   Hemdale, 1986
PLATOON ★★   Orion, 1986
WALL STREET   20th Century Fox, 1987
TALK RADIO   Universal, 1988
BORN ON THE FOURTH OF JULY ★★   Universal, 1989
THE DOORS   TriStar, 1991
JFK ★   Warner Bros., 1991
HEAVEN AND EARTH   Warner Bros., 1993
NATURAL BORN KILLERS   Warner Bros., 1994
NIXON   Buena Vista, 1995
U-TURN TriStar, 1997

CAROLINE THOMPSON

Although we're still waiting for Caroline Thompson to direct a great movie, all indications from her past achievements point to the fact that it's only a matter of time. One of the first words ever spoken by Thompson was "aminal"—close enough to the real thing to indicate her future passion for those creatures of a non-human aspect. And throughout her life, Thompson has maintained strong emotional connections not only with "aminals," but also with the child who felt such a powerful empathy for them. Thus, it's unsurprising that Thompson's first two forays as director—BLACK BEAUTY and BUDDY—were both about the powerful relationships between humans and animals.

It was only natural that the celebrated writer of such films as EDWARD SCISSORHANDS, THE ADDAMS FAMILY, THE SECRET GARDEN, HOMEWARD BOUND: THE INCREDIBLE JOURNEY and TIM BURTON'S THE NIGHTMARE BEFORE CHRISTMAS should choose BLACK BEAUTY and BUDDY as her first two directing efforts. The stories of a besieged equine hero, and a 1920s eccentric socialite who raised a gorilla as if her own child, certainly fit into the overall framework of Thompson's previous work. Every one of her scripts has dealt with the bittersweet alienation that is part and parcel of being a member of the animal, human child or in the case of EDWARD SCISSORHANDS and THE NIGHTMARE BEFORE CHRISTMAS, monster kingdoms.

Thompson was born and raised near Washington, D.C., the daughter of a lawyer and a teacher. After graduating from Amherst College, she moved to Burbank, California, with a few horses and other household pets. Her first work to be seen by the public was a novel, First Born, which Thompson describes as a "dark tale of the ultimate outsider." She then met another famed outsider—director Tim Burton-a kindred spirit who helped launch her film career with the acclaimed gothic fairy tale EDWARD SCISSORHANDS. Now Thompson's career has taken on a life and character of its own, demonstrating the writer/director's uniquely. . . animistic. . . approach to life.

MICHAEL SINGER: Was directing something that you had always planned on doing throughout your writing career, or was it a decision that you came to during that process?

CAROLINE THOMPSON: Well I wish I could say I'd planned to do anything I've done in my life, but I can't. So I didn't really plan it so much as. . . as kind of fell toward it. Which is to say that, other than EDWARD SCISSORHANDS, my writing career has been filled with frustration, in terms of the execution of my work. And that's not to say that it hasn't in places been executed brilliantly, but I usually found that I didn't even hear my dialogue on screen the way I heard it in my head. I didn't see the same pictures I saw in my head. . . and it's a very frustrating feeling. I'm sure every writer feels it. In the execution of EDWARD SCISSORHANDS, that's the one place where the director and I saw the same movie to a "t", so it was a completely satisfying experience creatively. Short of that, it hasn't been a completely satisfying life. And I would also say though, that the other thing is that when you're a writer of screenplays, just generically, it's not an end. Finishing a script is not an end of finishing something, you know? If it's going to live, it's going to live on film, and the desire to follow through my own work became really, really strong. Plus, the particulars of this were such that I was asked by Warner Bros. to do BLACK BEAUTY, it hadn't been my idea. And I was really sort of sorry it hadn't been, because it was a great idea to do it. But I couldn't think of a director who I would want to do it. And I love this animal so much—I mean, I am a complete horse nut and have been since I was a little kid.

Q: The smell of horses literally surrounds this movie.

A: I'm really happy to hear that, because that's what I'd hoped. And I just couldn't—I ran through the people in my mind, and there was nobody who I would trust with it. And I don't mean "trust" in a grand way, I mean really in a micro way because so much of it is about the deliberate and actual details of these animals' presences, and you have to know horses to know what you're going for. I mean, I know enough about their behavior to know how to get what I want, and that made it a very efficient process as opposed to a horrifyingly inefficient process, which a person who didn't know horses could have found themselves stuck in to begin with. And also, again, the particulars of the details of the way they behave to me is endlessly fascinating, and to a person who doesn't love them, I don't see how it could be.

Q: To the uninformed—namely the person who either didn't see HOMEWARD BOUND or had no idea of your long-held love for horses—it might have seemed an offbeat choice for a first directing effort from one who had become known for unconventional scripts.

A: Well, it was considered a very conventional choice by some people, and I really resent that. . . In fact it's a very unconventional film. To me, that's just the kind of reaction people have when they're looking at the surface of things and not thinking underneath.

Q: Why do you consider BLACK BEAUTY to be an unconventional film?

A: Well, it's unconventional in that first of all, if you turned off the sound, you'd understand everything that was going on. It's very emotionally powerful. To me, it's exactly the same movie as EDWARD SCISSORHANDS. It just has a different protagonist. And okay, the production design doesn't twist your brain the way it would on EDWARD SCISSORHANDS, but it's not about production design. But emotionally it's exactly the same movie. I mean, they're all the same movie, but literally those two are the same movie. It's about coming into a world where you feel completely welcomed at first, and then it turns against you, and yet you keep your sweetness throughout. It's the same character. . . but on the other hand, it always made me laugh for them to see EDWARD SCISSORHANDS as "weird" and "quirky" and "unconventional." I mean, to me, it's just another metaphor for feeling like an outsider. . . you know, you can see any dog in the world and say, "Gosh, the world wasn't made for that dog. How weird would it be to be that dog?"

It's been interesting to be asked about where things come from, because then you think about it, right? And I finally realized, because people were always saying, "Boy, you must have had an unhappy childhood", and I didn't, or, "Boy, you must have had a weird life", and I didn't. But what I do carry around is a really really really strong feeling of what it was like to be, say three or four years old and two-and-a-half feet tall, and try to sit in a chair. . . and your feet don't touch, and you can't reach the table. In other words, I have a really strong sense memory of the disproportion of the world to me, and I think that everything I do comes from that. And, okay so you're either a character with scissors for hands, or you're a horse. . . you're still a creature in a world that isn't made for you. To me, they're the same. I get really angry when people tell me that BLACK BEAUTY is conventional material. I mean, to me, THE SECRET GARDEN's a far more conventional story. . . far more.

Q: *Well, considering the fact that it's a multi-character piece—told from the point of view of an animal—that in itself is highly unconventional.*

A: I suppose that's literally unconventional, and it hurt me when people couldn't go with that. I loved seeing the world as best I could through the eyes of this creature that, to me, is the most bizarre creature on earth. I mean, think about it . . . they actually want to be part of our lives. Only a dog is the other creature that wants to be part of our lives. And people think they're stupid.

Q: *So, you were asked to do the movie by Warner Bros., and you go over to England, and it's the first time you've directed, and you're working with a highly experienced British crew. Was it daunting?*

A: Well, I trust my "bullshit" meter completely, and that's sort of what I hoped would carry me through, and in fact, it did. I knew that I would be far better off if I could afford to hire people who knew what they were doing. And luckily I'm not insecure enough that I couldn't hire them.

Q: *It's not like, "Oh, I can't hire someone as experienced as John Box. Let me hire somebody who. . . "*

A: . . . who I can tell what to do. No. John Box and I told each other what to do, you know what I mean? John Box, who I must say was the single most enthusiastic of all the production designers I interviewed, brought such devotion to me and the project, that I was astonished. I mean, I was surrounded by Academy Award winners, from Jenny Beavan, the costume designer, to Claire Simpson, our editor, John Box, and Simon Kaye, who did our sound. They were so devoted and so enthusiastic every single day that I just felt blessed to have them there.

And I'm also not afraid to ask people's opinions. That doesn't mean I'll always do what they suggest, but I'm happy to ask, "What do you think, what do you think, what do you think?" Some people at first took that as a sign of lack of leadership, but they quickly came to realize that it was an honest question, but not an insecure question. You know, not a question of "please tell me what to do. I was just asking, "What do you think?" You know, at first some of them were afraid to answer because they're not used to having their boss say, "What do you think", but it really became a wonderful sort of large partnership with a lot of people. And I'll try to run every set that way.

I have seen directors—and I won't name them—who will tell the sound guy how to do his job. Well, you know what? That sound guy knows his job a lot better than the director knows the sound guy's job. What's the point of hiring the sound guy if you're going to tell him how to do his job? I want to make an atmosphere in which I inspire people to do their jobs the best they can do them. And that was really how I saw the goal, from the horse trainer to the production designer.

So, there was no intimidation or anything like that. I didn't have time to be intimidated either. It's just too much work. And casting, I was really lucky that people like David Thewlis were unknown here. And I tried in each instance to cast slightly against type, slightly against expectation, because I wanted it to be a rich movie. I didn't want it to be a conventional movie. I didn't want it to be a sentimental movie, which was its greatest risk. I wanted it to be filled with sentiment but not "ooky" sentimental.

Q: *Your re-creation of Victorian England was, I thought, visually rich. Much of it reminded me of Hogarth.*

A: Oh, how cool. Thank you. We had Hogarth prints all over the walls in the production office. Actually, our riskiest and most successful choice was using Blenheim Palace for Victorian London. It worked like gangbusters because you really felt the claustrophobia, yet we were in this not so big, very controllable space. And so we got to roll camera all day instead of direct traffic all day, which was essential on a schedule like ours.

Q: *Logistically tough movie. . .*

A: Very tough movie. A big movie, and a scope that I've never written before.

Q: *Was the writer at war with the director at that point?*

A: Oh, not at war. . . it was just the director was going, "Damn you! Damn you!" Because when you think about it, my movies really haven't been chock full of action sequences at all. But again, I just sort of. . . put my head down and marched forward and did my best.

Q: *So, you make the movie. You get it done. It gets good reviews. It opens, and. . .*
A: It dies.

Q: *Why?*

A: Well, it's not a summer movie. And it was released not just in the summer but at the height of summer. It came out the same weekend as THE MASK. It wasn't marketed honestly in my opinion. I'm being straight. It was sold both too coldly and too fuzzily. It wasn't sold as a story with any balls, or any spirit. And it has both of those things. I felt that it was misrepresented in its advertising. It wasn't sold aggressively. I think the studio was in a quandary having only me to promote, because I'm not exactly well known, and so, you know, given that—I mean, David Thewlis did come for a day of publicity in New York, but he's not exactly a household word here. And, so I think that was a problem for them.

BLACK BEAUTY was brought out the week after LASSIE, and if you look at the two posters, they're identical. The campaigns are identical. There's nothing that distinguishes this film in its campaign to make you think, "Oh, that's different," which it is. And, as I said, to bring it out at the height of summer is just foolhardy. This is a movie that should have been platformed, in my opinion— given a chance to build as opposed to just go wide. And it should have come out in the autumn or at a down time, not at the hottest time of the year. And maybe then, it would have had a chance in the marketplace. You know, I can't say that the audience would have gone for it, I have no idea. But I don't think an audience was given a chance to go for it.

Q: *What do you think of the explanation that American kids raised as they are these days can in no way relate to a story that takes place in Victorian England?*

A: Well, THE SECRET GARDEN did a heck of a lot better than this movie. It made $32-million dollars. So, you know, so much for that. I mean, that's not huge numbers, but it's certainly respectable numbers. So, I don't really think that's true. And if it is, well, who knows what any of us is doing? On the other hand, I will always be grateful to Warner Bros., for letting me make the movie I wanted to make. They were absolutely great to me in the sense that they really creatively left me alone to make the best film I could, and not every studio in town will do that. And I will be grateful 'till I die to them for that.

Q: *You've had a kind of a special relationship with Warner Bros.*

A: Well, yeah, I've done two films there now. Yeah. . . I mean, they've been great to me. . . they've been wonderful. They really have believed in me, and that's been real important.

Q: *Obviously, you're not discouraged by the. . .*

A: No, I'm saddened, you know? I'm sad. I went from shock to the kind of depression where you sleep 20 hours a day. I did that for a week or so. On the other hand, first of all, I'm not a person easily embittered. And secondly, so many people whom I respect enormously have really genuinely loved the movie. You know, you can tell when somebody's bullshitting you, and to feel that, okay I've made something—and I'm not inclined to love my own work, by the way. I actually hate most of the things I've done—and I loved this film. I was very proud of it. But to get the kind of confirmation from people who I really respect has meant tons. So, you know, it's not—it's like you say to yourself, okay, how would I have rather this happened? Well, I would obviously have rather had it done really well at the box office. Okay, well if you had to put yourself in a situation where you had a choice of making a movie you were proud of or having it do well at the box office, which would you rather? Make a movie you're proud of, obviously. And I got to do that. And that's not nothing—that's a huge thing.

Q: *Your career is a living example that what industry wisdom would never think would work . . . works.*

A: Well, that's true. Tim Burton is the prime example of it, I think. Especially starting with EDWARD SCISSORHANDS. I mean, that never would have gotten made except under very special circumstances. Yeah. And I'm pleased with that, only because it makes me proud of the audience. It makes me proud of the people out there who want to see things that are good and different and strange.

Q: *So now, at this point on, are Caroline Thompson the screenwriter and the director two different people. Do you have separate careers?*

A: Well, not really, because I learned so much about screenwriting from directing. I mean, I learned about things that I hadn't really even thought about, like how do you get from one scene to the next—what's the cut? And I learned—you know, there's certain things, certain sort of tricks I'll do in a script to get myself out of trouble that would put the director straight into trouble, you know? And so, the two people in me know exactly what I'm doing now, and when I'm doing it.

Q: *So you're not leaving your career as screenwriter separate from directing behind. . .*

A: Well, in terms of just work, when I'm a writer, I lead the best life in the world. Which is to say I write about two thirds of the day and then I horseback ride the other third of the day and then I go out in the evening and see a movie or something. I mean, it's the best life in the world. And when I'm a director, I'm leading the worst life in the world.

Q: *Up at five. . .*

A: Up at five—and you know, I only stopped dreaming about the shooting of BLACK BEAUTY about three weeks ago. And so, we're not talking about an 18 hour a day job, we're talking about a 24 hour a day obsession. And not that I don't get obsessed about my screenwriting work—I do—but on the other hand, I always have been able to leave it at the desk. This I couldn't leave at the desk. It totally took me over and ruined parts of my life. And I'm happy to have my life ruined sometimes, but I can't have it ruined all the time. Just for me. . . I can't do it. And so, for example, I'm doing an adaptation of an E.B. White book, STUART LITTLE, for Columbia right now, for fun. You know, to me that's fun. It's almost relaxing to be able to do something that I'm not going to direct. It was never intended for me to direct it, I don't even want to direct it, but I'm having fun doing the writing on it. It's like a vacation. And then I have scripts that I very much want to direct. So, I'm just trying to find the balance. You know, I cannot become a movie monk. I cannot give my whole life up to working on movies every day all day. I mean, some people might say that means I'm not the real thing. I say it means I'm a human being. But no, it's true. . . it's like, what kind of devotion do you have? And I say I have a tremendous amount of devotion, and it's a very very deep devotion, but it's just devotion that is measured by desire to lead a good life as well. So, I'm greedy.

Q: I want to ask one more question, and it's this tremendous empathy you have, not just for animals, but also and I think, or course, the two are very strongly related—for children.

A: Yeah, I love kids. First of all, I think they're way smarter than adults. I think they're way more honest than adults. Both as themselves and as an audience. I love them as an audience. They're very pure in their reactions. But I think it goes back to what I was saying about that feeling of disproportion. My strongest feeling in my life is a feeling of disproportion—of the world not being in proportion to me. And kids feel that all the time. I mean, that is the definition of being a child. I don't have any kids myself. Maybe it's because I still feel like one of them and it wouldn't make any sense. But I do find if I'm in a room with adults and children, that I go to hang out with the children. Because to me, their imaginations are much more interesting. It's like they're on acid all the time. And I just love their brains, and I love the way their thoughts work—you know, they are far more witty in their illogic than so-called adults are in their logic. They track things sensationally and they track things emotionally rather than tracking things logically. And the kind of discoveries that they make about the world every day just by the nature of their minds is paradise to me.

Q: Well, I don't know if you believe the whole Wordsworthian concept—which is also prevalent in Balinese culture—about children coming directly from God, and therefore wiser than adults.

A: Well, exactly. I think that we get stupider as we get older because out of fear, we try to organize our lives so desperately. And children don't have that fear. Innately they don't have that fear. The most touching thing that's happened to me lately is I've been asked to be the honoree for an organization that's for child abuse victims. And that's touched me more than anything I've been asked to participate in. I mean, if I have contributed to kids, that's the best compliment I could ever have been paid. I really do think that they have a magical vision of our world.

F I L M O G R A P H Y

C A R O L I N E   T H O M P S O N

BLACK BEAUTY   Warner Bros., 1994, British-U.S.
BUDDY   Columbia, 1997

$\mathcal{M}$ARIO $\mathcal{V}$AN $\mathcal{P}$EEBLES

It's (unfortunately) a great rarity. . . two generations of Black American film directors, not an easy accomplishment in an industry that until very recently was highly successful in excluding African Americans from such positions of creative power. The block that begat the chip is Melvin Van Peebles, the take-no-prisoners pioneer whose 1971 classic SWEET SWEETBACK'S BAADASSSSSS SONG signaled the birth of a completely uncompromising black American cinema. And the chip is Mario Van Peebles, whose first feature—NEW JACK CITY—carried its own controversy.

Simultaneous with the growth of his acting career, Mario Van Peebles cut his creative teeth by directing several plays and 16mm shorts before moving into television, where he directed several episodes of primetime fare (including several hours of 21 Jump Street, Wiseguy and Sonny Spoon, the series in which he starred). For Malcolm Takes A Shot, an Afterschool Special, Van Peebles received a nomination from the Directors Guild of America.

Influenced as much by contemporary European films as it was by classic gangster movies, NEW JACK CITY took stylistic risks in pursuit of story and content, and went on to become Warner Bros.' most profitable film of 1991. After this interview was conducted, Van Peebles went on to direct the retro-western POSSE; PANTHER, another controversial slice of fictionalized Black American history written by father Melvin Van Peebles; and then collaborating once again with his father as co-director of the cable television movie GANG IN BLUE, before returning to the feature arena with LOVE KILLS, the first venture of his new company, Ivan Cain Productions.

MICHAEL SINGER: *Before I saw* NEW JACK CITY, *I expected a very gritty neo-documentary urban street drama. What I saw, though, was a highly stylized and very carefully designed film with lots of attention to color and camera movement. You seemed to go in very prepared.*

MARIO VAN PEEBLES: Well, when I was a kid, and my dad did SWEET SWEETBACK, he had only 21 days to shoot. That's not a lot of days. By those standards, I had all the time in the world—36 days—which is still pretty short by today's standards. You either have to have a good idea of what you're doing or start praying. Although I must add that as comforting as plans are, the ability to improvise is also key. You will have those "what can go wrong, will go wrong" days, man.

Q: *Especially since you were a first time feature director.*

A: Yeah, being a first time feature director is sort of like having three bullets in your .38. You've got to pick your targets carefully. Maybe even lose a few battles, but hopefully win the war. My first fight was to get a cinematographer who could move and yet provide the edgy, dynamic visual style I felt the piece required. The joke when we were shooting the film was that it would win the Oscar for Best Foreign Film. I tried to take realistic, gritty characters and then juxtapose them against a background of heightened urban reality. Medium being part of the message, I used sort of classic PUBLIC ENEMY-ish gangster silhouettes but gave them a distinctive New Jack twist. I shot it with the sort of color saturation that you might see in a DIVA or a LA FEMME NIKITA, which I married to great African rhythms by using music not only to enhance a mood, but to push the narrative. In the scene at the drug treatment center, it became edgy cinema verite docu-drama-ish. But at other times the movie is polished, glossy and almost epic.

The second fight was to turn our budget constraints or fiscal shortcomings into cinematic strengths. For example, a lot of people commented on the high energy bike chase that jump-starts the film. Well, it was originally written as a fairly standard car chase. But on our budget, I felt that a through the "hood" killer bike chase would be more original and far cheaper than the car chase that has become a staple of most action films. So, I rewrote it, necessity being the mother of invention, right? Also, scriptwise, it was very important to give the film its balance. If we wanted kids to emotionally "say no" to the gangster, I felt we needed alternative role models to "say yes" to. In most gangster films the audience emotionally links up with the gangster.

In NEW JACK CITY, the audience ended up cheering in support of the black and white cops. In fact, during the sequence where the victim "Pookie" was getting addicted to crack, a kid stood up in the theatre and yelled "Just say no, fool!" So that was the moment for me, man. After that, if it makes money, fine, but we reached them. In NEW JACK CITY, my third bullet or battle—I forget which metaphor I'm rolling with here—was rehearsal. Real rehearsal time was key. It allowed us to tailor the roles to the actors, utilizing their strengths. All anyone that had a brilliant idea had to do was tell me, and I'd pretend it was mine. I was also lucky enough to have Barry Michael Cooper, the writer, during most of the rehearsal time. We both saw the script as a living thing. Rehearsal really allowed the actors to artistically exhale, to rehearse without having to perform. And I can't say enough about how their contributions enhanced the movie. So when you ask about how much of NEW JACK CITY was pre-visualized, I would have to say a lot of it was. And when you've got only 36 days and you're not Coppola yet—they can still fire your ass—you've got to plan like hell, be ready to improvise, and be lucky.

Q: *Did you use any storyboards?*

A: Yeah, I did. I had a guy come in and do some boards, but I draw myself as well.

Q: Were you ever worried about sacrificing performance for technique?

A: No. Because I'm an actor and I direct from the inside out, my actors motivate the camera movement. So if an actor has a change of thought that's going to carry him somewhere, then that's what's going to drive the camera. Style is nothing without character and story.

Q: As an actor in NEW JACK CITY, you sort of took a backseat to Wesley Snipes, Ice-T and Judd Nelson.

A: In NEW JACK CITY, I needed a New Jack cop to take down a New Jack gangster, and it's Judd and Ice-T who are the New Jack heroes. I was sort of a service character in the film, but my ego is not with having 90 more close-ups of Mario. The director in me is stronger than the actor. I had to ask myself, "Wait a minute, are you the best person for this particular role?" I went to Columbia University and had a whole different set of socio-economic advantages than someone like Ice-T, who was in a gang and finally said no to violence and drugs. So Ice-T playing the hero cop who really came up from that sort of neo-hip-hop Protestant work ethic of pulling yourself up by the rapping bootstraps and making something of yourself has a lot more resonance than me doing it.

Q: Although NEW JACK CITY works well on a straight action level, the movie made a lot of salient socio-economic points.

A: Perhaps the overriding consciousness of NEW JACK CITY is best reflected in the final courtroom scene, when Nino Brown, on the witness stand, says, "Hey, we don't make Uzis in Harlem, we don't have poppy fields in the ghetto. How do you think this massive amount of narcotics gets here?" Every urban dealer knows that the real gangsters are affiliated with the Noriegas of the world—who by the way, had serious CIA ties—they're in the BCCI scandals. The real drug lords are white-collar guys largely involved in government, but they're connected and thus above the law. It's the little black guy with the gold chain that goes to jail. It's not unlike The Boxer Rebellion in China at the turn of the century, when China was flooded with opium from the British, who were trying to (a) make lots of money and (b) keep the Chinese a subjugated people. And a lot of people don't think that it's any accident that drugs are allowed to flood the black communities in that quantity. It's the great neutralizer. When you're on crack, you don't vote. So they don't vote more money for education, versus more money for the Gulf War. We're getting to a real interesting place in this country, because when people who grow up with nothing watch unfortunate shows like Lifestyles of the Rich and Famous, which tells them "you've got to have lots of gold and a big car to be somebody in our society," well, they want to get it one way or another. The have-nots buy into that consumerist doctrine just like the rest of us, but without the means of which to obtain it. Nino is someone who says "Hey man, I'm not Mike Tyson, I can't box my way out of the 'hood.' I can't sing or rap my out. I'm not Michael Jordan, so I can't dribble my way out. But I can be a gangster. And I'd rather live fast and die young." A tragic kamikaze version of a Michael Milken, or Gordon Gekko-type character from WALL STREET. I tried to give each character his or her own truth. That's Nino's truth. The truth of Ice-T's character is that Nino is killing his own people. The bad guy is wrong, but he also has a perspective.

Q: The problem was, when NEW JACK CITY opened, the points you were trying to make got swept away in major controversy about the violence that occurred in some theatres on the first night of the movie's run. How were you able to get beyond that?

A: In NEW JACK CITY, we said that drugs are not a black thing, it's not a white thing, it's a death thing. Well, perhaps Hollywood's not a black thing, not a white thing, as much as a green thing. It's the color of money. We had a situation—a sort of riot—in Westwood on opening night. The media said that it must have been because of the film, that NEW JACK CITY was a call to arms of sorts. But what actually happened was that people came down to see the movie and couldn't get in. They bought tickets but couldn't find seats. At the same time, what was on TV every day, all the time? The Rodney King beating tape, which had just occurred. So you have opening night of NEW JACK CITY, all these kids show up, and so do the police. Someone yelled out, "Let's get them back for Rodney King." And they hadn't even seen the movie! Now, the media was responding not to the movie, but to the poster. They didn't see a white guy with a big gun, they saw a black man with a big gun. He didn't have a basketball. They said "Aha! That must be it. You give the natives a gun and you're gonna have problems." In the end, ironically, the movie did more for the positive image of cops than the LAPD did with their Rodney King video. Because again, unlike most gangster pictures, ultimately NEW JACK's heroes were cops, not criminals. But eventually folks saw the movie and got the message. In fact, one reviewer said, "NJC has a just-say-no message that would warm Nancy Reagan's heart." They have had violence at soccer matches in England. Is soccer a call to arms? We've had violence at rock concerts. It's probably an unfortunate reflection of society more than it is a reaction to a one-sheet or a soccer match. Initially, 20 years ago, only two theatres in the United States would play my dad' s film SWEET SWEETBACK'S BAADASSSSS SONG. It broke house records in both and eventually became Variety's top grossing independent hit in 1971. By comparison, the 825 theatres NEW JACK opened at ain't bad.

Q: I can pretty well guess that you find this stereotyping of black films more than a little upsetting.

A: They're still looking at us as one sort of big black cinematic basketball team. But you know, it's like when black music first came out back in my mother's day it was called "race music." Now it's "race movies." And until the film business sort of mirrors the progress of the music business, you still have to suffer those sort of slings and arrows of cinematic misfortune. But the movies of Spike Lee and the Hudlins and John Singleton and Mario Van Peebles are really vastly different. There are relationships, but they're really different.

Q: What about those eight years of directing that preceded NEW JACK CITY? When did you decide to direct in addition to acting?

A: Well, I have been very lucky because I grew up with "Melvin Van Movies," who really took some chances and opened the doors for the second generation of black filmmakers. Looking back, I probably had two distinct advantages. One, because I grew up with a director I had no illusions about what the job entailed, i.e. how much work it was. For me, practicing one's craft was a must. And secondly, because dad was a boss and he happened to be black, I never really had a color chip about what I could do. You know, if you're Margaret Thatcher's daughter—whether you like the politics or not—you're a woman who grows up thinking that a future in politics is possible. So I grew up thinking, "Hey, this is something that's possible—if I have the talent." Now that's a big "if." I didn't write NEW JACK. I didn't produce NEW JACK. I didn't star in NEW JACK. I was invited as a director. And to get to that point where someone might invite me to direct, I really had to develop and practice and develop a body of work. In order to do that, I directed a lot of shorts, some rock videos, and plenty of theatre. Stephen Cannell did for my directing what Clint Eastwood did for my acting. They both gave me a shot, Clint by casting me in Heartbreak Ridge and Cannell by letting me direct episodes of 21 Jump Street, Wise guy and Top of the Hill. And the man really let me stretch creatively. I'd direct traffic for that guy if he asked me to.

Q: *What turns you on so much about film?*

A: I wasn't in London in the 19th century, but I was there in David Lean's version of OLIVER TWIST. I've never been to China, but I was there in THE LAST EM-PEROR. I'd never been to Sweden until recently, but I was there in MY LIFE AS A DOG. I don't care what color the director is, or what color the actors are. . . if they can take me somewhere, film can take me in and immerse me in a world that I don't know. Make me understand people that I wouldn't have understood. It's interesting that film is the final frontier, in that it's the last product that Ameri-cans make that folks all over the world want. I was just in Brazil, and when you go to some guy's shack in the middle of the jungle, and instead of sending his kids to school he's buying a color TV and a VCR to watch the movies we make here, it makes you think about what we're saying and how what we're saying echoes around this global village. American film and American music are everywhere, and just look at the African-American influence in music. Anything to do with music in this country really has African rhythm at its root. The slave traders took the drums away from the Africans when they reached America. The drums were a means of communication, and thus probably pretty intimidating to outsiders. But they couldn't take away the rhythm. That African rhythm went into the guitar, the bass and Armstrong's trumpet, see? That became the blues and rock and roll and rap and hip-hop and jazz and gospel. This rhythm was so important to NEW JACK CITY. So if that's what kind of influence African-Americans had on music, think of what they can do for film. This new blood isn't an invasion, but a truly American blending of influences, the cinematic melting pot.

Q: *And now, post-NEW JACK CITY, what kind of directing work are you being offered?*

A: Thus far a variety of things, not just "There's five black guys in high-top sneakers fighting over radios, so Mario'll have a special genetic understanding of this." And I'm still trying to push the envelope in terms of what they're willing to accept from black filmmakers, so that we're not just into shoot-'em-ups or dancing-rap-ping sequel movies. The key is to diversify and avoid Seventies-itis, where we get stuck in the SHAFT GOES TO THE 7/11 PART VI sequel syndrome.

Q: *Do you actively solicit your father's opinions when you're directing? I know that the two of you collaborated on a film a couple of years back called IDENTITY CRISIS.*

A: Some of the surrealistic aspects of NEW JACK were almost a homage to SWEETBACK. And if you look closely, them' s even a scene from SWEETBACK in

NEW JACK, when Nino Brown is watching television. Melvin Van Movies is not only my buddy and my pop, he's one of the sharpest brothers I know, and I'd work with him anytime. He's the godfather of "Do it yourself cinema," man.

Q: Can you talk about your next film?

A: Well, I could, but that's all it would be is "talk." You know, Hollywood is a strange place. One day you're on a billboard, the next day you're on a milk carton. But right now I seem to have them fooled.

Q: Not the worst position to be in at this point.

A: Hey, it's not bad. It beats working at the post office. . .

F I L M O G R A P H Y

M A R I O   V A N   P E E B L E S

NEW JACK CITY   Warner Bros., 1991
POSSE   Gramercy Pictures, 1993, U.S.-British
PANTHER   Gramercy Pictures, 1995
GANG IN BLUE (CTF)   co-director with Melvin Van Peebles, Robert Lawrence Productions/Van Peebles Films, 1996
LOVE KILLS   Trident Releasing, 1998

$\mathcal{M}$ELVIN $\mathcal{V}$AN $\mathcal{P}$EEBLES

If you're looking for a key to the Life and Philosophy of Melvin Van Peebles, you'll have to look for those two tattoos on his neck, and another on his rear end. After making his first million bucks (on his 1970 big studio comedy hit WATERMELON MAN), Van Peebles suddenly became worried that he would forget the meaning of life. . . so he had it forever imprinted on his anatomy (unecessarily, he says in retrospect) one fine day at the Dorchester Hotel in London. One one side of his neck, you can read in French, "*Couper sur la ligne*"— roughly translation as "Cut on the dotted line." On the othe side, in English, "Lynch here." And on his derriere, there's a warning in Bamboura, an archaic African language—"N*e* B*essie*"—which means, in the vernacular, "If you can, motherfucker."

The saga of Melvin Van Peebles—and I use the word "saga" advisedly, since he's often been up against the worst fire-breathing dragons and demons— is so unpredictable, ribald, heroic and dramatic that it could easily make a great movie in itself. Absolutely acknowledged as the "godfather" of modern black American cinema, Van Peebles is an outrageous iconoclast and style-setter who's always been too hip for the room. . . the room, of course, being the rest of the world.

Van Peebles has lived several lives in his 66 years. As a filmmaker, he is best known for SWEET SWEETBACK'S BAADASSSS SONG (1971), probably the most uncompromising black film ever made, a movie that has been enormously influential on the current generation of black American directors. In the theatre, Van Peebles created, wrote, composed and directed two successful Broadway musicals in the 1970s—AIN'T SUPPOSED TO DIE A NATURAL DEATH and DON'T PLAY US CHEAP, which heralded an authentic black American theatrical voice. For television, he wrote (among other things) the brilliant four-hour drama THE SOPHISTICATED GENTS (in which he also co-starred) and the telefeature JUST AN OLD SWEET SONG. As a composer and singer, Van Peebles stylistically predated rap and hip-hop by about two decades. During time spent in Paris during the 1960s, Van Peebles wrote several novels in French, one of which—L*a Permission*—he adapted into his first feature film, THE STORY OF A THREE-DAY PASS.

You want more? In the 1980s, this latter-day Renaissance man became the first black trader on the American Stock Exchange, which resulted in his 1986 book *Bold Money: A New Way to Play the Options Market*. And oh yeah. . . he's also an astronomer. . . and the father of second generation director/actor Mario Van Peebles, with whom he's collaborated on the features IDENTITY CRISIS and PANTHER and the cable telefeature GANG IN BLUE.

In 1990, the Museum of Modern Art in New York held a major retrospective of Van Peebles' films, with the American Cinemateque in Los Angeles following suit a couple of years thereafter; a retrospective of his amazing life would take considerably longer, and the following interview only scratches the surface. In 1997, a documentary directed by Mark Daniels, entitled MELVIN VAN PEEBLES CLASSIFIED X, premiered at the Sundance Film Festival. . . further insuring that the man's work and life will not retreat into obscurity.

And lest one think that the passing of the years has emerged in a milder, mellower Melvin Van Peebles. . . *Ne Bessie!*

MICHAEL SINGER: *In his Encyclopedia of Film, James Monaco wrote that SWEET SWEETBACK'S BAADASSSSS SONG was "one of the very first films to define an African American aesthetic." Was that your conscious intention?*

MELVIN VAN PEEBLES: Interesting. But that is not at all how I thought about it. I thought about it as saying what I wanted to say, how I wanted to say it, with hope that it would be a success. I was not aware that my take was the Everyman psyche's take. But it was really a culmination of many years' work, and I just have to recount that experience.

Q: *Be my guest.*

A: I originally was a painter, but I discovered after the first little exhibitions that I wasn't reaching my audience. Well, I thought maybe writing is where it's at, so I began to write. And again, I was not reaching my audience. I realized the people I wanted to talk to were going to the movies to neck and try to cop a feel from each other. So I decided that's what I was going to try and do: make movies. Now, it seems logical and intelligent perhaps at this stage of the game, but at that time it was considered close to insanity. I mean, I don't know why they didn't lock me up and give me a lobotomy.

And I remember so well. . . I was working on the cable cars in San Francisco—I mean, many of these things become almost symbolic, you almost don't want to tell them because they think oh come on, you made that up. It was the Fourth of July in 1958 when I was fired from my job. I went up on a hill, and I sat there just thinking. I was fired because I had written my first book, which was about cable cars. I used to be a gripman, so I published a photo essay book about cable cars. And the head of the barn, who was racist, was very pushed out of shape by me having done this. He didn't think black people should read, let alone write.

Anyway, I had gotten in the post office at the Lincoln Annex. Suddenly, at that juncture, I decided that I was going to—what does Bob Dylan sing?—"They stone you when you're. . . " You're gonna get stoned anyway, so you might as well do what you want to do. And I decided to make films to reach my public. So I made my first three feature films in San Francisco, which turned out to be 11 minutes long each, because I knew nothing about film. I just knew a guy who had a windup camera available. I said that I wanted to make a feature. He said, "Well, 16 or 35 millimeter?" I said, "What's that?" So I just taught myself as I went along. And then someone came to me and said, "We hear you're making a movie. Who do you like, Kurosawa or Einstein or Welles?" And I said, "What are those?" Those were people I had never heard of. So I came pretty fresh to this filmmaking thing. My cinema education consisted of a guy teaching me how to take nail polish and glue two pieces of film together. That was it. All the rest I learned the hard way.

Anyway, jump cut. I made this film, my first film, no sound or anything like that. And it didn't make much sense. The guy said, "Well, you've got to put the scenes together. It's called editing." Anyway, I cut this masterpiece down, and it ended up, like I said, being 11 minutes long. And I took it to Hollywood, wanting to show it, hoping to get into the business. The guy said "What do you want to do?" I said I'd like to write, direct. And he offered me a job as an elevator operator. I said "No, no, no, I want to write and direct." So they upgraded the offer to dancing. But I had gone through this before. I had been in the Strategic Air Command as an officer when I was 20 years old in the Air Force. And I sensed a lot of this, I sort of knew the music. What often happens is you think any time you come to a stone wall, it's indigenous to the place. So I thought, well, maybe in the military it was like that, but you're often taught in the entertainment industry that everything is open. And it isn't.

Q: *Back then it sure wasn't, and it isn't much more so now.*

A: We were allowed to do a little dancing and singing and things like that, but behind the controls. . . I mean, they just got blacks as quarterbacks, you understand? Anyway, long story short, they did not take to this. And so I went back to my second career, which was astronomy. I went to Holland to get my Ph.D. in astronomy. And on my way there to study some very esoteric orbits, I stopped in New York and leased my film to a fellow named Amos Vogel. He would go from place to place and show these things, sort of a dog and pony show. This was certainly outside the fringe. Anyway, I was in Holland and I got a letter from the Cinematheque in France. Amos Vogel showed my film in France, and these people said, "Gee, this is great, who is he?" That was my first word of encouragement. So I hitchhiked from Holland to France, and began to work in France as a beggar, because I didn't have a visa. I spoke no French. I had nothing; I just sang in the street with my cap. However, I discovered that there was a French law that said that a French director or writer could have a director's card. It didn't require money to become a writer, so I wrote a couple of novels. . . which I didn't get published. But one day I saw something in a newspaper and I thought, "That's not right, I don't believe that." And I went to one of the major newspapers and said "I don't believe that murder happened like that. I'd like to investigate it." The guy stopped, looked at me, and said, "Okay, go investigate the murder." What I didn't' t realize was that it was August in Paris, and in August everybody in Paris disappears. The editor needed to fill up news space. If it happened in January, this never would have occurred. Anyway, I go investigate the murder, and stumble onto a scoop. Three days from that, there's my story on the cover. Suddenly, I began to get calls from people. Calls doesn't mean you had a telephone. . . calls meant they called somebody else who would come up and knock on your door in this little room and say, "Ah, didn't you have a book in here? We should look at it again." So I got my first books published, and then I got other books published.

Q: *Wait a minute. . . didn't you indicate before that you didn't know French when you got to France? But you wrote those novels in French, right?*

A: Mm-hmm. It's not as hard as it sounds.

Q: *It does to me.*

A: No, it isn't. I just learned it as I went along. What happens when you go to a foreign place, if you go there and you hang with the people that speak the same language you do, you end up not learning anything. But if you only hang around other people and you want to take a leak, you will learn. The second time around, you'll learn how to say, "Where can I take a leak?" in the language of that country. Anyway, I wrote very street French, cause that's all I knew. And I'm still always having trouble with masculine-feminine, but so what, everybody understood. And then, hell, people had to correct my English, so it wasn't a big deal if somebody corrected my French. Anyway, after my novels were published, I went and asked for a director's card. And then all I needed to do was find the zillions of dollars to make a film. Anyway, I found the money, and wrote. . .

Q: . . . THE STORY OF A THREE-DAY PASS.

A: Which was meant to be flattering to the French. I'm crazy but I'm not stupid. And then luck stepped in again, and I was invited to the San Francisco Film Festival in 1968 as one of the French delegates. Of course, everybody freaked out, but the French wanted to show how liberal they were. I looked like I just stepped off a construction site or something. A woman at the festival was quite surprised. I spoke to her in French. She asked, "Where are you from, Gambia?" And I said "Naw, I'm from Chicago." But it accomplished exactly what I wanted to do. It put into context the fact that there were no black Americans making feature Films. Then the search for the Great Black Hope was on, and I got offers to make Films in Hollywood for the studios. I didn't have a job, but I turned them down. I felt that if I accepted, they would have had their very own black genius, and nobody else would get a shot. However, when I didn't do this, two other black directors were suddenly discovered. People older than myself, and with much larger names, who had been trying to break the doors down for the longest time, and who had credentials up the kazoo. And that was Ossie Davis with COTTON COMES TO HARLEM and Gordon Parks with THE LEARNING TREE.

Meantime, Hollywood was still talking to me, and I agreed after those two shots I would make the film with the caveat that we'd shoot in Hollywood. Because, you see, COTTON COMES TO HARLEM and THE LEARNING TREE were both shot on location, where they didn't have to worry so much about blacks breaking into the unions.

Q: And that was Columbia's WATERMELON MAN.

A: Right. Now, when I looked at the shooting schedule for WATERMELON MAN, I realized in many ways that I had been programmed for failure. Because the shooting schedule was for 23 days. Hey, no big problem. I shot it in 21 days.

Q: And your next movie, which was made independently, was SWEET SWEETBACK. Where did it come from?

A: Jump cut again, back to 1957. I was sitting in a movie theatre in San Francisco, and there's some black guy on screen humming spirituals. And I thought, that was not the reality that I knew. It was not the reality that any other black people knew, or for that matter, many of the counter-culture white kids. In those days, if a black guy did anything half-ass brave or smart, he had to die by the end of reel nine. Those were the thoughts that I had when I shot SWEETBACK. So what I did cinematically was just tell it the way it is. The use of clashing colors, and so forth. . . that's the way I saw color. The jive talk. . . that was the way I heard people speaking on the street. I didn't know enough to know it was wrong. I knew the major point was I liked it.

The title of the movie in "White-ese" would have been THE BALLAD OF THE INDOMITABLE SWEETBACK. But in Black-ese, it comes out SWEET SWEETBACK'S BAADASSSSS SONG. Then to sell the movie, I had to hire a white front man because I couldn't go through those doors myself. When we were getting ready to sign the distribution contract, it said SWEETBACK, formerly known as SWEET SWEETBACK'S BAADASSSSS SONG. And I said "Whoa, wait, wait, wait." He said, "We're gonna change the title." I said, "Whoa, kiss my ass." He said, "But I don' t understand the title." "Who gives a fuck if you don't understand it," I said. "My audience will understand it." They relented. They were generally well-meaning, and they wanted to make money. But the cultural bias kept intruding itself in many ways.

At first, only two cities in the United States would show the picture: one in Detroit, and one in Atlanta. The first night in Detroit, it broke all the theatre's records, and that was only on the strength of the title alone, since nobody had seen it yet. By the second day, people would take their lunch and sit through it three times. I knew that I was finally talking to my audience. This is why the Hudlin brothers, Spike Lee, Robert Townsend and everybody else says that I'm the godfather of modern black cinema. SWEET SWEETBACK'S BAADASSSSS SONG made a zillion dollars before four white people had ever seen it.

Q: I remember that incredible ad campaign after the MPAA tagged it with an X rating: "Rated X by an All White Jury."

A: Yeah. I put that on T-shirts.

Q: The movie wound up grossing $14 million from a budget of half a million. . . and that was in 1971. It should be mentioned at this point that you produced, directed, wrote, starred in and composed the music for SWEETBACK. I imagine at that point, Hollywood came knocking again.

A: No. I never had an offer from a major to make a film. You see, first, I wasn't controllable in their way at the time. Two, they figured that they would take a knockoff of the product but not go to the source. That's when "blaxploitation" movies came in. They figured they could get a black girl as the lead, like CLEOPATRA JONES, have her say "motherfuck" three times, and there, you have a black film. Not only that, you allow her to beat up on some white guys who put little babies' eyes out, and dip rabbits in acid. But in the final analysis, who did all of these black heroes work under? Bwana, that's who. Each one really worked under the law, so these movies still had the message that white law knows best. Then they discovered that they didn't even have to hire blacks to direct those films, so they began to hire hip white kids just out of film school and said "Here, learn to cut your teeth on this. And when you learn, we'll give you a real film."

Q: Was Mario (Van Peebles) around when you were directing your films and on Broadway shows?

A: Mario has always been very, very creative. But it's very important for a person, a child, to know that he did it on his own. He was around and worked on SWEETBACK, and he worked for me on many of the shows. Mario also sees it as a business, and that's been a great advantage to him. Because the golden rule is that he who has the gold makes the rules. I raised the money for all my projects. I put together the packages, which was really impossible to do. You think creativity went into the color or the sound? You ought to see the creativity that went into the financing of the impossible.

Q: So the ultimate question, of course, is this. . . are things really any better right now?

A: Oh no. I wouldn't say they're better. Remember what the woman said in AIN'T SUPPOSED TO DIE A NATURAL DEATH? Every time you get hip to the old one, the man lays a new hype on you.

F I L M O G R A P H Y

M E L V I N   V A N   P E E B L E S
(Melvin Peebles)
b. August 21, 1932 - Chicago, Illinois
THE STORY OF A THREE-DAY PASS *LA PERMISSION* Sigma III, 1968, French
WATERMELON MAN Columbia, 1970
SWEET SWEETBACK'S BAADASSSSSS SONG Cinemation, 1971
DON'T PLAY US CHEAP Movin On Distribution, 1973
IDENTITY CRISIS Block & Chip Productions, 1989
EROTIC TALES co-director with Bob Rafelson, Susan Seidelman, Ken Russell, Paul Cox & Mani Kaul, Regina Ziegler Filmproduktion/Tele-Munchen/Westdeutscher Rundfunk, 1994, German
GANG IN BLUE (CTF) co-director with Mario Van Peebles, Robert Lawrence Productions/Van Peebles Films, 1996

PETER WANG

I wish I knew what Peter Wang has been up to since his last released film nearly 10 years ago. Perhaps he's returned to the world of science, from whence he came before turning to film, and if so their gain is our loss, because Wang's first film—A GREAT WALL in 1986, when I met and spoke with him in the lobby of the Chateau Marmont in West Hollywood—was one of the most auspicious first features of the latter part of that decade.

An admitted cross-cultural hybrid of having been born in Mainland China, raised in Taiwan, educated in America and working out of both Hong Kong and the U.S., Wang began his professional life as a science professor before making the unlikely leap to independent filmmaking.

First coming to the attention of American audiences of specialized films as the wry cook who sings "Fry Me to the Moon" (sic. . . intentionally) in Wayne Wang's (no relation) CHAN IS MISSING and the lead/co-writer of Allen Fong's early new-wave Hong Kong drama, AH YING, Wang managed to strike the first co-production deal between the United States and the People's Republic of China for A GREAT WALL. He thereby created one of 1986's authentic sleeper hits, a humanistic, ironic and utterly charming film of cross-cultural misunderstandings and reconciliation that delighted audiences and critics alike.

However, his output since has resulted in only two films: THE LASER MAN (1988), which appropriately, utilized a scientific backdrop for another comic tale, and the made-in-Taiwan, and unfortunately little-seen (in the U.S. anyway), FIRST DATE (1989). Nonetheless, his ground-breaking achievement with A GREAT WALL still stands tall, both artistically and historically, swinging open the gates of the Middle Kingdom for other filmmakers seeking to film there. . . including Bernardo Bertolucci, who followed Wang into China for THE LAST EMPEROR.

MICHAEL SINGER: *After all the talk during the last few years of US/Chinese co-pro-ductions, you were ultimately the first one to do it, ironically enough on a low-budget indepen-dent feature. How was this accomplished?*

PETER WANG: It was not as hard as it seems to be, but we took a different route. We didn't go to China pretending we were the big boys. Instead, we were approached by one of the Chinese companies who expressed interest in a co-production. We told them we were independent filmmakers with zero money, but that we would probably make a better film than the majors. Somehow we con-vinced them, and it was really quite easy. We told them that we had a very simple story idea. Definitely not political. People to people. A slice of life. The Chinese had no objections to the story, so we got started.

Q: *Did you use Chinese technicians or bring your crew from the United States?*

A: We used a lot of Chinese technicians, about sixty or seventy people. Only twenty of us, including actors, were from the States or Hong Kong. Of course, the key personnel such as director of photography, gaffer, first assistant director, were from the US.

Q: *Did the crew stir up a lot of interest in Peking?*

A: Constantly. Crowd control was a big problem. Most of the scenes were not even usable, with people staring at the camera, including a lot of policemen. Quite a frustrating experience. Later on we used a Chinese cameraman and a second unit crew to try and pick up all sorts of things, and that worked out very well.

Q: *Did you shoot on all practical locations, or did you have to build any sets in Peking?*

A: All of the existing scenes in the film are real locations. We shot a number of scenes in the studio with very elaborate set designs. The were dream sequences. . . the Chinese father's idea of the United States.

Q: *Sounds like Kafka's Amerika. . . someone's vision of the United States who has never actually been there. Why did you decide to edit those scenes out? They sound fascinating.*

A: They were fascinating, but I have to back up my decision to cut them. In the script it worked very well, but considering the flow of this film from beginning to end in the editing room there was a problem. A GREAT WALL is very episodic, and there's no strong narrative plot to carry the story. It depends on mood and music and editing, which make the whole story flow unconsciously. . . very tricky and very delicate. And whenever we threw in those dream sequences, we imme-diately felt that the film didn't flow well at all. And also, A GREAT WALL is a more realistic portrayal of life, and the dream sequences were just off-pace and out of place. They just weren't very original. I was unconsciously trying to imitate Fellini. As much as I loved those dream sequences—which were very well shot they just didn't belong. I'd like to sell them to MTV. Does anybody want an MTV video with a lot of Chinese?

Q: *Do you like shooting loosely and then finding your movie in the editing room?*

A: No. That was not my intention. I started as a writer and I like telling strong stories.

Q: Were the Chinese actors in A GREAT WALL professionals or amateurs?

A: The young actors are amateurs. They never acted before. The father and mother were professionals.

Q: What kind of equipment did you use in China? Did you bring it from the States or rent it there?

A: We rented some from Peking Studios, who had some brand new cameras. We brought in some Nagras from Hong Kong, as well as a small dolly. We also rented a generator from the Chinese, which was left over from the mini-series, MARCO POLO.

Q: A GREAT WALL looked much more expensive than it actually was. What was the final budget?

A: The official number is under two million dollars.

Q: American audiences first saw you as the singing cook in CHAN IS MISSING, and then some of us had the chance to see AH YING, in which you starred and also co-wrote the screenplay. The first film was shot in San Francisco, and the second in Hong Kong, yet you're based out of New York. What's your background, and how did you come to be such a filmmaking gypsy?

A: I was born in China, brought up in Taiwan and educated in the United States. To begin with, I thought I was a person who didn't belong anywhere. The Chinese term for this feeling translates as, "half a person" or "marginal person." There are a lot of people in my generation who have shared similar experiences. We were exposed to many different cultures and places. At times we don't really understand or feel our identity, but eventually we have to graduate from that. It's okay if you feel that way. . . the whole world is turning that way. . . your home base, who you are, what language you speak, what culture you identify with, are becoming less and less important. This is a fact of life. You really have to accept that in order to be a modem man. And that is the only way you can create, I believe.

Q: By being slightly uprooted?

A: Yes. The more you're uprooted, the more complex you are, and the greater possibility that you will create something. That's my definition, anyway.

Q: Then you prefer being uprooted?

A: It is not by choice. At this stage, I'm more American than people realize. I have a very, very heavy Chinese background from my family, because my father was a Chinese literature professor. He made it very clear that there were no ifs, ands or buts about it. If you didn't know your own culture, you didn't eat at the family table. I was trained as a scientist, which was another complication. So with all this mixed together, I think something new will always happen in my mind.

Q: That transition from scientist to filmmaker is not something we often encounter.

A: I think I made the Guinness Book of World Records as the only American filmmaker who switched from a science professorship to director.

Q: You were a professor of what branch of science?

A: Physics and engineering. I had a job at George Mason University in Fairfax, Virginia, which is a very good school.

Q: What happened? Why did you make the switch?

A: I think God originally wanted me to be a filmmaker or actor, and my father's wish was for me to get a very secure position in a field of science. I tried to please both. I think I did. In Asian family traditions, it's very important to go with your parents' wishes. Otherwise, they lay a guilt trip on you which you're never going to get out from!

Q: When you decided to make this transition, did you suddenly just leave your professorship?

A: It was a gamble, and I was thinking about the switch for some time. Also, I happened to hit the mid-life crisis, or something like that—where I had been X number of years in my profession and wondered if I really wanted to stay on the job. The money and job security were great, but in the meantime I felt that there was something else unfulfilled.

Q: How did you begin seeking this new career? You must have moved from Virginia to a place where you could make films.

A: I've been involved in filmmaking for a long time, and before that I was involved with theatre and writing. I made 16mm documentaries, so I had some knowledge of film production. I also had the advantage of scientific and engineering training, so that the technical aspects of filmmaking were no big deal to me. But from what you think you can do to what you can actually do takes another quantum leap. The process of making AH YING in Hong Kong was very educational, very inspiring.

Q: Was AH YING the first feature you were involved with as a filmmaker? You had acted in CHAN IS MISSING a couple of years before.

A: Yes. I was heavily involved in the whole process of developing and filming AH YING. After that, I thought I was ready to direct my own film.

Q: This burgeoning community of Asian-American filmmakers—whether in San Francisco, Los Angeles or New York—and the new wave directors in Hong Kong and Taiwan, all seem to know each other. It seems to be a mutually supportive community. I know that you all have different commitments and ideas of the Asian image. Some of you feel that you have to make your own statements without regard to social necessity. What are your own feelings about this, in terms of pressure from the community to make the "right" kind of movie?

A: Unavoidably, as Asian-American directors, we have to carry this load. Either we are self-appointed or our community appoints us to carry it. There's not doubt we will do as much as we can. I certainly want to be part of the force that eventually will bring up the image of Asian Americans on the screen. That is undeniably one of the goals of making films. However, I want there to be more Asian-American filmmakers so the responsibility will be equally shared. The other aspect that I'd like to comment on is that it's even more important to be a man than to be a good Chinaman. There's something broader, there are issues and ideas that probably can apply to every human being, not just the Asian-American image. It's part of my mission, but I see something larger. So in the future, there will be films which call for Caucasian actors. And I won't feel guilty using them.

F I L M O G R A P H Y

P E T E R   W A N G
(Wang Zhengfang)
b. Beijing, China
A GREAT WALL   Orion Classics, 1986, U.S.-Chinese
THE LASER MAN   Original Cinema, 1988
FIRST DATE   Peter Wang Films, 1989, Taiwanese

$\mathcal{W}$AYNE $\mathcal{W}$ANG

It's pleasing to report that since this conversation with Wayne Wang—which took place after the release of his third movie, DIM SUM: A LITTLE BIT OF HEART—this bi-cultural filmmaker has continued a staunchly independent path that has resulted in eight more features on both sides of the Pacific.

With his first independent features, CHAN IS MISSING and DIM SUM: A LTTLE BIT OF HEART, Wang opened a window to the East for audiences, as he would continue to do with EAT A BOWL OF TEA, LIFE IS CHEAP. . . BUT TOILET PAPER IS EXPENSIVE, CHINESE BOX and his most commercial film to date, the beautiful and poignant THE JOY LUCK CLUB, based on Amy Tan's best-selling novel. With unyielding insight and loving observation, Wang put many aspects of Chinese and Chinese-American life into focus for filmgoers accustomed to blurry stereotypes.

But Wang hasn't limited himself to films solely on Asian themes. For SLAMDANCE and his two successful collaborations with New York writer Paul Auster, SMOKE and its spinoff BLUE IN THE FACE, the director stepped outside of the bounds of the Chinese experience, further breaking through preconceived notions of what an "ethnic" director is supposed to be. And most recently, ANYWHERE BUT HERE sees Wang swimming in a more mainstream but no less ambitious direction.

Wang's style has understandably altered through the years, from the austere, Ozu-influenced meditations of CHAN IS MISSING and DIM SUM to the more extravagant, but entirely appropriate, romanticism of THE JOY LUCK CLUB, and then back to the rueful Brooklyn-based musings of SMOKE and BLUE IN THE FACE, and verité stylings of CHINESE BOX. Once thing that hasn't changed is Wang's stubborn determination to go his own way, without bending to the expectations of either the studio or independent systems.

MICHAEL SINGER: *Silence is a rare commodity in modern American films, but you make extensive use of it in your films. What are the influences, either cinematic or cultural, that allows you to utilize silence in such a way?*

WAYNE WANG: I think the use of silence is influenced by a lot of Asian films, obviously, and also some German films that may actually be influenced by Asian films themselves. For example, Wim Wenders' films are all influenced by the Yasujiro Ozu films. The non-action balances the action, which is why I think silence is just as important as dialogue or action. One of my favorite scenes in CHAN IS MISSING is one where the two main characters just sit in a bar. Thirty seconds goes by and nothing happens. In DIM SUM there are two direct references to directors who have had an influence on me—one is Frank Capra, and the other is Ozu. Capra was my father's favorite director and I truly love his films. I still religiously watch IT'S A WONDERFUL LIFE every Christmas. And Ozu, because I think he truly represents an aesthetic and sensibility that's more Asian than anything I've ever seen.

Q: *You and Ozu seem to share a belief that space without people still carries an essence of those who reside there. That seems to be a very Asian concept.*

A: I really like those empty shots. They're almost like after-images that you sometimes see on television. They collect the experiences of the characters in a movie and also give room for the audience to think a little about their own lives in relation to what they're seeing on the screen. And sometimes they have a slightly mysterious and magical quality about them.

Q: *I know you've been influenced by Capra on the American side and Ozu on the Asian, but what about Chinese film?*

A: Well, there are a lot of good filmmakers of my generation who are working in Hong Kong, Taiwan and China. They have made some very good films. But I don't think these films have truly matured in terms of finding a language for themselves, and none of these directors have developed a whole body of work that are truly masterpieces. There is a lot of research, and people talking about Chinese movies, and trying to find out what is really Chinese about them. . . but I think everybody is in the early stages of probing. I try to explore that in my films too, because with the composition in my films I'm pretty much working with some very basic concepts. For example, our DIM SUM cinematographer, Michael Chin, and I were pretty consistent in insisting that any one image not take over the movie. It's the simplicity of the whole body of work. Also, we wanted to put the camera in a comfortable objective position to observe the action, rather than go real tight or have very dramatic angles. Everything is shot basically from a position that's parallel to the plane of action, so it allows for things to happen in a more balanced way within the frame.

Q: *I really loved your water shots in CHAN IS MISSING, where you would just hold the camera on a body of water with, it seems, nothing else happening. Mood and feeling become more important than narrative.*

A: Water for me is so wonderful, because I used to swim a lot. And the lesson I learned is that I had to go with the flow of the water and not fight it. Water could be incredibly gentle or incredibly powerful and vicious. . . it had all the ingredients of saying "this is nature, this is the world, and we're only one very small part of it." There are recurrent images of water in CHAN IS MISSING and DIM SUM, and water will probably persist in different ways through my other films. The Russian director Andrei Tarkovsky said that water is the blood of the universe.

Q: *Tell me about your personal background.*

A: I was born in Hong Kong in 1949, and left there at age 18. I've been here for 18 years. So next year I become more American! I studied painting at Foothill College in the California College of Arts and Crafts, and also did some photography and other things. I laid all the groundwork to get into films, because deep down inside I always wanted to make movies. In graduate school I shifted into filmmaking and television, and from there made my first feature film with two other friends after we got out of school. We had twenty thousand dollars and made a film called A MAN, A WOMAN AND A KILLER, which was shown at festivals and was well-received in Europe. Then I went back to Hong Kong to direct a television series which was sort of like All In The Family Hong Kong-style. But I got frustrated because I was stepping into the shoes of another director who had made it one of the most popular T.V. shows at that time, and I was just picking up on what he did. So I came back here and left film for a little while, working as an administrator and a teacher in the Chinese community-mainly because I felt that it was relevant not only in life but also as a director. In 1979 I quit, wrote some proposals, and that's how CHAN IS MISSING came about. CHAN was a success, which I didn't expect, and that made it easier for me to do DIM SUM.

Q: CHAN IS MISSING *was ridiculously inexpensive for a feature, wasn't it?*

A: Yes, it cost about twenty thousand dollars.

Q: *And for* DIM SUM *the budget took a massive leap to. . . ?*

A: Five hundred thousand dollars.

Q: *And it was shot in color and thirty-five millimeter?*

A: Right.

Q: DIM SUM *had something of a false start, didn't it?*

A: Yes. We shot some material with a different script, in which the story of the finished DIM SUM was only one of five stories. Originally it was sort of a Chinese-American women's St. Elmo's Fire.

Q: *When did you know it was going wrong?*

A: If we had written more drafts of the script we probably could have pulled it off, but going into shooting I felt that some of the stories weren't as well-developed as others. I felt very strongly about the mother/daughter story, and the other stories were getting a little too slick. There were elements in them that were probably very commercial, and may have sold tickets, but what does that all mean? That's when I did a very risky thing. . . I told my producer that we should stop and start again clean with that one story.

Q: *Your producer, Vincent Tai, is an architect who had not been previously involved with films. It's nice that he had faith and allowed you to finish the project.*

A: There's a part of Vincent Tai that is truly an artist. The reason he went into architecture is because he felt he could do something truly artistic, and I'm glad that he has supported the movie. Otherwise there would have been no independently produced Chinese-American movie for at least a few years down the line.

Q: *The story of DIM SUM in its finished form is the story of a mother and daughter who are played by a real life mother and daughter, Kim and Laureen Chew. How much of the story we see on screen is actually their story?*

A: A lot of the information came from Kim and Laureen. We took all that information and created our own drama. The conflict actually comes from facts that they told us. For example, the mother thinking that she's going to die after visiting a fortune teller, the mother wanting the daughter to get married, the way she puts pressure on her daughter, the daughter having a boyfriend in Los Angeles that she's been seeing for years. But it's like research material, and we literally had to put all this information on three by five cards and create scenes and plot points. It's a fictional dramatic script based quite a bit on the real events.

Q: *How did Laureen and Kim Chew react to the film?*

A: I think Kim, who played the mother, had no idea what kind of film we were making. She sort of thought it was a home movie or student project. At the premiere screening in San Francisco there were five hundred invited guests and she got a five minute standing ovation. People wouldn't let her sit down. I think that's wonderful for somebody after forty years of being basically a housewife and working as a seamstress. Laureen also went through a lot, living a character that's very close to herself on the screen. The last line of the movie, where she says, "I made some decisions while you were gone" to her mother, is pretty much true for Laureen too. After shooting the movie she made some decisions about her own life and moved out of the house for half of the week. Half the time she's there, half the time she's not. So she's still maintaining that same relationship with her mother, yet at the same time having a more independent life.

Q: *Laureen's reaction at the end of the film was wonderfully enigmatic. We weren't quite sure she was crying out of anger, relief, joy, mortification. . . or all of those things.*

A: That's right, and that's why I like it so much. It's a combination of the complexity of all those different elements. I love tears that come out of feelings you can't put your finger on.

Q: *Do you have any desire to return to Hong Kong and make a film there?*

A: I have a lot of offers. But now that I've worked over here and seen more quality films, I really don't want to do schlocky commercial movies. If I can find the right conditions to do a good movie in Hong Kong, I would certainly consider it. Because I think there's a part of me that's still in Hong Kong, and still in China. Right now, I'm actually looking for a love story that's maybe set in Shanghai in the 1940's with an international cast. But it's got to be a great CASABLANCA-like story.

Q: Why is it so difficult for Hong Kong filmmakers to strike out independently? Is there a complete monopoly of the industry by the larger studios?

A: Yes, and also the demand for very popular films is what the whole market goes after. If you look at the films in Hong Kong they're either full of action, or totally slapstick. It's the extremes of commercialism, even more than here. There's very little characterization, very little story. There are a few filmmakers who work against all of that, one of whom is Allen Fong, who's made FATHER AND SON and AH YING. There's another young director named Yim Ho, who made a wonderful recent film called THE HOMECOMING.

Q: Do you have any plans of edging into big-budget commercial features, or do you have a commitment to independent filmmaking?

A: I have a commitment to independent filmmaking, and I'll always do independent films on my own terms. But at the same time I want to try doing some so-called mainstream Hollywood movies. Mainstream in the sense of THE KILLING FIELDS, for example. . . movies that have strong stories and great characters.

Q: What about American-made films about Asians made by non-Asians. . . is it up to Asian filmmakers or Asian-American filmmakers to tell their own stories?

A: No, I don't think so. It's up to producers and directors who are willing to take a little bit of risk to write three-dimensional characters and get away from typical dramas that tend to stereotype Chinatown and the Chinese-American community. I'd love to see the day when someone writes a script for Meryl Streep but thinks, "Boy, there's this wonderful Chinese actress. . . I mean, she's born in America, speaks English without an accent and is just as American as Meryl Streep". . . then takes a risk and casts the Chinese actress. Not only would you have a great actress playing the part, but also a whole other dimension, which is the final acceptance that any Chinese born in this country is just as American as Joe Blow down the street. I may be idealistic, but I think that somewhere along the line producers, writers and directors will take certain risks, do their homework and make real films with three-dimensional characters.

F I L M O G R A P H Y

W A Y N E   W A N G
b. January 12, 1949 - Hong Kong
A MAN, A WOMAN, AND A KILLER   co-director with Rick Schmidt, 1975
CHAN IS MISSING   New Yorker, 1982
DIM SUM: A LITTLE BIT OF HEART   Orion Classics, 1985
SLAMDANCE   Island Pictures, 1987
EAT A BOWL OF TEA   Columbia, 1989
LIFE IS CHEAP. . . BUT TOILET PAPER IS EXPENSIVE   *LIFE IS CHEAP*   Silverlight Entertainment, 1989, U.S.-Hong Kong
THE STRANGER (CTF)   co-director with Joan Tewkesbury & Daniel Vigne, HBO Pictures, 1992
THE JOY LUCK CLUB   Buena Vista, 1993
SMOKE   Miramax Films, 1995
BLUE IN THE FACE   co-director with Paul Auster, Miramax Films, 1995
CHINESE BOX   Trimark Pictures, 1997, French-Hong Kong-Japanese-U.S.
ANYWHERE BUT HERE   20th Century Fox, 1999

$\mathcal{K}$EENEN I VORY $\mathcal{W}$AYANS

When I first sat down with Keenen Ivory Wayans in his office one afternoon ten years ago, he was a rising young actor/director/writer. Now, he's a household name, thanks to his late night talk show and previous Fox Television comedy program IN LIVING COLOR, which also catapulted Jim Carrey and several other Wayans family members to the stars.

I spoke to Wayans following the release of I'M GONNA GIT YOU SUCKA— for which he served as director, writer and star—an outlandish but sweetly affectionate send-up of '70s black exploitation films. Featuring a cast that included such hardened genre vets as Jim Brown, Isaac Hayes, Bernie Casey and Antonio Fargas, I'M GONNA GIT YOU SUCKA took freewheeling and lighthearted comic punches at virtually everything that tickled Wayans' funnybone—including street pimp fashions, dubious athletic competitions for gang members, hyper-macho superheroes tripping over their own ineptitude, syrupy romance, disco dancing, threatening midgets and bumbling would-be badasses. His sophomore directing effort, A LOW DOWN DIRTY SHAME, didn't fare quite so well, but was certainly no embarrassment either.

Wayans had previously co-written and co-starred in Robert Townsend's irreverent comedy HOLLYWOOD SHUFFLE, following years as an actor and stand-up comedian. He moved from New York poverty to Hollywood glory in just a few years, planning and executing each new career goal with military precision ... and then setting his sights on further ambitions. It's interesting, in hindsight, to note how successful that game plan has been.

MICHAEL SINGER: *An obvious first question would be: Where did you derive the inspiration to make a film which spoofs a long-dead genre? Did you really love black exploitation movies when you were a kid?*

KEENEN IVORY WAYANS: As a kid I was enthusiastic about these films, but as I got older I'd be sitting around with a bunch of friends, just talking about how bad some of them really were. Now that they're on videocassette, you get a chance to see them again. And from a filmmaker's point of view, and an adult's point of view, you can really see how terrible some of them were. Now, the unfortunate thing is that there were a lot of great films that got tagged along with the really bad ones, but the really bad ones were just hysterical. Then I saw AIRPLANE and realized that its genius was that the filmmakers took another genre that was short-lived and parodied it for all it was worth. I thought it was a brilliant satire, and eventually the idea came to me, "Wow, I could do something like AIRPLANE! based on black exploitation movies." The concept of I'M GONNA GIT YOU SUCKA started out as a strict parody, but I think the movie has grown into its own as a little action adventure comedy with references to some of those films. It now lends itself to a much broader demographic because you don't have to have seen those films to get the jokes. Most of the humor is pretty broad and there in your face. I tried to satirize everything from my generation, in addition to the films. I pulled some of the politics, the clothing, the dances, the whole atmosphere of the '70s, but tried to do it in a way that would be contemporary. And I think, based on the reactions that I've been getting, that we accomplished that.

Q: *One of the delightful things to me about* I'M GONNA GIT YOU SUCKA *is that the character you play as the lead, Jack Spade, is really someone out of a typical Hollywood home-from-the-war drama of the 1940s rather than a tough black hero of the 1970s.*

A: Yeah, Jack is the kind of guy you don't see in films anymore. He's the naive do-gooder. Originally, I had written him as a badass combat soldier, but I decided to give him a different character. I just wanted to give him certain values that you don't see anymore, and I don't think there's ever been a black male who's played that type of character. He's so against the grain, so different from the tough guys whom he idolizes.

Q: *Watching you play that character in the movie reminds the audience of how limited black characterizations have been in film.*

A: What's missing from film nowadays is the innocence. Not that I'm an innocent guy and all my films will be of that nature, but innocence is something that is almost looked upon negatively—and it's really not. There's something warm and fun about watching innocence before it's tarnished by the realities of life. Once I started acting out the part, I made the choice to make him a very childlike character. For example, I gave him a military jacket with all these medals on it, but they're all secretarial medals. The guy has never been in combat in his life, which is my joke on today's army. There hasn't been a real war since Vietnam, but half the guys who go into the army come back like they're real badasses. The movie, for me, was just a chance to poke fun at everything.

Q: I'M GONNA GIT YOU SUCKA *was your first directing effort. What in your background gave you the confidence to direct a feature?*

A: Well, I had done my homework as an observer. I spent a lot of time with Robert Townsend when we were doing HOLLYWOOD SHUFFLE, and then we did RAW with Eddie Murphy. But I think what prepared me most was the fact that I'm a standup comic, and that's what I nurtured first in terms of talent. When you do standup comedy, you're your own writer, director, actor, producer and editor. You wear all the hats while you're on stage, so when it was time to take this written piece called I'M GONNA GIT YOU SUCKA to the next phase, I wanted to be the director and the actor so that I could keep the vision clean. Because it's the kind of film, which, if misinterpreted, could really work against me—and I didn't want that to happen. So I said, "Okay, this is the one I'm going to do."

Q: *I often ask this of first-time directors. . . were your cast and crew supportive, or did they test you day-to-day?*

A: I was very lucky. I got excellent people to work with me—especially the producing team. There were people who took cuts in pay, who had far more credits than I did. But they liked the script and the fact that I wanted to direct it, and they were truly supportive—the cast, my editor, the director of photography—it was a very warm and creative environment. That was the thing that motivated me the most—the fact that all these people wanted me to succeed. There were no undercurrents of envy or competition. It was a very paternal environment as well. All the cast members like Jim Brown, Bernie Casey and Isaac Hayes, guys who had done tons of film. . . whether they were good or bad, they had gone the distance . . . all gave me great advice and caring. That was a good feeling. And they were so into the spirit of having fun themselves. I think they felt comfortable about what they were doing. Because of that, they didn't have to second guess themselves and knew they could trust me, because they knew that I had the same sensibilities and wouldn't exploit them in any way. They were very uninhibited about being funny and going out on a limb. You can take Jim Brown, who's not known for being the funny and spontaneous guy, and in the film he's very, very funny. He has a good time. I was shocked and delighted that he was such a dry, funny guy and that he had ideas on how to be inventive. The support system of the cast and crew is what really enabled me to take my vision and make it a reality.

Q: *How much criticism may you be in for in terms of people accusing your film of confirming damaging black stereotypes?*

A: I don't think my film allows that to be a valid criticism, because what I do with the stereotypes is ridicule them to such a degree that they cannot be looked at as reinforcement. The pimp character, for instance, is so ludicrous, so out there, that he's even ridiculed in the context of the film. There's no way he can be looked upon as a reinforced stereotype. That type of criticism has no foundation to stand on.

Q: *Were you criticized at all by people who saw early screenings of the film?*

A: Based on the title, a lot of people approached me negatively prior to seeing the film. But anyone who does that just doesn't get it. The title is supposed to be a joke on titles like THE HIT, SHEBA BABY and T.N.T. JACKSON. So if you don't get the joke, it's very easy to sit back and go, "Hey, what's that brother trying to do there?" But once people have seen the film, their attitude changes.

Q: *Well, the movie really disarms an audience with its own good-natured fun.*

A: I think that if anything, the criticism will be why didn't I make a more profound film of social relevance, or something like that. But my feeling is that in order for black film to progress, we have to get out of the art film trap that we're in right now. Every movie we make can't be a social commentary. There has to be a level of entertainment or else you have nothing to market, if that's where your head is at, I applaud and support you. But it's not where my head is at. I want to make movies that have black people in them, not just make black films. I don't want to make films that only a small faction of the audience is going to patronize, because no one wants to pay seven bucks to see a movie that reminds them of how oppressed they are. They know that. . . they've lived that. They want to see things that either present an alternative or gives them some kind of relief. I enjoy making people laugh at things that aren't necessarily funny, to give them a sense of relief, to make today a little bit brighter for the two hours you sit in the theatre. I guess I'm more commercially oriented. That's how I perceive myself as a filmmaker.

Q: *Would you say that your friends and colleagues Eddie Murphy and Robert Townsend more or less share your point of view?*

A: Yeah, I think so. I know Eddie does for sure. We've discussed this at length and again, it's just two different schools of thought. Some people think that film is to teach, other people think film is to entertain. You, as a filmmaker, choose which side. I think you can do both, but I also think that if you lose the humanity of your film, then it just becomes preaching. No one's going to hear you, they'll just turn you off. But if people can lock into a character, then they can experience what he is experiencing and get a better insight into whatever story the film-maker is trying to tell, as opposed to a character on screen just talking at them.

Q: *Let's talk about how all this got started. You were born and raised in New York. . . what kind of family do you come from?*

A: They're a great source of inspiration to me, and there's a lot of talent in my family. There were ten children—five boys and five girls, and seven of us are pursuing careers in show business. We'll be like the King Family of comedy.

Q: *Who were the parents of this extraordinary brood?*

A: They are two people who never stifled us creatively. My mother, especially, was very supportive of us.

Q: *Were your parents themselves in show business?*

A: No. My mother used to sing when she was younger, but she never really pursued it. My father was the sole supporter of ten kids. We were very poor. The only thing we ever really had was laughter. But we never knew that we were poor—we just thought my mother was cheap! We didn't have things that other kids had, but then again, there were kids who were far worse off than we were. My parents never made us feel deprived or imprisoned by our poverty, but always encouraged us to accept what was given and move on. My father passed his tenacity on to us. He's a guy whose belief has always been—if you fall down, get up, brush yourself off, and keep going. And again, my mother nurtured us creatively. When I would come home with a finger painting, she made me feel like I was Van Gogh. She'd put it on the refrigerator and if anybody came in she'd say proudly, "Oh, look! Keenen did that!" It's an objective of mine to some day help the whole family by creating a film that we'll write and act in together.

Q: *When did you start thinking about going into show business?*

A: I was an avid fan of Richard Pryor from age six, and he was the one person that I think inspired me to go into show business. I remember watching him back then, and what intrigued me was that he was able to take things that were painful experiences, things that I had experienced myself, like poverty and being bullied and not being liked and not getting the girls and being an outcast. . . and he made fun of it. In fact, he made it funny. Even at six, I thought he was a genius. I locked right in and said, "That's what I'm gonna do." But I didn't actually pursue it until I was about 19. I was already in college in Alabama as an engineering major, and I would spend most of the day hanging out at the campus fountain telling stories about New York. I would always have a crowd around me. In Alabama, they were always curious about New York. There was another guy from New York who came up to me and said, "Hey man, you should go to The Improv." I didn't know what he was talking about, so he told me all about The Improvisation in New York. So when I went home for the summer break, I went there, and that's where I met Robert Townsend. By the third time I auditioned for The Improv, I finally got passed by a guy named Chris Albrecht, who was then the manager of The Improv with Budd Friedman. Later on, when Chris moved from New York to Los Angeles, he got a job as an agent at ICM and took me, Joe Piscopo, and three other guys as his five clients. We all moved out to L.A. I started doing standup there and got a TV show called "For Love and Honor." Then I did "The Tonight Show," and that was—other than directing I'M GONNA GIT YOU SUCKA—the greatest experience of my life. Doing Johnny Carson's show is something that all comics dream about. We would watch Johnny every single night, looking for the comedian to come out and do his thing. It's that moment that you live for, it's every comedian's objective. I don't care who they are—you haven't made it until you do your five minutes on Carson. Well, I finally got mine. It was a great shot, and Johnny invited me to come over and sit down on the sofa. I was in a dream. . . it took me days to wake up. I did it. . . I had my five minutes of immortality—I guess that was ten minutes less than Warhol had in mind—but who cares!

Q: *That must have given you the confidence and encouragement you needed to push on even further.*

A: See, I approached this business very methodically. I understood this business long before I really knew anything about it. That's because I paralleled it to any other business. I've always been a believer that the easiest way is the right way. Once you learn what the right way is, you pursue it. Show business is really no different than working for IBM or any other corporate structure. There are different levels and different steps up the ladder. You have to be prepared to take the different steps. Everybody pays their dues one way or another. Either you make it fast and bum out, or you prepare yourself for longevity, so each year I would give myself specific goals. The first year I was in L.A., I said, "I'm gonna get on TV whether it's a commercial or a one-liner." And I was able to do that. The next year I said, "Okay, now I want to get a pilot." Then the next year, "Okay, I want to get on a series." I got on a series. The next year I said, "I want to do Johnny Carson's show," and I did Johnny Carson. I was very methodical about the different steps that I took and all this led me to here. The nice thing is that I feel confident about being here. So I don't regret taking the time and paying the dues, and the wonderful thing is that the poverty I knew came in handy, because I knew how to live on nothing. So it wasn't a big deal to struggle. I've been doing that all my life and was happy anyway.

Q: Has it been tough learning to live with success? Has that presented its own problems?

A: Well, I was kind of prepared for that because being friends with Eddie Murphy, I got a chance to watch him and see what went on around him, all the nuances that come with success and how manipulative people can be. So now I can see what's coming if it happens to me. But I don't really view myself as being successful. I think I'm on my way to being successful, but I still have more steps to take. But I am getting closer to where I want to go.

Q: So now that you've accomplished all of these methodically chosen goals, what's next?

A: I want to branch out. I want to be an entity that is respected and looked upon as a possible source for others—family, friends, other talented people, people who normally wouldn't get a chance to break in. I want to continue making my own films and really taking what are now looked at as "black movies" to the level of just being "movies." That's really what my goal is—to allow black actors the same diversified roles that white actors have, and allow myself as a director to be as diverse as Oliver Stone, John Hughes, and all the other guys I admire. And I want others to be able to do the same kind of thing. I am a firm believer that there are certain things that are a given, and one is that racism exists in America. And it's something that's not going away. Fine. . . . deal with it and move on. It's not something that I think has to be such a great obstacle that we cannot find our dreams. It just means that it may delay them a little longer.

Q: I've resisted asking you about what the press has conveniently dubbed "The Black Pack," of which you're a conspicuous member, along with Eddie Murphy, Robert Townsend, Arsenio Hall, Paul Mooney, and your brother Damon Wayans. What does The Black Pack actually mean? Does it represent a new black power in Hollywood which can make its own demands and get what it wants because there's a power in unity between several "bankable" guys who happen to be black?

A: See, that's the myth. That is not what The Black Pack is at all. That is what The Black Pack should be. But the reality is that power is relevant to its environment, and we will never be more powerful than Hollywood. We will never be able to demand anything from Hollywood, because that power makes or breaks you, and if you don't understand that, you're in for one hell of a ride. What we can do together is offer something to Hollywood that they want, and based on that, utilize that creative power to negotiate with them. But it's not like this raging fury of black power blazing through Hollywood. I would never want to perpetuate a myth like that. I never want to give false hope to other black filmmakers who think that all they have to do is come together and knock the walls down, because this is not about that. The Black Pack is a group of creative people who happen to be good friends, who support each other, who network with each other, and eventually we'll get to a level where we will be able to create an environment for other black creators to come in and do the same type of thing. At least, that's our hope.

. .

F I L M O G R A P H Y

K E E N E N I V O R Y W A Y A N S

b. June 8, 1958 - New York, New York

I'M GONNA GIT YOU SUCKA   MGM/UA, 1989

A LOW DOWN DIRTY SHAME   Buena Vista, 1994

SIMON WINCER

Although he had directed more than 200 hours of television (winning an Emmy Award in the process) and no fewer than seven feature films, it took a 7,000 pound aquatic mammal named Willy to really put Simon Wincer's name on the map of top Hollywood directors hailing from Down Under. . . joining a list that had already included George Miller, Bruce Beresford, Phillip Noyce and Fred Schepisi. The huge success of FREE WILLY in 1993 (the film spawned two sequels directed by others) left little doubt that Wincer's ease with actors of various species on rugged outdoors locations marked him as a filmmaker comfortable in surroundings that would make other directors scurry back to their Winnebagos in a flash.

Of course, this came as no surprise to anyone following Wincer's 20 year-long career in long-form filmmaking. Early efforts in Australian television for the Sydney-born Wincer naturally led to a feature career, and he enjoyed his first big home country hit with 1983's period horseracing opus PHAR LAP, which also won many fans stateside. Lured to the U.S. in 1985 to direct the science fantasy D.A.R.Y.L. for Paramount, Wincer then stayed to direct two TV movies before returning home for the historical feature THE LIGHTHORSEMEN, which rivaled such epics of old as THE CHARGE OF THE LIGHT BRIGADE and GUNGA DIN in scale.

In 1989, Wincer's cross-Pacific career culminated with his Emmy Award-winning direction of the mini-series LONESOME DOVE, one of the most acclaimed and honored programs in television history. Based on Larry McMurtry's best-selling novel, it recreated the American West and its inhabitants with an almost primal power that transcended the genre, particularly for that medium. After the entertaining Aussie western QUIGLEY DOWN UNDER, Wincer took a lighter look at the American frontier in LIGHTNING JACK, for which the filmmaker was the first to recognize Cuba Gooding, Jr.'s considerable comic talents. . . which were later parlayed into an Oscar-winning turn in JERRY MAGUIRE. In between QUIGLEY and JACK, Wincer fit in a few well-received episodes of George Lucas' YOUNG INDIANA JONES series.

Returning to the big screen, Wincer returned to exotic locales to film the Disney adventure OPERATION DUMBO DROP in Thailand, and returned to that country (as well as Australia and the U.S.) once again for THE PHANTOM. Launched in a particularly brutal summertime movie battlefield, THE PHANTOM failed at the box office despite some wonderful reviews which noted Wincer's deft and unpretentious handling of the film's comic book origins.

As is typical for Australian and British filmmakers, who see no contradiction in devoting their skills to both features and television, Wincer then directed a few movies-of-the-week, for Disney and the Showtime Network, among others, while preparing future theatrical projects.

I spoke with Wincer shortly before he left for the Northern Thailand location of OPERATION DUMBO DROP.

MICHAEL SINGER: *Hollywood tends to stereotype directors, and at this juncture in your career, you are seen as a "great outdoors" filmmaker, specializing in wide open spaces, animals and action.*

SIMON WINCER: I think these days everyone tends to get pigeonholed a bit. Maybe they think I'm the large mammal guy because of FREE WILLY and OPERATION DUMBO DROP, but if my films have a strength, it's a strong emotional line, whether it's got to do with animals or humans or both. And I would like to be thought of, when I've finished my filmmaking career, as a person who has made a whole range of films of all different genres and subject matters. I suppose I made a good western with LONESOME DOVE, so I was perceived as a western guy. Then FREE WILLY, so I'm the animal and kid guy. But my career goes back to 1972 when I started directing for television, and I've done a wide body of work, some epic, like the YOUNG INDIANA JONES TV episodes and THE LIGHTHORSEMEN, more contemporary melodramas, like the mini-series BLUEGRASS and THE LAST FRONTIER.

Q: *You seem to work in a solid tradition of telling the story at hand in a clear, cohesive way on film with few fancy frills.*

A: It's very rare that you go to the movies and you don't see a fine looking film, but what makes a successful film is script, story and character, always. The script is where it starts and finishes, and it doesn't matter how technically fine it is. If you don't have a good script and story, you don't have anything. When you first start directing, you tend to worry a lot more about what the camera's doing than the form and content, which are actually the most important things. The biggest mistake a director can make is to be so busy worrying about moving the camera and getting pretty shots that he or she forgets about more important things like pace. It's very rare to see a film these days that isn't atmospheric. . . but if it's atmospheric and dramatic and moving and the story and character are right, than you've got something really special.

Q: *Every thirty second TV spot you see these days is technically gorgeous, so with the talent working behind the camera nowadays, it no longer seems to be such a remarkable accomplishment to make your movie look like a painting.*

A: I think there's a bit too much emphasis on technical filmmaking, and we've all got to keep up with it because every film is competing for its place in the market. Then suddenly you get a film that doesn't rely on technical razzle-dazzle—like FOUR WEDDINGS AND A FUNERAL—and it takes the world by storm because it's not high concept. That's what I love to see. Certainly the projects that I'm developing are more along that vein.

Q: *You directed, what, somewhere around 200 hours of television before your first feature?*

A: Oh yeah. . . probably closer to 250. That's great mileage, just in terms of directing experience, working behind the camera, a great learning process. So many great American directors have come up through that school: Steven Spielberg, Sydney Pollack, Richard Donner, Sidney Lumet, John Frankenheimer. When they got in the field of feature films, their technical knowledge was like driving a car, second nature. What they concentrate on is script and story and this is why those guys keep making successful movies—because they know what makes films work.

Q: *But for the last twenty years or so, we've seen a trend toward giving every other successful screenwriter who's never shot a foot of film an opportunity to direct a feature.*

A: Well, there's a universal shortage of good scripts, and sometimes the only way a studio can get it is to offer the writer a chance to direct either that one or another But there's a danger in this because, if you've never worked on a set before, it's daunting. It's not an easy job. Just through growing up in television, I found it amazingly difficult to achieve the day. It's still challenging. So how anyone who has sat at a computer writing a script can just walk onto a set even having been through film school—and direct a movie, to me is awesome. You can have a visualization of how a movie should be, but the reality is that filmmaking is about making decisions and compromise and knowing when to say yes and knowing when to say no. That just comes through experience and miles under your belt. I think that's why so many of these inexperienced filmmakers get into trouble. . . they rely on the people around them, and the people around them don't always have the answers because they're used to servicing more experienced directors.

Q: *The Australian directors of your generation—Bruce Beresford, George Miller, Phillip Noyce, etc.—have accomplished an extraordinary degree of success in the United States. Why do you think that happened?*

A: I think we all grew up making films and television commercials and television series on very very limited budgets, and were very disciplined about the amount of film we were able to shoot and the number of set-ups we had to achieve in a day and the number of pages we had to shoot. We learned to do it economically and efficiently—we had to— and when we got a chance to direct pictures in America, we leapt at it and proved that we could do the job without too much drama.

Q: *When you were growing up in Australia and getting interested in film, what were the movies and filmmakers that inspired you?*

A: I've loved the movies all my life, but I never knew that I was going to have a career in film until quite late. Television came when I was a young boy at school in 1956, and that was the year of the Olympic games in Melbourne. This whole new world lit up before my eyes, and it seemed like what I wanted to be a part of. I wanted to be a television director, doing variety shows, outside broadcasts and stuff like that. And I achieved that fairly early in my career.

Then I started working part-time in theatre to gain more knowledge of working with actors, and I decided that film was the way to go. But as a kid growing up, there were Saturday matinees at the Rose Bay Winter Garden, a suburban theatre in Sydney, always a great serial with a cliffhanger ending to start things off, then a "B" picture and an "A" picture. I had fairly eclectic tastes, I guess. But the first film that really had an enormous impact on me was LAWRENCE OF ARABIA. I was about 18 years old when I saw it, and absolutely bowled over. It was just so far ahead of anything I'd ever seen before. And to this day David Lean is the filmmaker I most admire. He made such an extraordinary range of films.

Q: *You've made several films in that epic mode, including* THE LIGHTHORSEMEN, *your* YOUNG INDIANA JONES *episodes and* LONESOME DOVE *which really brought you great attention in the States.*

A: I knew I was the perfect person for LONESOME DOVE, but I had to prove that. I had just finished THE LIGHTHORSEMEN as a feature, and they needed somebody who could handle a high-powered cast, big landscapes and story on a TV schedule. It was like a perfect marriage for me, because I was doing a genre that I loved, and I think I do have a good eye for landscapes. Although I grew up in the city I spent half my life in the Australian bush on horseback.

Q: *You still maintain a ranch in the Australian countryside, which reminds me of some of the great American western filmmakers, who were cowboys themselves.*

A: When John Ford went out to make a western, he would camp out there on location. That's the sort of filmmaking that I love. One of the happiest working experiences of my life was on the YOUNG INDIANA JONES series, when we lived under canvas for seven weeks in Kenya. It was very remote, five hours from the closest major town. It was just wonderful to be there making a movie in the most exotic location, and to eat, breathe and sleep nothing else but making a movie in a great place. You can't help but be influenced by everything that's going on around you.

Q: *Your historical films tend to be both very realistic and romantic at the same time.*

A: LONESOME DOVE was a good deal dustier and sweatier than the others. I'm a stickler for detail, but only to the point where it doesn't interfere with the drama. If a hat's too big for an actor and it looks like it's wearing him, then I would rather go with a smaller hat that's not necessarily historically correct.

Q: *Let's talk about* FREE WILLY *for a bit. It was a bonafide sleeper smash that sort of came out of nowhere. But did you know during production what kind of potential it had?*

A: During production, everyone at Warners tended to think of FREE WILLY as the "little" kid and whale movie, and because it was being produced by the Donners and ran very smoothly, they tended to leave us alone. It wasn't until my first cut preview that the studio realized what we had—we scored higher than any previous Warner Bros. movie, including BATMAN and the LETHAL WEAPON films. From the second day of the shoot, Nick Brown, the film's editor, kept nagging me that we really had something special, this kid and this whale. His enthusiasm was boundless. And as I started looking at the cut material early on, I realized that it was indeed very special. I did have confidence, but I never quite thought that it would be as successful as it turned out to be. The first time I saw the rough cut, which was 154 minutes long, we were all absolutely flabbergasted. I looked across at Nick and Basil Poledouris, the film's composer, and we all had tears running down our cheeks. It's always exciting when that happens because the first cut is usually so depressing. It's often the worst moment in a director's life when he sits down to look at the first cut and can only see the problems.

Q: *How would you characterize your work with actors? Do you like to give them a lot of room?*

A: I see myself as a conductor, if you will. Usually, a week or two before we start shooting, I just like to sit in a room and talk—first individually and then as a group—so that we're all of a like mind about characterization and the tone of the movie. Then I like to give the actors a lot of freedom in terms of both movement and blocking, so that it's very loose. We sort of workshop the blocking, and obviously with action it has to be more specific, but I'm always open to suggestions. But actors ultimately understand character even more than the director. And as long as they're not running off the rails, I think it's nice to give them as much freedom and flexibility as possible within the overall framework that you have to set for them.

Q: *You're not exactly Hitchcockian in that approach.*

A: To me, the director is the audience. And if the actor's doing something that you think the audience isn't going to respond to, then I tend to suggest something here and there. But I tend to arrive at everything through quite a lot of rehearsal, particularly on the set before you shoot the scene. You can rehearse before you start, but it's never the same until people arrive in costume on the set.

Q: *Technically, you seem to favor the anamorphic format, which seems to suit not only the subject matter of your films, but your compositional eye as well.*

A: I do like shooting anamorphic. It's great for actors because they've got a lot more freedom within the frame. You can have five actors in a very tight shot in an anamorphic frame, and when you're doing something for television, they're all sort of standing on each other's toes.

Q: *Are there any films you would make differently if you shot them today. . . and are there some films you wish you hadn't made at all?*

A: Oh no. . . they're all part of your life and you love them for one reason or another I suppose the film that I have the most regrets about is HARLEY DAVIDSON AND THE MARLBORO MAN, yet it keeps popping up as one of those movies that people enjoy as a guilty pleasure.

Q: *By the time this interview appears, you will already have finished shooting a Vietnam-set film—OPERATION DUMBO DROP—in the wilds of Northern Thailand. What attracted you to the project?*

A: First and foremost, it's just a wonderful story about a group of men who keep a promise. It's about two men in particular—one who wants to leave a positive mark behind before he leaves the country—and the other guy who is sent in to replace him. This group doesn't necessarily start out by sharing the same philosophy, but by the end they're all united in their cause, and put their lives on the line to do it. OPERATION DUMBO DROP is a really joyous movie, and if I do it right, it will be a great adventure, fun and very emotional.

Q: *It sort of sounds like the perfect Simon Wincer movie.*

A: Yeah, because there's an elephant in it, right? Well, okay. Action, humor, an exotic location. . . and a large mammal.

F I L M O G R A P H Y

S I M O N   W I N C E R

b. Sydney, Australia

TANDARRA (MS), 1976, Australian

THE SULLIVANS (MS)   co-director with David Stevens, 1976, Australian

AGAINST THE WIND (MS)   co-director with George Miller, Pegasus Productions, 1978, Australian

THE DAY AFTER HALLOWEEN *SNAPSHOT*   Group 1, 1979, Australian

HARLEQUIN   New Image, 1980, Australian

PHAR LAP   20th Century-Fox, 1983, Australian

D.A.R.Y.L.   Paramount, 1985

THE GIRL WHO SPELLED FREEDOM (TF)   Knopf-Simons Productions/ITC Productions/Walt Disney Productions, 1986

THE LAST FRONTIER (TF)   McElroy & McElroy Productions, 1986, Australian

THE LIGHTHORSEMEN   Cinecom, 1987, Australian

BLUEGRASS (TF)   The Landsburg Company, 1988

LONESOME DOVE (MS) ☆☆ Motown Productions/Pangaea/Qintex Entertainment Inc., 1989

QUIGLEY DOWN UNDER   MGM/Pathe Communications, 1990, U.S.-Australian

HARLEY DAVIDSON AND THE MARLBORO MAN   MGM-Pathe Communications, 1991

THE YOUNG INDIANA JONES CHRONICLES: CONGO, 1917 (TF)   Lucasfilm Ltd./Paramount TV, 1992

THE YOUNG INDIANA JONES CHRONICLES: SOMME, 1916 (TF)   Lucasfilm Ltd./Paramount TV, 1992

FREE WILLY   Warner Bros., 1993

LIGHTNING JACK   Savoy Pictures, 1994, Australian-U.S.

OPERATION DUMBO DROP   Buena Vista, 1995

THE PHANTOM   Paramount, 1996

FLASH (TF)   Walt Disney TV, 1997

ESCAPE: HUMAN CARGO (CTF)   Neufeld-Rehme Productions/Showtime

THE ECHO OF THUNDER (TF)   Hallmark Hall of Fame Productions, 1998, U.S.-Australian

$\mathcal{R}$OBERT $\mathcal{W}$ISE

It was tremendously gratifying when Robert Wise was honored with the American Film Institute's Lifetime Achievement Award in early 1998, for it was official acknowledgement of this legendarily quiet and low-keyed director's enormous contribution to cinema. When I spoke with the unfailingly polite and astute Wise in his Beverly Hills office, he had just suffered the disappointment of having French-based financing drop out of a project entitled AND MILES TO GO, a World War II drama which he hoped to film in Poland for a miniscule $11.5 million. It was a sad commentary on the industry in general that the man responsible for some of the biggest hits in the history of the medium couldn't mount a film for the equivalent of some movies' special effects budgets. It's indicative not only of an endemic amnesia that affects most contemporary studio executives, but also of a rampant ageism that denies our living national treasures access to their art.

Since his first directorial effort—Val Lewton's chilling 1944 production of THE CURSE OF THE CAT PEOPLE—the name "Robert Wise" has been synonymous with films that entertain and enlighten, of all genres and sizes. It's been a courageous career, filled not with one landmark, but several. The Indiana native made his way to Hollywood in 1933, winding up in RKO's editing department, working his way up to cutter on such notable films as THE HUNCHBACK OF NOTRE DAME (1939) and projects of no less import than Orson Welles' CITIZEN KANE and THE MAGNIFICENT AMBERSONS. Given his first shot at directing by Lewton, Hollywood's resident master of atmospheric terror, Wise proceeded to learn his art by directing eight more features for RKO during the '40s. These included another well-received Lewton production, THE BODY SNATCHER, the *noir* western BLOOD ON THE MOON; and the gritty and powerful THE SET-UP, considered by many to be the best boxing movie ever made until, and possibly since, RAGING BULL. Early on, Wise established a strong streak of humanism in his work that informed every genre he attempted-which was virtually every genre invented for the cinema.

Throughout the 1950s, Wise worked for several major studios on war films (THE DESERT RATS; DESTINATION GOBI; RUN SILENT, RUN DEEP), westerns (TWO FLAGS WEST; TRIBUTE TO A BAD MAN), melodramas (THREE SECRETS;

THE HOUSE ON TELEGRAPH HILL; THE CAPTIVE CITY; EXECUTIVE SUITE; UNTIL THEY SAIL), science fiction (the undisputed classic THE DAY THE EARTH STOOD STILL, which helped the maligned genre to gain respectability), costume spectacle (HELEN OF TROY), boxing biopic (SOMEBODY UP THERE LIKES ME), romantic comedy (SOMETHING FOR THE BIRDS; THIS COULD BE THE NIGHT), suspense (ODDS AGAINST TOMORROW) and topical drama (I WANT TO LIVE!), which brought Wise his first Oscar nomination.

But it was really WEST SIDE STORY that lifted Wise to true superstardom at the dawn of the '60s, a rich decade for the filmmaker which was to see him at the helm of several remarkable films, both large and small. Following the gigantic success of WEST SIDE STORY—for which Wise won Oscars as Best Director and as the Best Picture producer—with the more intimate TWO FOR THE SEESAW and THE HAUNTING, Wise then filmed THE SOUND OF MUSIC, won his third and fourth Academy Awards for directing and Best Picture producer, and created a timeless family classic.

For those who feared that Wise had shucked off the more serious examinations of the human condition for which he was known, THE SAND PEBBLES (1966) was a return to form, albeit on a massive scale. One of the bravest American films of its time, Wise dared to utilize three hours of a big studio, roadshow picture to tell a relentlessly downbeat story of Jake Holman (Steve McQueen in his best performance), a doomed sailor who becomes an existential victim of foolhardy U.S. military intervention in 1920s China. For contemporary audiences, the parallels to a more recent and equally foolhardy U.S. military adventure in Asia were unmistakable. The film, now available on laserdisc in an uncut, letterboxed format, continues to gain in reputation.

Wise's next film, also on a grand scale, was 1968's STAR!, toplining Julie Andrews as British musical star Gertrude Lawrence. A failure in its day, the film's stature has also been revived due to its recently restored video and laserdisc release. Wise's work since then has included the compelling science "fact" thriller THE ANDROMEDA STRAIN (1971)—still one of the best adaptations of Michael Crichton on film—and the first STAR TREK feature, a huge success in 1979.

Hopefully, Wise's AFI award and tribute will lead to more work behind the camera for this great filmmaker. He certainly expressed no intentions of hanging up his spikes and retiring his number, and Wise has, after all, only directed 39 features. . .

MICHAEL SINGER: *I read a couple of weeks ago that you've been in some stage of preparation for another film. Is this a project you want to talk about at this point?*

ROBERT WISE: Yes, I can talk about it. Like so many of us, we have projects that sometimes take a long time to get off the ground. I've had an option on a book called AND MILES TO GO, which was first published in 1963 or '64, and then republished in the early '80s. I've had an option for about five years, and last fall, I got a French company interested in financing the picture. They read the treatment and liked the idea. I first met with them in Paris in October '93, after I'd been encamped in Belgium at a film festival. Two months later, I flew back to Paris with a screenwriter, Carmen Culver. The story is centered around a very famous Polish Arabian stallion that was born in a stud farm outside of Warsaw just before the start of World War II, and tells his whole story during the entire war. It's a true story about a real horse and the interesting people involved with him.

Anyway, we had a very good meeting and went on to Warsaw for research. The writer went about her work, writing a first and then second draft script, and I returned to Poland and selected a cinematographer, production designer, costume designer, assistant director. I met with actors in Poland who could work in English, also did some casting here in Los Angeles. Everything was going fine until the latter part of April '94, when we turned in the budget. And then everything stopped. It was about $3 million more than they anticipated, although interestingly enough, all along the line, nobody from the French company had ever asked me how much I thought the film was going to cost. I didn't get myself too concerned about the budget, because they didn't seem to be concerned. So now everything's on hold, and it looks like they're not going to go ahead with it, so we're trying to set up the project someplace else.

Q: *It seems that in this day and age, $3 million sounds like a diminutive amount of money to prevent a film from being made.*

A: Yes, this was not a big budget, only $11 million and a half or so. But they're used to $7 or 8 million, I guess. Anyway, we have reasonable hope and it's already in the hands of a German producer who's expressed a lot of interest in the project. And my associate in Paris says that two or three other sources in France may be interested, so it's very possible that we'll get it in turnaround and get it set up someplace else. But in the meantime, we've obviously had to postpone the start. I was planning on. . . I should be in Poland right now. We'd be just a week ahead of shooting, actually. We were supposed to start on the 16th of August.

Q: *This must be a great frustration to you.*

A: It is.

Q: *It's rather amazing to consider the difficulties you've had in mounting this project with your incredible background, but these days, the American industry seems to think that film history began with JAWS. Have you been frustrated by this as well?*

A: Well, I suppose I've been frustrated by that to a certain extent, because I haven't been doing any films in recent years. And that would seem to be an indication that the studio executives now—so many of them younger people—really don't know my track record. A lot of them think I've been in the business too long now, and there can't be much juice left. And so, yes, I've been pretty conscious of that, you bet—and a victim of it, in some sense.

Q: *Ageism has become a big problem in Hollywood.*

A: Sure. It's all over town, and not just with directors. It's with writers, who have an awful time. I understand that it got so bad with writers, that there seemed to be some kind of onus against any writer over 35 years old, and they set up a special committee at the Writers Guild to look into this whole thing. What they've been able to do about it, I don't know.

Q: It certainly infuriates me, because for me, your films were seminal experiences that started to teach me what a film director really was, and what they do.

A: Well, I'm glad that my films brought something to you—made you start thinking about films, how they get made, what goes into getting them up on screen. You know, most people don't realize all the planning, the work, the preparation, above and beyond the script, that goes into making a film, and that's absolutely as it should be. . . it should look like it's just happening up there on screen. People shouldn't be thinking about how it got there, how you were able to manage it. It should all be seamless and together, and all the work and sweat and strain and effort that we put into making it should never show. Hopefully, this moving image up there that captures you, gets you involved. . . that's all it should be.

Q: Your work has never had a showboating quality to it, with technique dominating substance. To some degree, we never really emerged from the period when auteurist critics like Andrew Sands were dumping great craftsmen like yourself, Lewis Milestone and William Wyler into negative categories. Do you have an opinion on this?

A: Well, I do have an opinion, and I feel very strongly that those of us who were not necessarily "auteurs" were rather badly treated. And I don't think this was a reflection of the general movie-going public. So, it seems to me that some of those critics were a bit out of step with the vast viewing public who seemed to relate more to the kind of work that we were doing.

Q: When I was young and fell in love with movies, the name "Robert Wise" was more a symbol than something flesh-and-blood. It was an emblem for movies that were larger than life, yet entirely human. And all I knew was that I was going to have one hell of a great time at the movies . . . and learn something to boot.

A: What you've just said that's important to me is "learn something to boot." Because I've been asked many times what the steps are to my taking on a given project, and I have to start off by saying that whether it will be based on an original screenplay book, play or short story.., how does it grab me as a reader? Does it catch me up? Because I'm the audience as I read it, and it has to be something that involves me with story and plot. That's primary, the initial reaction that gets me involved.

Next, as I think about it, what does it have to say about man and his world? But it must be said in terms of story, plot and character. It must not be said by getting on the soapbox. The message should flow from the story, the characters and the plot. My one prime exception to that, of course, was THE DAY THE EARTH STOOD STILL, in which the conclusion was the message.

The next step, of course, is whether the story is cinematic. Is it a story that can be put on the screen? And the last step is that I have to start thinking about what the cost would be, because that's the first thing that's going to be asked by the front office.

Q: One of your strongest films, I think, was THE SAND PEBBLES, which packed a very powerful message within its narrative. It was an expensive roadshow picture which nonetheless was essentially a downbeat story about American military intervention in Asia, and you actually made it during. . .

A: The Vietnam War. I had always been fascinated by Mainland China, which was the setting of Richard McKenna's book. I had never been there, and couldn't go there even when I did the film. At that time, we weren't even allowed to visit China. I had to do all my research on the story from newsreels, books, pictures and stories. But when I first read the book, I thought to myself that it seemed time for the American public to be reminded that the phrase, "Yankee, Go Home!" didn't start just in World War II. It had been happening throughout the 20th Century when we were showing off our military might here and there. And in the case of THE SAND PEBBLES, other countries besides the United States had gunboats patrolling the Yangtze.

At the time I got the project underway, Vietnam was still on the back burner, and my then wife and I decided to take some time off after shooting THE HAUNT-ING in London and take a three-month trip around the world. This was 1963. We went to Saigon—because I knew I was going to do THE SAND PEBBLES and wanted to see if there were any possible locations there. And I'll never forget that when we landed in Saigon, there was just row after row of American Air Force planes at the airport. Saigon was filled with American soldiers, what we then called "advisers"—about 10,000 of them—and we could see the foreshadow of what was to come. By the time THE SAND PEBBLES got made and was released, the war in Vietnam was in full swing and people thought that Vietnam was what we had in mind for the film all along. It wasn't, but it turned out to be quite prophetic in terms of what was happening once again in Asia.

Q: *I understand that the shoot was quite a logistical nightmare in Taiwan and Hong Kong.*

A: The places we could shoot were so limited. Even getting the okay to shoot in Taiwan took a long time. We had all kinds of terrible weather problems, winds that would switch all the time. Every day we would have five or six different call sheets, depending on the weather, wind direction and river currents. And several times during the shoot, the weather would change so fast that I'd have to get all my extras—perhaps a thousand of them—changed from summer to winter clothes because we had to change sequences. It was in every way the most difficult film I've done so far. It was a monster fighting us every minute, and all of us who were on it all the way through thought that it didn't matter if it was successful in the-atres or with audiences. . . it was just a real triumph to get it done and up on the screen.

As a matter of fact, when Francis Coppola was over in the Philippines shoot-ing APOCALYPSE NOW, I guess he heard about some of the problems we had on THE SAND PEBBLES, because his office called and asked if we could possibly get a 16mm print over to him in the jungle so he could show it to the crew. I guess he said "Hey guys, let's hang in there and get it done. . . they did.

Q: *You mentioned THE HAUNTING just before. To me, it's still the most innovative and frightening horror movie ever made. But I've recently read that someone plans to remake it, which I find even more frightening.*

A: Me too. I've had so many people tell me over the years that THE HAUNTING was the scariest picture they'd ever seen, because it didn't really show anything, and they want to know how I did it. Well, it all comes from Val Lewton and the power of suggestion. The greatest fear that people have is fear of the unknown.

Q: *Of course, you directed your first two pictures for Val Lewton at RKO in the early 1940s. What about WEST SIDE STORY? That changed film musicals forever.*

A: WEST SIDE STORY was a challenge, of course. It was extraordinary on stage. I don't know of any stage musical that told so much of its story through dance. Not just song, but dance. Jerry Robbins' choreography was revolutionary on the stage, and we had to figure out how to adapt it for the screen, and even improve on it if possible. The two mediums are different. . . that's the challenge. With the stage, you have the proscenium arch, so you're not quite into reality. You're removed from reality so actors can go out of dialogue into song, or out of dialogue into dance without the audience feeling a little tinge of embarrassment. The screen is a very real medium, and it doesn't take kindly to stylizations unless it's an utter fantasy like THE WIZARD OF OZ.

The challenges that Robbins and myself and our associates had was how to take all the stylized aspects of WEST SIDE STORY and put them against the most authentic backgrounds. I was the one who insisted that we had to go to New York for all the daytime scenes. We had to shoot them on real city streets. The studio wanted me to see if we could find something in Los Angeles, but I said "No way." Once we're through the daytime scenes, the rest of it's all sunset and night, where we could do effect lighting on stages, that's alright. And I remember Jerry Robbins saying to me, "Bob, I agree with you about going to New York, but boy, you've given me the biggest challenge in the world. . . to take my most stylized dancing, which is in the prologue, and put against real backgrounds. We knew we had to deliver New York to start with, and I didn't want to do that same opening shot across the river with the bridge and the skyline. So I started thinking, and wondered what New York would look like from straight down! And that ended up as the very opening of the film, with a real New York that even New Yorkers hadn't seen, a bit abstract. That was the genesis of that opening in WEST SIDE STORY.

Q: *And thereby, you pretty much invented* MTV.

A: [laughs] I suppose so. Forgive me.

Q: *But immediately after* WEST SIDE STORY, *which was a giant roadshow film that was a huge hit and won 10 Academy Awards, you made two intimate pictures,* TWO FOR THE SEESAW *and* THE HAUNTING, *rather than another epic. Why?*

A: Well, I did WEST SIDE STORY, so I thought, fine, I've done my musical. So I went on about my business making other films. TWO FOR THE SEESAW came to me prepackaged in a sense by The Mirisch Company. They had already signed Bob Mitchum and Shirley MacLaine, and then I liked the script by Isobel Lennart, whom I'd worked with before.

I had my hands on THE HAUNTING for quite awhile. That's one I actually was very instrumental in getting. So many of my films have come to me from producers and studios, sometimes with a first draft script already done. But this one I found. I was at Goldwyn Studios doing post-production work on WEST SIDE STORY and I read a review of Shirley Jackson's novel The Haunting of Hill House in Time Magazine. I looked it up and found out that it hadn't been picked up by any of the majors, so I read it, loved it, and thought that there was a hell of a picture in it. In a way, making THE HAUNTING was kind of a tribute to Lewton. Finally, we took it to MGM. But they only wanted to put $1 million into the film, and the best budget I could get out of Culver City was one million and four, and they didn't want to go ahead. But I was going over to London about that time for a command performance of WEST SIDE STORY, and someone said, "Hey, you know, MGM has a nice little studio over in England at Borehamwood. . . maybe they'd be able to get you a better price on this. So I gave the script to them in London, and they came back with a budget of one million and fifty thousand, and the studio went for it. That's how I happened to make THE HAUNTING in England, even though it has a New England backdrop.

Personally, THE HAUNTING is one of my favorites. I've done 39 pictures and I have about a dozen favorites, but THE HAUNTING is always one of them. I think it's one of my very best directorial jobs. I'm very proud of what I got up on the screen.

Q: *You did several historical films, but really only one costume epic—HELEN OF TROY.*

A: Yeah, that was my first and last venture into spectacle. People have asked me many times what my favorite genre is. I don't have a favorite, but I have two unfavorites: westerns and spectacles. I haven't made a western since the mid-'50s, because they were being done to death as both movies and TV series. And I found out that the spectacle wasn't a genre that I enjoyed when I shot HELEN OF TROY all over Italy.

Q: *But a lot of people did enjoy HELEN OF TROY. I understand that the film had a big impact on Oliver Stone when he saw it as a youngster.*

A: [laughs] Yes. He once approached me at a Directors Guild function and told me that. I was quite flattered.

Q: *I've also heard that the film is, unfortunately, in a deteriorated condition and in dire need of restoration.*

A: That's true. And even though I didn't exactly enjoy making it, I would be very pleased if HELEN OF TROY could be restored.., but such an expensive task needs some sponsorship.

Q: *Let's talk a little about your background, if we may. You began working at RKO in 1933 as a messenger?*

A: A film carrier, really. I was carrying prints of films to the projection rooms for executive screenings, checking prints, patching leader and stuff like that.

Q: *Had you been attracted to editing, or was it something you just fell into?*

A: No. I dropped out of college after one year at Franklin College near Indianapolis. It was the height of the Depression. I couldn't go back the second year. I had an older brother who was working at RKO, in the accounting department, and my family told me to go Los Angeles to join my brother, get a job and earn a decent living. It was just that basic. . . I had to work. Had I been able to go on in college, I wanted to be a journalist.

So in July of '33, my brother David got me an appointment with Tommy Little, head of the property department. And fortunately for me, he didn't need anybody right then. So another week went by and he got me an appointment with Jimmy Wilkinson, head of the film editing department, and he said he could use another kid eager, a strong back and willing to work hard—in the shipping room. So that was my break. Then I had to work my way up through all the aspects of editing and finally into directing.

Q: You put in more than a few 24 hour days, I understand.

A: Yeah, a lot. Particularly in sound effects editing.

Q: I can't let this conversation go by without asking you at least one question about CITIZEN KANE, although by now it's probably the most chronicled film in history.

A: I would imagine so.

Q: But when you were editing the film, you had to be aware of just how extraordinary it was.

A: I've been asked many times if those of us working on KANE realized at the time that we were making something that would be thought of 50 years later as perhaps the greatest picture ever made, and I have to say no, none of us did. I don't even think that Orson—who had a pretty good size ego—felt that. But you couldn't look at those dailies coming in every day and not realize you were getting something quite extraordinary. It was just thrilling. We couldn't wait to see the dailies every day. They were so different, so unusual, so strong, so dynamic. Full of marvelous performances, from people we didn't know, because in fact none of those actors had been on the screen except in bit parts. The camerawork, the setups, the angles, the dynamics. . . we knew it was extraordinary, but we didn't anticipate the fame down through the years.

Q: You've worked with a lot of good cinematographers. Did you have a personal favorite to collaborate with?

A: No. Many directors like to work with the same DP, but I never felt that strongly. I don't think there's any DP that I worked with on more than two films. Bob Surtees did two of mine, and Dick Kline did two, I think. I like to cast my cinematographer for the given project and the cinematic style that I feel is right for it. And although they're all very professionally capable, some are stronger for one kind of film than the other. For instance, Curly (Lionel) Linden did I WANT TO LIVE for me. I wanted a very documentary realistic, grainy look in black and white, and I didn't know Curly, but I'd seen some of his work at Paramount. But I would never have used Curly for THE SOUND OF MUSIC because that was not his forte. I wanted somebody to give it a softer, more romantic look, and that was Ted McCord.

Q: Your visual style always adjusted to the material.

A: Yes.

Q: Rather than the other way around.

A: I guess that's why esoteric critics have accused me of not having a style. But I've done so many genres, and I've tried to address each project in the cinematic terms that I think are appropriate to each.

Q: Rather than ask another question, I wonder if you have anything to say to the American film industry at this point in time?

A: Well, the only thing I would say is that I think this industry should—if it can keep the box office coming in—try and do fewer action pieces with gratuitous violence. I would hope that we would tend to have fewer and fewer of those and

more adult, mature, dramatic stories that don't rely on effects, but instead rely on human interaction. That would be my hope.

Q: *I'd like to point out, though, that you've never shied away from violence on-screen. I think in particular of* THE SET-UP *and* THE SAND PEBBLES. *However, your intent was to show the impact of such violence on the human body and spirit.*

A: Right! I think humanity has to come through strongly in all films. . . no matter what the genre is.

F I L M O G R A P H Y

R O B E R T   W I S E
b. September 10, 1914 - Winchester, Indiana
THE CURSE OF THE CAT PEOPLE   co-director with Gunther von Fritsch, RKO Radio, 1944
MADEMOISELLE FIFI   RKO Radio, 1944
THE BODY SNATCHER   RKO Radio, 1945
A GAME OF DEATH   RKO Radio, 1945
CRIMINAL COURT   RKO Radio, 1946
BORN TO KILL   RKO Radio, 1947
MYSTERY IN MEXICO   RKO Radio, 1948
BLOOD ON THE MOON   RKO Radio, 1948
THE SET-UP   RKO Radio, 1949
TWO FLAGS WEST   20th Century-Fox, 1950
THREE SECRETS   Warner Bros., 1950
THE HOUSE ON TELEGRAPH HILL   20th Century-Fox, 1951
THE DAY THE EARTH STOOD STILL   20th Century-Fox, 1951
THE CAPTIVE CITY   United Artists, 1952
SOMETHING FOR THE BIRDS   MGM, 1952
THE DESERT RATS   20th Century-Fox, 1953
DESTINATION GOBI   20th Century-Fox, 1953
SO BIG   Warner Bros., 1953
EXECUTIVE SUITE   MGM, 1954
HELEN OF TROY   Warner Bros., 1955, Italian-French
TRIBUTE TO A BAD MAN   MGM, 1956
SOMEBODY UP THERE LIKES ME   MGM, 1957
THIS COULD BE THE NIGHT   MGM, 1957
UNTIL THEY SAIL   MGM, 1957
RUN SILENT, RUN DEEP   United Artists, 1958
I WANT TO LIVE! ★   United Artists, 1958
ODDS AGAINST TOMORROW   United Artists, 1959
WEST SIDE STORY ★★   co-director with Jerome Robbins, United Artists, 1961
TWO FOR THE SEESAW   United Artists, 1962
THE HAUNTING   MGM, 1963, British-U.S.
THE SOUND OF MUSIC ★★   20th Century-Fox, 1965
THE SAND PEBBLES   20th Century-Fox, 1966
STAR! *THOSE WERE THE HAPPY TIMES*   20th Century-Fox, 1968
THE ANDROMEDA STRAIN   Universal, 1971
TWO PEOPLE   Universal, 1973
THE HINDENBURG   Universal, 1975
AUDREY ROSE   United Artists, 1977
STAR TREK - THE MOTION PICTURE   Paramount, 1979
ROOFTOPS   New Century/Vista, 1989

CHE-KIRK WONG

Every bit as brash, steam-driven and entertaining as his movies, Che-Kirk Wong is the most recent Hong Kong filmmaker to make a splash in the United States, and with the exception of John Woo, thus far the most successful. THE BIG HIT, starring Mark Wahlberg, Lou Diamond Phillips and introducing China Chow, turned out to be an apt title for the modestly-budgeted studio film that both turned a profit and won attention for a director already well known to Hong Kong movie fans for such action spectacles as CRIME STORY, ORGANIZED CRIME & TRIAD BUREAU and ROCK N' ROLL COP. A decidedly lunatic adventure comedy, THE BIG HIT was appreciated for its adherence to the principles of Hong Kong moviemaking. . . anything goes, and the wilder, the better.

What follows is Wong's own story, told in his own inimitable way over several cups of coffee in the incongruous setting of a Jewish-style deli restaurant in Los Angeles' Westwood. (On the other hand, the setting was entirely appropriate, considering Wong's entirely engaging *chutzpah*). Much of it reads like the hilariously tangled plot of a Hong Kong comedy about the odyssey of an ambitious young man who dreams of making movies, and by hook, crook and the skin of his teeth, accomplishes that goal. . . and more.

MICHAEL SINGER: *What kind of contribution do you think directors from Asia can make to American cinema?*

CHE-KIRK WONG: Just bring something different. A new kind of attitude, because we came in from a totally different background. In fact, it varies from director to director. I mean, what John Woo may have in mind is probably totally different than what I have in mind. Being from Hong Kong, our first considerations are always commercial. You've got to survive first, right? So directors tend to protect investors. They don't go over budget intentionally. And they do want to make a film that's successful, not only for themselves, but so that the investor or the producers can make money and allow the directors to continue making films. So it's basically an art of survival.

Q: So what's the draw of coming here to the United States, in addition to the economic benefits?

A: The other aspect of it, which is the art. Because of our cultural background, the way we think is different, and what we create is different. For example, a lot of people say that Hong Kong movies are "over the top." But I *see* things over-the-top, it's sort of altered reality to us. Film doesn't have to have documentary realism. I mean, most of my films are based on true stories, but the way I tell them, it's much more intense than reality. See, in Hong Kong, we don't have research screenings, we have a midnight show where the movie is watched for the first time. The people who go to these midnight shows are your average people from the street, and they go to a movie expecting to be entertained all the time, every minute. And if they see something they don't like, they'll boo and scream at you, knowing that you're the director. I mean, I've been to shows where people would be pissed off, standing up and shouting "Who the hell is the director? I want him out here," or "Who the hell wrote the script? Go get that stupid asshole!" But at the same time, if they go to a good show, they'll be cheering, clapping, it's like a riot. So once you're a director, you've got to get through this experience. You get nervous, man. You know you're gonna face that crowd, eventually. So you've got to make sure your film is good. And I mean *damn* good!

Q: A lot of people felt that THE BIG HIT was one of the purest U.S. films made by a Hong Kong director in that you didn't compromise your style at all to suit American tastes. Were you consciously trying to hold on to your style, or was it even an issue?

A: It wasn't an issue. I simply saw it the way I felt best. There was no other way to shoot it, even if I was asked by the studio.

Q: How was it working with an American cast and crew? In Hong Kong, directors often perform more functions on their own.

A: There isn't a whole lot of difference. American crews are greatly efficient. But one thing I have to say is that because we come from a film industry which is much smaller, it's almost like being in a family. Like it or not, you love each other, you hate each other, just like a family. You can call them 24 hours a day. They're there for you to do anything within reason. You can call the prop guy at three in the morning and say "I want sixty chickens at 6:00 a.m. tomorrow," and he'll say "Okay." They don't care how they do it, even if they go to a farm and steal them. I remember one time I walking down the street with my propmaster and said "Hey, you know, we have that scene this weekend where we're looking out the window, and wouldn't it be great if we had a lamppost by the window?" And the lamppost would show up on the set. They stole it from the city!

Q: But here, you're dealing with unions, SAG observers, all kinds of stuff you wouldn't think of in Hong Kong.

A: Which I also like, because it's very organized. And crews here work very hard for you. You just have to tell them in advance. You can't just conjure something up and have it on the set in an hour. Things take more time, you have to go through physical production people, and they have to be approved. You have to go through the system. But ultimately, the crews will do whatever they can for you. They're good people.

Q: When did you decide to come to the States?

A: It's kind of hard to figure out when the decision was made, but many years ago I was working for Cinema City in Hong Kong, which was extremely successful at the time. This was in the mid 1980s, when they were king. I told them that they ought to expand to both Japan and China, because the cultures were similar, and at the same time try to set some link with Hollywood because there's a huge amount of money to be made there. They were sort of half-convinced, and sent me to Hollywood. I met with some agents, who probably thought, "Oh, this guy's from Hong Kong, he doesn't know shit." So they sent me some seemingly popular actors, who were all on drugs or alcoholic or not working.

Q: They were really setting you up, weren't they?

A: So that didn't work out. But I always felt that there were strong similarities between Hong Kong and American movies, because Hong Kong re-invented American movies in the first place.

Q: And now you and other Hong Kong directors are coming here to re-invent American action movies.

A: It's so funny, because I remember telling Terence Chang—John Woo's partner—that the only reason John could make all of these over-the-top action films is because he has no fricking idea about how to handle guns. But Americans are cowboys, they know how to handle a Colt .45. Americans aren't going to buy John's stuff, they'll think it's ridiculous. But to my surprise, they love him here.

Q: Well, a lot of Americans thought that Woo's films were influenced by Peckinpah, who they were already familiar with.

A: Who isn't influenced by Peckinpah?

Q: You didn't set out to be a film director in the first place, did you?

A: No, I never thought I could. As a kid, drawing comic books was my first passion. But my father told me, "Hey, you're not going to make any money trying to be an artist. You should get a good job." But I always liked to draw. On open day at school, when the parents would visit, hundreds of my drawings would be all over the place. I never thought about becoming a director. I always thought that I'd be a painter. So I decided to study fashion and set design in the U.K. I sort of taught myself set design in Hong Kong with jobs like window dressing. I'd just walk into a shop and say, "Hey, you know, your shop windows look shitty. Why don't you let me do something about it?" And they loved it. I got to work on some of the really chic, trendy boutiques and shops in Hong Kong. And every two weeks, you've got to come up with an idea and change the window. You had to stay on top of the trends. I think that might have been some kind of training ground to become a director, because when you direct, you observe, always looking out for an interesting slice of life.

I was working for a boutique which was selling these T-shirts, and I said, "Hey, you know, these aren't interesting T-shirts. I can make better T-shirts than these." So I set up in their shop making T-shirts, and they were so successful that I moved on to making dresses, jeans and shirts. I had no formal training. I just got a book and learned how to make a pattern. I can make a pair of jeans in five minutes. I made thousands, thousands. Then somehow, I thought that I should go abroad and widen my horizons. So I decided to just pack up everything and go to school in the U.S.

Q: *I like the irony of the fact that with all the macho action films that you've made, you started in fashion design.*

A: I can sew. Can you imagine?

Q: *So how did it go from there to film?*

A: I did my set design in England, but didn't think I was very good, comparing my work to the other students. I wasn't top in my class. And I didn't think they'd hire a guy from Hong Kong to design A MIDSUMMER NIGHT'S DREAM. So I did a little course in film and television at the same school, and started making student films. I just shot and shot and shot. Back home in Hong Kong, I went for job interviews at a TV studio as set designer, and they said "Okay, show us your films." After they saw them, they said "No, we don't think we can give you a job as a set designer. But we want you to direct."

Q: *Which is the opposite of every else's story.*

A: I told them that I knew I could direct, but I wanted to go through the whole process. I wanted to be a designer, a continuity person, a propman, a lighting man. And they said, "No, we're short on directors right now. You've got to direct."

Q: *You should have made a T-shirt saying "But what I really don't want to do is direct." So you became a television director. How long did you stay in that arena before moving on to features?*

A: A little bit more than a year. They didn't like me. I had a nightmare the other night that I was still shooting with three cameras. I hated that. I kept asking things like, "Can you have another camera up on the ceiling?" I just kept coming up with ways to try and make it more interesting, like shooting on location instead of inside the studio. So after a while, they said "Hey, this guy is always shooting on location. We're wasting a lot of money and time. The crew is into a lot of overtime, the actors are tired." I think they were about to fire me, but instead demoted me to another department. I didn't shoot dramas anymore, but documentaries instead. It was a show called BANG BANG, sponsored by a very successful brand of jeans. They buy a half-hour slot, and you can pretty much shoot whatever you like. There were no rules.

Anyway, the financier of BANG BANG decided to make films, and he had a movie set up called THE CLUB. Then one Saturday night, he went to a disco, and ran into the director who was supposed to direct the film, and found him drunk and bahaving badly. THE CLUB was supposed to shoot in a week, but the financier fired the director. . .

Q: *And hired you?*

A: Yes. But when I read the script, it was terrible, the worst you've ever seen. Nothing made sense, everything was a cliche, and there was no story. But we had to shoot in a week. So I did something drastic. I told the producer, "Okay, I need the best hotel in town, facing the swimming pool. And I need a couple of writers to be with me 24 hours a day, from this moment on, and we'll stay in the hotel room and not go out. . . except to the swimming pool, of course." So we worked around the clock before we started shooting, but never finished the script. We were always re-writing during shooting.

Q: *How was the experience of shooting your first feature?*

A: Well, THE CLUB is about a gangster who runs a club, and our line producer really was a gangster. And you know, when you work in Hong Kong, you live and die with your crew. And in that case I literally lived and died with my crew, because they were all gangsters. It was like living the movie. All of the people in the film were real, and that's why it's so interesting to watch.

Q: *It was as if Coppola made THE GODFATHER with real gangsters. How did THE CLUB do at the box office?*

A: Pretty good. And after that every studio and independent producer wanted me to work for them.

Q: *Did you continue with this kind of dangerous realism, or did you back off from reality a bit after THE CLUB?*

A: Well, it kind of evolved, I suppose.

Q: *What's your personal favorite of the films you've made?*

A: Actually, I never look back. I don't have a favorite. When I finish a film, and after it's released, I never look at it again.

Q: *Were you happy with your collaboration with Jackie Chan on POLICE STORY?*

A: Well, yes and no. We were great friends, but it got ugly later on, because of the studio system, and his entourage. People became jealous of how close we became. When you have a star and a director working that closely, nobody else has any control.

Q: *That's too bad, because I think it was one of Chan's best films.*
A: I agree.

Q: *In a recent article in Asiaweek, Chan was expressing a little disappointment at working in the American system.*

A: That's total bullshit. I think the American system is very sophisticated, and allows you to do a lot of things. I'll tell you the difference between the Hollywood system and the Hong Kong system. In Hollywood, making movies is like riding in a stretch limo. They're very expensive, very comfortable, very classy, but you have to tell the chauffeur where you want to go. While you're driving around in that limo, and see a donut stand, you tell the driver to stop because you want to buy a donut.

The chauffeur would say, "Sir, we should call my boss first, because I have to deliver you on time at twelve o'clock. If I don't have you there by twelve, you're going to get into trouble, I'm going to get into trouble, and both of us are going to get fired." So I would say, "Make that phone call. I'm going to spend five minutes in that donut shop, but I know a short cut we can take afterwards, so we'll still be on time."

So if you're going to stop by that donut shop, you better have a game plan. You don't just fucking go off and buy a donut and be late for that date. Making a movie in Hong Kong is like driving in an old, beat-up Honda. You hardly have any gas, not even enough to get where you're going. There's no air conditioning, no radio, no tape player. The car may break down, but you can repair it if you have to. In fact, you can do anything you want. You can stop and buy a donut. And if you're half-an-hour late, what's the big deal?

But once you're used to riding in that stretch limo, can you go back to your little Honda? I don't know, man. You have two or three cell phones in that limo, and you can call anybody in the world from that car. And you can stretch your legs. Right now, I want a fleet of limos. Maybe one in front. . . and another one behind [laughs].

F I L M O G R A P H Y

C H E - K I R K   W O N G
(Wong Che-Keung)
b. 1949 - Hong Kong
THE CLUB   1981, Hong Kong
HEALTH WARNING   1983, Hong Kong
LIFELINE EXPRESS   1984, Hong Kong
TRUE COLOURS   1986, Hong Kong
GUNMEN   1989, Hong Kong
TAKING MANHATTAN   1991, Hong Kong
CRIME STORY   1993, Hong Kong
ORGANIZED CRIME & TRIAD BUREAU   Sky Point Film Investment, 1994, Hong Kong
ROCK N' ROLL COP   Sky Point Film Investment, 1994, Hong Kong
HOTLINE - THE ICAC FILES   Sky Point Film Investment, 1995, Hong Kong
THE BIG HIT TriStar, 1998

JOHN WOO

The filmmaker at the crest of the cinematic tidal wave crashing upon American shores from points east in the last few years is John Woo, the undisputed godfather of Hong Kong cinema and now one of Hollywood's most sought-after directors. With an incredible flair for highly stylized action and dramatics, Woo's full power has finally been seen to its best advantage in his third American film (following HARD TARGET and BROKEN ARROW), FACE/OFF, which featured two stunning leading performances by Nicolas Cage and John Travolta.

Woo's best films—which often seem as influenced by such archetypal American directors as Peckinpah and Hawks as they are by Chinese traditions and mores—have explored moral duality, honor among thieves, retribution and redemption, set against backdrops of beauty and violence. His more noticeable Hong Kong efforts—A BETTER TOMORROW (parts one and two), THE KILLER, BULLET IN THE HEAD, ONCE A THIEF and HARD-BOILED—influenced not only other filmmakers there, but in the U.S. as well, impressed by the sheer power of Woo's poeticized, choreographed imagery. Woo's first two U.S. entries were just warm-ups for FACE/OFF, which was hugely successful both critically and at the box office. Woo also continues to work in television on occasion, directing the pilots in Canada for both JOHN WOO'S ONCE A THIEF (a remake of his earlier feature) and BLACKJACK.

But even more extraordinary than John Woo's movies is his life story, which combines Dickens, Alger and ANGELS WITH DIRTY FACES, roiling them together and re-setting them on a Hong Kong backdrop. Transcending almost unbelievable odds, with a poverty-stricken childhood and zero prospects, Woo has either achieved every goal he pitched for himself, or fully intends to. With partner Terence Chang, Woo has helped open the floodgates not only for other talented Hong Kong filmmakers eager to work in a freer market, but homegrown directors as well. Together, they've become a powerful force in Hollywood that, for a change, works for the common good rather than hoarding all of the goods for themselves.

"Inspirational" is a word that's freely thrown around, but in Woo's case, it's the only one to describe the contents of the following interview.

MICHAEL SINGER: Is it true, as I read in a story in Asiaweek, that your main reason for coming to the United States was as much about family as it was about filmmaking?

JOHN WOO: Yes, it's true, but there are so many reasons. First of all, my wife is an American citizen and two of my kids were born here. At one time, I had never dreamed of coming to Hollywood, I was only interested in working in Hong Kong. But you know, Hong Kong is a place that will drive you crazy. It's very competitive, lots of pressure, people don't respect your privacy. You always have to work faster and smarter than the other guy, or else you'll get beaten down. Hong Kong people train for that. You work seven days a week, and it's really unhealthy. I spent all, or most of my time, in the office and the studio. I was never able to give enough time to my children, and my family was being torn apart. I finally realized that my family is the most important thing in my life, and once I got the opportunity to work in the States, I decided to move them here.

There's pressure here, of course, but it's normal pressure. People have to work hard and do a good job, but everyone is more respectful of each other's lives. I can have my own privacy, and not work on weekends to spend more time with my wife and children. My children have become happy. My real responsibility is for them, to give them love, support, encouragement and guidelines. That's what they needed. Even if I fail in the United States, I still don't want to go back— even though I love the place, and love the people in Hong Kong—I couldn't stand that kind of lifestyle anymore.

In Hong Kong, if you fail just once, you're finished. No one cares about you, no one calls anymore. But in this country, even if you fail once or twice, you can still keep your reputation and position. What people respect more than anything is your work, not if you're a winner all the time. In Hong Kong, no way. If you fail. . .

Q: You're out.

A: Yes. And especially in the film business, and especially if you're a star. You know, by the time a star reaches the age of 30, they're considered old.

Q: When you first came to the U.S., you really weren't sure what your fate would be?

A: I wasn't sure. I just wanted to learn and experience, because I've always liked challenges. I've always believed that all of mankind is pretty much the same. We have a similar style of work, a similar kind of feeling and thinking, you know? We have the same kind of dreams. We just do it in different ways. I see myself as a bridge. I've got the responsibility to bring concepts from the East to the West, the best from my country and the United States, and put them all together into one film. I'm looking for the harmony between the two. That's why people have said that my kind of movies are intenational.

For my first American movie, HARD TARGET, I thought I knew enough about this country, but I didn't. It really plays pretty much like a Hong Kong movie. That's why I spent a couple of years after that not writing or directing. I took the time to learn more, to keep in touch with the people and see how they talk, how they feel, what they like. To learn both the good and the bad. And finally, FACE/ OFF gave me a great opportunity to combine what I learned in both the East and West.

Q: Did you realize, when you were still in Hong Kong—or even when you first came to the United States—how many admirers you had in America?

A: I was really surprised and shocked to realize that there were so many fans in this country. I never knew. Before I came here, I only went to one or two film festivals. I knew that some people were interested in my work, but I never knew how many. That really encouraged me, and also made me feel a great responsibility to keep my own style and not let people down. . . especially the critics and journalists here who gave me full support.

I don't see them as "fans." I see everybody as my friend. And every movie I make is a bridge to send my regards and feelings to my friends. Movies seem like a good method of communication. So no matter where I work, I have to keep myself, my own style, my own character. I also received so much support from the film community in the United States. A producer once told me that nobody in the film industry was jealous of me. Everyone seemed very excited about me to come here. Everybody wanted me to be successful, and no one wanted to see me fail. I was so moved, so moved. . . I figure that if people love my movie, then they'll also love me [laughs]. I feel so lucky. It's just like getting a new life. In Hong Kong, all you can make are action or comedies. It's hard to try anything new, and I felt that my style was beginning to go down. I wanted to try something new, something human, real drama, find more things to express on film.

Q: *So you see yourself moving away from action films?*

A: Yes. I would like to try comedy, and would also love to make a musical.

Q: *John Woo wants to make a musical!!??*

A: That is my biggest dream. You know, when I was a kid, I was so crazy about musicals, and was so influenced by them. I'm sure you can see that I'm inspired by musicals in my camera movements, which is choreographed like a musical. I found the real beauty in musicals when I was a kid. I was raised in a Kowloon slum, a neighborhood called Shek Kip Mei. It was much more awful then. I felt like we were living in hell, with drug dealers, gangsters, gamblers. There was a lot of crime in the '50s and '60s. I had to fight very hard to survive, and I always dreamt about flying away from this hell to another, better place, where there was no crime, no hatred, where people loved and trusted each other.

Then, I found his dream in two places. One was the church. The church saved me, gave me good guidelines. Whenever I got beat up, or felt upset or lonely, or did something wrong, I would go to the church to make my confession, and feel safe insde.

The other place was the movie theatre, where I found my dream in the musicals. The people were so charming, so full of life and colorful, with the singing as lovely as angels. The first two musicals I ever saw were SINGIN' IN THE RAIN and SEVEN BRIDES FOR SEVEN BROTHERS. And then, in the '60s, my favorite musical was Jacques Demy's THE UMBRELLAS OF CHERBOURG and THE YOUNG GIRLS OF ROCHEFORT. From his movies, I learned about love and romanticism.

The problem was, when I was a kid I was so shy, and never learned to use the proper language to deal with people. Even now, I have a problem expressing myself in words. That's why I like action, which substitutes for language. That's why, as a kid, I loved dancing and singing. I've always tried to use body language to express myself. I love using visuals to tell a story, rather than language, which I suppose is why my visuals are the strongest element in my films.

Q: And now I know why churches play such a prominent role in your films.

A: Oh yes. I'm a Christian, and I have a very strong relationship with the church. I don't know what would have happened to me and my parents without the church. In the '50s, when I was growing up, ninety percent of the people were poor. We all came from China with nothing, and had to struggle very hard. My parents were very strict and very tough on me to keep me a decent person. They taught me a lot about Chinese culture. We were so poor, homeless for a couple of years, living on the street. And just before I almost joined a street gang, the church helped me and my family. An American family sent money, through a church, to support my school fees. That's how I got educated. My family couldn't afford for me to go school until I was nine years old, but the American family sent us money every month. They supported me for six years, and also helped my younger sister and brother.

When I was in high school, my first dream wasn't to be a filmmaker. I wanted to be a minister, to pay back society and help others. I wanted to share the great message with other young people, and I also respected all of the other religions. That's why there's so much religious imagery in my movies.

Q: When did you switch ambitions from the ministry to the movies?

A: Well, when I was young, I also discovered that I had a gift for art. I was good at drawing, painting, music, dancing and writing. I used art to express myself. My parents were a little disappointed in me, because they were afraid that I wouldn't get a good job. But for me, it was a struggle to discover myself. In the '50s and early '60s we started seeing a lot of movies from Europe and Japan. I discovered the French new wave, so original, so intelligent, like Hitchcock, who was always experimenting and making something new. I discovered that the movies were a perfect tool for me to express my feelings. A movie can be a painting. A movie can tell a story. A movie can be very spiritual, or very intellectual. So I made the decision. Of course, I had already been rejected for missionary school, because they said I was too artistic and wouldn't be able to concentrate on a mission.

Q: They knew you could help people in a different way.

A: [laughs] Yeah, maybe. But my father passed away when I was 16 years old, and my mother pounded rock on a construction site to take care of her family, so she really couldn't afford to send me to the film school. There was no film school in Hong Kong, so if you really wanted to study, you had to go to the United States or Europe. But it was like a dream, you know? But I didn't give up. I learned by watching every classic in the art movie theatre. I studied film books, arts books, philosophy books. That's how I finished my college education [laughs]. I had no choice. I had no money. I had to steal film books, to learn. I'm not encouraging others to do this, it's not a good thing. But in the old days, most of the people did the same thing. Then I got together with other young people who were also crazy about movies, and we made an experimental film together.

Then, I was 26 years old, I got lucky with the support of a friend of a friend who all of a sudden made a lot of money from the stock market. So he gave us a little bit of money to form an independent company to make my first film. The next year, in 1973, I directed YOUNG DRAGON.

Q: *What was the first film that you directed that you really like?*

A: I'd say it was PRINCESS CHEUNG PING, which I made in 1975. That movie made me finally feel like I was a real filmmaker. Before that, I was still pretty unsure of myself. It was like practice work. But PRINCESS CHEUNG PING gave me a very strong feeling. That was the first time I was really in control and making the movie with my own personality.

After that, I made several comedies, which I felt were too silly even though they made money for the studio, Golden Harvest. Finally, A BETTER TOMORROW in 1985 was the next movie that I was really happy with.

Q: *And it was that film that started to bring you to the attention of filmgoers overseas, wasn't it?*

A: I really think it was later on, with THE KILLER.

Q: *THE KILLER increased your visibility, but people I knew who were interested in Asian cinema already took notice of you through A BETTER TOMORROW.*

A: I certainly didn't know it at the time. Not many people expected A BETTER TOMORROW to be a hit. They just saw it as another gangster film. When I made that film, I was down. I had quite a few failures, and some people even said that I should retire, or go home for a couple of years. I was so sad, because I knew that I was a good director, and felt that I was letting people down. Remember, there's some dialogue from A BETTER TOMORROW which goes something like 'I failed for three years. If I get a chance, I will get back to fame from my own hand.'

Q: *I never knew how personal a statement it was.*

A: So then, after the film was a huge success, lots of people were so shocked and surprised. And suddenly, I got back everything. Friends, reputation and money. And also, of course, a lot of jealousy. So when my movie got attention from over-seas, people working in the studio never let me know about it. They never showed me press clippings from other countries. They were trying to cover it. I didn't care, you know? I just wanted to keep making my movies. I was told later on that I was invited to some film festivals, but the studio never let me know about it, just to hurt me. Some people even said that I didn't direct the film, that it was the pro-ducer, not John Woo. I was so mad. But that's typical Hong Kong, you know?

So I left that company, and made another film, THE KILLER, with my own hand, to try and prove myself one more time, to test my work. I didn't care about producers, studios, or anything else. And that movie got even more attention from the international community than A BETTER TOMORROW. My friend Terence Chang—what a great man—knew that some people were jealous of me, so he brought THE KILLER to Cannes, to Canada, to Italy, to Sundance, to let people know about my work and introduce me to the world. I still feel lucky and ex-tremely grateful to Terence, who's now my partner.

Q: *And now the two of you are conquering America.*

A: My opportunity to work here is mainly all because of Terence. He made the path for me. . . he did all the hard work.

Q: And now you're making the path for other Hong Kong filmmakers to work in the United States.

A: It's not only for Hong Kong filmmakers. I actually want to do something for anyone who really has a gift of making movies, but no opportunities. That's one of the reasons we formed our company, is to help others to produce or direct movies. If we can provide some opportunities for young filmmakers, and let them express themselves, then it can change the face of American film.

Q: So in a way, you've fulfilled both dreams. . . to work in film and help others.

A: I know how to be grateful. I'm not looking for a great fortune. I'm not crazy about fame and money. I know how to appreciate. If somebody does me a favor, I will pay back double or triple. I like America because I've gotten so much help from people here. Also, it comes from our Chinese culture. In ancient China, we had so much honor, loyalty and chivalry. If you got from others, you paid back double. That's our spirit, and that's what my movies are about.

Q: You even made a movie in the late '70s called LAST HURRAH FOR CHIVALRY.

A: I've got my work. I've gotten my family back. I've made several successful films. It's time to do something for others. I'm looking for an even bigger family, for everyone to learn from each other. In the film world, as in the "real" world, we are not living alone.

F I L M O G R A P H Y

J O H N   W O O

(Ng Yu-Sum/Woo Yu-sen)

b. 1946 - Guangzhou (Canton), China

YOUNG DRAGON   Golden Harvest, 1973, Hong Kong

THE DRAGON TAMERS   Golden Harvest, 1974, Hong Kong

PRINCESS CHEUNG PING   Golden Harvest, 1975, Hong Kong

HAND OF DEATH   *COUNTDOWN IN KUNG FU*   Golden Harvest, 1975, Hong Kong

MONEY CRAZY   Golden Harvest, 1977, Hong Kong

FOLLOW THE STAR   Golden Harvest, 1977, Hong Kong

LAST HURRAH FOR CHIVALRY   Golden Harvest, 1978, Hong Kong

FROM RAGS TO RICHES   Golden Harvest, 1979, Hong Kong

TO HELL WITH THE DEVIL   Golden Harvest, 1981, Hong Kong

LAUGHING TIMES   Cinema City, 1981, Hong Kong

PLAIN JANE TO THE RESCUE   Golden Harvest, 1982, Hong Kong

SUNSET WARRIOR   *HEROES SHED NO TEARS*   Golden Harvest, 1983, Hong Kong, released in 1986

THE TIME YOU NEED A FRIEND   Cinema City, 1984, Hong Kong

RUN, TIGER, RUN   Cinema City, 1985, Hong Kong

A BETTER TOMORROW   Film Workshop/Cinema City, 1986, Hong Kong

A BETTER TOMORROW PART 2   Film Workshop/Cinema City, 1987, Hong Kong

THE KILLER   Film Workshop/Golden Princess, 1989, Hong Kong

JUST HEROES   co-director, Magnum, 1990, Hong Kong

BULLET IN THE HEAD   John Woo Productions/Golden Princess, 1990, Hong Kong

ONCE A THIEF   Milestone/Golden Princess, 1991, Hong Kong

HARD-BOILED   Milestone/Golden Princess, 1992, Hong Kong

HARD TARGET   Universal, 1993

BROKEN ARROW   20th Century Fox, 1996

JOHN WOO'S ONCE A THIEF   *ONCE A THIEF* (CTF)   Alliance Communications/WCG Entertainment, 1996, Canadian-Hong Kong-U.S.

FACE/OFF   Paramount, 1997

BLACKJACK (CTF)   Alliance Communications/USA Network, 1998, Canadian

$\mathcal{R}$OBERT $\mathcal{M}$. $\mathcal{Y}$OUNG

In the knockabout world of commercial filmmaking, Robert M. Young has always presented a refreshing alternative voice. Firmly rooted in a strong humanist tradition, Young has nevertheless turned a clear eye to humanity's more aggressive instincts in such films as SHORT EYES, THE BALLAD OF GREGORIO CORTEZ, EXTREMITIES, TRIUMPH OF THE SPIRIT and ROOSTERS.

Following a distinguished career as a documentarian, Young entered feature filmmaking in the mid-1960s with the groundbreaking "minority" films NOTHING BUT A MAN and ALAMBRISTA!, beginning a lifelong concern with telling stories of America's underprivileged and unchronicled. His other films have included ONE-TRICK PONY, a wry collaboration with singer/songwriter Paul Simon, the tender DOMINICK AND EUGENE and very recently—representing something of a departure—two of cable network TNT's foray into biblical filmmaking, SOLOMON + SHEBA and SLAVE OF DREAMS.

I met with Young just before the theatrical release of TRIUMPH OF THE SPIRIT, an accomplishment of which he seemed deservedly proud.

MICHAEL SINGER: *You are one of the few filmmakers working today working from a staunchly humanist tradition. There seems to be a determined effort on your part to avoid becoming involved with any projects which in any way would be antithetical to what must be a strong personal code.*

ROBERT M. YOUNG: I suppose that's true. At the time we are infants in the crib and learning things from our mother's face, we begin to read things about life. And these are things that really inform us. We have to try and pay attention to the things that we think are true about life. So I think that film, of course, is based on that. We look at behavior on the screen and we in the audience are reading something and get insights. I think that it's wrong to be misinforming people and putting their values askew. I think that with such a powerful medium, we have a great influence on people. So it's not that I'm some kind of goody-goody. I'm the same as anyone else. It's just that I believe things have to be psychologically true. It's just that simple.

Q: *Do you feel that you're ever held suspect by, say, the critical establishment for making films that take—as much as possible—a positive view of the human condition?*

A: Well, sometimes I feel a little bit discouraged when I see things that are false so widely accepted, or even hailed. I think that I'll never be that successful. But when I hear myself say that, I think, "What, are you feeling sorry for yourself? You don't have to be judged by somebody else's standards. You just have to be judged by your own." But the danger in this area is that I don't take myself that seriously. When I sound that sober, I have to make fun of myself. To me, when I make a film, I'm making it for myself in some deep way. Not in the sense that I don't care what anyone else thinks. It's not that at all. I'm really interested in communicating with other people. What I mean is that the lessons or experimental things in the film are things that I'm trying to understand and explore in a personal way.

Q: *You began as a documentary filmmaker, and many of your dramatic films have a sense of documentary-like realism. What was it in your background that encouraged you to take this approach to moviemaking?*

A: I don't know how to do it any other way. As a filmmaker, you have to operate from inside yourself. How do you, in fact, judge whether something is true or false? How do you look at a performance and how do you reflect back to the actor what you see and possibly make some suggestions as to how something might be changed? It's your own reaction. If I have to do something and I can't trust myself, then how can I direct? I don't do it according to some kind of formula. I don't know how to be a director operationally. In other words, I don't do masters. I don't have that kind of approach. I try to put the camera where I think the story is. That's a difficult thing. I want to put the audience in a certain place where they should be experiencing the situation. And what is the situation that they are to be experiencing? What is the nature of it? Is it true? Am I taking them into a process or is this just telling them a result, because I don't like things that are result-oriented. I'm not a political filmmaker in the sense that I'm making any statements. I don't like to make statements. I like taking you into an experience so that you are put in a position where this experience is seen and made new again. I want to take people on some kind of a journey. I think every story is some kind of a journey, just as I think our lives are journeys. The process for me, hopefully, is to have more understanding as I get older so I can bring to bear whatever kind of insights I have.

Q: *Your films have a visual and dramatic immediacy which seems to be a direct outgrowth of your experience as a documentarian.*

A: The outgrowth of that background, I suppose, is my feeling that the camera should be in the place where the camera should be and should only see what you are supposed to see. That doesn't mean the eye shouldn't have the kind of freedom inside the frame to move around. But it's not as if it's just to cover something. That's just too formalist for me. It's not where the story is. When I started making documentary films—and I continued to do it for a number of years—I was a cameraman, but I always took the responsibility for the material. In other words, I never worked as a cameraman where somebody else told me what to do. Strange, but I couldn't shoot that way. I'd ask difficult questions like "Who is this guy?," and someone would say "Just shoot him, it's not your job to ask questions."

I always wanted to know why I was shooting a particular person. That influenced the way I'd shoot him and the way the light would be on his face, what I would emphasize in the shot. To me it was about seeing. It was about knowing, not about just reproducing an image. The next thing I had to understand in making documentaries was what was going on. I'd move in on a situation. What was happening? What is the relationship between these two people? As soon as I find the situation, the situation has the dynamics of the relationship. Then I learned very quickly to capture the pieces, the surfaces of the reality, that when they're cut together are going to give you the dynamics of the situation. So for me, the aesthetic was to understand what are the facts, who are these people, what is the situation, what are the facts of the situation and what is the situation I'm going to be using.

The situation was what was tremendously important, but I would try never to indicate, never try to tell about it, but rather allow it to unfold and let the audience really come inside and decide for themselves. There's negative space in film, just as there is in architecture. You're making a film that's two hours long. It's a construct. It can't be everything. So I want it to be alive and for it to be alive, it has to have this negative space. It has to have the room for the audience to come inside. As soon as you try and tell something completely, you've told a lie. I think it has much more verisimilitude to life if you capture the fragments that pull the audience into this negative space by suggestion.

Q: *Your camera seems to be a participant or an observer, rather than an intruder. I've never see a sequence in any of your films where one is studying the camera movement rather than what's happening dramatically.*

A: I don't want to draw any attention to the camera, yet the camera may be moving tremendously. In EXTREMITIES, for example, I didn't want to allow the audience to be in a safe place to watch what's happening, which is an attempted rape. That would be obscene. So I explored the space between the people in the film, and it's all choreographed so that it's one shot against another shot. I don't want the audience to sit back and watch. I want them to participate.

Q: SHORT EYES *was one of the most difficult films I've ever seen in terms of the intensity and realism of its violence. I actually had a lot of trouble sitting through it.*

A: Some of the critics couldn't even watch it. But if you compare SHORT EYES with other films about men in similar situations, I think you'll see that it has much less violence in it. There's a great deal of psychological violence, and that's what I think it should be about. I think that is what film is tremendously effective at accomplishing. Film is a psychological medium. When Charlie Chaplin is about to sit down on a chair, and there's a hypodermic needle on that chair, your body tightens up. But as wonderful as LAWRENCE OF ARABIA is, you don't get heat prostration by watching it. You're not affected by those things. That's not what works in film. You can tell people about cold, but you don't make them feel cold. You can turn up the air conditioning. . . that's more effective.

Q: In TRIUMPH OF THE SPIRIT *you were walking a very thin line, because you were making a film about a subject which some people, like Elie Wiesel, feel is inevitably trivialized in the movies. . . the Holocaust.*

A: I felt that we approached TRIUMPH OF THE SPIRIT in the spirit of Wiesel's book Night, and in the spirit of Primo Levi and Frankel's books as well. I feel that we had avoided obscene images in the film, like naked bodies being thrown into furnaces. I don't want to put those kinds of images into people's heads. That's not what the film was about, and I thought it would just push people away. And as I said, I'm interested in taking people into something, not showing them or telling them. We showed Elie Wiesel the film and he was very affected by it. He thought it was elegant, done with delicacy and was the finest movie that had been done on the Holocaust.

Now, nobody knew that he saw it. Some of the negative reviews that we've gotten even quoted Elie Wiesel, without knowing that he admired the film!

We've had curious reviews. On the one hand we've gotten fantastically good notices, and then we have some that I cannot understand. Siskel and Ebert complained that we didn't show bodies being put into the ovens and so we weren't being horrific enough. Another critic said the movie was unfeeling and cold. Actual survivors have put their arms around us and said that the film is real and they're glad it was made so that people won't forget. This is a good lesson for me to find out how vulnerable I am. You do still want to be praised and have people like your work and say what a good boy you are. I'm putting it in those terms because I have a certain amount of contempt for my own vulnerability about that. That doesn't mean that what I've done is right, because I know I'm very small and insignificant and see things from a very limited point of view. But I believe very deeply that we were very much in touch with our subject matter in TRIUMPH OF THE SPIRIT, and operated out of our deepest feelings and sensitivities. We always tried to solve our problems in the most honest way we could. There was a collaboration of actors and myself on the film which was really at the highest level. Willem Dafoe, Edward James Olmos and the others were rooted in their characters. When you somehow bring things to that level, I can take some kind of credit and responsibility in helping to make it happen.

Q: *There are a lot of wonderful performances in your films. What kind of atmosphere do you create on the set to allow that to happen?*

A: There is a back and forth, but it is the actor who ultimately does it. It's about an honesty, not violating the truth. We're trying not to violate your sensibilities of what really is true. The ones that you started out with when you were in the crib and you get so that you know by that look on your mother's face just what she's thinking and feeling. I call up my wife and I hear the first word she says and I know from the timbre of the voice what kind of day she's had. That's what I'm interested in, that kind of truth. I think we have to build on truth and not subvert it. You need escape when going to the movies, sure. I love seeing something funny. But I also think it's like going and plugging in your charger and coming out feeling more alive and in touch with the world and yourself. And I think that's the function of art, quite honestly. It's to center you. If you've had a hectic day and you need some good laughs and you go to a movie that's funny, you come out and now you have another perspective. What is laughter? Laughter helps you put things back into perspective. When you see how ridiculous we are, it's a very healthy anecdote to the pomposity and self-importance that we tend to fall into. By the same token, drama that takes you into being in touch with how things really are, with the truth and the best of our ability to render it, is to make us more in touch with being alive.

Q: In *other words, you won't be directing* RAMBO IV?

A: I wouldn't be the right director to try and make something which is built on conceits. If it's a conceit, I'm not interested in it. If it could be funny—if you prick the balloon and see that it's a conceit—yes, then I'm interested. I'd love to do a comedy. I enjoyed making RICH KIDS. It did have some very funny things in it. I hope this new film, TALENT FOR THE GAME, will have some funny things in it, too. God knows, I'm dying to do something funny after movies like TRIUMPH OF THE SPIRIT, DOMINICK AND EUGENE and SHORT EYES.

Q: TALENT FOR THE GAME *is set against the backdrop of professional baseball, which is something of a change of pace for you. Have you been a fan of the sport?*

A: I've never been a baseball fan. Forgive me, but I've been so oriented toward work or doing something "meaningful." I always thought that watching a baseball game would be a waste of time, and what's been exciting for me is that I found that I've been wrong. As I learned about the game, as I've been reading about it and talking to players and seeing baseball, I'm watching it now with new eyes and learning a fantastic amount. The game is really a metaphor for life, what our values are.

Much of the film will have a humorous edge, but it will also ask questions about business practices and ethics in baseball. I'm really excited.

F I L M O G R A P H Y

R O B E R T   M .   Y O U N G
(Robert Milton Young)
b. November 22, 1924 - New York, New York
THE INFERNO *CORTILE CASCINO, ITALY* (FD) co-director with Michael Roemer, Robert M.
    Young Film Productions, 1962
NOTHING BUT A MAN co-director with Michael Roemer, Cinema 5, 1965
ALAMBRISTA! Bobwin/Films Haus, 1977
SHORT EYES The Film League, 1978
RICH KIDS United Artists, 1979
ONE-TRICK PONY Warner Bros., 1980
THE BALLAD OF GREGORIO CORTEZ Embassy, 1983
SAVING GRACE Columbia, 1986
EXTREMITIES Atlantic Releasing Corporation, 1986
WE ARE THE CHILDREN (TF) Paulist Pictures/Dan Fauci-Ted Danson Productions/The Furia
    Organization, 1987
DOMINICK AND EUGENE Orion, 1988
TRIUMPH OF THE SPIRIT Triumph Releasing Corporation, 1989, U.S.-Israeli
TALENT FOR THE GAME Paramount, 1991
ROOSTERS I.R.S. Releasing, 1993
SOLOMON + SHEBA (CTF) Dino DeLaurentiis Communications, 1995, U.S.-Italian
SLAVE OF DREAMS (CTF) Dino De Laurentiis Communications/Showtime Entertainment,
    1995, U.S.-Italian
CAUGHT Sony Pictures Classics, 1996

EDWARD ZWICK

When the 1989 Civil War spectacle GLORY won critical praise, success at the box office and a slew of Oscar nomnations, a lot of heads turned in Hollywood. Not only were historical epics out of fashion at that time, but GLORY's director—Edward Zwick—had until then been known as a prime explicator of the way we live *now* rather than *then*.

The co-creator and co-executive producer (with Marshall Herskovitz) of TV's primetime sensation *thirtysomething*, Zwick's only previous feature directing credit was the contemporary comedy-drama ABOUT LAST NIGHT. . . about romantic commitment (or lack of same) in America today. But with GLORY, Zwick pulled the rug from under conventional industry analysts, demonstrating a strong grip on his subject matter and a fine flair for poetic visual action.

Zwick followed with a much smaller piece, the bittersweet LEAVING NORMAL, and then returned to a more elaborate canvas with both the period piece LEGENDS OF THE FALL—which helped consolidate Brad Pitt's position as America's golden boy of the screen—and then the Gulf War-set COURAGE UNDER FIRE. I spoke with Zwick following the release of GLORY; at the time of this writing, the director had just completed the contemporary spectacle AGAINST ALL ENEMIES, envisioning a New York under siege by Middle East terrorists.

MICHAEL SINGER: *What gave you the confidence to approach a film on such a huge scale as GLORY, considering the fact that your previous work in both film and television has been on a much more intimate scale?*

EDWARD ZWICK: I would never presume to suggest that I would be able to accomplish anything in the same league as people like David Lean, John Ford, Akira Kurosawa and so many others, but I've always been taught that directing is about overreaching. All that I want to do is to challenge myself in order to grow. If I had made a choice that in some sense was in the same arena in which I've been working, not only would others have presumed that's all I wanted to do, but I would have been in danger of somehow limiting myself and inhibiting growth at what is still a very early moment in my career. Also, I would say that these last couple of years doing THIRTYSOMETHING have created an extraordinary opportunity, because I have shot hours and hours of film. What directors have no opportunity to do these days is to direct. They do one film and a couple of years go by, and the stakes immediately rise so high that the second film they do is based on having shot only two hours. But as a director of television, or executive producer of a show like this, I've had the sense of having the growth I may have made as an artist between the first and second films with the number of hours and thousands of feet of film having been shot.

Q: *Would you say that in some way television—whether episodic or TV movies—has become the contemporary equivalent of the way two-reelers functioned in the old days, as a training ground for directors?*

A: I would say absolutely. I think there are other equivalents. I think there are certain kinds of low-budget films that accomplish the same thing. But I'm about to direct another episode of THIRTYSOMETHING tomorrow. It may be another year before I do another film. But a director directs, just as a writer writes.

Q: *In American but not in England or Europe—there seems to be something of a professional stigma attached to making a successful feature and then returning to direct TV.*

A: Less and less, though. Jim Brooks is doing it. So have Dick Donner, Joe Dante, Steven Spielberg and others.

Q: *Do you think we're finally growing up?*

A: Right. I think the English model is a much more legitimate one. Those guys go back and forth from television to films to the theatre to commercials with impunity. It's about a difference in form, and there are virtues and liabilities in each of the forms. Television is limited by time and money. It is also, however, visceral and intuitive and often it is anonymous, which promotes risk-taking and growth. The subject matters allowed on television are either immediate or intimate in a way films can't be. Conversely, the scale and canvas of a film are unlike any you can approach in television. Everything has its merits. It's just a difference in form.

Q: *The stereotyping of directors is probably even more prevalent than the stereotyping of actors. Is this something you specifically fought against when you chose to make GLORY?*

A: I just think it's something that everyone is aware of. I don't think that I've cynically chosen this film to avoid stereotyping. I chose GLORY based on the power and the wonder of the story, how compelling it was to me that I could presume to recapitulate that for an audience. But I am aware of stereotyping, and I think it's a real and destructive thing. It's for those who are too busy to think, or are unwilling or lazy. They want things made knowable, and artists are much more complex than that.

Q: *Do you think that some directors actually fall prey to that stereotyping, and can't break their own molds?*

A: I don't presume to know what goes on in other artists' heads, but I suppose there are those who fall prey to a stereotype and then there are those who have such a singularity of vision that it makes them wonderful as artists. I don't think that David Lynch thinks of himself in any stereotypical way, yet his sensibility is so unique as to insist that the work he does is distinctive. I think it's also true of people like Brian De Palma and Martin Scorsese.

Q: *Your background was more theatrical than cinematic, wasn't it?*

A: I was trained in repertory theatre, and that meant you would do Strindberg one night and Sam Shepard the next and Shakespeare the one after that.

Q: *What compelled you to eventually go into film?*

A: I learned very early that if you have a vision and the ability to articulate it to those around you, then you can indeed realize those things. But why does one artist begin with pastels and end up with oils? I don't know. I can't even speculate.

Q: *In discussing some filmmakers who influenced you, the names of Hawks, Ford and Kurosawa are mentioned. But would you say that their movies or techniques have had direct impact on your work?*

A: I don't know. I have to say that there's a promiscuity of influence in my life, and not just having to do with fill. I do know that at a very young age I saw a lot of European cinema and was affected by the humanist traditions of Truffaut and Bergman. On the other hand, I know that paintings had a lot to do with GLORY. I kept looking at Goya, for example. And the Pulitzer Prize-winning novel Killer Angels by Michael Shaara was somehow very important to me in making the movie. It brought you inside an historical moment and let you understand the personal context of the larger canvas. That was an extraordinary accomplishment.

Q: *You used the great Freddie Francis as your cinematographer on GLORY, a man who's worked with a lot of other greats in the past. . . including David Lean, perhaps the most famous of all living directors who specialize in historical epics. What kind of working relationship did you have with him? Were you intimidated by his vast experience?*

A: Well, I obviously wanted somebody who had been through everything and would be undaunted by the scale and the demands made on us. He really has been everywhere and done everything. Our collaboration, however, was very typical of any I've had with other cinematographers. We'd talk about an idea—I'd tell him very specifically what I had in mind—and then he'd go and do exactly what he wanted to do!

Q: *In the look of GLORY, you and Francis chose a very clear palette rather than a muted "period" sepia tone.*

A: I felt that sepia would be a cliche and distract the viewer from the story. We felt that we could use smoke from fires, smokestacks and oil burners, which would be a natural diffusing element. And we also very carefully art-directed the palette to be monochromatic with the blues and browns and greens.

Q: *The white protagonist in GLORY, Robert Gould Shaw, writes a letter to his mother in which he expresses some feeling of distance from the black men under his command. Did you, as a white director working with a mostly black cast, share any of those emotions?*

A: I have to say that I don't subscribe to that kind of thinking in general. I do believe that a director's function is interpretive, that a director has to be able to project himself into Shakespearean England, or outer space. Those things are what distinguishes a director in terms of his ability to recognize the commonality of experience, or the humanity in everyone, and to project himself firmly into that. As far as the issue of race, I'm a third generation American Jew—not the child immigrant but it's easy for me to lapse into a kind of fond Yiddish inflection and emulation of that culture in a way that is done without baggage and trying, amidst the humor, to find the dignity in that. For Denzel Washington, Morgan Freeman, Andre Braugher and the other actors in GLORY, I suspect they did that with extraordinary ease. Not to say they weren't grappling with some of the pain of remembrance of the real indignity of slavery. . . but they did it, as far as I was concerned, with a real generosity of spirit. There was never any baggage. They read the script, knew my purpose for being there, and made themselves vulnerable to me in the process. I also, in turn, opened myself to their contributions in order to get it right. I didn't presume to tell them things that they knew much better and more profoundly than I. I also believe that their performances in GLORY had to do with a sense of purpose. I was humbled by that, and knew that sometimes the best thing to do was to get out of the way and let those performances unfold and have their moment. I think there are some parts of GLORY that are indeed inspired.

Q: *You've said that GLORY is not so much a film about the Civil War as it is a film about passion.*

A: I think there was a certain fervor of the Utopian ideal, the abolitionist zeal that had a legacy, and some of that legacy was unexpected. It was contradictory, too. But it was also about an extraordinary opportunity of men being given the occasion to fight for something they believed in. To have that occasion, to strike a blow against that which has oppressed one, is quite rare. The fight to be in that situation is very beautiful. And certainly, young people now don't quite understand the context of political passions. I think to tell a story about a nation seized by passion, good and bad, was very contemporary to me.

Q: *How do you answer charges that the film actually glorifies war?*

A: The title GLORY is deliberately ironic. It does suggest that there are moments in which the only response against oppression is to fight it. . . there is a certain dignity in risking everything for that which one believes. But on the other hand, we went to such extraordinary lengths to try and portray the savagery and horror of what war is. My interest was to do anything but glorify war.

Q: *The battle scenes in GLORY really do portray a terrible beauty.*

A: I guess if the first battle in the movie was somehow narrative, and the second very subjective—to try and capture the inside feeling of combat—then the third and final battle was trying to address what that terrible beauty is. And I suppose that certain elevated tone that it takes on is what I was going for. . . the myth after the fact.

Q: *James Horner's music was very important in that mythical elevation. Was he involved with the film from inception?*

A: From the very beginning, James and I knew that the sound of The Boys Choir of Harlem had to be heard in the film. We felt that boys are always fighting wars, and we wanted to somehow juxtapose the sound of those beautiful voices against some of the atrocities that are depicted in the film.

Q: *GLORY was refreshingly free of cliches that one usually finds in historical films, such as extraneous romantic subplots. Was there any pressure from the studio to include some of those more conventional elements?*

A: Remarkably, no. We did begin to film some sequences between Robert Gould Shaw and a woman who, in historical fact, did have a friendship and possibly a romance with him. But the scenes just weren't working in the context of the story we were telling, so they were cut.

Q: *ABOUT LAST NIGHT. . . and GLORY are totally different from each other in both setting and tone. Is either one closer to the kind of film you really want to make?*

A: To answer that question, I'll tell you my favorite joke. Mrs. Feingold wants her Miami Beach apartment re-decorated. So she calls the decorator, who asks "What would you like?" Mrs. Feingold answers, "I want it should be done period." And he asks, "Well, what kind of period? Louis the Fourteenth? Second Empire? Restoration?" And she responds, "No, no, no! It should be so beautiful that when my friends come, they take one look at it and drop dead. . . period!"

Q: *Your next feature project is LEAVING NORMAL, which is based on an original screenplay by Ed Solomon. What attracted you to the script?*

A: It's very rare for me to come to a script that I wasn't personally involved in creating, but when I found LEAVING NORMAL, I was very struck by the one thing that I look for in any film. . . a voice. I think every film re-invents the universe, and those that do it best create behavior and rules for their characters to observe. And what this script did was present a whole world view that was slightly pixillated, eccentric to be sure. And it was aggressively a reaction against what I see around me now-films in which people have stated goals which they strive for and win. Films in which people overcome all odds. Here is a story that says the opposite. . . that the journey you take is not the journey you expect, and indeed, while you think nothing may happen, in the end everything might happen. I was also very moved by Ed's presentation of women in LEAVING NORMAL, which does not necessarily involve men, or rape, or chases or any other elements of genre other than the effect of one character upon the other.

Q: *Do you feel once again, as with GLORY, that you're swimming against the tide? And do you enjoy that?*

A: Well, I don't know, but I've always subscribed to Casey Stengel's theory. . . "Hit it where they ain't!"

FILMOGRAPHY

EDWARD ZWICK

b. October 8, 1952 - Winnetka, Illinois

PAPER DOLLS (TF)   Leonard Goldberg Productions, 1982
HAVING IT ALL (TF)   Hill-Mandelker Films, 1982
ABOUT LAST NIGHT. . .   TriStar, 1986
GLORY   TriStar, 1989
LEAVING NORMAL   Universal, 1992
LEGENDS OF THE FALL   TriStar, 1994
COURAGE UNDER FIRE   20th Century Fox, 1996
AGAINST ALL ENEMIES   20th Century Fox, 1998

ABOUT THE AUTHOR

MICHAEL SINGER has worked in motion pictures for more than 25 years in various capacities, currently as a unit (production) publicist and author of books about film.

Singer makes his home in San Francisco, California, with his wife and two daughters.

OTHER FILM & ENTERTAINMENT BOOKS
FROM LONE EAGLE PUBLISHING. . .

■ SPECIAL FEATURES ■

SCHLOCK-O-RAMA
The Films of Al Adamson
by David Konow

The films of Al Adamson captured the '70s drive-in era and reflected the time and culture in all its glory. Often compared to zany director Ed Wood, Adamson gave a twisted version of what was going on in America, told with the wildest characters imaginable. Adamson is the only film director who ever gave Colonel Sanders a part in a movie in exchange for all the chicken the crew could eat. David Konow documents how a maverick filmmaker with a few bucks made a fortune on his own terms. Includes never-before seen photos, insider stories and interviews.

$19.95 ISBN 1-58065-001-5, original trade paper, 8.5 X 11, 160 pp, illustrated.

THE HOLLYWOOD JOB-HUNTER'S SURVIVAL GUIDE
An Insider's Winning Strategies For Getting
That (All-Important) First Job...And Keeping It
by Hugh Taylor

Hugh Taylor offers insider's advice on getting that all important first job, Setting up the Office and Getting to Work, the Script and Story Development Process, Production, Information, Putting It all Together, and Issues and Perspectives.

HUGH TAYLOR received his MBA in business from Harvard's School of Business Administration. He has worked as an assistant to one of Hollywood's top producers moving up from the job of "gofer" to Vice President.

$18.95 ISBN 0-943728-51-7, original trade paper, 5.25 x 8, 250 pp, illustrated.

THE ULTIMATE FILM FESTIVAL SURVIVAL GUIDE
The Essential Companion for Filmmakers and Festival-Goers
by Chris Gore

Learn the secrets of Sundance, Telluride, Slamdance and over 300 film festivals worldwide in this comprehensive and eye-opening guide. Packed with information, this book reveals how to get a film accepted and what to do after acceptance, from putting together a press kit to putting on a great party to actually closing a deal. Includes chapters on The Players (festival directors, agents, PR pros, acquisition experts and others), The Parties (the single most important event at a festival besides your own screening), and The Politics (networking, how a juror thinks, self-promotion). Also contains complete directory listings of hundreds of film festivals, cross-referenced indices, plus resource appendices for screening rooms, affordable video dub facilities, agents for independent filmmakers, attorneys, public relations firms and travel agents.

CHRIS GORE has been called everything from "the Gen-X Leonard Maltin" to the "pit bull of journalism." He is the publisher of *Film Threat* magazine and has been a judge at the Florida Film Festival, the Athens Film Festival, the Slamdance Film Festival and for the American Film Institute.

$14.95 ISBN 1-58065-009-0, original trade paper, 6 x 9, 304 pp, illustrated.

To order or for more information,
call 1-800-FILMBKS (345-6257) or go to www.loneeagle.com

OTHER FILM & ENTERTAINMENT BOOKS FROM LONE EAGLE PUBLISHING. . .

■ DIRECTING ■

FILM DIRECTING:
KILLER STYLE & CUTTING EDGE TECHNIQUE
by Renee Harmon

This book is written for the director who, though skilled in basic directing techniques, wants advice on achieving the emotional and visual impact demanded by today's motion picture industry. Renee Harmon explores the relationship of the director with the star, producer, writer, production manager, editor, composer and all the major film craft professionals. Includes straight-from-the-hip advice, helpful hints, plus important do's and don'ts of filmmaking.

RENEE HARMON, PH.D., is the author of eight best-selling and critically acclaimed books on various aspects of the film business.

$22.95 ISBN 0-943728-91-6, original trade paper, 6 x 9, 224 pp.

■ ACTING ■

MAKING MONEY IN VOICE-OVERS
Winning Strategies for a Successful Career in Commercials, Cartoons and Radio

by Terri Apple
Foreword by Gary Owens

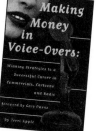

This book helps the actor, radio DJ, vocal impressionist and amateur cartoon voice succeed in voice-overs, no matter where you live. From assessing one's competitive advantages to creating a demo tape to handling initial sessions, Apple provides a clear guide full of insider tips and strategies helpful to both beginners and experienced professionals.

TERRI APPLE is one of the top paid, award-winning voice-over actresses whose work is heard everyday all across the country. She lives in Los Angeles, California.

$16.95 ISBN 1-58065-011-2, original trade paper, 5.5 x 8.5, 224 pp.

NEXT!
An Actor's Guide to Auditioning
by Ellie Kanner and Paul G. Bens, Jr.

Written by two of Hollywood's hottest casting directors, NEXT! is the definitive insider's guide to successfully navigating the complicated maze of auditions and landing that all-important role in a movie or TV show. NEXT! details the common errors that most inexperienced actors make when auditioning.

ELLIE KANNER cast the TV pilot of *Friends* and *The Drew Carey Show*. **PAUL G. BENS, JR.** is a partner in Melton/Bens Casting.

$19.95 ISBN 0-943728-71-1, original trade paper, 7 x 9, 184 pp.

YOUR KID OUGHT TO BE IN PICTURES
A How-To Guide for Would-Be Child Actors and Their Parents
by Kelly Ford Kidwell and Ruth Devorin

Written by a top talent agent and a stage mom with three children working in film, TV and commercials, YOUR KID OUGHT TO BE IN PICTURES explains what the odds of success are, how to secure an agent, where to go for professional photographs, the auditioning process, lots of photographs, plus much more.

$16.95 ISBN 0-943728-90-8, original trade paper, 9 x 6, 280 pp.

To order or for more information, call 1-800-FILMBKS (345-6257) or go to www.loneeagle.com

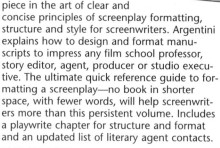

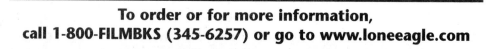

OTHER FILM & ENTERTAINMENT BOOKS
FROM LONE EAGLE PUBLISHING. . .

▄▄▄▄▄▄▄▄▄▄ SCREENWRITING ▄▄▄▄▄▄▄▄▄▄

WRITING GREAT CHARACTERS
The Psychology of Character Development
by Michael Halperin, Ph.D.

This valuable book identifies and solves a major problem for writers, creating characters who are so real they literally jump off the page. Halperin has developed an easy to understand, logical system which gives all screenwriters a foolproof and failproof method of developing great characters. WRITING GREAT CHARACTERS is a book for all writers, from the expert who is looking to polish his techniques to the novice who wants to learn the craft from an expert.

MICHAEL J. HALPERIN, Ph.D., has taught screenwriting at UCLA and currently teaches at Loyola Marymount University in Los Angeles, CA. He has written numerous popular television programs and has authored several bestselling computer based interactive media programs. He has given seminars for executives of television and film. He holds a BA in Communications from USC and a Ph.D. in Film Studies from the Union Institute in Cincinnati, Ohio.

$19.95 ISBN 0-943728-79-7, original trade paper, 6 x 9, 208 pp.

WRITING SHORT FILMS
Structure and Content for Screenwriters
by Linda J. Cowgill

Contrasting and comparing the differences and similarities between feature films and short films, WRITING SHORT FILMS offers readers the essential requirements necessary to make their writing crisp, sharp and compelling. Emphasizing characters, structure, dialogue and story, WRITING SHORT FILMS dispels the "magic formula" concept that screenplays can be constructed by anyone with a word processor and a script formatting program. Writing a good screenplay, short or long, is a difficult job. Citing numerous examples from short films as well as feature films, the author teaches strategies to keep a short film on track and writer's block at bay. Chapter headings include The Three Part Nature of Film Structure, Proper Screenplay Format, and Dialogue–The Search for the Perfect Line.

LINDA J. COWGILL received her Masters in Screenwriting from UCLA, after winning several screenwriting awards and Fellowships. She has taught screenwriting seminars at the Boston Film Institute, the American Film Institute, and the prestigious Kennedy Center in Washington, D.C. Currently Ms. Cowgill teaches screenwriting at Loyola Marymount University in Los Angeles. Ms. Cowgill has written over 12 features and teleplays.

$19.95 ISBN 0-943728-80-0, original trade paper, 6 x 9, approx. 250 pp.

TOP SECRETS: SCREENWRITING
by Jurgen Wolff and Kerry Cox

"TOP SECRETS is an authentic stand-out. The combination of biographies, analyses, interviews and actual script samples is a real winner."
–Professor Richard Walter, UCLA

"TOP SECRETS provides an excellent addition to screenwriting literature. It conveys what it takes to be a screenwriter: the passion, the discipline, the art, the craft, the perseverance."
–Dr. Linda Seger, Author of *Making A Good Script Great*

$21.95 ISBN 0-943728-50-9, original trade paper, 6 x 9, 342 pp.

To order or for more information,
call 1-800-FILMBKS (345-6257) or go to www.loneeagle.com

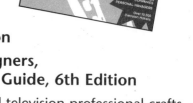

545 B2 FM 141
04/15/99 39255 SCLB
INFORMATION CONSERVATION, INC.